6-6-72

American Communism

AMERICAN COMMUNISM

A Critical Analysis of its
Origins, Development and Programs

by

JAMES ONEAL

and

G. A. WERNER, PH.D.

New and Revised Edition

GREENWOOD PRESS, PUBLISHERS
WESTPORT, CONNECTICUT

The Library of Congress has catalogued this publication as follows:

Library of Congress Cataloging in Publication Data

Oneal, James, 1875–
    American communism.

    1. Communism--U. S. 2. Socialism in the United
States. 3. Political parties--U. S. I. Werner,
Gustave Adolph, 1879-   joint author. II. Title.
HX89.05 1972   335.4   75-138170
ISBN 0-8371-5627-0

Copyright 1947 by E. P. Dutton & Co., Inc.

Originally published in 1927
by James Oneal

Reprinted by arrangement
with E. P. Dutton & Co., Inc., New York

First Greenwood Reprinting 1972

Library of Congress Catalogue Card Number 75-138170

ISBN 0-8371-5627-0

Printed in the United States of America

PREFACE

THE first edition of this work appeared in New York in February, 1927, and was favorably received by reviewers and the press. Communist publications gave expression to the usual maledictions always hurled at any critical presentation of the Communist movement. The author of the first edition, James Oneal, has often been urged to bring out a new edition but poor health made it impossible to undertake the task alone. Believing that a new edition extending the history to the current period would serve a useful purpose, Prof. G. A. Werner volunteered his cooperation and the result is this new and expanded work. 1690446

The first edition contained thirteen chapters and two appendices; the second contains twenty-two chapters and five appendices. In reviewing the material in the first edition we found that it had survived the test of nearly twenty years of Communist history. The only changes made in using that material has been adding to a few footnotes and as the author had written so close to the events he discussed we have substituted the past for the present tense. The titles of two chapters were also changed.

Chapter XII, Neurosis of Communism, is an expansion of the same chapter in the first edition and Chapter XIII, Financing Communism, is an expansion of the same chapter in the first edition. The| new chapters are: XIV, Trotskyism in America; XV, Communism and American Youth; XVI, Dissolution of the Comintern; XVII, Under Two Flags; XVIII, Strategic Retreats; XIX, More Fronts and Splits; XX, Summation; XXI, Post-War Trends; XXII, Alternatives.

The additional Appendices are: III, Instructions for Communist factions; IV, Constitution of the Third International; V, Nazi-Communist Parallels.

We have endeavored to cite reliable sources for every important statement made and, believing that what the Communists say of themselves and their aims is more convincing than what any critics may say, we have let them speak in the following pages.

It has also been necessary to consider the European backgrounds of American Communism during the second World War and the postwar period in order to understand the bizarre conduct of the "comrades" in responding to the needs and desires of the Russian dictatorship. Journalists and radio news commentators have often been perplexed to explain the peculiar behavior of Moscow in its relations with the rest of the world and we are hopeful that our presentation of the history of the amoral code observed by all Communists will also be helpful in understanding the Russia of Stalin and Molotov.

Finally, we wish to express our gratitude to all who have helped us to bring this work to completion, especially Algernon Lee, President of the Rand School of Social Science, New York; Boris Nicolaivsky, Russian scholar, historian and refugee from Russia; Liston M. Oak, Managing Editor of the *New Leader*; and to Lena Morrow Lewis, for clipping from various publications material that has been very helpful.

Phoenix, Arizona   J. O.
Stockton, California   G. A. W.
Spring, 1947

CONTENTS

Contents

INTRODUCTION

Not since the third and fourth decades of the nineteenth century has the United States observed such a confusion of tongues in politics as it witnessed following the end of the first World War. The war and the rise of the Bolsheviks to power in Russia served as an explosive hurled into American life, tearing asunder old mores and bringing a reaction that recalls the conservative terror of the last two years of the administration of the elder Adams. This earlier reaction was a by-product of the French Revolution. The ruling classes of England were also frightened by the spectre of French Jacobinism. In both countries the upper classes took refuge in espionage acts — spies, illegal raids, arrests, *provocateurs*, suppression of meetings, books, pamphlets and papers. Contemplating the rise of the Jeffersonian "levellers," Theodore Dwight could solemnly ask his Federalist friends whether their wives were to be "thrown into the stews." In England an association of aristocrats could resolve, "May the tree of liberty be transplanted from France to hell."

Professor Prince, in his *Catastrophe and Social Change* (p. 20), observes that when the matrix of custom is shattered by catastrophe "mores are broken up and scattered right and left." Hysteria becomes the normal state of the overwhelming majority of mankind. Myth becomes fact and rumor certainty. At the same time, the classes who have big stakes in the social order direct the popular illusions into channels that will serve their own interests. Their intellectual retainers rise to the occasion, appealing to the old patristic gods against the imagined hosts of imps and goblins who have invaded the fatherland. The underlying population comes to accept the leadership of the most reactionary groups in society, and these groups proceed to tear down the priceless structure of civil rights that has cost generations of sacrifice to erect. Only to the extent that the mythology of reaction breaks down is the work of the destroyers checked, but survivals of the reactionary mood continue into the more normal period.

In this study of American labor and politics the American Communists easily stand out as the most conspicuous group because of their frequent appearance in the headlines of the daily press, and yet little is known by the readers of this press regarding American Communism. One reason for this lack of knowledge is the absurd stories of the movement that have appeared in American periodicals. Another reason is that American Communism has had such a tortuous and complicated development that for each year since its organization in 1919 it must be studied to know what were its ideas in each phase of its evolution. Because of its rapid and frequent changes from one phase to another, it can only be undrstood by considering its entire history. It is something entirely different from what it was as the "Left Wing" in 1919. Its official publications of that period offer no explanation of the movement known as the Communist Party today.

In order to comprehend the program of American Communism, it has been necessary to consider also some prewar European and American backgrounds and origins. In the Socialist and trade union organizations here and abroad there have been certain tendencies manifested from time to time which did not find complete expression until the organization of the first Communist parties. It has been necessary to trace the origin and development of these ideas and tendencies, although they have been of minor importance and generally of minor influence in the Socialist and trade union organizations. Then, with the appearance of the Communist organizations and their attempts to establish relations with other movements, it has been necessary to consider these other organizations and their reactions to Communist approaches. The rapid and frequent changes by Communist organizations in their maneuvering to establish contacts with other organizations have also made the history of American Communism more complex and hence less understood. As a phase of social, political and economic history the movement is especially interesting as a study in psychology, having its immediate origins in one of the greatest wars in all history.

The study is based upon original sources, and these show that the estimates of millions of organized Communists in the United States are grotesque absurdities. At its very inception in 1919 the movement never had over 35,000 or 40,000 members. All the numerous organizations that appeared in the period of 1919-1921 had been gathered into one by 1927, and the sole survivor then had less than 8,000 members. Moreover, practically all but a thousand of the organized Communists were of immigrant origin. After six years of devoted service, the movement made few converts among American workers. That this small band could have so thoroughly frightened our bourgeois classes at that period is due to the myths which they cultivated during the first World War and the immediate post-war period.

Within recent years the Communist Party has claimed as many as 100,000 members. There is no way of checking this statement and it is probably very much exaggerated. We do know that in 1923 when the Communists founded the Federated Farmer-Labor Party they reported 500,000 members to Moscow but within less than a year it was evident that the party had "captured" only its own members as the result of their seizure of another organization. Subscribing to the policy of using falsehood against their opponents, the Communists also employ it in their own movement. Hence the obviously false report to Moscow.

The study shows that, owing to the sacrifices made by American Socialists in behalf of their anti-war position in 1917, they accepted the call for a new International to replace the old one which had collapsed in the first World War. They voted to affiliate with an organization which the Soviet leaders proposed to organize, but when the Russians issued their Twenty-one Points and sought to impose them upon organizations in all countries, the American Socialists steadily moved away from any official relations with the Communist International. They believed that the Russian program was suicidal and that it also implied Russian control of the new organization. As successive manifestoes came from Moscow, their views were confirmed.

The action of American Communists was the reverse of this. They also approved the new International before any terms were announced and then expressed complete satisfaction when the Twenty-one Points became known in this country. They accepted Russian leadership, not only in the International but accepted "statutes" of its executive which required affiliated organizations in all countries to accept decisions of a small body stitting in the capital of Russia. Brains were superfluous, thinking impossible for all affiliates.

So complete had the Russian dictatorship become that the Workers' (Communist) Party had to get the consent of this executive to hold a convention, and if consent was withheld, no convention was possible. Or if a convention is permitted, the Moscow body may set aside its decisions. It has nullified not only convention decisions, but even the results of a referendum of the members. The party was compelled by one such decision to reorganize on a "nuclei" basis, a plan that made its own leaders apprehensive and which, according to their admissions, brought a heavy loss in members.

Thus the American Communist Party is not a political party in the American sense. It is an offshoot of the counter-revolution against the democratic Republic of Russia and an agency of that counter-revolution in this country, an agency pledged to carry out the orders of the Russian dictatorship and awaiting "the day" when it believes that it can afford to risk an attempt to do the same thing here.

As this movement is the subject of controversy, we have permitted its advocates to speak for themselves in the following pages, while the reader will find in the footnotes authority for every statement made.

American Communism

CHAPTER I

FORCE TENDENCIES IN THE AMERICAN
LABOR MOVEMENT

SOME misconceptions of Communism must be considered if we are to understand the modern Communist movement and its American offshoot. Communism, that is, common ownership or possession of property or goods, was an early phase in the evolution of society, but modern research has shown that there was also considerable private possession of things by the side of things held in common. Communism as a form of human association implied the absence of private property and the sharing of goods in common. In its purest form it probably has never existed outside of some early Christian communities, but as an ideal it captivated the imagination and the support of workmen and peasants in many periods of history.

The class antagonisms and struggles of the medieval period generally took the form of a religious movement. Time after time various sects appeared, questioning the ruling status of property and law, demanding a reorganization of society on a basis of Christian Communism, often denouncing the ruling classes and occasionally becoming a menace to the established order. Open conflict with religious and secular authorities sometimes followed, accompanied by bloodshed and often by the literal extermination of a rebellious sect.

Another form which this ideal took was the organization of communistic societies in the nineteenth century, especially those organized in the United States. The religious motive was also prominent in the organization of these societies. Force, however, played no part in the founding of these communities. History appeared to their founders as a series of blunders of which clever men took advantage, and they believed that they could change society by organizing miniature models of a "perfect society."[1]

While these societies were being founded, Karl Marx and Frederick Engels were taking the leadership in organizing the modern Socialist movement in Europe by founding the First International which was organized in London in 1864. They had also founded the Communist League in 1847 as a secret society because of the general reaction of that period. They chose to call themselves Communists in order to distinguish themselves from a variety of sects and groups known as "Socialists." They sharply defined their views in the *Communist Manifesto* which became a classic statement of the Socialist view of history, society and the problems of the working class. The reaction of the period and the almost complete disfranchisement of the masses rendered party organization political action impossible and the *Manifesto* clearly justified the use of force. When the trade unions acquired stability and the masses won repeated extensions of the suffrage, this extension of political democracy no longer justified the appeal to force, and the Marxians participated in the organization of Labor and Socialist parties.[2]

The First International was a loose federation of trade unions and radical societies and parties. No sectarian dogmas were imposed and no rigid rules were adopted and enforced by a central authority. The organization had scarcely got under way when Michael Bakounin, the founder of Communist Anarchism, became a guiding spirit of groups believing in conspiratory methods for the overthrow of the bourgeois order. He had spent six years in a Russian prison, was exiled to Siberia from which he escaped, and

[1] For primitive Communism, see Lowie, *Primitive Society*. For the ancient and medieval periods, see Beer, *Social Struggles in Antiquity* and *Social Struggles in the Middle Ages*. For the American communities, see Hillquit, *History of Socialism in the United States*, Part I.

[2] *The Communist Manifesto*, Chicago, 1912.

arrived in England in 1861. Bakounin and his associates organized
what the modern Communist would call secret "nuclei" in the
First International. His first step was the organization of a secret
international which included the following three orders: (1) the
International Brothers; (2) the National Brothers; (3) the International Alliance of Social Democracy.

There is a remarkable resemblance between this organization
and the Communist International which we shall consider later.
Even the phraseology is similar to the manifestoes issued by the
executive of the Communist International. The International
Brothers were limited to one hundred who were to direct revolts
and serve as a secret executive with supreme power over the
other two organizations. "In their hands alone should be the making of programs, the rules, and the principles of the revolution.
The National Brothers were to be under the direction of the
International Brothers, and were to be selected because of their
revolutionary zeal and their ability to control the masses." Bakounin designated himself the supreme lawgiver. The organization
was to "accelerate the universal revolution" and to create a "sort
of revolutionary staff" to direct the world revolution. In 1869
Bakounin's Alliance was admitted to the International and there
began a series of intrigues and the beginning of a struggle between
Marx and Bakounin which eventually disrupted the First International. At the Hague Congress of 1872, Bakounin was expelled
by a vote of 27 for, six against, and seven abstentions. A resolution
favoring political action was adopted by a vote of 36 for and five
against. It was then decided to transfer the seat of the General
Council from London to New York. This action meant the formal
dissolution of the International and it is likely that Marx and his
associates desired it. The organization had become so identified
with the absurd and dangerous ideas of Bakounin and his friends
that it could not live down the reputation it had acquired as a
conspiratory society. In his *Revolutionary Cathechism*, Bakounin
had also outlined an infamous code of conduct which in many

respects is similar to a code which modern Communists accept and which we will consider below.[3]

The seed that Bakounin had sown came to the United States and culminated in a tragedy. Among the refugees from Europe in 1848 and later were Socialists and Anarchists, but the main division in this country was between the followers of Marx and Ferdinand Lassalle. In a famous letter to the organized workers of Germany, Lassalle gave first importance to political organization. The American Lassalleans accepted this view, believing that they should organize politically regardless of whether the economic organizations of the wage workers had become stable and enduring. The Marxists insisted that to attempt political action before the trade unions had become stable was premature and would lead to disappointment. Sound economic organization should always precede any attempt at political action. The First International was built chiefly upon economic organizations of the working class with the expectation that as rapidly as they became rooted in the soil of each country political action would follow. Commons and Associates, in considering this controversy in the United States, present this distinction between the views of the International and the Lassalleans: "The distinction between the ideas of the International and of Lassalle consisted of the fact that the former advocated economic organization prior to and underlying political organization, while the latter considered a political victory as the basis of economic organization. These antagonistic starting points are apparent at the very beginning of American Socialism as well as in the trade unionism and Socialism of succeeding years."[4]

Experience was to prove that the Lassalleans were wrong. A political movement in New York in 1871 failed, but the panic year of 1873 seemed to the Lassalleans an opportunity for political action. The unions were prostrated, and the Lassalleans organized

[3] Hunter, *Violence and the Labor Movement*, pp. 1-26, 196-200.
[4] *History of Labor in the United States*, II, p. 206.

a Labor Party in Illinois in 1874, but it received hardly a thousand votes in Chicago. In the fall it polled still less. In the same year the Social Democratic Workingmen's Party was organized and this merged with the International and two other organizations into the Workingmen's Party of the United States in 1876. Even the Marxians united with the Lassalleans in founding the party which assumed the name Socialist Labor Party of North America in the following year. "It is estimated that not more than 10 per cent of the members of the Socialist Labor Party, during the period described, were native Americans," says Hillquit. "All the rest, including the most active and influential leaders, were men of foreign birth, insufficiently acquainted with the institutions, customs and habits of the country of their adoption, and frequently ignorant of its very language."[5]

Failure to rally any large number of workers to support the party brought pessimism in its ranks which led to a struggle between Marxians and Lassalleans for control of the organization. This struggle resulted in internal prostration for a number of years during which education, organization and propaganda were almost completely neglected. The Anarchist movement is generally born of a sense of futility and failure, resulting in an impatient desire to find a "short cut" to the promised goal. The local political disappointments led the Lassalleans to question political action and to turn Anarchist, gradually accepting force as a means of social transformation. The Marxian members, with their belief in a long period of preparartion, were regarded as timid and conservative by their opponents.

While the struggle within the Socialist Labor Party between Socialists and an increasingly influential Anarchist group continued, the great railroad strike of 1877, accompanied by street battles of organized and unorganized masses with the police and militia in several states, seemed to confirm the view of the advocates of force. It appeared that large numbers of workers were

[5] *History of Socialism in the United States*, Rev. Ed., pp. 193-4.

ready for a mass revolt against the present order and all that they required was courageous leadership that would prepare them for an assault on capitalism. A few years later the German Lassallean organ, *Verbote*, of Chicago, was urging plunder of the rich and the "propaganda of the deed."[6] It had abandoned political action and its contents did not differ from *Die Freiheit* established by Johann Most, the German Anarchist, after his arrival in New York in 1882. Fraud in elections also stimulated the drift towards force. In Chicago an Agitation Committee of the Grand Council of the Armed Organizations in December, 1880, issued a call to "all revolutionists and armed workingmen's organizations" to offer "armed resistance to the invasions by the capitalist class and capitalist legislatures." In July, 1881, the "Black International," as it was called, was organized in London. Its real name was the International Working People's Association and an American section was organized. The following October it held a national congress in Chicago and seated delegates from fourteen cities. The congress approved organizations that "stand ready to render armed resistance to encroachments upon the rights of workingmen," endorsed the "Black International," and rejected a resolution in favor of political action.

A few political actionists remained in the organization, but at the next congress held in Pittsburgh in October, 1883, a document known as the "Pittsburgh Manifesto" was adopted. It declared in favor of "organization for the purpose of rebellion," that "all attempts in the past to reform this monstrous system by peaceable means" had proven futile, and that there "remains but one recourse — FORCE." The manifesto went on to declare that its authors desired "destruction of the existing class rule, by all means, *i. e.*, by energetic, relentless, revolutionary, and international action." The break with political action was complete. The Anarchists had captured a majority of the members of local or-

---

[6] See Ely, *The Labor Movement in America*, pp. 256-7, for excerpts quoted from *Verbote* and other publications of this period.

ganizations of the Socialist Labor Party in St. Louis, Milwaukee, Cincinnati, Cleveland, Omaha, Brooklyn, New York, Philadelphia and Baltimore.[7]

The trade unions in many of the larger cities were involved in a factional war over force as a weapon. In Chicago two central labor bodies appeared, with the force advocates in control of one. In October, 1885, this body adopted a resolution calling upon the working class to "arm itself," and concluded with the words, "Death to the foes of the human race." In November it entered into the eight-hour agitation. The strikes at the McCormick Reaper Works occurred the following May, and as a result of a brutal assault on the strikers by the police, a protest meeting was called in Haymarket Square for May 4. A bomb was thrown by some person unknown, seven policemen were killed, some 60 people injured, and a terrible reaction set in. The Knights of Labor lost over 178,000 members within a year, members of labor organizations became intimidated because of a press campaign against trade unionism, Socialism and Anarchism. Years passed before passions cooled and the work of education and organization could be resumed. Anarchism itself disappeared. It was the first to fall a victim to the reaction which it had invited.

The evolution of Lassallean Socialists into advocates of force was the logical result of an illogical interpretation of historical development. The Pittsburgh Manifesto affirmed that all attempts at reform of the social order "by peaceable means" had failed. This failure was evident from experience in elections. Only a small fraction of the voters had responded to the appeal to support independent party action. The fact that the masses did not rally to this appeal would suggest that they were not as yet interested in any activity or any organization pledged to the reorganization of society. If the masses were not prepared for a trial of peaceful means it was not likely that they could be won to the use of force.

[7] See Commons and Associates, *History of Labor in the United States,* II, pp. 290-300, for a more detailed account of the development of the idea of force.

On the contrary, it was certain that when political action was abandoned for physical force the change from peaceful to violent methods would estrange some who would otherwise remain with the movement. A rational analysis of history and experience could not justify the course taken by the Pittsburgh Congress. Later we shall see the American Communists repeating this history in 1920.

In 1889 a peculiar variation of Lassalleanism appeared in the Socialist Labor Party. This grew out of a difference of opinion between that organization and the American Federation of Labor as to whether central labor bodies should admit delegates of local Sections of the S. L. P. A debate of nine hours followed in the Detroit convention of the A. F. of L. in 1890 and the S. L. P. was defeated. The former body declined to give such representation to the S. L. P. It could not concede this without giving representation to Greenbackers, Single Taxers, and other political organizations that might be formed and in which trade unionists were active. This was the beginning of a bitter campaign of denunciation against the A. F. of L. and in 1895 the S. L. P. organized a rival in the Socialist Trades and Labor Alliance. The S. T. and L. A. never obtained more than a few thousand members. It dragged out a precarious existence until it joined the I. W. W. organized in Chicago in 1905. The S. L. P. itself "split" into two factions over this policy, the larger one rejecting the policy of dual unionism and joining with other Socialist organizations to found the Socialist Party in 1901.

The Lassallean aspect of this phase of Socialist history differs from the preceding phase although both had one thing in common — impatience with the organized working class. In the earlier period this impatience found expression in premature political organization, followed by pessimism because of meager political results, which in turn brought a tendency to question the value of political methods and finally ended by choosing physical force. The later phase of impatience took the course of trying to coerce the trade unions into assuming a position subordinate to the Socialist Labor Party, serving this party as an auxiliary, and providing that all officers of trade unions, local and national, shall "not support any political action except that of the Socialist Labor Party." Like the earlier Lassalleans, the economic organizations of wage workers were considered of secondary importance.

The S. L. P. not only declined but the S. T. and L. A. which it nursed failed to make any impression upon the established trade unions. Eventually the party turned to introspection and, in part, repeated some of the experience of the earlier Lassalleans by considerably modifying its emphasis on political action and supporting a qualified form of force. This stage was reached when the S. T. and L. A. helped to organize the I. W. W. in 1905. A few years later members of the S. L. P. were engaged in a heated discussion as to whether it would not be best to disband the party, give up political action, and organize industrial unions for the seizure of all industries through a series of strikes leading to some final conquest of power and the expropriation of the possessing classes.

The Preamble of the I. W. W. declared that the struggle between capitalists and workers "must go on until all the toilers come together on the political as well as the industrial field, and take hold of that which they produce by their labor through an economic organization of the working class, without affiliation with any political party."[8] Immediately after the adjournment of the convention Daniel DeLeon, the most brilliant exponent of the S. L. P., delivered an address on the Preamble in Minneapolis. He proclaimed the mission of the industrial unions to "take and hold" the powers of production and assigned a minor role to political action. The moment the workers acquire control of the State through political action they will adjourn! To hold political power any longer than it takes to accomplish this adjournment would be usurpation. Control of the State is only obtained

---

[8] See Brissenden, *History of the I.W.W.*, Appendix II.

in order to "abolish" it. The headquarters of the I. W. W. then becomes the capital of the nation. If the possessing classes resist the seizure of industry by the unions, so much the worse for them, for the I. W. W. "will be in position to mop the earth with the rebellious usurper."[9]

Three Syndicalist ideas are expressed in this address, seizure of the machinery of production and distribution by the unions; immediate abolition of the State, and, though not rejecting political organization and action, merely employing political action to obtain control of government and then abandoning this power. Syndicalism had its origin in France and was the result of the ascendancy of Anarchism in the French trade union.[10] The fear of the state and the use of power even during a transition period from the old order to the new one is characteristic of French Syndicalism, the Socialist Labor Party and the I. W. W. The coercive character of the State is the cause of this aversion. Within two years after the founding of the I. W. W. that organization as well as the S. L. P. were discussing whether political organization was necessary. The I. W. W. moved on to the logical conclusion of opposition to political action. The S. L. P. became involved in a heated discussion. It began as early as November, 1906, seventeen months after DeLeon delivered his Minneapolis address. The first attack on political organization was made by a member of the party and was followed by others in *The People*, the party organ. The history of this controversy has been preserved in a publication[11] which enables us to trace its development

The first critic urged that all references to politics in the I. W. W. Preamble should be stricken out because "political

[9] DeLeon, *The Preamble of the Industrial Workers of the World*, New York, 1905.
[10] Levine, *The Labor Movement in France: A Study in Revolutionary Syndicalism*, p. 95.
[11] *As to Politics. A Discussion upon the Relative Importance of Political Action and of Class Conscious Economic Action and the Urgent Necessity of Both.* New York, 1921.

activity may justly be considered of little or no value for the over-throw of the capitalist system." The census reports show that the working class does not constitute a majority of the voters. The obvious conclusion to be drawn from this alleged fact, but not mentioned by the critic, is that the working class, although a minority, should impose its will on society. But assuming, he continues, that the workers have a majority, can one hope to gather them "under one revolutionary banner?" It is very doubt-ful because of bourgeois control of bread and butter, of schools, press and pulpit. Even granting a national electoral victory, what hope is there that a ruling class would acquiesce in it? The workers would be considered rebels anyway if they used the power of an industrial organization to enforce the will of the voters. Assume further that, following an electoral victory, the masses are per-mitted to take control of the government and organize an adminis-tration, what then? The critic answers that "the new form of society, which we are preparing for, does not recognize private ownership; it proposes to recognize production and distribution on collective lines, a function which cannot possibly be filled by politicians." (DeLeon had himself said that "it does not lie in a poltical organization, that is, a party, to take and hold the machinery of production. Both the 'reason' for a political party and its 'structure' unfit it for such work.") [12] The critic concluded that political organization and government control are unneces-sary. Step by step he had come to the conclusion that although he believed that workingmen were a minority of the population, they could in some manner acquire control of industry by ignoring city councils, state legislatures, Congress, courts, police and the army.

The views of other critics did not vary much from the views of the above writer. In his answers to each critic DeLeon empha-

[12] In his Minneapolis address. Here DeLeon confuses a political party with government control by a party. So far as I know, there has never been any sug-gestion that a party should "take and hold the machinery of production."

sized the conviction that for a class striving for public power to make any progress it must, time after time, submit its claims to the judgment of the voters. Where public agitation and peaceful submission to the counting of the ballots are the normal processes of political life, "the man or organization that rejects them does so at his or its peril." We are no longer "barbarians," he insisted, who settle these questions with fists. The ballot is a civilized substitute for the barbarian code of action. Those who talked of "revolutionary means" or "methods" were brushed aside as absurd. "Means and methods may be good or bad, wise or unwise, timely or premature — 'revolutionary' never."[13] The force tendency in the S. L. P. was checked but not without some desertions to the I. W. W. which became anti-political.

The S. L. P. had prepared for this episode in its history by its approach to another problem. Labor and Socialist party programs have a twofold character, their affirmation of a fundamental goal and their attitude towards immediate questions related to the time and place and circumstances in which a party functions. In the minds of some Socialists the question arose, "Shall we pause to give attention to problems intimately related to the system which we seek to reorganize on another basis, or shall we ignore these questions and emphasize the necessity of the complete reorganization of capitalism?" To some this question appeared as a conflict between the present and the future, between reform and revolution, and that a reconciliation between the two is impossible. The platforms of the S. L. P. down to and including 1896 had solved this problem as practically all Socialist parties of the world had solved it by deciding that there was no conflict between the two. Beginning with the year 1900 the party made a change. It omitted the section devoted to measures of reform, and has continued this policy since that year. By this action its members tended to give their attention to a coming social catastrophe through which the workers were to be vested with power

[13] *As to Politics*, pp. 1-12.

to completely alter the basis of society. The psychic result of this attitude is to prepare many of its advocates for some "short cut" to the ideal and to become impatient with political action itself. It is not surprising that the S. L. P. lost some of its best spokesmen to the I. W. W. and that it has become a shadow of what it was twenty years ago. In spite of this experience American Communists repeated this history.

The Socialist Party, excepting for the period immediately following the first World War, had been least affected by tendencies leading to a philosophy of force, but the end of the war found it facing an upheaval of this type that easily made up for its comparative absence of force advocates in its previous history. Organized in 1901, it brought into it some veterans whose experience included a struggle with the force Anarchists of the eighties. The organization of the party was also a repudiation of the S. L. P. attitude of antagonism to the established trade unions. The Unity Convention of 1901 adopted resolutions urging Socialists to strengthen the trade unions, but also appealed to members of the unions to "sever their affiliation with the capitalist parties." This continued to be the policy of the party.

But in this convention there appeared the old conflict between reform and revolution. A group led by the Chicago delegation proposed that all references to reform measures be stricken from the report of the Platform Committee. A. M. Simons, the leading advocate of this proposal, favored it on the ground that nowhere else in the world had "the struggle between capital and labor narrowed down to as . . . clear an issue as it has in America." The implication was that a final struggle between capital and labor was imminent. The vote cast on this proposal is interesting. Each delegate had as many votes as there were members assigned to him to represent and the votes of 6,801 members were cast. Of these the vote was 1,321 in favor and 5,480 against.[14]

[14] The proceedings of this convention were never printed. My information is obtained from a typewritten copy.

This decision remained the policy of the Socialist Party although it has been questioned by small groups in succeeding conventions. In the convention of 1904 a decided Lassallean view regarding the trade unions appeared and it provoked the exciting debate of the convention. Its representatives came chiefly from the agricultural states of Kansas, Wyoming and Oregon where trade unions were few in number. The earlier Lassalleans accepted the trade unions as a factor in the struggle for social transformation but gave party organization first consideration. The Lassallean group in the 1904 convention denied that the trade unions had any importance in the labor struggle and fought for a repeal of the party's expressed position regarding its relation to trade unions and their struggles. The Lassalleans insisted that the trade unions contended merely for "petty reforms," such as wage increases and shortening the hours of labor. To support struggles for these aims was to make the party "reformist." Every member of a union was leaning on a "crutch." Not until it was broken would he come to the Socialist standard. This neo-Lassalleanism was defeated by a vote of 100 to 51 with nine abstentions.[15] The 51 votes of the minority do not represent the strength of the anti-union view. This view at the most did not have more than a dozen supporters while the remainder of the minority favored the unions but wanted the party ranged in favor of industrial unions.

Eight years later a Left Wing had appeared in the Socialist Party which represented a complete reversal of the Left Wing of 1904. A marked Syndicate tendency appeared in the convention of 1912. Translations of Syndicalist literature had been appearing in the United States for a number of years and a Syndicalist organ, *The Toiler*, was being published in Kansas City. Some active members of the Socialist Party were writing favorably of Syndicalism and the *International Socialist Review* of Chicago published much of a Syndicalist character. The I. W. W. had

[15] *Proceedings of the National Convention of the Socialist Party*, 1904, pp. 175-214.

become bitterly anti-political. Most of the prominent Socialists of this tendency left the Socialist Party to support the first World War. Sabotage became a theme of discussion. It was subtle in that it involved support of a method in labor struggles which included actions ranging from the most harmless to the most dangerous and violent. It was a method that irresponsible individuals might use or masses of men organized and disciplined might carry out. It might be legal or illegal. It might endanger the life of the person who practiced it, the lives of others, or both. Sabotage was an illusive and evasive word. It meant what any exponent of it meant and all exponents did not mean the same thing. Moreover, its supporters, unlike the Left Wing of 1904, were overemphasizing the power of economic organizations and most of them regarded the political organization merely as an agency for collecting funds for use in industrial struggles.

The storm broke when the Committee on Constitution reported Article 2, Section 6, as an amendment to the party constitution. As finally adopted it read:

Any member of the party who opposes political action or advocates crime, sabotage, or other methods of violence as a weapon of the working class to aid in its emancipation shall be expelled from membership in the party. Political action shall be construed to mean participation in elections for public office and practical legislative administrative work along the lines of the Socialist Party platform.

The amendment was adopted by a vote of 191 for to 90 against.[16] Eugene V. Debs was not a delegate to the convention but he expressed the general view embodied in this decision. "I am opposed to sabotage and direct action," he wrote. "I have not a bit of use for the propaganda of the deed. These are the tactics of the Anarchist individualists and not of Socialist collectivists. If I regarded the class struggle as guerrilla warfare, I would join

[16] *Proceedings of the National Convention of the Socialist Party*, 1912, pp. 123-135.

the Anarchists and practice as well as preach such tactics. If sabotage and direct action, as I interpret them, were incorporated in the tactics of the Socialist Party, it would at once be the signal for all the *agents provocateurs* and police spies to join the party and get busy."[17]

Following this decision, a small group left the Socialist Party, but in the following November the party received the largest vote in its history. Its membership also increased. William D. Haywood was recalled from the National Executive Committee in February, 1913, and he became a pronounced anti-political actionist. That sabotage, in the view of some of its advocates, included banditry had become evident from an article written by Haywood in 1911. He wrote from Paris in that year, quoting an editorial by Gustave Hervé, a French Syndicalist, with approval. This editorial extolled the deeds of a pick-pocket who, after serving his sentence, armed himself with a revolver and knife and murdered one of the policemen who had arrested him. Individual vengeance is praised to the skies in the editorial in the name of a movement that seeks a transformation of society.[18] This force tendency in the Socialist Party was checked in the convention of 1912 and it rapidly declined.

William Z. Foster, who became a leading American Communist, was also a leading founder of Anarchist-Syndicalism in the United States. He collaborated with Earl C. Ford in the authorship of a pamphlet[19] which served as a textbook for the Syndicalist League of North America. They regarded the Socialist Party as a "usurper," rejected political action, relied on direct action and sabotage, and declared that the ruling classes can be overthrown and expropriated by a general strike. Foster anticipated the Communist conception of ethics in the labor struggle as early as 1912. In choosing weapons, he wrote, the Syndicalist "is

[17] *Miners' Magazine*, June, 1912.
[18] Haywood, in *The International Socialist Review*, March, 1911.
[19] Ford and Foster *Syndicalism*, Chicago, 1912.

no more careful to select those that are 'fair,' 'just,' or 'civilized' than is a householder attacked in the night by a burglar. . . . With him the end justifies the means. Whether his tactics be 'legal' and 'moral,' or not, does not concern him as long as they are effective." He opposed organization of rival trade unions but favored planting of "nuclei" in them to "standarize their policies, instigate strike movements, and organize their attacks on the conservative forces in the unions. A fighting machine is thus built up which enables the Syndicalists to act as a unit at all times and to thoroughly exploit their combined power.[20] Thus, six years before the organization of the Communist International, Foster outlined the ethics — if they can be called ethics — and the tactics which Communists were to pursue in the trade unions and of which he is a conspicuous representative today.

Foster had been a member of the I. W. W. but he left that organization to agitate for the methods outlined above. The I. W. W. had its origin in dissatisfaction with the conservative policies of the old unions. It suffered from desertions and splits almost from its beginning and when it became definitely anti-political it came more and more under the control of migratory workers whose mode of life was such that they could not exercise the franchise. Its philosophy represents an attempt to shape the whole labor movement upon the status of one group of the American working class. Its members being unable to use the ballot they insisted that all other organized workers should refrain from using it. The migratory faction gained control in the convention of 1908 and forced out the political actionists and the political clause was stricken from the I. W. W. constitution. Under the control of this group the I. W. W. entered upon its stormy career and, like the S. L. P., it has declined to a shadow of what it was in 1905.

We have observed the tendency of political and economic organizations of workers at times to seek a "short cut" to a realiza-

[20] Ford and Foster, *Syndicalism*, pp. 43-44.

tion of fundamental aims. This tendency has generally been the result of insisting on one form of action to the exclusion of others, ending in sterility and disappointment. Frequently the overemphasis on political or economic action has led to the adoption of physical force as a method of social transformation. No form of the Labor movement, whether political or economic, has been completely free of the lure of force. When the Russian Revolution burst upon a world involved in the first World War and the Russian Communists took the leadership in organizing the Communist International, the latter found factions and groups in nearly all countries ready to respond to its program. Moreover, the ruling classes had also submitted their rival claims to dominion to armed conflict and had hurled millions of workers into it. The Socialist and Labor movement in all countries had anticipated the war of the imperialist powers for many years and had protested against the sinister interests that were bringing it on. The hysteria of the war years had also prepared a psychic mood for armed insurrection to overthrow the capitalism out of which the first World War had issued. The greed of the victorious powers, their peace of desolation, their cynical division of the booty of the war, their revolting treatment of the famine-stricken populations of the defeated nations, and their use of conscripts and Romanov generals against Soviet Russia contributed much to convince many workers that an era of physical force was at hand and that the laborer who declined to accept violence as a means of social and economic liberation was either a conscious or unconscious agent of reactionary classes. By their conduct and their policies the ruling groups in the victorious nations made a marked contribution to the organization of the Communist International and its affiliated national sections all over the world.

CHAPTER II

THE SOCIALISTS AND THE FIRST WORLD WAR

ALTHOUGH, as we have seen, there were various tendencies in American Labor and Socialist organizations that were receptive of violent views, the Socialist Party was the only organization immediately affected by the program of the Russian revolutionists. This organization since its appearance in 1901 had successfully combatted divergent ideas that inevitably lead to a force philosophy while at the same time affirming its aim of social revolution in the sense of a complete transformation of modern society. However, it had never resorted to general expulsions when members disagreed with the party position unless the disagreement was of such a fundamental character that it constituted a rejection of fundamental aims or methods. This wide tolerance of differing views left within the Socialist Party small factions not in full accord with its program, but they generally accepted decisions of conventions and referendums while continuing to agitate their views. This democratic procedure had contributed considerably to unity in organization work and political campaigns.

The Socialist Party had received 897,000 votes for its presidential candidate in 1912. Its dues-paying membership had increased to 118,000. In 1915 it had thirty members in the legislatures of twelve states and nearly 1,000 municipal officials, including mayors of twenty-two cities. Its growth in votes and membership may be seen from the following table:

Year	Vote	Membership
1900	87,814	10,000
1904	402,283	20,763
1908	420,713	41,751
1912	897,011	118,045
1916	590,294	83,284
1920	915,302	26,766

The misfortunes of the organization began with the outbreak of the first World War. In August, 1914, its executive issued two statements, one condemning "the ruling classes of Europe," who had demonstrated their unfitness "to administer the affairs of the nations." The other warned the nation of a possible food shortage and urged the Government to seize the food industries in order to "starve the war and feed America." In 1915 the executive strove to organize an International Socialist and Trade Union Congress, to meet either in Europe or the United States. Failing in this, it formulated a peace program which provided for no indemnities or transfers of territory; self-determination, disarmament and the organization of an "international congress, with legislative and administrative powers over its affairs." In 1917 it renewed its efforts to get an international congress of the organized workers of all countries to meet at The Hague in June. As German submarine activities developed, the executive urged President Wilson to place an embargo on all shipments to the belligerent countries. When the United States Government broke relations with Germany, the Socialist Party executive urged the Socialists to organize meetings of protest against the nation entering the war, and on the eve of the special session of Congress it urged the President and Congress to refer the question of war to a referendum of the people. As Congress assembled in April, the Socialists gathered in an emergency convention at St. Louis and issued their statement opposing the war.[1] 1690446

This statement is known as the Majority Report. It was signed by eleven members of a special Committee on War and Militarism. Two minority reports were also submitted, the first signed by three members and the second by one member. Of the nearly 200 delegates, 140 voted for the Majority Report. The first minority statement received 31 votes and the second five votes. To obtain a referendum of the party members for one of the defeated reports fifty signatures were required and neither report could obtain the required number, whereupon another statement was drawn up by dissenting delegates and this obtained the required number of signatures. However, a number of delegates favoring the Majority Report signed the dissenting document in order that a test of the opinions of the party membership might be made. The Majority Report was approved by the members.[2]

The adoption of this manifesto against the war immediately gave it marked publicity and singled out the Socialists for indignant attacks. The following paragraphs gave especial offense: "WE brand the declaration of war by our Government as a crime against the nations of the world. In all modern history there had been no war more unjustifiable than the war in which we are about to engage. No greater dishonor has ever been forced upon

[1] All the statements of the party executive and the Majority and Minority reports of the convention were reprinted in *The American Socialists and the War*, New York, 1917. In the above I have drawn largely upon my article on "Changing Fortunes of American Socialism" in *Current History*, April, 1924.

[2] The detailed vote of the members on the Majority and Minority reports was printed in *The Socialist Party Bulletin*, Chicago, July, 1917. Each report was divided into eight important sections and members were required to vote "Yes" or "No" on each section. There was, therefore, no vote for each report as a whole, and the vote on each section naturally varied, but there is little doubt that the Majority Report was favored by a big majority of the members. Every section of the Majority Report but one received over 21,000 votes, while the "Nay" votes with one exception averaged 350. The interest in the Majority Report is also evident from the fact that nearly 23,000 members voted on it, while less than 8,000 members voted on the Minority Report. The organized Socialists were evidently overwhelmingly anti-war.

a people than that which the capitalist class is forcing upon this nation against its will." The Socialists were immediately attacked as "pro-German" although the manifesto itself called upon "the workers of all countries to refuse support to their governments in their wars" and indicted the ruling statesmen of all the warring nations. The program of action outlined in the manifesto included public demonstrations, mass petitions and "all other means within our power"; opposition to conscription and work for repeal of any conscription act passed; opposition to censorship of the press and mails or any restriction of speech, assemblage, organization or the right to strike. It urged propaganda against military training and militaristic teaching in the schools, encouraged political and industrial organizations to shorten the war, and favored educational propaganda to enlighten the masses regarding capitalism and the war. It urged restriction of food exports and fixing of maximum prices, demanded socialization and democratic management of the great industries, land and other natural resources held out of use for speculative purposes.

Another action of the convention caused considerable comment. Article II, Section 6, of the party constitution was repealed. This was the section inserted in 1912 prohibiting any member from advocating sabotage and the general opinion of the press was that the repeal was intended as covert instructions to the membership to practice sabotage. The proceedings of the convention were never printed, but the minutes of each session were printed for the delegates. The record of the seventh day session shows that Delegate Kennedy, for the Constitution Committee, moved to strike out the section with the understanding that "the committee expresses neither approval nor disapproval of the phrases eliminated, but rather, that, in the judgment of some of the committee the educational purpose of the adoption in 1912 of this section has been accomplished, while still others of the committee believe that such questions are more properly within the domain of the economic organizations." The Massachusetts delegation presented a statement, saying that in voting for the repeal they did so "with the express understanding that the elimination of the section does not express an endorsement of methods of individual violence as means (a form of?) of the class struggle or the propaganda of such methods, nor does it mean a repudiation of the stand of the party that political action is one of the basic principles of the party." However, a motion to repeal the section without any accompanying statement was adopted by a vote of 78 to 42. The Massachusetts statement was representative of a large majority of the convention and sabotage itself had by 1917 become almost an extinct word in the vocabulary of the Socialist organizations.[3]

Within a month after the delegates had returned home the Indiana Socialist state headquarters was raided and it became known that W. R. Gaylord, a former Socialist State Senator in Wisconsin, and A. M. Simons, former editor of the *International Socialist Review*, had written Senator Husting of Wisconsin advising him of the "treasonable" character of the Majority Report and suggesting that steps should be taken to prevent its general circulation although permitting the members of the Socialist Party to vote upon it. The Indiana raid by the Federal authorities was the beginning of raids and arrests of Socialists.[4]

Congress passed the Espionage Act on June 15, and the national organ of the Socialist Party *The American Socialist*, issue of June 30, was denied transit through the mails because it carried an advertisement of a leaflet bearing the title, "The Price We Pay." The June issue of the party's national bulletin was also declared

[3] *Proceedings, Emergency Convention of the Socialist Party of America, at St. Louis*, 1917, seventh session, morning, pp. 8-10.

[4] The Gaylord-Simons letter appeared in *The Congressional Record*, May 11, 1917, and *The New York Call*, May 19, 1917. The same issue of the latter publication carries a symposium of the opinions of prominent Socialists regarding the action of Gaylord and Simons, who automatically ceased to be members of the party. One contributor quoted the opinions of Mr. Simons on the war since September, 1914, showing that he had been a militant opponent of the war down to the period when he joined with Mr. Gaylord in sending the letter to Senator Husting.

unmailable. On July 15 a peace demonstration and parade of 10,000 people organized by the Socialists in Boston was broken up by a mob, the state headquarters was raided, its records and literature were thrown into the street and burnt. The first meeting of the executive of the party on July 6 was largely given to a consideration of the suppression of Socialist meetings and publications.

Following the adoption of the anti-war program certain prominent members left the Socialist Party and associated with the advocates of the war. The most conspicuous leaders of this group had been extremists and advocates of sabotage. The Socialist movement in all countries has frequently witnessed this peculiar psychological type. Its representatives have often gone over to the most conservative views when some crisis faced the movement and the United States now witnessed this phenomenon. Sorel, the French philosopher of revolutionary Syndicalism, became an admirer of the Italian monarchy. Briand and Viviani became noted exponents of French imperialism. Hervé, who as a Syndicalist had urged insurrection against militarism, became one of the most extreme chauvinists and nationalists during the war. Most of the leaders of the bolting Socialists, like the European type, have abandoned their Socialist views.

This group made no impression on Socialists in general. Its members organized the Social Democratic League, but this organization attracted few members and it died. So did the National Party, organized by a few of this group. The dissenting leaders found their way into the American Alliance for Labor and Democracy, inspired by leaders of the American Federation of Labor in Minneapolis, in 1917. Mr. Samuel Gompers and his associates conceived the idea of founding a special organization to aid in the prosecution of the war and to combat all views not consistent with a "knockout" victory. A few years before the war Mr. Gompers had visited Europe. He was aware of the forces that were making for war, and, upon his return, wrote his approval of the anti-war attitude of the organized masses. "They intend to resist stubbornly any reckless heads of State," he wrote, "that may set out to employ them as mere counters in a clash of force over questions which are alien to their own great interest in social justice. On this point 'the workingman has no country.' "[5] As late as 1916 the American Federation of Labor had also affirmed its "fraternal spirit and worldwide sympathy and kindly regard for the welfare of our fellow-workers, regardless of where located or of what nationality." It opposed militarism and military training in the schools, warned against "pseudo-patriotism" and a large standing army, and appointed a committee of five to report on these matters.[6] However, the appointment of this committee was abandoned, and in March representatives of the unions, meeting in Washington, were presented with a document declaring full co-operation of the unions with the Government in prosecuting the war, if declared.

Certain evidences of dissent within the unions induced Mr. Gompers and his official colleagues to found the American Alliance for Labor and Democracy in September at Minneapolis. The deserting Socialist group found a place in this organization. Although homage was paid to freedom of discussion as an abstract principle, the alliance declared that utterances that could be construed as obstruction of war aims "should be repressed by the constituted authorities."[7] The abandonment by the American Federation of Labor of what it had stood for and its acquiescence

[5] Gompers, *Labor in Europe and America*, New York, 1910, pp. 274-78. In this book Mr. Gompers fully shared the internationalist and anti-militarist views of the organized workers and Socialists of all countries. These workers "will forever refuse to kill one another merely because authority has put them in different uniforms" (p. 277). He ridiculed wars of either "defense or aggression" (p. 276).

[6] *American Federation of Labor History, Encyclopedia, Reference Book*, pp. 121-22. Also Gompers, *American Labor and the War*, documents and reports, pp. 289-329.

[7] Encyclopedia, etc., p. 74. Mr. Gompers' collection of public addresses in the preceding citation reveal an intolerance that was not exceeded by any other man during the war, and a recklessness in attacking those who disagreed with him that ignored facts in the most amazing fashion.

in arbitrary suppression of dissenting opinions gave the Government authorities a free hand in "controlling thought." In the intolerant atmosphere that followed, not only did Socialists find it difficult to express their opinions, but many others as well.

In international relations the Socialists faced other difficulties. In all the warring nations, those who maintained their ideals of international fraternity were deprived of their contact with each other. At the same time the "war Socialists" were patronized by their respective governments. They were provided with passports and given missions abroad. An example of this was the relations maintained by the American Federation of Labor with W. A. Appleton, Secretary of the General Federation of Trade Unions of Great Britain. This organization was an insurance society to provide strike benefits for members of unions affiliating with the General Federation. It had no power to formulate policies or to speak for British Labor. These functions belong to the British Trade Union Congress, the Labor Party, and their executives. However, Mr. Appleton, who for years had been opposed to the general policies of British Labor, was singled out by the British Government as the spokesman of British Labor. Mr. Gompers also accepted him in that capacity. In their standard history, the Webbs speak of "the resentment at the ever-widening range of subjects at home, on which Mr. Appleton, the Management Committee, and the conferences of the General Federation claimed to voice the feelings of organized labor. . . . It looks as if the General Federation must in future either restrict itself to the limited range of its original purpose or else run the risk of being financially weakened by the secession of influential trade unions."[8] Mr.

---

[8] Sidney and Beatrice Webb, *History of Trade Unionism* (Rev. Ed), New York, 1920, pp. 554-56. Mr. Gompers' defense of his negotiations with British and European trade unions during the war may be consulted in his *Seventy Years of Life and Labor*, Vol. II, pp. 387-472, but he presents little documentary evidence. Kellogg's and Gleason's *British Labor and the War*, New York, 1919, presents the views and negotiations of the British workers, and its value lies in the informing excerpts it reprints of important communications that passed between Mr. Gompers and the British leaders.

Gompers' views appeared to have the support of British Labor, while in England the real representatives of Labor protested in vain at the usurpation of Mr. Appleton and his colleagues.

Meantime many Socialist and radical publications were being deprived of their mailing privileges. In September, 1917, the head office of the Socialist Party at Chicago was raided by Federal officials, and in February, 1918, Adolph Germer, National Executive Secretary; J. Louis Engdahl, editor of the party's national publications; William F. Kruse, Secretary of the National Young People's Socialist League; Irwin St. John Tucker, former head of the party's literature department, and Victor L. Berger, of the National Executive Committee, were indicted under the Espionage Act. They were tried in the following December, convicted in January, 1919, and sentenced to twenty years' imprisonment. In June, 1918, Eugene V. Debs, the party's presidential candidate in every presidential election since 1900, spoke in Canton, Ohio, and was indicted. In September, 1918, he was convicted and sentenced to ten years in prison. Victor L. Berger was elected a member of Congress in November, 1918, and was expelled. In November, 1919, five Socialists were elected to the New York Legislature, and in the following January they were called before the Speaker of the Assembly, who informed them that they had been "elected on a platform that is absolutely inimical to the best interests of the State of New York and of the United States." This was followed by a "trial" and the expulsion of the Socialists. The raids, arrests, throwing publications out of the mails and even refusal to mail circulars appealing for funds to insure legal defense of those indicted left the Socialists without their usual channels of information. Many local organizations disappeared and public meetings became almost impossible, except in the larger cities.

The Bolshevik revolution in November, 1917, had in the meantime made an impression upon the trade unions and Socialist organizations in many countries. Following the collapse of the

Central Powers, the Russian Communists arranged for an international conference, which was held in March, 1919. Socialist groups in nine countries signed the call for what proved to be the first congress of the Communist or Third International. This congress issued a Manifesto to the Socialists and revolutionary workers of all countries.[9] This document presented a searching analysis of the causes of the war and with bitter invectives denounced the political and economic organizations of the masses that supported their governments, as well as the lead rs of these organizations. This document served as the basis for organizing a "left wing" in the Socialist Party. It did not have that positive character and certainty of program which characterized later Bolshevik pronouncements, with the result that the "left wing" program was just as uncertain.

This first Manifesto of the Communist International declared that Communist Russia had created "a higher working-class democracy," but that "in those countries in which the historical development has furnished the opportunity, the working class had utilized the regime of political democracy for its organization against Capitalism. In all countries where the conditions for a workers' revolution are not yet ripe, the same process will go on." Where the institutions "of political democracy represent bloody ruins" the proletariat must create its own democracy, which "is represented in the Workmen's Councils." Where possible, workers, soldiers and peasants through these councils must "oppose them to the State apparatus of the bourgeoisie." The imperialistic war was "passing into the civil war, which lines up class against class." Therefore, "the Third International is the International of open mass action of the revolutionary realization, the international of deeds." The proletariat must concentrate all its energies

---

[9] A number of reprints of this Manifesto appeared in this country. One translation appeared in *The Nation*, May 31, 1919. A translation by Ida Ferguson appeared in *Truth*, Duluth, Minn., July 18, 1919, which the notorious Lusk Committee of the New York Legislature reprinted in Vol. I of its report on *Revolutionary Radicalism*, Albany, 1920.

upon "mass action, with its logical result — direct conflict with the governmental machinery in open combat."

Although all the energies and resources of the organized Socialists were being devoted to the defense of various members who were indicted or were being tried for alleged offences under the Espionage Act, the receipt of this Russian Manifesto was followed by the bitterest factional quarrel they had ever faced. This document was made the basis for the accusation that the Socialists, especially their representative spokesmen, were "reformist," too "moderate," and had failed to represent a real Socialist movement. This indictment of the Socialist Party by a faction of its own members was formulated in a Manifesto of the New York Left Wing, which served as a model for similar action by small groups in the lesser cities and large groups in the alrger cities, especially where the party had a considerable number of members of foreign birth. As the members of alien birth played a conspicuous role in the organization of the Left Wing as well as the numerous Communist parties, it is important to consider them.

In addition to its English-speaking branches, the Socialist Party had permitted various nationalities to organize into federations, with the expectation that they would be better adapted to teaching their members American history and American problems than by admitting these members into American branches, where they would find it difficult to understand the language. All the local organizations, including those attached to the federations, were Socialist educational clubs. Only those members who are citizens, of course, function as such in the political committees recognized by the election laws of each state. The admission of such federations began in 1907 by permitting the Finns to have a Translator in the head office of the party. The national convention of the party in 1908 adopted a resolution in favor of the organization of foreign-language branches and having them affiliate with the party but not until the Convention of 1910 was the party constitution amended so as to clearly define the relations between these federations and the various divisions of the organization. The development of these foreign-language federations may be seen from the following table showing the years when each was admitted:

Finnish	1907
Lettish	1908
South Slavic	1911
Italian	1911
Scandinavian	1911
Hungarian	1912
Bohemian	1912
German	1913
Polish	1913
Jewish	1913
Slovak	1913
Ukrainian	1915
Lithuanian	1915
Russian	1915

A few years' experience developed the fact that these federations often tended to act as a unit in affairs of the organization, and they were occasionally disturbed by differing opinions on questions arising in the homelands of the members. In practice, some of the federations constituted small national Socialist parties attached to the American organization. Others, like the Finns, the Germans and a majority of the Jews, performed real service in acquainting their members with American conditions and aiding members to become citizens. On the whole, the federations were always a problem for American Socialists, and no satisfactory solution of it was ever reached. It was these federations which, responsive to the upheavals that occurred in Europe at the end of the first World War, contributed the bulk of the membership of the Communist parties. Each federation had a publication in its own language, but to reach the American members it was necessary to establish publications in English. In New York City, Chicago, Cleveland and Boston this was accomplished by liberal financial contributions.

A substantial number of American members were also attracted to the Left Wing, but they did not all continue the course that led the Left Wing into the underground organization that soon followed. A few returned to the Socialist Party, but many, disillusioned, uncertain and dissatisfied, did not affiliate with any organization.

There was also a general belief among the members of these federations that the United States was on the eve of a social revolution. They were confirmed in this belief by every declaration and manifesto that arrived from Moscow, and these declarations were numerous. The revolutions in Europe following the end of the war had also convinced the Third International that the bourgeois order had reached its end in all countries. The "world revolution" was at hand. Indeed, it appeared that most of the European nations were collapsing and that the organized working class in each were to fall heir to the power of the old ruling classes. The statesmen of the victorious powers feared this and it brooded over their deliberations in the peace conference in Paris.

But while all this was true of Europe, there was not the slightest evidence of any great social changes in the United States. Unlike the European nations, American capitalism and, to a large extent, American workers thrived upon the war. Americans were not within the immediate zone of the conflict, and its agonies and sacrifices were not felt by them as they were by the masses abroad. Famine did not impend, cities were not shelled or bombed, and American forces took part in the fighting only a few months instead of years. We had no great masses made desperate by the war and no soldiers transformed into determined revolutionaries. There was no peasantry made desperate by their sufferings, ready to unite with mutinous soldiers and urban workers in setting up councils after the Russian fashion. All the factors that accompanied the revolutions in Europe were absent in the United States. All indications were that America would emerge from the war self-satisfied, its profiteers fat with their gains, the workers satisfied with war wages, and the returning soldiers confident that "we won the war." Yet the members of most of the foreign federations attached to the Socialist Party sincerely believed that the United States was entering a revolutionary crisis, that the revolution would drift into physical conflict through "mass action" and "civil war" and end by the "overthrow of the bourgeois State." It was a period of intoxication and thrills, a foretaste of revolutionary frenzy, that could not be reasoned with. It was a delirium that had to run its course.

It is true that the number of strikes had increased in this country. The average number of strikes each year in the quarter century 1881-1906 was 1,470. There was a marked increase after the United States entered the war. "In the two years 1917 and 1918 the number of strikes was 7,572, and in the period 1916 to 1921, inclusive, there were 20,062 strikes, an average of 3,343 strikes each year." [10] But the majority of these strikes were voted by members of conservative unions, who at no time displayed any interest in or sympathy with any program of social transformation. What political dissatisfaction developed outside the Socialist Party was not Communist. It took the form of a Labor Party, which was organized in Chicago in November, 1919, by over a thousand delegates representing trade unions. However, Left Wing publications regarded the strikes as significant of a drift towards physical revolt. "Mass strikes," they were called, although they did not differ from any other strikes that had occurred before we entered the war. It was expected that these strikes would increase in number and eventually involve many millions of wage workers who in turn would come into conflict with the "apparatus of the bourgeois State," seize power under the leadership of Communists, and establish a proletarian dictatorship based on the Soviet form of organization.

[10] Fitch, *The Causes of Industrial Unrest*, New York, 1924, p. 4.

CHAPTER III

THE LEFT WING SOCIALISTS

PROFESSOR SUMNER was of the opinion that "Revolutionary leaders expect to carry the people over to new mores by the might of two or three dogmas of political or social philosophy."[1] This is generally true, because a period of social revolution reduces all issues to one of power and organization for a rising social class, and the Left Wing which emerged from the Socialist Party verified this truth. It framed a program based upon the conception of a society facing a catastrophe. It indicted its opponents for failure to recognize that the social order in the United States had entered a period of collapse that imperatively required a few simple slogans which the masses would understand and to which they would respond.

Within a few months after the end of the first World War the Left Wing was organized in New York City, and early in the spring of 1919 it adopted a "Manifesto and Program."[2] The first section of this document was devoted to a review of the Socialist movement in general, and in particular to the alleged failings of

[1] Summer, *Folkways*, p. 86.
[2] *Manifesto and Program of the Left Wing Section Socialist Party*, Local Greater New York, 1919. See Appendix I for the Left Wing Program.

the American organization. The Left Wing denounced the Socialists for not having converted "an imperialistic war into a civil war — into a proletarian revolution." They either openly favored the war or adopted a policy of "petty bourgeois pacifism." Why had this happened? Because, this Manifesto declares, the Socialist Parties had for years concerned themselves with reform measures and social legislation, with the result that "dominant moderate Socialism accepted the bourgeois State as the basis of its action and strengthened that State." This moderate Socialism was intended to attract "tradesmen, shopkeepers and members of the professions," and forgot the proletariat. Compromising with the bourgeois State, this Socialism "fell a prey to social patriotism and nationalism." [3]

But "revolutionary Socialism" was certain to eventually burst through this fraudulent thing. Fortunately, the Russian Communists had shown the way by establishing a proletarian dictatorship. If we turn to the United States, we observe the opportunities that moderate Socialism was missing. There was "formidable industrial unrest, a seething ferment of discontent, evidenced by inarticulate rumblings which presage striking occurrences." Moreover, the "temper of the workers and soldiers, after the sacrifices they have made in the war, is such that they will not endure the reactionary conditions so openly advocated by the master class," while "strikes are developing which verge on revolutionary action." A Labor Party was in process of organization, but "Laborism is as much a danger to the revolutionary proletariat as moderate Socialism." The Socialists must reorganize. They must "prepare to come to grips with the master class during the difficult period of capitalist readjustment now going on." The Left Wing did not abandon political action, but considered it as "a struggle for the capture and destruction of the capitalist State," and yet this State must also "be destroyed by the mass action of the revolutionary proletariat." In fact, the "bourgeois State must be completely

[3] *Ibid.*, pp. 3-7.

destroyed" and a new State — the State "of the Federated Soviets" — must take its place.[4] We, therefore, understand the gulf that separated the Left Wing from the moderate Socialists.

The Manifesto, in its reference to "rumblings which presage striking occurrences," is reminiscent of religious sects that see "signs" and "omens" of fearful things to come. Its expectation of returning soldiers, dissatisfied and likely to be swept into some revolutionary agitation, is amusing, considering their activities in the American Legion. The strikes were based upon the usual demands for more wages or organized resistance to wage reductions. There was no evidence whatever at the time this was written or at any period thereafter that strikes were tending towards some form of revolutionary action. The Manifesto was merely a response to what had occurred in Russia. As an interpretation of the year 1919 it is absurd.

Turning to the Program presented in the Manifesto, we find that organization of Workmen's Councils is recommended as "mass organizations of the working class" for the "immediate struggle" and as "instruments for the seizure of power of the State"; workmen's control of industry to be exercised by "industrial unions or Soviets"; repudiation of all debts, "with provision to safeguard small investors"; expropriation of the banks; expropriation "of railways and the large (trust) organizations of capital," provision to be made "during the transition period for the protection of small owners of stock";[5] the socialization of foreign trade. These were not to be regarded as "immediate demands," but imply "a revolutionary struggle" against the State

---

[4] *Ibid.*, pp. 7-12.

[5] *Ibid.*, p. 13. The contradiction between the safeguards urged for "small investors" and "small owners of stock" and the ultraproletarian character claimed for this program was immediately detected by its opponents, who ridiculed its authors and supporters. The Left Wing was so embarrassed by this that, in a later edition, they eliminated references to small investors. The program was practically copied from a Russian document. It represents the stage at which the Bolshevik program had evolved in Russia early in 1919.

and the coming of "the new Soviet State" with its "dictatorship of the proletariat."

The Program concluded with ten short paragraphs, which may be summarized as follows: (1) a uniform declaration of principles and the "aboltion of all social reform planks"; (2) "the party must teach, propagate and agitate exclusively for the overthrow of Capitalism and the establishment of Socialism through a proletarian dictatorship"; (3) Socialist candidates must adhere "strictly" to the above provisions; (4) the party must engage in propaganda for "revolutionary industrial unionism"; (5) the party press must be party owned and controlled; (6) party educational institutions must be so owned and controlled; (7) the party must discard obsolete and publish new literature in keeping with the new policies and tactics; (8) demands an emergency convention "to meet the present crisis"; (9) demands repudiation of the Berne Congress and any other congress of moderate Socialists; (10) demands election of delegates to the international congress proposed by the Russian Bolsheviki and participation only in such congress that includes Communists, Spartacists and Left Wing parties.[6]

This Manifesto and Program caused the "split" in the Socialist Party a few months later. As early as March, 1919, a Chicago group organized the "Communist Propaganda League" and adopted a program similar to that of the New York Left Wing.[7] The measures and policies demanded of the Socialist Party were urged with religious fervor as a final program that would correct numerous mistaken policies and insure steady progress in winning the support of the American working class. In presenting it to party gatherings, the Left Wing would not agree to any amendments or substitutes, nor would it consent to a consideration of it item by item. It must be accepted or rejected as a whole. The parent Left Wing in New York was organized in February, 1919, by certain delegates who left the Central Committee of Greater

---

[6] *Ibid.*, p. 14.
[7] The Chicago Program appeared in *The Communist, Chicago*, April 1, 1919.

New York and organized within the Socialist Party. They adopted this Manifesto and Program, opened headquarters and proceeded to issue membership cards to those who joined it.[8]

This action presented not only an issue involving program, policy and methods, but also whether the Socialist Party could permit some of its members to organize within it, establish their own dues system, issue membership cards, and thus constitute an organization within the organization. In reality, the "split" occurred when the Left Wing took this course. While it gave formal allegiance to the Socialist Party, it pledged its members' allegiance to the Left Wing and enforced strict discipline to maintain this Left Wing allegiance. It served as an organized bloc, and even adopted its own constitution. As an organized group, it set aside the rules, decisions, membership obligations and procedure of another organization, taking over its powers and functions without obtaining a mandate from that organization or its members.

The divergence of opinion between the insurgents and the regulars had gone so far that the Left Wing objected to the circulation of petitions and holding of mass meetings to obtain amnesty for political prisoners. The Left Wing was so confident that a social revolution was at hand in all modern countries that it had no

[8] The Left Wing application blank will be found in the Lusk Committee's report on Revolutionary Radicalism, Vol. I, p. 681. The first two volumes of this report contain many documents of various organizations which would be difficult to find elsewhere. Most of this material is reliable, but the editorial matter accompanying them is generally malicious, false in interpretation, and betrays an ignorance of working-class movements that is amazing. For example, an attemt to form a Central American Union of five Latin-American republics is declared in this report to be an attempt to organize "a single Communistic State." (Vol. I, p. 497.) The report lists hundreds of organizations and individuals as "dangerous," or "Socialists," "Communists," "Anarchists," etc., without any regard to facts. Even the Ford peace ship is given a number of pages, and a number of post cards and letters that passed between members of the Ford peace party are solemnly photographed and reprinted in facsimile. No reliance whatever can be placed on any editorial statements that appear in this report, and many of the documents that are printed have no relation whatever to "revolutionary radicalism." The committee itself was later discredited when its insufferable arrogance provoked resentment and its most conspicuous members were laughed into oblivion.

patience with these "bourgeois" methods. The Massachusetts convention of the Left Wing in May, 1919, resolved to liberate political prisoners by "general political strikes and demonstrations." [9] A Left Wing editorial also declared that in the matter of such prisoners "we don't want amnesty for them. We want them to be released by the industrial might of the proletariat, by class-conscious action." [10] In the same month five of the foreign federations, through their representatives, protested against holding an amnesty convention and demanded of the executive of the Socialist Party that the call for this convention be rescinded and the convention abandoned. [11] In the publications of both groups it was being admitted that both could not remain within the organization. The Left Wing strategy was to remain within the organization and obtain control of it and its publications.

But the Left Wing itself soon revealed divergent tendencies, and it was unable to maintain the discipline and unity necessary to accomplish its intentions. The foreign-language federations constituted a Left Wing within the Left Wing, and this unexpected development forced the insurgents to turn from the regulars and give attention to their own internal troubles. Out of this internal quarrel came two Left Wings. Late in May the National Executive Committee of the Socialist Party met in Chicago and took a series of actions that brought all issues to a crisis. The executive consisted of fifteen members, of which two were in prison, three others absent and ten were present. Two of the members present were committed to the Left Wing. In his report to the executive, the National Executive Secretary, Adolph Germer, called attention to a rapid increase in the membership of the foreign-language federations within a few months, especially those representing the various Russian nationalities. In a recent referendum of the party members for the election of national party

[9] *The Revolutionary Age*, Boston, June 7, 1919.
[10] *Ibid.*, May 24, 1919.
[11] *The Bulletin*, National Office, Socialist Party, June 15, 1919.

officials, he had observed that many members of these federations had voted as a unit and in some instances ballots were marked by the same person. The unprecedented increase in the membership of the federations was presented in the following table:

Federations	Dec., 1918	April, 1919
Russian	2,373	7,824
Ukrainian	2,400	3,836
South Slavic	1,200	3,115
Lithuanian	4,760	6,049
Lettish	1,353	1,606
Totals	12,086	22,430

Under ordinary circumstances, he continued, the average membership of the party, which for the first four months of the year was 104,656, would be encouraging, but the character of the increase was a matter of much concern. The membership for April showed that 57,248 members were in all the foreign federations, and as the total membership of the party for that month was 108,504, the figures showed that 53 per cent., a majority, were members of these federations. This, he concluded, was a dangerous situation, as the federations were already showing that they could not rise above "nativistic and nationalistic prejudices."

He next directed attention to the state organization in Michigan which had in a state convention adopted a provision that all local organizations in that state should refrain from adopting or supporting any reform measures and that any such organization supporting such reforms would have its charter revoked. Another resolution of the Michigan convention also required all speakers and organizers "upon all occasions" to discuss and explain religion, the assumption being that they were to give the party in that state a special anti-religious character. The Executive Secretary contended that these two actions of the Michigan organization ranged it in conflict with the national organization.

J. Mahlon Barnes, the Director of the American Freedom Convention, the special department created by the Socialist Party for holding a national amnesty convention, also reported that six foreign-language federations had announced their intention to oppose any amnesty convention, and that they had used "their office machinery to send out mimeographed resolutions to their branches . . . to obstruct and oppose the convention," while all the Left Wing publications did "everything possible" to characterize the proposed convention as "reactionary" and to "break up the movement for the release of political prisoners." While this obstruction was going on, he complained, a Federal agent had entered his office and seized thousands of letters announcing the proposed convention, while 2,300 other letters of a similar character mailed a week before were being held in the local office. With this practical cooperation between the Left Wing and Government officials, the Director doubted the advisability of proceeding with arrangements for the convention.

These were the more important questions that faced the executive, which was in session seven days. All important issues were decided by a strict partisan vote of eight to two. The important actions taken were, (1) the suspension of seven foreign-language federations and referring this action and the reasons for it to a special national convention; (2) revocation of the Michigan State charter; (3) instructing the Executive Secretary not to tabulate the vote cast in the referendum for party officials and "to call in all the original ballots of the federations in question, send them to the National office, and that a committee be elected to investigate the whole question of the election and report to the national convention"; (4) that a national Emergency Convention be called, to meet in Chicago on August 30; (5) that the membership be urged not to initiate any referendums on controversial matters, as they "can only be settled after consulting a mass of testimony and documentary evidence, which cannot possibly be sent to the party membership and which are essential to intelligent decisions"; (6) that members in Michigan opposed to the two objectionable actions taken in that state be organized so that they would not be deprived of representation in the national convention; (7) refusing a request of the two Left Wing members that they be permitted to print a statement in the party's *National Bulletin* regarding their position on questions decided by the executive.[12]

A state convention of the party in Massachusetts early in June was easily controlled by the Left Wing. This was due to the large foreign-born population of the state, which contributed a majority membership to the state organization. By a majority of 117 to 40, the convention voted to send two delegates to a National Conference of the Left Wing, which was to meet in New York on June 21, and all local organizations in the country were urged to send delegates. Sixty-eight delegates withdrew from the convention and appealed to the National Executive Committee for recognition. By a vote of eight to one, this committee revoked the charter of the Massachusetts organization, cancelled the election of delegates to the national convention, granted a state charter to the 68 regulars and instructed them and local organizations adhering to them to elect delegates to this convention.[13]

Meantime the Left Wing in Ohio endeavored to obtain a referendum of the members in all states. Local Cuyahoga County (Cleveland) presented the initiative, but the National Executive Committee refused, by a vote of seven to three, to send it out for a general vote on the ground that it carried with it comment of a character prohibited by the constitution of the party.[14] This decision made it certain that all issues would be settled in the national convention to be held in August.

[12] The complete minutes of this meeting, together with considerable documentary material, appeared in the party's *National Bulletin*, June 15, 1919. On the more important controversial questions, the Left Wing members presented in each case a carefully written statement of their views, which appeared in this issue.

[13] The proceedings of the Massachusetts Left Wing convention appeared in *The New England Leader*, June 10, 1919. The action of the National Executive Committee in revoking the Massachusetts charter and reasons therefor appeared in the *National Bulletin*, July 15, 1919.

[14] *National Bulletin*, July 15, 1919.

The National Conference of the Left Wing in New York on June 21 divided into two wings. A minority, dominated by the foreign-language federations, desired the immediate organization of a Communist Party, while the majority favored a national convention in Chicago at the same time the Socialists were to meet, believing the latter might abandon their convention and thus leave the Left Wing to fall heir to delegates that came to Chicago; or if the Socialist convention was held, the Left Wing hoped by propaganda to "split" it or obtain the allegiance of some of the Socialist delegates. The minority, favoring immediate organization of a Communist Party, was defeated by a vote of 55 to 38, and 31 delegates left the conference. The majority elected a National Council of nine members and issued a call for a national convention, to meet in Chicago on September 1, to include "all revolutionary elements willing to unite with a revolutionized Socialist Party or with a Communist Party that may be organized by Left Wing delegates seceding from the convention of the Socialist Party to be held August 30." The conference adopted a long and tedious manifesto, couched in obscure verbiage, and a number of other documents, including one devoted to the "moderate" Socialism of the Socialist Party, and then adjourned.[15]

In the meantime the Left Wing obtained what it claimed to be the returns on the disputed Socialist Party referendum on the election of national party officials which had been held up by the National Executive Committee. These returns included 26 states and the District of Columbia, and showed that the Left Wing had elected all its candidates by heavy majorities, including one who

---

[15] The proceedings of the Left Wing conference, including the Manifesto and other documents, appeared in *The Revolutionary Age*, New York, July 5, 1919. The constant use of the word "moderate" in this period recalls the rebuke administered by William Cobbett against the inappropriate use of this adjective. "Amongst a select society of empty heads," he wrote, " 'moderate reform' has long been a fashionable expression; an expression that has been well criticized by asking the gentlemen who use it, how they would like to obtain 'moderate justice' in a court of law or to meet with 'moderate chastity' in a wife." — Cole, *The Life of William Cobbett*, p. 271.

was practically unknown outside of Chicago. This convinced the regulars that the foreign federations had voted practically as a unit and according to instructions.[16]

Late in June the Left Wing captured the state convention of the Socialist Party of Ohio, but also elected delegates to the Socialist Party national convention. They were instructed, however, to support the Left Wing program in the convention if seated, but if the program was not carried out, they were to "bolt" the convention and unite with other sections of the Left Wing in organizing a Communist Party. How obsessed with world events these delegates were, was demonstrated in a Municipal Platform which they adopted for all Ohio cities. Two paragraphs were devoted to the cities, one stating that Left Wing candidates elected to public office in the cities shall "use their special position to carry on a propaganda for the establishment of the proletarian dictatorship" and the other favoring municipal ownership of city industries. The remainder of this long document was devoted to the causes of the war, the development of capital, imperialism, the League of Nations, internationalism, and the dictatorship of the proletariat! [17]

[16] This Left Wing tabulation of the referendum vote appeared in the *Ohio Socialist* (Cleveland), June 18, 1919. The figures showed that a little over 16,000 of the 104,000 members had voted. Many of the American members had become discouraged by the factional quarrel and did not vote, but most of the members of the foreign federations were mobilized to vote in this referendum for the Left Wing candidates. See below, pp. 61-62.

[17] Proceedings of the convention were reported in the *Ohio Socialist* (Cleveland), July 9, 1919.
The utterly irrational Left Wing psychology was demonstrated a few months later when the New York Left Wing contested the Socialist Primaries in October. In a number of districts its candidates were nominated. They declined, but, due to some complication in the election law, the declinations were not accepted. The Left Wing then engaged in a campaign, urging the voters to boycott the election, including its own candidates! *The Communist* (Chicago) issue of October 4 rejoiced over this decision and attempted to provide a "scientific" basis for what it believed to be a new proletarian tactic which had issued from this New York incident. We quote, word for word, a number of paragraphs from this long

Within a few weeks of the meeting of the August 30 convention there were three Left Wings — (1) the parent Left Wing, that had controlled the conference of June 21; (2) the insurgent Left Wing, which consisted largely of the foreign federations

editorial, which is without sense and which defies intelligent interpretation, but is typical of much that appeared in Left Wing and Communist publications:

"Campaigns and elections are not necessarily interwoven: they may be separated. There is, in fact, a clear distinction between campaigns and elections; there are moments when the Communist Party will participate in the campaign, but boycott the elections, in order to emphasize the mass character of the proletarian struggle. . . . The Communist Party participates in the political campaigns for purposes of propaganda and in order to emphasize the political character of the class struggle. The workers must be convinced of the futility of the isolated strike against the employers and of the necessity of action against the State by means of general political strikes, culminating in the conquest of the power of the State by the revolutionary proletariat. The Communist Party, accordingly, uses parliamentarism to emphasize the political character of the class struggle, but equally to emphasize the impossibility of parliamentarism conquering the power of the State.

"This being our general policy, at particular moments the Communist Party will participate in the political campaign in order to emphasize the objective — conquest of the power of the State; but will boycott the elections in order to emphasize the means necessary to attain this objective — the general political strikes of the proletariat and the development of proletarian organs of State power.

"The proletarian revolution is a process, each phase developing its own problems and requiring the application of appropriate tactics in accord with Communist fundamentals and life itself. It is the characteristic of the Socialist betrayer of Socialism to evade all actual problems of the revolution. The proletarian revolution is a process; it has its own peculiar problems at particular stages of its development; our tactics, accordingly, must be pliable, living, in accord with the problems of each phase of development. In preliminary stages, we shall find it necessary to boycott the elections while participating in the campaign; in the final stage it may become necessary to boycott parliamentarism completely, as did the Spartacan-Communists of Germany during the elections to the Constituent Assembly. . . .

"The Communist Party must develop the consciousness of action against the State, of the political character of the class struggle which we accomplish by means of participation in political campaigns and our general agitation — but simultaneously the Communist Party must emphasize the impossibility of parliamentarism and elections realizing the conquest of power — and this we accomplish by means of a boycott of the elections. The American workers . . . must not depend upon parliamentarism, but must bend parliamentarism to the requirements of the mass struggle. The Communist Party, accordingly, urges: Boycott the elections!" All of which may be profound, but we submit that the reader must boycott reason if he attempts to understand what it means. It is impossible to argue with such obscurantism, yet it is typical of Communist literature.

which withdrew from this conference; (3) Left Wing members elected, in the disputed Socialist Party referendum, as members of the National Executive Committee and who met in Chicago on July 26, organized as the Socialist Party executive, and issued a proclamation to the members of this party. The whole insurgent movement was largely demoralized by the factional quarrels, and the Socialist Party was in little better condition. The third Left Wing presented a demand upon the Executive Secretary of the Socialist Party for the surrender of the national headquarters, which was refused, whereupon it planned to take possession of the Socialist Party convention on the ground that it was the only legal National Executive Committee.[18] But, in August, the plan to capture the Socialist Party convention was abandoned, as the parent Left Wing had decided not to pursue this policy further, and this decision liquidated the third Left Wing, just two weeks before the Socialist convention met.[19] In the meantime the second Wing — the June insurgents — had organized and issued a call for a national convention to meet in Chicago on September 1. Seven of the foreign-language federations, a Minnesota Left Wing convention, the expelled Michigan organization, and twelve city Left Wing local organizations issued the call. They bitterly criticized the parent Left Wing and the Socialist Party, and affirmed their determination to organize the Communist Party of America because: "The present is the period of the dissolution and collapse of the whole capitalist world system, which will mean the complete collapse of world culture if capitalism with its unsolvable contradictions is not replaced by Communism." [20] Late in August the parent Left Wing agreed to go to this convention.

[18] The third Left Wing issued one Socialist Party Bulletin, August 1, 1919, which carries a record of the one meeting held by this committee.

[19] The reasons given for this change of policy on the part of the parent Left Wing were stated in full in *The Revolutionary Age*, New York, August 23, 1919.

[20] The convention call and reasons therefor of the June insurgents appeared in *The Communist*, Chicago, July 19, 1919.

When Socialists, Left Wing members and Communists gathered in Chicago there were three conventions, two of which organized Communist parties. We shall consider the new parties in the next chapter. There was considerable confusion of opinion among the delegates to the Socialist convention, owing to the mass of conflicting statements and claims with which all factions had been flooded since the end of the war. Some were sympathetic to the Left Wing, but a decided majority were opposed, while in the center were a group seeking information before deciding their course. The party executive had also challenged the claims to seats made by a number of delegates. The result of the contests was the seating of four Left Wing Oregon delegates, three of whom went to one of the Communist conventions. Two Left Wing Nebraska delegates were voted seats and also "bolted." The same thing occurred in the case of two Utah delegates. Six from California were given seats and "bolted." The Ohio delegation appeared before the contest committee, but left before their case could be considered. This conduct on the part of so many Left Wing delegates convinced a wavering section of the convention that pronounced Left Wing members had no desire to present their case to their party associates, and this impression proved to be a turning point in favor of the regulars.

However, a report of the National Executive Committee reviewing, in general terms, the troubles which had faced the organization was not satisfactory to the convention. It ordered the committee to report on each specific controversy that involved suspension and revocation of charters. The charter of the Ohio state organization had also been revoked a few weeks before the convention met, and as this state had a large membership, interest in the reasons for this action was keen. The supplementary report of the committee went into detail on these matters, quoting Left Wing documents and decisions, clauses in the party's constitution which, it claimed, had been violated, and justified all its actions on the general ground that the Left Wing movement had acted as a "supreme court without any mandate from the members" in setting aside constitutions, platforms and resolutions, and creating a separate organization in conflict with the Socialist Party while still claiming the privileges of membership in the latter.

The Ohio case was considered in detail by the committee. It quoted the record of the Ohio convention to show that it had voted to affiliate with the Left Wing; that it had accepted branches of the suspended foreign federations in Ohio; that it had ordered the proceeds of the sale of stamps for the payment of the expenses of delegates to the national convention be turned over to the state organization instead of forwarding the funds to the national office; that the Ohio organization had permitted its state secretary to send to local organizations in all other states an urgent appeal; that they also withheld such funds from the national office, and that this official had also served as National Secretary of the "rump" executive which had demanded the surrender of the national office on July 26. The action of the convention on this report was to agree "that the administration of discipline was necessary and justified" but that the executive had not made "sufficient effort to acquaint the membership of the suspended and expelled organizations with the facts and endeavored to have them repudiate their officials." This was carried by a vote of 63 to 39. The minority agreed that the executive had been justified in its disciplinary measures but was opposed to the note of censure which the resolution contained.

The report of the committee entrusted with the investigation of the returns of the vote on the disputed referendum for the election of national party officials confirmed the charges of widespread frauds committed by the Left Wing organizations. The committee consisted of four members one of whom was sympathetic with the Left Wing and who later became a member of the Communist parties. This committee was unanimous in its findings. The report was documented with reports of various party officials who reported frauds in their organizations, samples of fraudulent returns, and a digest of all the material that was presented to it. The report complained that most of the suspected organizations either ignored the request that they send all individual ballots to the committee or refused to send them, but a sufficient number had complied with the request to enable the committee to reach the unanimous conclusion that gross frauds had been committed. The committee's conclusions were: (1) In certain branches of the Russian, Ukrainian, Hungarian and Lithuanian Federations the members signed their names to ballots previously marked by the secretary or some other person; (2) in certain Russian branches the ballots given to members were marked to indicate how they should vote and the members voted as indicated; (3) in certain Russian branches the secretary or canvassing committee fraudulently reported a full vote for the Left Wing slate when votes had been cast for other candidates; (4) a large number of branches in the suspended federations cast more votes than their average membership for the preceding four months; (5) a large number of branches in all the suspended federations cast an absolutely uniform vote, generally for the same candidates, the so-called Left Wing slate; (6) in view of the "fraud and irregularities discovered in the suspended branches from whom we have received ballots it is reasonable to suppose that such fraudulent or irregular practices existed to even a greater extent in those branches which refused to furnish individual ballots as requested by the National Executive Committee." This report was accepted without a dissenting vote.

The question of international affiliation had been referred to a committee of twelve members. The Socialist Party had been impressed by the anti-war position of the Russian Soviet leaders and Socialists in other countries and before the Russians had formulated any general and rigid terms for admission to a new International the American Socialists had been discussing the reconstruction of the international organization. In May, 1919, the general membership of the party voted upon a referendum and by a large majority had agreed on a policy expressed in the following resolution: "That the Socialist Party shall participate in an international congress or conference called by, or in which participate, the Communist Party of Russia (Bolshevik) and the Communist Labor Party of Germany (Spartacan)." The Second International, which had collapsed at the outbreak of the war, had met in Berne, Switzerland, the previous February. Much of the time of the conference was consumed in heated debates on "responsibility" for the war and it contributed practically nothing to the reconstruction of the International. By the time the Socialist convention met, the Third (Moscow) International was sowing discord in the ranks of Socialists and trade unions in all countries. The result was that the convention was not satisfied with either the Second or the Third International.

The Committee on International Relations brought in a Majority and a Minority report. Both agreed to repudiate Berne, that a new international organization was necessary, and that it must take in the Communist and Socialist parties that subscribed to the class struggle and that opposed coalition with the bourgeoisie. But the Minority report went further by recommending that the Socialist Party "declares itself in support of the Third (Moscow) International, not so much because it supports the Moscow programs and methods," but because Moscow "is really challenging world imperialism"; it is threatened by the combined capitalist forces of the world simply because it is proletarian" so that no matter "what we may have to say to Moscow afterwards, it is the duty of Socialists to stand by it now. . . ."

The report was signed by J. Louis Engdahl and William F. Kruse. The Majority report was adopted, but the convention voted to send both reports to a referendum of the members. By a vote of 3,475 to 1,444 the Minority Report was adopted and later forwarded to Moscow. The latter never sent an answer to the National Office, but in the Russian *Press Review* (a weekly bulletin issued by the Soviet Government) there appeared in October, 1920, what was intended to be an answer by the Executive Committee of the Third International. The Socialist Party was attacked and the application rejected.

A New National Executive Committee, except for one hold-over, was elected and the convention adjourned.[21] The Socialists, however, had been severely weakened by quarrels and desertions. On the other hand, the two Left Wings were meeting in other halls in the same city and negotiations between their conventions demonstrated that cohesion was impossible. The foreign-language federations which had contributed the shock troops that waged war within the Socialist organization were now an important factor in the Communist Party. They had practically become the masters of this party and were to play an important role in all the devious history of American Communism in the ensuing years. The Communist movement was no longer hampered by Socialist obstruction and henceforth it was free to choose its own ways, demonstrate its capacity to inspire and organize American workmen, and replace its enemy, the Socialist Party. Its first phase in this role is the theme of the next chapter.

[21] The proceedings of the Socialist Party convention, with accompanying documents, are in the *National Bulletin*. Socialist Party, Chicago, September 15, 1919. See also *The American Labor Year Book*, 1919-1920, New York, Part Six. The answer of the Executive Committee of the Third International to the Socialist Party application was printed in full in the *New York Call*, November 30, 1920.

CHAPTER IV

THE FIRST COMMUNIST PARTIES

ALTHOUGH the United States was the farthest removed from the scene of the first World War and the American Socialist Party had, at great sacrifice of its organization and its members, maintained the historic position of the Socialists against war, it was the first section of this international organization to divide into warring groups following the end of the war. The Socialist and Labor parties in England and Europe had developed opposing groups before the end of the war because of different attitudes towards the war, one favoring support of their governments and the other opposing such support. In the United States support or nonsupport of the war was not an issue among American Socialists except for a very few who left the party after the adoption of the St. Louis anti-war resolution. The "split" in the American organization was a direct outcome of the Russian Revolution and the attacks made upon pro-war Socialists by the Russian Communists. Even the "Manifesto and Program of the Left Wing" which formulated the grievances of the insurgents did not charge the American Socialists with support of the war. This document was a pale reflection of Russian Communism which attracted the Anarcho-Syndicalist tendencies that had flared up in the American organization in 1908, reaching their highest point in 1912, and then subsiding until early in 1919 when the Russian Revolution served as a hothouse for their rapid development.

Thrown upon their own resources in Chicago, the Left Wing elements and June insurgents began a course that has produced more Communist organizations than any other country in the world. They began with a schism which in turn produced numerous sects and organizations, each one in conflict with all others. At the outset it was necessary for the two wings to unite as both were out of the Socialist Party. This they attempted to do and failed. They conferred with each other through committees and exchanged formal documents expressing their respective views of their past relations with each other and the problems that faced them in forming one organization. There was practically no difference of principle between the two organizations. What they contended for was what they had sought in the Socialist organization, special advantage for their respective groups. The June insurgents had already organized their convention as the first national conference of a Communist Party while some of the Left Wing delegates were caucussing and awaiting the results of the contested seats in the Socialist convention. They came to the conclusion that this convention was controlled by a "machine" and at an opportune moment they announced that they were withdrawing from the convention, taking with them a small fraction of the delegations from 21 states. Meeting in the hall below, they met as "the regular convention of the Socialist Party under the direction of the newly elected National Executive Committee." Negotiations were then opened with the Communist Party convention for a union of forces.

The Communist convention desired the Left Wing delegates to present a complete list of such delegates, their instructions, and how many members each claimed to represent. This formal request was followed by a long document critical of the Communism of some members of the Left Wing which resulted in a documentary war as to which convention represented the truest Communism. Left Wing leaders were charged with having "carried on their campaign against the old party upon legalistic grounds" rather than "upon an understanding and acceptance of Communistic principles and tactics." The Left Wing was told that among its suspects were also those who "made use of revolutionary phrases" without understanding the difference between the Right and the Left; some who merely had personal grievances which they were nursing, and others whose Communism could be questioned. It is evident from the documentary exchanges that the Communist convention desired to scrutinize each Left Wing delegate rather than invite all of them to sit as a body in the convention. The Communist convention also claimed to have 128 delegates and nine fraternal delegates representing 58,000 members.[1]

When the negotiations had reached this stage the Left Wing convention had chosen the name "Communist Labor Party." Possibly the delegates believed that by assuming the status of a political party — the Communist convention having already chosen the name "Communist Party" — they would have more prestige in the negotiations. In its answer the Communist Labor Party asserted that a caucus of all Left Wingers following the Socialist Party suspensions in May had decided to continue the "legalistic" struggle in that party and that criticism on this score was "unworthy of those who make it." Moreover, that decision was ratified by the National Left Wing Council and it was the leading members of the Communist Party convention who had violated the decision and organized another convention. The C. L. P. also retorted that "we see inconsistent elements in your convention" and as for membership it had 92 delegates who "represent an overwhelming majority of the Socialist Party's membership."[2]

As for individual delegates presenting themselves to the Com-

[1] This claim is an exaggeration. It is impossible to give accurate figures of the membership of either convention, but a careful study of all claims, including those of the Socialist Party, and making allowance for thousands of members who declined to pay dues to any organization, a rough estimate, and a fair one, will give the whole insurgent movement about 35,000 members at the period of the two conventions.

[2] This is also an exaggeration. Of the 21 states, these delegates could not really be said to represent a majority in more than three or four states, and even these are doubtful, as the strong Left Wing states were fighting ground for both Left Wings. These delegates represented uncertain fragments. The Communist Party conceded them 15,000 members, but even this was too generous. The C.L.P. delegates themselves did not know what or how many members they represented, so they made the claim of a "majority," without mentioning any number.

munist Party convention, this was emphatically declined because they were "Left Wing delegates regularly assembled in an emergency convention and have permanently constituted ourselves the Communist Labor Party." They represented a "permanent and stable organization." They offered the counter proprosal that "the two conference committees shall constitute a joint credentials committee to go over the roster of both conventions to see whether they really contain irreconcilable elements and, if possible, agree upon a joint recommendation to both conventions."

This proposal was curtly refused by the Communist Party convention and the negotiations came to an end except for the adoption of a resolution by the Communist Labor Party convention extending a "standing invitation to the Communist Party to meet, on a basis of equality, in a unity conference." Those who made this advance claimed later that they never received an answer to it. With the adjournment of both conventions war began in the organs of the two parties, a war not only on the question as to which represented Communism, but a war to obtain members from hesitating groups and from each other.

The foreign federations constituted the overwhelming bulk of the membership of the Communist Party convention and easily controlled its deliberations. The few representatives of English-speaking organizations favored a conference with the Communist Labor Party but this conciliatory policy was blocked by the foreign federations. The Michigan state organization which had joined in issuing the call for the Communist Party convention had the largest number of English-speaking members. It had 20 delegates present but they did not vote on the program and other documents presented to the convention as the proceedings convinced them that it was hopeless to venture an opinion not acceptable to the federations. The defection of the Michigan organization really meant the organization of a third Communist organization, for it soon took the initiative in founding the Proletarian Party which we shall consider later. Three Communist parties were the outcome of the Left Wing insurgency in the Socialist Party.

The constitution of the Communist Party created an Executive Committee, elected by the convention, and five alternates to fill vacancies. Applicants for membership were required to read the constitution and the program of the party and accept the "principles and tactics of the party and the Communist International," but no person could become a member "who has an entire livelihood from rent, interest or profit." Applications for membership must be endorsed by two members and proposed members must wait two months before action is taken on their applications. In the meantime they were required to pay an initiation fee and dues and attend meetings.

The main features of the Program were the declaration to overthrow capitalism and the "destruction of the bourgeois State," the Communist Party directing the "workers' struggles against capitalism, developing fuller forms and purposes in the struggle" and "culminating in the mass action of the revolution . . . and the establishment of a dictatorship of the proletariat." If the Communist Party elects any members to legislative bodies they "shall not introduce or support reform measures." Their work was to "expose the oppressive class character of the capitalist State." The party prohibited nominations for executive offices such as for mayor, governor and president as "participation in elections are limited to legislative bodies only, such as municipal councils, state legislatures and national congress." In order to emphasize its "uncompromising character" the Communist Party "in campaigns and elections, and in all its other activities, shall not cooperate with groups or parties not committed to the revolutionary class struggle, such as the Socialist Party, Labor Party, Nonpartisan League, People's Council, Municipal Ownership Leagues, etc." Mass strikes are of supreme importance and must be encouraged and the party "must engage actively in the struggle to revolutionize the trade unions." Wherever possible "councils of workers shall be organized in shops . . . for the purpose of carrying on the industrial union struggle in the old unions, uniting and mobilizing the militant elements; these councils to be unified in a Central Council wherever possible." Of course, the convention voted to affiliate with the Communist International.

The Communist Labor Party convention brought forth an interesting and somewhat heated debate regarding political action. The Platform Committee had brought in a document which appealed to workingmen to unite with the party "on the political field." This was amended to urge the workers to unite "for the conquest of political power, to establish a government adapted to the Communist transformation." This amendment was carried by a vote of 46 to 22. This appeared to some delegates as an evasion of the whole question of political action. A few left the convention and some dissenters remained practically as observers rather than delegates. Later in the proceedings the convention defined political action as "action taken by the workers to impose their class will on the capitalist State." Preceding the section in which this statement is found was also a declaration that "the most important means of capturing State power for the workers is the action of the masses, proceeding from the place where the workers are gathered together — the shops and factories." Moreover, the year 1919 was considered "the period of the dissolution and collapse of the whole system of world capitalism."

Under the caption of "Recommendations" the convention advised alliance with the Communist International. Considering that "this is the historic period of the Social Revolution," all Communist Labor Party platforms must contain "only one demand: the establishment of the dictatorship of the proletariat" and "association with other groups not committed to the revolutionary class struggle" was prohibited. Shop branches were to be organized in factories wherever possible. Locals and Branches were required to elect committees on Labor Organizations to "initiate, or support the creation of, Shop Committees in every industry in their district, the uniting of these committees in Industrial Councils, District Councils, and the Central Council of all Industries."

The constitution of the party revealed some differences from the constitution of the Communist Party. It created a small National Committee of five members and the members could come from any section of the country. No time limit of membership was prescribed for election to this committee. The most important difference, however, was the relations established between the party and foreign federations whose branches were required to be an integral part of local city organizations and pay dues to local and state organizations. The reason for this change, as stated by John Reed and Benjamin Gitlow, two delegates who reported to their New York constituents, was that the federations had been practically autonomous in the Socialist Party, "for they acted as organizations separate and distinct from the English-speaking body of the party." In passing it may be said that the Socialists themselves had made this complaint, but the Left Wing factions had defended the status of the federations in the Socialist Party.

After adopting a number of resolutions and a "Proclamation to the Membership" the convention finished its work. This document carried the statement that "the Socialist Party employed the Chicago Police Department to throw out of the national convention the duly elected delegates of the membership." As this alleged use of the police was made prominent in all the insurgent publications it may be noticed here. The Chicago Police Department sends patrolmen to all large gatherings and they were present at the Socialist convention. They also appeared at the other conventions. Passions were at a high pitch at the opening of the Socialist convention as the Left Wing had announced its intention to take it in charge. Many of its delegates were meeting in conference in the same building. Left Wing delegates began to appear at the entrance to the Socialist hall at the hour for calling the convention to order. A disturbance followed and the police ejected the Left Wing delegates. The Machinists' Union that owned the hall in a letter to the convention objected to the presence of the police. The convention ordered its secretary to write to the Machinists' Union explaining how the police came to be present. The Socialists claimed that the Left Wing had decided to start a disturbance in order to provoke interference by the police and then use the incident against their opponents.[3]

In the weeks following the conventions the Communist organizations made war upon each other. The official organ of the Communist Party explained that its opponents' delegates at Chicago had quickly organized a party "so as to be in a bargaining position with either the Socialist Party or the Communist Party." It denounced this action as "dastardly and traitorous," for about thirty delegates had been kept away from the Communist Party convention "by deliberate delay and misinformation." Moreover, "a dozen conscious misleaders" of the opposition "were notorious Centrists" while a few were "guided by personal venom." Therefore, "the Communist Labor Party has no vestige of principle, Communist or any other kind." What is to be said of a party that calls itself International, the organ asked, when it refers to the foreign federations as "autonomous?" It is evident that "it desires to be a revolutionary proletarian party without the prole-

---

[3] The information regarding these conventions is somewhat scattered, but the programs of the Communist conventions may be consulted in *The Labor Year Book, 1919-1920*. More complete reports, including a variety of documentary material, will be found in a number of publications, including the following: *The Communist* (Chicago), September 27, 1919 (C.P.); *The Ohio Socialist* (Cleveland), September 10, October 8, 1919 (C.L.P.); *Socialist News* (Cleveland), September 27, September 13, 1919 (C.P.); *Communist Labor Party News* (Cleveland), September, 1919 (C.L.P.); *Communist Labor Party of America, Official Report of the Chicago Convention* (New York, n.d.) (C.L.P.), the report of John Reed and Benjamin Gitlow to their Left Wing constituents, which contains a good digest of the proceedings; *The New York Call* (daily) issues during the week of the Communist conventions; also for the Socialist Party; the Lusk *Report*, cited above, reprints several documents in Vol. I, but the reader must again be warned against the accompanying editorial comments; *The National Bulletin* (Chicago), September 15, 1919 (S.P.), carries much critical matter regarding the Left Wings.

tariat." Nearly 60 per cent of our wage workers are of foreign birth and the Communist Labor Party "stands for an American movement — an American Communism!" Its conclusion was that "the Communist Labor Party is no organization with which the Communist Party could ever have any dealings."[4]

The Communist Labor Party replied in bitter terms, its chief grievance being that the other party had rejected its offers for a union of forces and it appealed to the members of the Communist Party to take the initiative for unity out of the hands of their leaders. These leaders, one organ complained, "deny our comrades the same respect as Communists that they demand for themselves. The only unity that they consider is the unity offered by the Pope of Rome: 'Join my church and then there will be only one church.' Some of the leaders of the Communist Party frankly admit their adherence to the split philosophy. This is, briefly, that the more you split, the 'clearer,' and stronger you become." This organ recalled that Hourwich, a New York delegate, had explained "that in order to have a group of uncompromising leaders competent to lead the working class when the final crisis comes, you must constantly 'split and split and split.' You must keep the organization small and constantly bring about situations within the party that will result in splits." In this way, it continued, the Communist Party hoped to so refine its membership that a small group will be "clear" and determine who are not "clear."[5]

The charge was not unfounded. The philosophy of "split" was becoming pronounced and when both parties were united in the Left Wing previous to the conventions they had subscribed to the philosophy of "split" as applied to their Socialist Party opponents. The campaign of the Left Wing was based on this plan. It was to capture the Socialist organization and expel the "moderates" or to "split" it if it was not conquered. After the Left

[4] *The Communist* (Chicago), October 4, 1919.
[5] *The Ohio Socialist* (Cleveland), October 8, 1919.

Wing broke into two wings, Alexander Stoklitzky devoted a page to recalling this plan.[6]

In fact, the philosophy of "split" was outlined by Gregory Zinoviev, President of the Third International, as a necessity of Communist development in all countries. In his report to the Third World Congress he reviewed his generalship in this work in various countries. The following reference to the French Socialist Party is typical: "We had to execute a 'forced march' into France in order to do in one movement what was done in other parties in two movements. We had to bring about two splits to disperse the Right Wing and the Center. This operation was carried out brilliantly and we immediately secured a purified party." Despite the "purified party" he obtained in France, Zinoviev observed that there may be "some wavering and a crisis," which implied that he might have to again "split" the organization.[7] The numerous Communist organizations that followed within the next few years caused some pessimism in their ranks whereupon a California organ proceeded to justify numerous "splits" on the basis of a biological analogy. "The law of life in biology is division of cells and so it is the law of social science," the editor observed. "The more active divisions, the larger the great body of trained men and women at the crisis." There were those who lament that "the past year has witnessed more division than at any time in the history of the movement," he continued, but this really should not be a matter of discouragement. "Don't worry about division; rather fear the opposite," was his conclusion.[8] This biological analogy may have placed the philosophy of "split" on a "scientific" foundation, but within a year after its acceptance Communists all over the world were required to discard it for its opposite — the "united front."

The emergence of the two Communist parties was also the

6 *The Communist* (Chicago), August 2, 1919.
7 *The New York Call,* May 30, 1921.
8 *The Western Worker* (Oakland, Calif.), May 20, 1921.

emergence of a movement committed to a veiled support of physical force as a method of social transformation. A Socialist organ as early as June had forecast what would happen to it. "The fact that the whole continent of Europe is going through 'revolutionary times' is no evidence that New York, California, Alabama and all other states are affected," it observed. "He who dreams of a 'dictatorship of the proletariat' in a single state of this country, to say nothing of the whole; who urges this in spite of the fact that only a tiny fraction of the 110,000,000 people are ready for any social change, invites all the powers of reaction and must eventually go underground. He cannot form a political party in this country and have it live six months on this basis. It must eventually become a secret society."[9]

In fact, the Communist parties did not live two months on the basis they had planned. They were driven underground by the nation-wide raids planned by Government agents on the night of November 7, 1919, in many cases carried out with ferocious brutality. In the following month, December 21, the "Soviet Ark," the ship *Buford*, left the port of New York with 249 aliens, sailing with sealed orders and her destination unknown to the newspapers. "So ends a chapter in American history," reads an editorial in a liberal weekly. "On December 21, 1919, one hundred and thirty years after the foundation of the American Government, the right of asylum was abolished, and the ancient institutions of banishment and exile re-established. That is what will be remembered of the voyage of the *Buford*. Of those who applaud or acquiesce today, many will in later years think back to this and feel the humiliation of it. They well recall that this is not the America that the world knew for over a century and believed in so profoundly."[10] The raids and arrests were likened by Senator Johnson to the "Law of Suspects" during the Reign of Terror in

---

[9] *The New York Call*, June 10, 1919.
[10] *The New Republic*, December 31, 1919.

the French Revolution. It was estimated that over 70,000 persons were taken in the dragnet.

That the official bureaucrats responsible for these arrests and raids in almost every instance acted illegally is certain. In the following year twelve distinguished lawyers issued, under the auspices of the National Popular Government League, a booklet of 67 pages in which they brought a convincing indictment of the illegal practices of the Department of Justice, accompanied by documentary material amazing in its revelations of how far scared bureaucrats will go in striking down the most elementary guarantees of civil rights. Even a forged confession of a suspect is found among these documents. In a few pages addressed "To the American People" they summarized their indictment:

"Under the guise of a campaign for the suppression of radical activities, the office of the Attorney General, acting by its local agents throughout the country, and giving express instructions from Washington, has committed continual illegal acts. Wholesale arrests both of aliens and citizens have been made without warrant or any process of law; men and women have been jailed and held *incommunicado* without access of friends or counsel; homes have been entered without search warrant and property seized and removed; other property has been wantonly destroyed; workingmen and working women suspected of radical views have been shamefully abused and maltreated. Agents of the Department of Justice have been introduced into radical organizations for the purpose of informing upon their members or inciting them to activities; these agents have even been instructed from Washington to arrange meetings upon certain dates for the express object of facilitating wholesale raids and arrests. In support of these illegal acts, and to create sentiment in its favor, the Department of Justice has also constituted itself a propaganda bureau, and has sent to newspapers and magazines of this country quantities of material designed to excite public opinion against radicals, all at the expense of the Government and outside the scope of the Attorney General's duties." [11]

The Department of Justice became the source of newspaper propaganda against "radicalism" which was based upon the

[11] *Report Upon the Illegal Practices of the United States Department of Justice, Washington, D.C. May, 1920.*

assumption that there were millions of Communists organized in
the United States.[12] Bourgeois delirium confronted Communist
delirium, but the former constituted the only real danger of the
period. It threatened to destroy all the civilized forms by which
human beings and social classes have learned to test their claims
and ideas. The fright of the ruling classes of England over what
was happening in France in 1792 was similar to the delirium of
our ruling cliques because of the Russian Revolution. What
Thomas Erskine May wrote of British reaction could just as well
have been written of the United States in 1919. Of the democratic
societies and their illegal persecution by Government authorities
May said: "In ordinary times, the insignificance of these societies
would have excited contempt rather than alarm; but as clubs and
demagogues, originally not more formidable, had obtained a
terrible ascendency in France, they aroused apprehensions out of
proportion to their real danger. . . . There is no longer room for
doubt that the alarm of this period was exaggerated and excessive. . . . The societies, however mischievous, had a small following. . . . None of the causes which had precipitated the revolution
in France were in existence here. . . . The influential classes, more
alarmed than the Government, eagerly fomented the prevailing
spirit of reaction. . . . The Government gave too ready a credence
to the reports of their agents and invested the doings of a small
knot of democrats, chiefly workingmen, with the dignity of a
widespread conspiracy to overturn the Constitution. Instead of
relying upon the sober judgment of the country, they appealed
to its fears and in repressing seditious practices they were prepared to sacrifice liberty of opinion. Their policy, dictated by
the circumstances of a time of strange and untried danger, was

[12] One piece of the department's propaganda was a pamphlet, *Red Radicalism,
As Described by Its Own Leaders; Exhibits Collected by A. Mitchell Palmer,
Attorney-General;* Washington, D.C., Government Printing Office, 1920. *The
Nation,* March 6, 1920, reprinted a facsimile of a page offered free to country
newspapers at the expense of the Department of Justice which was to be obtained
through the Western Newspaper Union.

approved by the prevailing sentiment of their contemporaries, but has not been justified, in an age of greater freedom, by the maturer judgment of posterity."[13] Fortunately one man in the Department of Labor, Assistant Secretary Post, was required to pass upon the legal status of the unfortunates caught in the dragnet of Attorney General Palmer. He declined to be an accomplice of the Attorney General in what William Hard described as "a reign of mass-law — of mass-inquiries, mass-searches, mass-seizures, mass-raids, mass-arrests, mass-incarcerations — violating in principle the spirit of law and violating inhumanly in practice the specific purposes of the Bill of Rights of the Constitution — all to the knowledge of members of the House of Representatives and all without impeachment by the House."[14] His effort to live up to his oath of office and to save innocent men and women from the extra-legal process of "administrative exile" provoked a demand in reactionary circles for his impeachment. Mr. Post[15] left a record of his experiences which no human being in possession of his senses can read without a profound sense of shame that high officials of the Federal Government can so abuse the powers of their office and be immune from punishment.

For a few weeks the Communist organizations disappeared.

[13] May, *Constitutional History of England* (ed. 1864), pp. 138-140. Referring to the arbitrary legislation of the period, Francis Place said that "Infamous as these laws were, they were popular measures." The same may be said of the American Espionage Act and similar legislation. Philip Anthony Brown's *The French Revolution in English History*, New York, 1924, is remarkable in the analogy it suggests to the reader between British fears of the French Jacobins and American fears of Russian Bolsheviks.

[14] William Hard, in *The New Republic*, May 12, 1920. See also editorial in the same publication, April 28, 1920.

[15] Post, *The Deportations Delirium of Nineteen-Twenty*, Chicago, 1923. Mr. Post asserted that Attorney-General Palmer was "the pivot" of a "powerful business and political combination" (p. 241). The oligarchs of finance and concentrated capital were very vocal in their support of Mr. Palmer's actions in office. For the legal and constitutional aspects of the raids, arrests, convictions and deportations, Professor Chafee's *Freedom of Speech*, New York, 1920, should be consulted.

They reorganized as secret societies. What had became a necessity was now proudly proclaimed a virtue. The underground organizations produced upperground offshoots in the form of literary societies, lecture forums, study clubs and the like, and through these they were able to engage in propaganda of "moderate" Communism. In a few months underground publications began to appear without any indication of the city or office in which they were published. "No longer were there party headquarters; neither national, state or local," reads an editorial in the first issue of an underground organ in June. "The active party officials were in jail or were fugitives. No meetings could be held without inviting arrests. Very little money could be raised even for defense and relief of prisoners. By February, 1920, the two thriving parties of October, 1919, had vanished."[16] The first phase of Communist organization had not survived two months and it had witnessed the delivery of three organizations at its birth, each one at war with the other two. From their hiding place came handbills with bristling appeals to the masses to use arms for the overthrow of the "bourgeois State." The few periodicals that were published gave considerable attention to all the "yellow Socialists" whose "petty bourgeois prejudice" against the use of physical force condemned them to sterile gestures of no value to the working class and stamped them as "betrayers" of that class.

Far from regretting their underground existence, the Communists appeared to enjoy it. To them it appeared as a mark of revolutionary honor. They threw aside all restraint and declared frankly for armed insurrection, the taking of industry and the powers of government by physical force, confident that the collapse of modern society was only a matter of a short time and that those who refused to prepare for the final catastrophe were in the last analysis ranged with the enemies of the working class. At the same time a union of divided forces was more imperative than ever and this we will next consider.

[16] *The Communist* (United Communist Party), June 12, 1920.

CHAPTER V

REUNION AND DIVISION

IN FOLLOWING the fortunes of the two main Communist parties we took no account of the development of the group represented by the Michigan delegates in the Communist Party convention.[1] This group and some sympathetic organizations in other states founded the Proletarian Party of America. It had its origin in a Detroit group of Socialists who were members of the Socialist Party. As early as 1916 this group had been active in propagating what it believed to be a literal Marxism in the hope of its replacing the "petty bourgeois" reformism of the Socialist Party. As the group grew in numbers it conceived the idea of founding a school for study classes in Marxism in Detroit and through correspondence in other cities. The "Proletarian University," as it was called, established classes and sent out occasional lecturers. It also founded *The Proletarian*, a monthly periodical, to expound its Marxian views. Under the influence of this group the Michigan state organization had been induced to take the actions which brought the revocation of the organization's charter by the National Executive Committee of the Socialist Party in May, 1919.

One of the main differences between the Proletarians and the two Communist parties was the objection of the former to the vague meaning implied by the words "mass action." The Proletarians emphasized the importance of party organization and political action and in June, 1920, they organized the Proletarian Party of America with branches in Detroit, Rochester and Buffalo, N. Y. Like its two rivals, the Proletarian Party insisted that it was the heir to genuine Communism in the United States. It also favored a union of Communist forces but, like the others, it

[1] See above, p. 68.

contended that certain of its fundamental principles could not be surrendered as they were essential to any lasting union. In November, 1921, this party held its second convention, adopted the long Manifesto that is customary of Communist organizations, and declared that "the Proletarian Party stands at all times for the unity of all revolutionary working-class elements on the basis of a correct application of Marxian principles to the class struggle in America. The convention authorized the National Executive Committee to appoint representatives of the party to negotiate with any elements to achieve unity. Any agreement for unity shall not be binding until approved by the membership of the party."[2]

This attitude of caution by the Proletarian Party had been justified by its experience with the Communist Party. It did not immediately separate from that party when it found the foreign-language federations in control of the Chicago convention. It remained in the Communist Party as a minority group, hoping that it would be able to change the view of the Communist Party which believed that a resolute minority could effect a revolution, modify its anti-parliamentary tendency and the policy of splitting away from the trade unions. But within a few weeks the Proletarians were expelled from the Communist Party and as they prepared to organize their own party the Palmer raids scattered their forces so that it was not until the following June (1920) that they were able to hold their first convention.

A delegate of the Proletarian Party had been sent to the Third Congress of the Communist International which met in June, 1921. He reported to the November convention that he was not seated but was accepted as a visitor, as one party, presumably the Communist Party, had been recognized in the United States. The convention declared itself in full accord with the Communist International and resolved to continue the organization of the Proletarian Party "until the Communist International is repre-

[2] *The Proletarian* (Detroit), December, 1921.

sented in America by a real Communist party." Such a party
did not exist, it asserted, "owing to the widespread confusion
fostered by various so-called Communist parties."

The Manifesto was the most sober and realistic of the Communist declarations of this period. While it declared that "world
capitalism is breaking down," it did not assume that the United
States was facing an imminent social catastrophe leading to a
violent social revolution, and this saved it from the delirious
expectations that swayed its rivals. The Manifesto included a short
but well-written review of the evolution of capitalism from the
period of the Middle Ages down to the contemporary era, including the revolutions following the end of the first World War. It
then proceeded to do what all Communist organizations before
and all those that came after it have done, denounce the Socialist
Party. Its criticisms on this score did not disagree with the criticisms of its two rivals. This antagonism to the Socialist organization is the only matter on which all the Communist groups could
agree. For the rest the Manifesto, while critical of the trade unions,
urged its members to join the unions and by "self-sacrificing devotion to the cause of the workers they must win the confidence
of their co-workers and wield a decisive influence in the organizations." It affirmed the necessity of the "dictatorship of the proletariat" during the "transition period between capitalism and
Communism," but not as a permanent institution. While em-
phasizing that "parliament is a bourgeois institution," it favored
nomination of "candidates for all political offices, for the purpose
of using elections as a means of conveying to the masses our
conception of the State and its function," that is, as an organ
of the ruling classes.[3] The Proletarian Party, unlike all other
Communist organizations, has maintained a consistent attitude,
never following the devious course of rapid change from one
position to another, each one offered as fundamental to Communist
growth and then forgotten for something else. So consistent has it

[3] *Ibid.*

been in this respect that it has never united with any other Communist organization and it survives as a denial of the claim that there is a united Communist movement in the United States.

Meantime the two underground organizations were negotiating for a union of their forces. This was effected probably in the following May in a unity convention where the Communist Party with 32 delegates, and the Communist Labor Party, with 25, and a representative of the Executive Committee of the Communist International succeeded in founding the United Communist Party of America. The first issue of its organ in June said: "Some time recently, somewhere between the Atlantic and Pacific, between the Gulf and the Great Lakes, two groups of elected delegates assembled as the Unity Conference of the Communist Party and the Communist Labor Party." They were in session seven days. Not one of the familiar names of Communists appear in the report. Following the custom of revolutionaries in the days of Czarist Russia, the Communists appear under assumed names. The proceedings as reported in this publication show the old maneuvering for power by the two factions, a threatened bolt, secret caucuses, ultimatums exchanged and, finally, a "split."

It will be remembered that the two parties had issued from the Chicago conventions the year before, each congratulating itself and the American proletariat that it had founded a genuine Communist party. The United Communist Party through its official organ announced that it entered "the working-class struggle in this country *as the first clear-cut expression of the revolutionary movement that has achieved a splendid victory in Russia.*" Still other Communist organizations were to be founded, each to make the same claim, while the Proletarian Party was also insisting that it alone had this merit. However earnest the men were who organized these movements they did not seem to possess a sense of humor. A union of forces was the object of this convention, yet with the knowledge that a group had "split" from the new party its organ could say: "When, after meeting as separate groups for a day the delegates from the two organizations were united, there quickly appeared upon the breasts of most of the delegates the words 'AT LAST' in great black letters. A circular bearing that caption had been distributed among the delegates and the words had been torn from it to give expression to their sentiment." The foreign-language groups again had been the obstruction to unity, as factions of these groups were represented by the delegates who "bolted." The Communists consoled themselves with the reflection that "the logic of the situation will compel them (the 'bolters') to join the united party or bring about the disintegration of their organizations."

The program of the party showed some marked changes. It abandoned the idea of obtaining the release of political prisoners by some form of "mass action" and which had induced Communists to oppose the efforts of the Socialist Party to obtain legal defense and amnesty. A resolution declared that "the United Communist Party favors every use of legal technique to save its members from prison or deportation, providing there is nothing pleaded in defense which contradicts or confuses the party principles" and members "shall refuse to answer questions or to supply information as defendant or witness concerning the party organization, its work, or membership." The program repeated the belief that capitalism "faces complete collapse" and that "civil war between the classes now holds the world in its grip." Curiously enough, although now an underground society, the party assured its members that it "participates in election campaigns and parliamentary action" but "only for the purpose of revolutionary propaganda." This is natural considering that the whole world order was facing "complete collapse." Nominations were to be made only for legislative offices and this because of the need of clever strategy. During great battles of "revolutionary potentiality the doors of the legislative halls are likely to be thrown open to the Socialist and Laborite betrayers of the workers' struggle." This will be the opportunity of the "Communist spokesmen" to confront the "yellow spokesmen of Labor," expose them, and keep "to the front the slogan: Down with the parliamentary sham of capitalism; hail to the Soviets and the real working-class democracy!"

While the Communists are exposing the "betrayers" in legislative bodies, they are not idle outside. There was much important work to do in the way of "mass action of the working class" to meet the "armed power of the State," which eventually would assume the character of a military dictatorship. But under the leadership of the Communists, "the class struggle, which so long appeared in forms unrecognizable to the millions of workers actively engaged in it, develops into open combat, civil war." At this stage the party "will systematically and persistently familiarize the working class with the inevitability of armed force in the proletarian revolution. The working class must be prepared for armed insurrection as the final form of mass action by which the workers shall conquer the State power and establish the Dictatorship of the Proletariat." Where the workers were to obtain the arms for this war and why untrained masses were expected to be victorious against trained troops using bombing planes, poison gas, machine guns, high-powered rifles and modern artillery was not considered in this program. However, what had been in the minds of the Communists since the organization of the Left Wing early in 1919 was openly stated in this program. Had the issue been as clearly stated at that time, the Socialist organization would not have suffered from the defections it did.

The constitution adopted by the convention showed that every precaution was taken in the admission of members. Applications may be accepted, but "only on recommendation of two persons who have been members for at least three months," and then only by a unanimous vote of the group. The new member was required to pay an initiation fee of one dollar and dues were seventy-five cents a month, both fee and dues going to the national organization. The unit of organization was a group "of approximately ten mem-

bers," ten groups to constitute a branch, not over ten branches
a section, not over ten sections a sub-district, and not over ten sub-
districts a district. A Central Executive Committee of ten members
was provided for and ten alternates, probably a precaution to
fill vacancies in case of any members of the executive being
arrested. No autonomous federations of language groups were
permitted, but branches of this type might form sub-district propaganda committees. These were the more important features of the
constitution of the "united" party.[4]

The insurgents who left the United Communist Party convention continued a separate existence under the name of the
Communist Party. In the following July this party held a secret
convention with 34 delegates in attendance and claiming to represent 8,000 members. The outsider would conclude that those who
favored the use of force as a means of social transformation would
be satisfied with the program of the United Communist Party
and its support of armed insurrection. Not so the Communist
Party. The convention gave its time to showing how "pink," how
utterly "bourgeois," the U.C.P. was! It charged that the U.C.P.
was led by "adventurers and charlatans" and that its platform
reeked with "*the bourgeois capitalist horror of the destruction
of property and lives. . . .* The use of the term 'Soviet rule under
a working-class dictatorship' shows a fundamental lack of understanding. . . . The Soviet Government is a form of proletarian
dictatorship." Another criticism was that "*The U.C.P. considers
the use of force as a purely defensive measure — not as an offensive*

---

[4] My source of information for the proceedings of this convention is *The
Communist*, June 12, 1920. It consists of sixteen pages, and the place of publication
is omitted. An editorial note on the last page states that resolutions on "abstention
from nominations in the 1920 campaign, re-affirmation of the declaration of the C.P.
and C.L.P. on the Debs nomination" and one on unity were omitted. They were
to appear in the next issue — promised for June 26. This issue did not come into
my possession, and whether it was ever published, I do not know; but the promised
resolutions are of minor importance and not essential to an understanding of what
the party represented. The reference to the "Debs nomination" probably referred
to a decision of the C.P. and C.L.P. not to support his candidacy because he had
accepted the nomination of the Socialist Party.

measure for which the Communists must consciously prepare," so that "here again the bourgeois horror of force emanates strongly from the U.C.P. camp." The latter only promises to "familiarize" the proletariat with the need of force instead of urging the masses to use it, which suggests how many times a hair can be split if this diversion suits you.

Moreover, the U.C.P. is suspected of not appreciating the revolutionary honor and necessity of staying underground. Its complete silence "on the question of an underground organization, either in their program or constitution, confirms the suspicion that the U.C.P. *may eventually give up any pretension of being an illegal, underground party.*" How can any real Communist organization unite with an organization guilty of such evasions? it asked. It summarized the U.C.P. program as "a typical centrist document, lacking both clearness and understanding of Communism. Framed by unscrupulous phrase-jugglers, it evades the fundamental issues. Phrases like 'civil war,' 'armed insurrection' and 'force' were mechanically inserted here and there, with no intention of permitting such insertions to change the tone of the document."[5]

The Communist Party convention reconciled itself to a "boycott" of political campaigns and elections because of its preference for an underground existence. Its organ described the party as "a highly centralized and well-disciplined underground organization" as well as the "military character of the organization in the time of revolution." Two sections from the constitution of the party are interesting:

"ARTICLE IV, SECTION 1: The Communist Party is an underground, illegal organization. It is highly centralized, with the convention as its supreme body and the Central Executive Committee as its supreme body between conventions.

[5] The critics also asserted that a "revolt" had begun in the U.C.P. and that "the Industrial or Independent Communist Party" was then in existence. If true, this would mean three parties issuing from the "unity" convention.

"ARTICLE V, SECTION 10:   The identity of the C. E. C. members shall not be made known, either by themselves or by those present at the convention."

The chief fact to be noted about the party membership is its Slavic character. The Lithuanian federation contributed 2,500 out of the 8,350 dues-paying members, according to the party's secretary; the Russian federation, 2,000; the Ukrainian, 1,500, and the Lettish, 1,000. Only about 500 members were said to have remained in the C.P. from among the English and non-federation language members, while the Polish, German, Hungarian and Esthonian federations had evidently left the party as a unit. Before the raids by the Federal Government, the party claimed 26,680; after the raids, 12,740, and after the split, 8,350. The secretary presented the following table of the membership of the original Communist Party before the raids, after the raids, and after the "split" in the U.C.P.:

	Before Raids	After Raids	After Split	Went to U.C.P.
English (including 800 Michigan	1,900	700	300	300
Non-Fed. Language members	1,100	400	200	200
Esthonian	280	140	...	140
German	850	500	...	350
Hungarian	1,000	...	...	...
Jewish	1,000	500	350	...?
Lettish	1,200	1,000	1,000	...
Lithuanian	4,400	2,500	2,500	...
Polish	1,750	1,000	...?	...?
Russian	7,000	3,000	2,000	1,000?
South Slavic	2,200	1,000	...	1,000?
Ukrainian	4,000	2,000	1,500	500?
Totals	26,680	12,740	7,850	3,490

The above table is of peculiar value, because it contains the only figures offered since the Chicago conventions of 1919 regarding the membership of the Communist Party. It verifies my estimate[6] that the two parties that issued from the Chicago conventions had about 35,000 members. In the above table the Communist Party admits that it had only 26,000 members at its origin instead of the 58,000 which it then claimed. Its rival certainly had a much smaller membership; and if we concede it 10,000 members when it was organized — and this concession is certainly generous — the total number of organized Communists in 1919 was not over 36,000, and it was probably less.[7]

This period of underground life was the nadir of American Communist delirium. "To talk with an American Bolshevik from early 1919 to the end of 1921," says one writer, "was much like talking with an asylum Napoleon."[8] Communist literature fairly reeked with talk of armed insurrections, strategic maneuvers and mass revolts to come out of the strikes of the period.

Disappointed over the "split" in May, 1920, and with nearly 8,500 members of the Communist Party fighting the United Communist Party as a "bourgeois" organization, the latter, with the assistance of the Communist International, tried to bring the insurgents into the "united" party. Early in 1921 the organ of the latter said that the dissenters were "taking a most asinine stand on important tactical questions." The American workers "are now willing to listen to Communist propaganda," and yet the Communist Party indulges in "criminal sabotage" and "cowardly evasion." However, it consoled itself with the belief that the U.C.P. "will not be thwarted by a native group of ultra-revolutionists who only stand in the way of revolution."[9]

[6] See above, Chap. III.

[7] My source for this criticism by the Communist Party of its rival is an article by Harry W. Laidler, "The Communist Party in Secret Convention" in *The Socialist Review*, New York (monthly), September, 1920.

[8] Benjamin Stolberg, "The Peter Pans of Communism," *The Century Magazine*, July, 1925.

[9] *The Communist*, No. 16, 1921. Several numbers of this publication are undated.

Early in the year 1921 negotiations began for a union. Both parties met in secret convention in February and documentary exchanges began. The U.C.P. elected a committee on unity of 25 members and asked the C.P. to elect a similar committee. The latter replied that it would not negotiate "upon the arbitrary basis of equal representation," and insisted upon a proportional representation of the two parties. As the C.P. had the largest membership, it is evident that proportional representation would give it a majority in any negotiations that might be undertaken. Anticipating this deadlock, the Executive Committee of the Communist International had appointed one member of each party to serve as a Unity Committee, with a representative of the Communist International to act in an advisory capacity. This representative was known by the name of "Yavki." The three agreed upon a plan for eventually uniting the two warring parties, but its language shows knowledge of a furious controversy raging between them. The report speaks of the factional struggle "growing more bitter," and the committee was convinced that "only further action by the Executive Committee of the Communist International can end this deadlock," but in the meantime "months will pass with disunity and factional struggle." The committee recommended a course of action including the following: (1) election of a National Council of three members from each party; (2) this council to function for both parties with the approval of their Executive Committees; (3) the council to publish one paper, with one editor from each party; (4) each party to contribute equal sums to finance the council; (5) the two parties to maintain their separate organizations and publications except their central organs; (6) all attacks of each party against the other to cease; (7) the Executive Committees of both parties were each instructed to "draw up a statement, complete and final, of why unity has not yet been accomplished and of what questions divide them — in armed insurrection, unionism, I. W. W., federations, forms of party organization, etc." These statements to be forwarded to Moscow for a final decision. The U.C.P. accepted three of these conditions, but agreed to the remaining four with certain important provisos. The executive of the C.P. rejected the proposals.

The two party members of the Unity Committee, in a report to both parties, regretted that they had "been unable to break the deadlock," and added: "We shall accordingly report to the Executive Committee that we cannot break the deadlock, and we shall make definite concrete suggestions to the Communist International on how to break the deadlock and how to realize actual unity — unity of a character which shall give factional control to neither party, but which shall be the unity desired by the International itself. In the meantime, we call upon the Central Executive Committee and the membership of both parties not to make factional capital out of our proposal, which was intended to end the factional struggle; we declare that to use our proposal in a factional spirit is to indicate desire for control and not for real unity." The negotiations had opened on February 17, and this document was signed by Louis C. Fraina for the C.P. and by Charles Ed. Scott for the U.C.P. on February 27.[10] In spite of the request for a

[10] The negotiations are reported in *The Communist*, No. 15 (U.C.P.), 1921.
Louis C. Fraina played a conspicuous role in the Left Wing movement, and following the Palmer raids he disappeared for a time. In fact, he was accepted as the leading exponent of Communism in this country, and as editor of *The Revolutionary Age* his denunciations of the Socialists were the most scathing to be found in Left Wing writings. For a number of years before the outbreak of the first World War, Fraina had also been identified with a small group in the Socialist Party who contended that this organization was too "reformist" to serve as a genuine instrument of the working class. He had written much in behalf of the general strike, "mass action," the "political strike" and similar themes which obsessed the Anarcho-Syndicalists of the period. To the extent that one man can be responsible for divisions in a movement, Fraina certainly had a greater share in bringing such divisions into the Socialist Party, and his activities in the Communist organizations also contributed to such divisions. All this is important, considering the sequel. On June 10, 1920, Santeri Nuorteva, Secretary of the Soviet Bureau in New York, issued a statement implicating Fraina as an agent of the Department of Justice. Nuorteva went into details, basing much of his statement on information he had obtained from one Peterson, who was such an agent and who had formerly worked on a Finnish paper with Nuorteva. Nuorteva's

informant reported that he had seen "in the files of the New York office of Palmer's department a returned check endorsed by Fraina." Although there were other charges, this one was the most damaging one. Fraina hotly denied the accusations, and the Communist Party made a thorough investigation of the charges, which was published as the *Stenographic Report of the 'Trial' of Louis C. Fraina*, 1920, place of publication not stated. The Central Executive Committee of the C.P. exonerated Fraina. However, about 1922, Fraina, who had gone to Russia, left that country with a sum of money intended for Communist propaganda abroad. He never reported to Moscow regarding his mission, and he completely disappeared from Communist circles. Communists themselves are silent regarding Fraina. They do not know, and nobody can know, whether he was really an agent of the Department of Justice or whether he had been a genuine Communist who had succumbed to temptation upon being trusted with some propaganda funds. The mystery of Fraina may some day be cleared up, but there were several queer cases of recantations and disappearances which are reminiscent of the old days of Czarist Russia when the revolutionary occasionally turned out to be a spy of the Czar. For the Russian type, see Mavor, *An Economic History of Russia*, Vol. II, Chap. xi, Police Socialism. In the report of the trial of Fraina, it appears that a member of the party by the name of "Jacob Nosovitsky" defended Fraina, and by questions he put to Nuorteva, it is evident that he endeavored to place Nuorteva under suspicion and direct attention away from Fraina. However, Nosovitsky asked some questions of Nuorteva which induced the latter to say: "I am very much astonished to hear questions asked which show a very close acquaintance with the doings in the Department of Justice." (*Trial*, p. 17.) Nosovitsky ignored this observation by Nuorteva and continued his questioning. But in November and December, 1925, the Hearst publications carried a series of articles by this same "Nosovitsky," who proved to be a spy of the Department of Justice and of Scotland Yard! In the *New York American* of October 4, 1925, "Nosovitsky" tells the story of this trial and quotes long excerpts from the printed record of the trial. "Nosovitsky" and Fraina left shortly after the trial to attend an international conference of Communists in Holland. Considering the disappearance of Fraina at a later period and his intimate association with "Nosovitsky," it is possible that Fraina may have been a spy in all the period when he was the most conspicuous and active man in the Left Wing and later in the Communist Party. C. E. Ruthenberg of the Communist Party then and of the Workers' Party now, gave some consideration to the "Nosovitsky" articles in the Hearst papers. Writing in *The Daily Worker* of December 19, 1925, Ruthenberg stated that "Nosovitsky" had been a member of the Russian Section of the Communist Party, but as he had been suspected as a *provacateur*, he was expelled. Ruthenberg claimed that "Nosovitsky" had frequently offered automatic pistols to "the members of the leading committee of the Russian section." The suspect later attempted to be reinstated in the party, but without success. Yet Ruthenberg admitted that "we needed his [Nosovitsky's] aid to make the arrangements for Fraina's trip" and these services of the expelled spy were accepted. After the Amsterdam conference of Communists "Nosovitsky" returned to the United States and renewed his attempt to join the Communist Party. Ruthenberg finally agreed to meet him in Washington Park, New York City. "Nosovitsky" asked to be permitted to meet the Central Executive Committee of the party, and was asked by truce and for the parties to refrain from attacks, the next issue of the U.C.P. organ carried an editorial of bitter invectives intended for the rival organization and its leaders.

In the meantime the qualified application of the Socialist Party for affiliation with the Third International[11] was rejected. This result was not known till November, 1920, when *The Russian Press Review*, October, 1920, arrived in this country. This may be summarized as follows: this document asserted that the International is "an organ of aggression, the General Staff of the World Revolution, for the forcible overthrow of the capitalist State everywhere," and that true revolutionaries must "prepare for revolutionary action, for merciless civil war." This the Socialists were averse to, which indicated that they were of the "counter-revolutionary" stripe. Of the authors of the minority report which favored affiliation, this group was characterized as being "permeated by cowardly compromise and petty bourgeois prejudices." The Socialists were considered a bad lot and unfit to associate with. "We answer by declaring war upon you traitors to the working class who, on the eve of the World Revolution, sold out to the enemy to save your skins," were the concluding words of this document.[12]

J. Louis Engdahl, William F. Kruse and two others who, in the Socialist convention in 1919, had framed the report applying

Ruthenberg to give his telephone number. After they parted, Ruthenberg called this number, and discovered that the spy was registered at the Hotel Commodore. As the spy had also pleaded poverty to Ruthenberg, the latter said "that was the end of 'Nosovitsky' so far as any relationship with the Communist Party was concerned." On the other hand, Ruthenberg made no attempt to explain the actions of Fraina.

Note: The above was written in 1927. A year or two later Fraina returned to New York where he became a contributor to several magazines and author of *The House of Morgan* and *The Crisis of the Middle Class*. He did not join the Communist Party but his contributions to periodicals and his books revealed the unreconstructed Communist.

[11] See above, Chap. V.

[12] This document was printed in full in the *New York Call*, November 30, 1920.

for admission, issued a statement which is interesting considering their later course. They observed that the conditions in the United States were fundamentally different from those prevailing in Europe, and that it would be suicide to accept the dogmas of the Third International. They commended the record of the Socialist Party and resented the arrogance of the reply. Moreover, they declined to "forego all chances of propaganda, save the conversion of police spies and the disturbance of proletarian mass movements that decline to wear our theoretical yoke." So far as they were concerned "the Socialist Party may not be ideally fitted to claim absolute political leadership today, but it is the organization [which] by history, structure and principles [is] better fitted for it than any other now in the field." They hoped that time would bring a better understanding of conditions in this country on the part of the Communists.[13] In spite of these views, Engdahl and Kruse were soon members of a Committee of the Third International, and later found their way into the Workers' (Communist) Party.

The Socialists had anticipated this answer, because in the previous September the famous "Twenty-one Demands"[14] of the Communist International had arrived in the United States. Bumptious and insolent in its tone, this document nevertheless clarified issues in all countries in every phase of working-class organization, policies and principles. It was an ultimatum addressed to all political, trade union and cooperative organizations of the working class in all countries, informing them what they must do. Its authors divided the world into two groups, Communists and anti-Communists, revolutionists and counter-revolutionists, and assumed that all who were really interested in a new social order would desire to be affiliated with Moscow. But to guard against

[13] The statement of this minority group appeared in the *New York Call*, December 16, 1920.

[14] This document was the work of the Second Congress of the Third International. It played such an important role in the Socialist and Labor movement in all countries as to make it of exceptional importance. It will be found in Appendix II.

the admission of "unsteady elements," "half-way methods" and "sabotage of the proletarian revolution," Moscow regarded it "as necessary to lay down very exactly the conditions for the admission of new parties and to direct the attention of those parties which have been admitted to the Communist International to the duties incumbent upon them."

In twenty-one sections the Third International made the modest demand that all organizations of the working class should place themselves under the guardianship of Moscow, and where organizations resisted this ultimatum the Communists should devote their time to obtaining the expulsion of all those who opposed this control. Should dissenters appear after such expulsions, the purging process should continue until the organization was sufficiently "purified" to be fit for service under the General Staff in Moscow. Communists must replace all other officials, editors, organizers, secretaries, executives, etc., and a war of extermination must be waged against all "reformists." There must be "iron discipline" and willing obedience, and legal organizations must also have illegal organizations, because in "nearly every country of Europe and America the class struggle is entering upon the phase of civil war." All parties must take the name of Communist. Between meetings of the Communist International, its executive acts and all its decisions are binding upon affiliated organizations unless modified by a succeeding congress. Some exceptions may be permitted in the application of these conditions, but the Executive Committee was the sole judge. Certain leading Socialists of a number of nations are mentioned by name for expulsion.

This bombastic ultimatum showed, as one writer expressed it, "the incorrigible tendency of the Moscow International to deduce from specific and casual Russian conditions infallible social maxims of universal applicability."[15] Having established a dictatorship in Russia by a few Communist leaders, these leaders

---

[15] Morris Hillquit, "The Moscow International," *New York Call*, September 23, 1920.

believed that the proletarians of all other countries, like the millions of *mujiki*, would welcome it. The program itself was based upon the assumption that the whole Labor and Socialist movement of the world could be shaped after a Russian pattern; that tribesmen of the desert and Chinese handicraftsmen; semi-serfs of Hungarian magnates and American miners; London dockworkers and Cossacks of the Don; Polish peasants and New York printers, with their variety of forms of labor and industry, historical backgrounds, folkways, customs, political traditions and culture, all have one path to follow, and that was in the keeping of a General Staff in Moscow. Certainly, the ridiculous in Utopia-building had been reached.

However, the Twenty-one Points gave great satisfaction to the Communists. To them the ultimatum meant that the doors were closed to all those they had fought as "counter-revolutionists," while it would force the warring Communist factions to unite. The "united" Communists believed that "not to have accepted these terms proved that the application of the Socialist Party for admission to the Third International was a bare imposture," but they were glad that "the hour of the Social Revolution is approaching. It is coming with speedy steps. Time is short wherein the revolutionists must prepare and organize the working masses for the task that the proletariat must perform."[16]

Before the Twenty-one Points were known in this country, the Finnish Federation of the Socialist Party began to show the effects of Zinoviev's various proclamations from Moscow. The federation inquired what the status of the party was regarding international relations in 1920. This inquiry was received late in the year, and the party had held a national convention in New York City in May. There were 143 delegates present, representing 26 states and the District of Columbia. The convention nominated Eugene V. Debs for President, although he was still in prison. Hundreds of party workers were imprisoned, many of its publi-

16 *The Communist* (U.C.C.P.), No. 14, about January, 1921.

cations had been destroyed by being deprived of mailing privileges and the remainder that survived were denied mailing rights. Three groups appeared in the convention on the matter of international affiliations. The Twenty-one Points were not yet known, and the first group favored adherence to the Third International, but was opposed to any "formula such as the dictatorship of the proletariat in the form of Soviets or any other formula for the attainment of the Socialist Commonwealth" that might be "imposed or exacted as a condition of affiliation." It also favored participation "in movements looking to the union of all true Socialist forces in the world into one International." The second group was led by Louis Engdahl, who again introduced the qualified resolution of affiliation alluded to before.[17] The third point of view was represented by Victor L. Berger, who opposed any international affiliation for the time being. After a long debate the resolution of the first group was adopted by a vote of 90 to 41. Forty-nine delegates signed the Engdahl report, and both were submitted to a referendum of the membership. The members adopted the majority report by a vote of 1,339 to 1,301, a rather small vote, and probably indicating that the members were becoming tired of the controversy, but the defeat of the Engdahl proposal which had been adopted in a previous referendum also indicated a decided drift away from any official relations with the Communist International.[18]

All this was in the background of the Finnish Federation when, a few months after, it sent its inquiry to the Executive Committee of the Socialist Party. In the previous January the federation members had in a referendum defeated a proposal to secede from the Socialist organization by a vote of 3,775 to 2,259, the strong minority desiring to affiliate with the Third International. The executive of the Socialist Party considered the inquiry of the

[17] See above, pp. 63, 93-94.
[18] A good digest of the proceedings of the convention and the resolutions in full will be found in *The American Labor Year Book*, 1921-22, Part Five.

federation early in November, citing the above facts. It had also met in August, and because of the small vote cast by the party members on the Majority and Minority proposals of the May convention, it had decided "that no action be taken by the Executive Committee regarding international affiliations until such time as the committee may have before it some definite proposal to be considered." The Twenty-one Points were also called to the attention of the Finnish Federation, and the opinion of Eugene V. Debs was quoted to the effect that "the Moscow program wants to commit us to a policy of armed insurrection," which was "ridiculous, arbitrary and autocratic." The committee added that the Moscow program would injure the Soviet Government itself, that it "tends to disrupt and disorganize the Socialist movement in other countries; it strengthens the reactionaries of all countries, gives them new arguments for reactionary measures of suppression, and impedes the growing tendency for resumption of trade relations." The committee decided to take no steps towards forming a suitable international until more favorable opportunities developed.[19]

In December, 1920, the Finnish Federation held a convention and by a two-thirds vote of the delegates it voted to withdraw from the Socialist Party. The insurgents carried most of the Western branches, while the regulars retained most of the Eastern branches and remained in the Socialist Party. Early in the following year the Italian Federation held a referendum and defeated a similar proposal, without any serious loss of members. The year 1920 was a period of failure of divided Communists to unite, although condemned to an uncertain and unpromising life underground, while the Socialist Party was disturbed by a few minor factions still lured on by the proclamations from Moscow.

---

[19] The statement of the Executive Committee of the Socialist Party appeared in *The Socialist World*, the national monthly of the party, issue of November 15, 1920.

CHAPTER VI

A MULTIPLICATION OF SECTS

THE YEAR 1921 brought a multiplication of Communist organizations, all of them having one thing in common. Each one presented a particular program which marked it off from the rest, the variation being mainly on how to approach the masses with the Communist message, but there was also the beginning of what may be called a "strategic retreat" on many matters which had been previously accepted as fundamental. The retreat became pronounced as the delirious mood receded in the underground organizations. Before the end of the year these secret organizations were longing for an "open party," that is, an organization not condemned to a precarious existence as underground propaganda societies hunted by the police. But the "open party" was impossible without the sacrifice of the propaganda for armed insurrection, a propaganda, as we have seen, which the Communist parties had insisted was essential for any genuine national section of the Communist International. The abandonment of this propaganda was not an easy matter, as the membership of the underground organizations had to be won for the idea of an "open party" before any attempt could be made to realize it.

Two other influences were at work, one independent of the Communist organizations and the other within the Socialist Party. The independents were apparently fragments of the Communist organizations which did not follow the latter underground, together with some radical unions whose members were largely of alien origin and were lured on by Communist propaganda. The influence in the Socialist Party was felt in a few of the remaining foreign federations in that organization and a few active members holding membership in the English-speaking organizations. As the underground organizations approached the necessary "strategic retreat" to an "open" existence, the independents and Socialist factions tended to drift towards a common center and coalesce in one "open party," an aim that was realized in December in the organization of the Workers' Party. However, this was not a "united" party, as a real union of Communist organizations has never been realized.

The first independent organization to appear was the Industrial Communists, who organized and adopted a national program and endorsed the Third International. Organized at Terre Haute, Indiana, in November, 1919, it soon changed its name to the Proletarian Socialist Party, and adopted the second paragraph of the Declaration of Independence as its "legal basis." Its program made no mention of dictatorship, Soviet form of organization or armed insurrection. It is therefore a unique variation from all other types of Communist organization. Its program was based on the idea that there are six basic industries in modern society — agriculture, transportation, mining, manufacturing, construction and education — and that the working-class party that is not built upon this fundamental idea is certain to fail in its aim. The party must be so organized that it will in miniature reflect the economic organization of society. In fact, "the Industrial Communists have been so organized that when it (the party) goes into power we will have Industrial Communism." Each local branch of the party must have members from the six basic industries, and national congresses of the party must also be representative of these industries. An appeal was made to all Socialist and Communist organizations to unite under the banner of the Industrial Communists. The party established an organ, *The Industrial Communist*, of which only a few numbers appeared.

In the seventh number of the official organ the editor explained why society had drifted into the maze of economic and political problems that faced it. "If the founders of this political republic," he wrote, "had understood how and had organized an industrial republic instead of a political republic, the new condition of life could not have appeared." They should have organized a republic on the six basic industries mentioned in the Industrial Communist program. If they had "provided for the organization of branch industrial heads in each community, composed of representatives from each department of industry in that particular community, setting forth the duties of the industrial officials — the organic law of the industrial republic could not have permitted the granting of private titles to land, or franchises to railroads, or mineral rights, or anything necessary in production, distribution and communication." On the other hand, he continues, the men who wrote the Constitution were all capitalists and served their own interests in writing it.[1]

Of course, it is a naive sociology that conceives of "six basic industries" in the colonial period. Mining was almost unknown; manufacturing was chiefly a household matter; transportation consisted of the sailing ship, the oxcart and the pack horse; education was in a rudimentary stage, and construction, in the modern sense, had no important social or economic importance. Even agriculture, the chief occupation, represented a variety of economic and sectional interests difficult to reconcile. The Industrial Communist program was based on the idea that has often characterized Utopia-builders, that is, the view that, because of some important "mistake" in a past historical period, mankind had been started on a wrong path and it becomes necessary to go back and begin right where others began wrong.

How many members the Industrial Communists gathered to their standard is not known, as the few issues of its organ present no data. At most, this organization did not have over one or two hundred members. Headquarters were established in Chicago in June, 1920, and in August an appeal was sent to Socialist and

---

[1] The information regarding the Industrial Communists, later the Proletarian Socialist Party, is scanty. My source is *The Industrial Communist* (Chicago), issues of September, 1920, and March, 1921. The Proletarian Socialist Party issued one large leaflet for general circulation, which seems to have exhausted its literary efforts.

Communist parties to meet in a unity convention in November, but nothing came of this proposal.

The Industrial Communist Party was succeeded by the Rummagers' League, and the eleventh number of the former's official organ, which appeared in January, 1922, was published as *The Rummager*, and became the organ of the league. The Rummagers abandoned the idea of party organization and organized as an educational society. They announced their purpose to be to "rummage the field of history and science so as to develop the keenest intellect possible. Special consideration given to present-day problems. Our object is to develop branches in every locality for the purpose of extending knowledge of the world's material and historical development. The main point of view is the highest possible working-class education."[2] The Rummagers proposed to establish study classes in the social and physical sciences, but in this they do not appear to have been successful. The Rummagers made no impression on other organizations and soon disappeared.

The Committee for the Third International appeared on the scene shortly after the 1920 convention of the Socialist Party. Its leading spirits were J. Louis Engdahl and William F. Kruse of the Socialist Party. As stated above,[3] these men and a few others constituted a group that favored affiliation with the Third International. They had recoiled from the attack made upon them by Moscow and asserted that acceptance of the Twenty-one Points was impossible. Nevertheless, they organized a group within the Socialist Party to popularize the idea of affiliation with the Third International. In April, 1921, the committee announced that such affiliation determined whether one was "for or against the revolution" and that the "Third International points the way." One year before they had said that affiliation would "forego all chances of propaganda save the conversion of police spies"; now they believed that the very preservation of the Socialist Party

[2] *The Rummager* (Chicago), January, 1922.
[3] See above 63-64.

depended upon adoption of "the principles enunciated by the Third International," and they favored "affiliation without reservations." This group urged its view in the convention of the Socialist Party in 1921 and was defeated. It was placed in the contradictory yet amusing situation of pleading against expulsion because of its position, yet urging affiliation with an international organization that was demanding wholesale expulsions. The group was not expelled, and its members participated in the organization of the Workers' Party.[4]

Meantime the Jewish Federation began to show signs of dissension over appeals from Moscow and sympathy with the Committee for the Third International. In January the federation decided in favor of affiliation with Moscow, but against leaving the Socialist Party, but after the June convention of the Socialist Party the executive of the Jewish Federation initiated a referendum of its members on the question of withdrawing from the party. The result was a special convention of the federation in New York in the following September, where a resolution favoring withdrawal from the Socialist Party was carried by a vote of 41-33. The minority delegates withdrew and organized as a federation affiliated with the Socialist Party. One week before this action the Bohemian Federation decided by a vote of practically ten to one to withdraw from the Socialist Party.[5]

New York City contributed another Communist organization in 1921 when "The Workers' Council" was organized in April, and began to publish a bi-weekly of the same name. This organization was founded by a number of Socialists in sympathy with the Committee for the Third International. It deplored the "ineffective reforms and parliamentarism" of the Socialist Party and believed that "the American working class undoubtedly offers a

[4] Proceedings of the convention are in *The Socialist World* (Chicago), July, 1921. See also *The American Labor Year Book, 1921-22*, pp. 405-407; *The Workers' Council* (New York), April, 1, 1921.
[5] *The American Labor Year Book, 1921-22*, pp. 406-407.

field for fruitful action. But this action can be undertaken only after all those who are today working as individuals and in groups for its culmination have been gathered behind a great driving force functioning on the political as well as the economic fields, reaching the working class in the shops and in meetings, in the labor organizations and through the press, in political campaigns and in political organizations." It proposed to accomplish what all other Communist organizations had attempted to accomplish — a union of all such organizations. It also desired affiliation with the Third International without any reservations, because the American masses had "shown a keen response to the appeal of the Russian proletarian revolution."[6]

In the meantime "The American Labor Alliance" was announced as another Communist organization early in the same year. This appeared to be an upperground extension of the underground United Communist Party because of the numerous foreign-language organizations which were attached to it as affiliated sections. According to its Cleveland organ, "The American Labor Alliance comes upon the political horizon at a most propitious moment." There were so many groups and organizations "working at cross purposes," which "calls for amalgamation, unity and close cooperation." It proposed to "become the voice of the hitherto voiceless" and to "unify, through a central body, the great mass of discontented 'left' political and economic forces of the country and to rally them about a common aim." In other words, it proposed to do what the Workers' Council desired to do. There was, therefore, every reason to expect cooperation between the two organizations, but they immediately attacked each other. The American Labor Alliance declared war on the Workers' Council and the Committee for the Third International. It believed that it was better to have "a minority of clear-minded workers" having "a revolutionary consciousness" and "an intellectually scientific attitude" than to have "a large party, unclear,

6 *The Workers' Council*, April, 1, 1921.

unscientfic and cowardly in the carrying out of its work." The Alliance had no confidence in the Committee for the Third International because of the belief that the latter would not meet the test imposed by Moscow.[7]

The underground United Communist Party also warned against what it considered these new usurpers. Its organ surveyed the field, and observed that the Socialist Party had bartered "with the revolution so long [that] the revolution has swept past and left it clutching the hand of the State." The Proletarian Party was no more satisfactory. It was not a party, because it rejected revolution "if it is not a *majority* revolution." It had no future, because it "labors under a complete misapprehension as to the nature and purpose of a revolutionary organization in the present epoch of capitalist society." The Workers' Council was still more hopeless, because it "is steeped in the philosophy and tactics of the Second International." Now, then, "what does Section 3 of the Conditions of Admission to the Third International say?" it asks. It says that "the class struggle in almost every country of Europe and America *is entering the phase of civil war.*" It was evident that the Workers' Council did not frankly accept the implications of Section 3. Moreover, "the open political party dare not be a bastard party, gathering about it the wavering elements. *It must be the open expression of the underground revolutionary party, analyzing and mercilessly criticizing the fakers and misleaders of the working class and helping to construct the revolution.*"[8]

Apparently these attempts at Communist unity introduced more confusion instead of dissipating it. For several months the Workers' Council ignored these attacks, and fell back upon the one resource of all Communist organizations — a continuous fire at the Socialist Party, which by all of them was considered the common enemy. The Workers' Council believed that it could modify the conditions of affiliation with the Communist Inter-

---

[7] *The Toiler* (Cleveland), issues of April 30 and August 6, 1921.
[8] *The Communist* (C.L.P.), No. 16, 1921. Italics in the original.

national once it was inside, a belief that was not justified by any
of the numerous pronouncements and manifestoes broadcast — by
Zinovief from Moscow, while the Twenty-one Points specifically
required affiliated sections to obey the judgments of the executive
of the Third International.

In September, 1921, the Committee for the Third International
announced that its members had severed their affiliation with the
Socialist Party. It made no claims regarding its membership.
There were twenty signatures to the announcement, two representing the Bohemian and Jewish federations and the rest signing
as individuals. The signers announced their emphatic approval of
affiliation with Moscow, denounced the Detroit convention of
the Socialists for not being recorded in favor of a dictatorship,
because it favored a survey of trade unions to ascertain whether
a Labor Party could be organized;[9] because it had considered a
resolution to expel those who favored affiliation with Moscow,
and finally, because the party had outlived its usefulness.[10] The
following month, the committee having been merged in the
Workers' Council, the latter took the initiative in a "strategic
retreat" by rejecting much that Moscow was insisting upon.
What is more surprising, it repeated many of the objections which
the Socialists had always made against the Communist parties!
Its October manifesto is a study in human psychology. Its authors
had just left the Socialist Party because the latter had taken
certain important positions against Communist principles and
policies, and now that they were outside, they were urging many
of the same objections against the Communist parties.

In what was intended to be a manifesto, the Workers' Council
said that the Russian Revolution "carried us off our feet by its
daring," and "its powerful romantic appeal bore us away from
a world of hopeless, cheerless realities, in a flood of enthusiasm."

9 Within a year after the appearance of this criticism the authors were themselves, and for a number of years thereafter, endeavoring to become affiliated with
a Labor Party and gave much time in an attempt to organize one.
10 *The Workers' Council*, September 15, 1921.

Moreover, "the Communist Party thought and acted as if the Russian Revolution had been bodily transplanted upon American soil." This was the period of Communist romanticism, but "romance has had to give way to brutal realities." Instead of a world revolution materializing, world imperialism "has emerged, for the moment more powerful than ever before." Still another view had been shattered. "The fantastic dream that a small minority of determined revolutionists may overturn capitalism and lead the proletariat into a Communist state of society, has vanished into thin air before the bitter experiences of the German and the Italian Communist uprisings." Even Russia was paying the price of romanticism, for there "the great mass of uneducated, indifferent and even counter-revolutionary workers and peasants is hanging like a millstone about its neck." The result was that the dictatorship may extend "over decades," because "the November revolution found the masses of Russia unprepared to receive its message." The idea of "a secret organization was not forced upon the Communist movement by Palmer and his cohorts," for it "had been lurking in the minds of most Communist enthusiasts ever since the outbreak of the Russian revolution." Now, it was time to abandon this secrecy, for even the Third International condemned agitation "for armed insurrection and open rebellion in countries where the revolution is still in the distant future." Moreover, "to demand unswerving allegiance to a set of doctrines that tomorrow may prove false, encourages unthinking, slavish obedience," while an underground existence "offers a rich field for the numerous romantic irresponsibles," and "illegality becomes the end and aim instead of a necessity." Yet, in spite of this tearing away of so much cherished by the Communists and a tearing away that the Workers' Council's recent Socialist associates agreed with, the manifesto went on to assert that "it is fundamentally in accord with the Third International," and it pleaded in behalf of an "open party."[11]

[11] *The Workers' Council*, October 15, 1921.

This self-criticism of Communist ideology appears to be the first evidence of a definite return to sane reasoning. Coming from its own camp for the first time, this criticism began to have some effect upon the Communists. In the same month, October, 1921, the New York Communists formed another organization as an experiment which might lead to an "open party." This was called "The Workers' League." Under this name candidates were nominated for mayor and other city and borough offices, and a "Manifesto and Platform" was adopted for general distribution as a leaflet. This program revealed a marked "strategic retreat" from Left Wing days when the demand was made of the Socialists that "the party must teach, propagate and agitate exclusively for the overthrow of capitalism and the establishment of Socialism through a proletarian dictatorship." The Workers' League, while urging the "establishment of a Workers' Soviet Republic in the United States," also declared that "the candidates of the Workers' League will agitate, organize and call the workers *to fight for the following immediate demands:* (1) Emergency legislation to combat and stop the reduction in wages. (2) Immediate legislation to protect the labor organizations against the capitalist open-shop drive. (3) Emergency legislation for the relief and amelioration of the condition of the unemployed. (4) Hands off Mexico, Haiti, Panama, Philippines, etc. (5) Recognition of and trade with Soviet Russia." [12] With the adoption of this program the Communist movement rejected the position it had adopted as a Left Wing in 1919 and which caused the "split" in the Socialist Party. It was back to "immediate demands," back to that "moderate Socialism" which it had scored as lacking in all that was required of an effective party organization of workingmen. In 1919 the cry

---

[12] The Manifesto appeared in *The Toiler*, October 29, 1921. It was also widely distributed as a leaflet in the same month. Sections 4 and 5, which consider foreign relations, are rather humorous when found in a municipal platform. They recall the municipal platforms provided by the Ohio Communists and which considered world problems for voters in city elections.

was, "Turn to the Left." Two years later it was, "Turn to the Right."

If we turn to the underground Communist Party, we observe a marked recovery from the delirious mood. In June the Socialists, in their convention at Detroit, had decided in favor of cooperating with trade unions in founding a Labor Party, while the Workers' Council was also criticizing the romanticism of its underground colleagues. Both factors made an impression upon Communists in general, although there still remained much friction, jealousy and personal animosity to overcome. Late in April occurred the arrest of three prominent members of the Communist Party in New York who had been followed from Pittsburgh, and the seizure of a number of secret documents which they carried. These documents revealed a secret code, or suggestions for communication by code and detailed instructions for Communists regarding their actions, writings, talk and relations with other persons, and advice on how to act if arrested.[13] The arrests placed much important information desired by the police in their hands, and it led to a number of other arrests. This disclosure of underground secrets, in spite of elaborate precautions to avoid such disclosures, probably made the appeal for an "open party" alluring for many members who were living in daily fear of what had actually happened.

As the action of the Socialist Party in its June convention in Detroit regarding political cooperation with trade union and other organizations for united political action was destined to play an important role in subsequent Communist history, it is necessary to understand what this action was. The convention conceived the idea of a political federation of Socialist, trade union, cooperative and farmer organizations modeled upon the plan of the British Labor Party, and, by a vote of 37 to 2, instructed the executive

---

[13] The documents were printed in the *New York Times*, May 1, 1921, and other New York dailies of the same date.

of the party to make a survey of such organizations. Its resolution ordered:

"that the incoming National Executive Committee be instructed to make a careful survey of all radical and labor organizations in the country with a view of ascertaining their strength, disposition and readiness to cooperate with the Socialist movement upon a platform not inconsistent with that of the party, and on a plan which will preserve the integrity and autonomy of the Socialist Party.

"Resolved, that the National Executive Committee report its findings, with recommendations to the next annual convention of the Socialist Party." [14]

This resolution was considered by all Communist groups as a final betrayal by the Socialists, and yet with that amazing inconsistency that has earned for Communists the title of "secular Jesuits" they were soon following the course advised in this resolution! In issuing a call to organize the Workers' Party, the Workers' Council announced that a "new era dawns in the political struggle of America's working class." One reason for this hopeful view was the Socialist "betrayal" at Detroit. When the executive of the latter organization met a few months later in Cleveland to carry out the instructions received at Detroit, the Workers' Council observed that the Socialist Party "has definitely gone over to labor reformism. This was predicted. Our prediction has come true. The Socialist Party has been swallowed completely in the swamp of reactionary opportunism," and for this reason the new party would enter "the field without a competitor." [15]

The Communist Party was just as emphatic. Considering the action at Detroit, its organ declared that "today the American Socialist Party stands unmasked, totally devoid of all revolutionary potentiality. . . . This [Detroit] resolution portrays a lamentable misunderstanding of the role of the political party in the prole-

---

[14] Proceedings of the convention are in *The Socialist World* (Chicago), June-July, 1921. See also *The American Labor Year Book, 1921-22*, pp. 405-7.
[15] *The Workers' Council*, December 15, 1921.

tarian revolution. . . . Such a policy is characteristic of the most degenerate centrism and opportunism."[16] Yet this resolution and other events mentioned above contributed to draw the underground Communists into an "open party," in which the resolution was to guide their conduct for a number of years. "With the present openly stated purpose of the party," observes the same publication, "that the use of armed force in the struggle to overthrow the capitalist State is an inevitable phase of the proletarian revolution," the Communist Party must remain an "underground organization," but to be of any service an "open party" must be organized and be "known to the masses as the legal expression of the Communist Party."[17]

This was a startling reversal of opinion for the party which had refused to join the United Communist Party on the ground that the latter had displayed a petty bourgeois prejudice against "the destruction of lives and property." However, the "strategic retreat" was proceeding so rapidly that a large part of one issue of its organ was devoted to explaining away former principles and preparing the way for an approach to the legal basis of activity and organization. The Communist Party had represented the most extreme swing to the Left and it was soon to display a tendency to the other extreme. By October it was frankly facing realities and openly endeavoring to bring its membership to a realization of the new era which the leaders desired to reach as speedily as possible. In that month its organ presented a remarkable survey of the adventures of the party, a candid admission of its failure to make any impression upon American workingmen, and considered the problem of how to create an upperground organization that would remain controlled by the underground party. The Twenty-one Points had declared this an imperative necessity and the good Communist was under obligation to carry out the program of the Third International.

[16] *The Communist* (C.P.), August, 1921.
[17] *Ibid.*

In taking stock of its adventures and failures, *The Communist* said that "it cannot be denied that the Communist Party of America practically does not exist as a factor in the class struggle. The truth of this statement can be inferred from the fact that the slogans, appeals and proclamations of the former two Communist parties never caused even a ripple on the surface of the class struggle. We called upon the workers to boycott the last national elections. We called upon the workers to demand recognition of Soviet Russia. We called upon the unemployed to organize. We agitated in favor of the Red Labor Union International. What has come of all this? What is there to show that our propaganda has not been in vain?" The answer to these questions is "almost complete failure" and after two years the party numbers "only ten thousand." If the reader asked why this failure the answer was that "we reasoned in a metaphysical manner" by creating a puzzling alternative, *i. e.*, "either we remain legal and betray Communism or save our Communist souls and go underground." Now a new truth was apparent: Communists "could be above ground and underground at the same time." As the isolation of the party had become "unbearable" it became necessary to "create a legal organization actively participating in every phase of the class struggle — on the industrial field, parliamentary field; *on a platform that will meet the requirements of the law as actually enforced by the ruling class.*"[18] This astonishing reversal of opinion was unthinkable a few months before and no leader could have retained his leadership had he expressed it then.

Naturally, these views would shock the members of the party and raise the question whether their acceptance would not mean a fatal compromise. Anticipating this reaction, "Roger B. Nelson"[19] boldly considered all the questions involved in the new attitude in an article entitled "Have We Retreated?" He observed

---

[18] *The Communist* (C.P.), October, 1921.
[19] An assumed name for one of the active underground leaders.

that Socialist opponents and "left" Communists regarded the proposed new policy as "treason to Communism." A thorough consideration of all questions convinced him that "a blanket declaration of revolutionary intentions does not make a party revolutionary" and it must lead in a struggle for "immediate necessities." Is this opportunism, the hated "moderate Socialism" of 1919? On the contrary, opportunists "are those who neglect and reject every opportunity for struggle, whether the struggle be for a modest immediate need or a broad political demand." And is this a retreat? Not at all. It simply means that Communists "are only coming to life. . . . *We are first beginning to understand Communist theory and practice.*"[20] Thus the sole and immediate aims of Communist striving, dictatorship and establishment of a Soviet government are replaced by a struggle for "immediate necessities." Anticipating the objection that this would be to concede the Socialist policy rejected in 1919 the writer asserts that the Socialists were "resorting to the most dastardly methods in order to prevent our winning the working masses" and while Socialists may stand for immediate measures, as centrists and opportunists, they "refuse to fight for even the minutest demands of the working class."[21]

It is clear that American Communists of all types were being profoundly affected by the barren results of their propaganda and policies. American Labor did not respond. A "moderate" section was approaching the most extreme section of the underground force group with the view of functioning as an "open" party. As late as October the American Labor Alliance was attacking The Workers' Council and yet it represented a half-way place between the two extremes. It also favored an "open" party, but it still believed that the "revolutionary temper of American workers is growing under the pressure of an arrogant capitalism that hesitates

[20] *The Communist* (C.P.), October, 1921.
[21] *Ibid.*

at no crime for the perpetuation of its own domination." It still professed belief in the view that "the experience of this revolutionary epoch, and particularly of the Russian Revolution, has demonstrated that the liberation of the working class is to be won not in parliaments but on the streets, not by oratorical discourses of Socialist statesmen but by mass action of the workingmen."[22]

Another organization claimed by Communists was the African Black Brotherhood which appeared some time in 1921. This was an organization of Negroes of which only a handful were avowed Communists, but it was hoped to use the organization to attract Negroes and win them for the Communist movement. Bishop George Alexander McGuire, who had been active in the Universal Negro Improvement Association, became a prominent leader in the new organization. The U.N.I.A. was practically ruled by Marcus Garvey who received a prison sentence for a fradulent transaction; and its program was the colonization of Africa by Negroes and the establishment of a Negro empire. Bishop McGuire said late in 1921 that he had joined the African Black Brotherhood because it stood for racial equality and a free Africa; because "it seeks to protect Negro Labor from exploitation by capitalism;" because it "welcomes into service strong intellectual men of the race without attempting to dwarf them before one giant [Garvey] master mind" and "erects no barriers to my religious freedom nor places any limitation upon my personal liberties and movements."[23] From this it appears that there was practically no Communism professed by the organization. It merely served as a means for a few Communists to carry on agitation among Negro workers, but it never made any impression and it probably did not survive a year after its organization.

The numerous Communist organizations were now approaching

22 *The Toiler*, October 29, 1921.
23 *The Crusader* (New York), December, 1921.

another period of maneuvering for a union of forces. The underground parties had failed to unite. They were now to attempt to unite all the upperground organizations into an "open" party with control retained by the underground chieftains in accord with the requirements of the Twenty-one Points of the Third International. The organization of the Workers' Party was the result of these efforts.

CHAPTER VII

THE WORKERS' (COMMUNIST) PARTY

By the end of the year 1921 no less than twelve Communist organizations had been formed of which eight were of a political character and intended to function as politicial organizations. Of these numerous organizations, seven had either died or had been merged with some other organization, leaving the following organizations as survivors: the Communist Party, the United Communist Party, the Proletarian Party, the American Labor Alliance and the Workers' Council. To these may be added the Arbeiter Bildungs-Vereine, consisting of former German Socialists.

The problem that faced these organizations was the establishment of the "open party" of Communism. Early in December a call was issued for a convention to meet in New York City, December 23-26, to organize the "Workers' Party of America." The official call stated that the "American capitalists are using the present economic crisis to increase their power of exploitation and oppression. The whole working class is being crushed under the iron heel of a brutal capitalist dictatorship." It went on to state that it is not necessary to create a desire for unity because unity "is already a living reality." Organizations participating in the convention were required to approve a statement of principles which accompanied the call. This statement was divided into five sections and it makes an interesting comparison with all former Communist programs as well as later programs which the Workers' Party adopted in other conventions. This statement reads:

1. *The Workers' Republic:* To lead the working masses in the struggle for the abolition of capitalism through the establishment of a government by the working class — a Workers' Republic in America.

2. *Political Action:* To participate in all political activities, including electoral campaigns, in order to utilize them for the purpose of carrying our message to the masses. The elected representatives of the Workers' Party will unmask the fraudulent capitalist democracy and help mobilize the workers for the final struggle against their common enemy.

3. *The Labor Unions:* To develop the Labor organizations into organs of militant struggle against capitalism, expose the reactionary Labor bureaucrats, and educate the workers to militant unionism.

4. *A Fighting Party:* It shall be a party of militant, class-conscious workers, bound by discipline and organized on the basis of democratic centralization, with full power in the hands of the Central Executive Committee between Conventions. The Central Executive Committee of the party shall have control over all activities of public officials. It shall also coordinate and direct the work of the party members in trade unions.

5. *Party Press:* The party's press shall be owned by the party, and all its activities shall be under the control of the Central Executive Committee.[1]

There is no trace in this program of the original Left Wing insistence on the one fundamental demand of proletarian dictatorship on the basis of Soviet organization of the masses and certainly no trace of the programs of the underground organizations. However, the last two sections are of special interest. They give "full power" to a Central Executive Committee over the proposed party and its press. This was intended to pave the way to compliance with the requirement of Moscow that the underground organization should control its uppperground off-shoot. It was expected that members of the underground organization would control this com-

[1] The call appeared in *The Workers' Council*, December 15, 1921. It was signed by the American Labor Alliance, the Finnish Socialist Federation, Hungarian Workers' Federation, Italian Workers' Federation, Jewish Workers' Federation, the Workers' Council of the United States of America, the Jewish Socialist Federation, and the Workers' Educational Association (Arbeiter Bildungs-Vereine).

mittee and guide the course of the new party. With this exception the "principles" announced in the call would have been called by its authors in 1919 decidedly "moderate."

The convention met at the appointed date and organized by seating 94 delegates and 14 fraternal delegates, the latter consisting of the Proletarian Party, 3; Jewish Socialist Party Left Paole Zion, 4; I.W.W. Committee for the Red Trade Union International, number not given; Young Workers' League, 2; Esthonian Uus ILm, 1; Columbiana Political League, 1; African Blood Brotherhood, 2; Amalgamated Metal Workers, 1. The groups that were represented as affiliated with the American Labor Alliance with 47 delegates were the Finnish Socialist Federation, Hungarian Federation, Irish-American Labor Alliance, Greek Socialist Union, South Slavic Workers' Federation, Spanish Workers' Union, Armenian Branch, Italian Section, Russian Section, and the Ukrainian Section. It would appear that the "American" alliance had almost everything but American workers.

The Workers' Council had 13 delegates but its racial composition is not given. The remaining organizations were: Arbeiter Bildungs-Vereine, 13; Jewish Socialist Federation, 12; Italian Marxist Federation, 4; Scandinavian Socialist Labor Federation, 2; Scandinavian Socialist Federation, 2; and Buffalo Socialist Labor Party Club, 1. From the composition of the convention it is evident that some fifteen foreign-language groups had gathered to organize an American political party.

The speech of James P. Cannon, the temporary chairman, was devoted to the adventures of American Communists for two years and the situation that now faced them. For two years there had been "much strife in our ranks," he said, but this was "natural and inevitable." Until the call for the convention was sent out many were "disheartened, discouraged and demoralized." Reaction was rife in the United States and political prisoners were still in jail. The release of these prisoners "should have been the rallying cry to arouse the workers, but the Civil Liberties Union, the Socialist

Party and the I.W.W." had failed in this task. The Workers' Party
would step in and "stem the tide" by putting up a program and
plan of action with a set of "fighting leaders" who would raise the
"rallying cry: Fellow workers, stand and fight!" Be assured that
the "workers of American will rally" to the new party. "They will
hail it as the morning star. They are looking for it. I say, comrades,
they are looking for it with longing eyes."

The speaker observed that he had talked to delegates who feared
"reformist tendencies" in the convention. The call for the convention lacked the revolutionary fire of Communist documents and it
was admitted that the Committee had not "put in many revolutionary words or foreign phrases," but this was because "that period
is past and the time has come for action." Moreover, there is no
danger of "reformism in a party that is organized and led by class-
conscious fighters." And what shall the party fight for? "The difference," he answered, "between us and the Socialist Party, or the
Farmer-Labor Party or the Gompers bureaucracy will not be
alone in the fact that we declare for the final revolution and they
do not . . . but because upon the basis of the class struggle, on
questions of bread and butter, on housing, on labor organizations,
wages and hours, they are afraid to fight, and the Workers' Party
says it will fight on every single one of these issues."

As the address was roundly applauded and the views of the
speaker were not challenged it marks a tremendous shift in Communist opinion since 1919. Except for the assertion that the Socialists and the trade unions did not fight for the things mentioned by
the speaker, an assertion which was not true, the address might
have been delivered before a radical Labor Party, including the
reference to Soviet Russia with which the speaker concluded. In
1919 and 1920 all Communist programs rejected the fight for
"bread and butter," for housing, etc., as "petty bourgeois" while
political prisoners were to be released by "revolutionary mass
action." In that period these demands constituted the worst type
of "reformism" but the new point of view asserted that the

demands were perfectly proper providing a movement fought really hard for them!

The labor program adopted by the convention also emphasized the "moderate" period reached by the Communist movement. By a process of elimination it relegated all other organizations to a position of unimportance and assigned the role of leadership to the Workers' Party. The Socialist Party was woefully inadequate and the Socialist Labor Party was "moribund." The Farmer-Labor Party had "utterly failed" and the Nonpartisan League represented "another failure." Up to the time of the convention there had been "no political organization that could lead and unify the workers against capitalism, "but with the organization of the Workers' Party "such an organization makes its appearance in American life." The party would immediately take up the burden of centralizing and directing "the struggle of the laboring masses" and "courageously defend the workers." Having done this it would also proceed to "consolidate the existing labor organizations and develop them into organs of militant struggle against capitalism, permeate the trade unions with truly revolutionary elements, mercilessly expose the reactionary labor bureaucrats and strive to replace them with revolutionary leaders." Then the party would turn to political campaigns and its representatives in office "will unmask the fraudulent capitalist democracy and help to mobilize the workers for the final struggle against the common enemy." It would always seek to "broaden and deepen" the workers' demands and "work for the establishment of a Workers' Republic." Such was the new Communist program at the end of the year 1921.

The general program was of the same type except that it largely considered international questions. It did not propose affiliation with the Communist International but expressed the opinion that it is growing rapidly and is "the citadel and hope of the workers of every country" and the new party "looks to Soviet Russia for leadership in the struggle against world imperialism." It condemned the opposing Second International because it "is continually splitting the ranks of labor and betraying the working masses to the enemy," an amusing statement when contrasted with the Twenty-one Points of the Communist International which ordered a factional war in all political and economic organizations of the masses in all countries. Anticipating the Congressional elections of 1922, the party framed a "moderate" program. The program included: (1) protection of trade unions and the right to picket and strike; (2) municipal funds to be used to relieve the unemployed and to be disbursed by unions and councils of the unemployed; (3) obedience by capitalists to their own laws and the laws won by organized labor before the war;[2] (4) protection of the lives and rights of Negroes; (5) cessation of preparation for new wars; (6) withdrawal of military and governing forces from Haiti, San Domingo, Puerto Rico; independence for the Philippine and Pacific Islands.

The convention also provided a program for the trade unions of the country and congratulated them and itself that comprehensive work had been "laid out" for these organizations. "The Workers' Party of America," reads one sentence, "rejoices to be able to point out that, for the first time in labor history, an adequate and comprehensive program has been laid out for the militant workers in the labor unions."

The Constitution of the Workers' Party offered an interesting study in that it embodied what the Communist organizations in all countries at this period called "democratic centralization." The phrase continued to appear in Communist publications for years after this convention, the assumption being that the genius of the new revolutionaries had formulated some new principle in organization by which democratic control is maintained by members at the same time that large powers are assigned to a central executive committee. In the constitution adopted by the convention demo-

---

[2] The language is that of the original. It implies that any labor laws enacted after the beginning of the war are unimportant. What was in the minds of its authors is difficult to tell.

cratic control is reduced to a minimum and centralization of power is conspicuous. Instead of democracy and centralization being reconciled the former is sacrificed for the latter. This was essential if the underground organization was to really direct the organization and administration of the new party. Power was placed in the hands of a central committee elected by a convention whose delegates are not chosen directly by the membership. No referendum was available for the members except that an emergency convention may be called "upon demand of district organizations representing 40 per cent of the membership." Branches elect delegates to district conventions and the latter elect delegates to national conventions. In its mode of election the convention is twice removed from the membership, thus following the "democratic centralization" of the bourgeois parties. This refined convention elects the Central Executive Committee of seven members which is supreme between conventions and which has the power to fill vacancies from a list of seven alternates elected by the convention. This central executive appoints district organizers, has all press and propaganda activities under its control, and all actions of district conventions must receive its approval before they can become effective. It is empowered to choose an Executive Secretary, Chairman, and "all other officers." The administrative machinery created by this constitution insured control of the party by the underground movement. For this reason there was no resolution considered by the convention affirming affiliation with the Communist International.[3]

[3] The convention proceedings, including the minutes, resolutions, program and constitution, were mimeographed, and this document is my chief source for the Workers' Party convention. The convention elected seventeen members for the Central Executive Committee instead of the seven provided for by the constitution. This action was taken upon a motion to elect all of seventeen members who had been nominated. The minutes do not show any constitutional objection being raised to the motion, which was made in the afternoon of December 26, and the constitution was adopted that morning. See also *The American Labor Year Book, 1923-24*, p. 159. The official name of the party a years or two later became the Workers' (Communist) Party.

The Proletarian Party declined to enter the new party. It held its second convention in Detroit in November and while it refused to endorse the call for the Workers' Party convention, it decided to send delegates who, as we have seen, were accorded the status of fraternal delegates in the convention. The Proletarian Party decided that the organizations signing the call were of such a character and represented so much "confusion" that the convention would be of doubtful value. It also contended that the Proletarian Party was already the "open" party of Communism and that there was no need of organizing another party.[4]

There was considerable rejoicing among Communists in having gathered a number of warring organizations in the Workers' Party, but it's program was so "moderate" that it was still necessary to win wavering elements who hesitated to make concessions in the matter of professed beliefs that were so much in conflict with the Communist period of 1919. For a time the organ of the former American Labor Alliance served the new party and it waged war against the old illusions. It contended that "a radical change from the policy pursued by the Left Wing" was necessary. Communists had "attempted to straddle the gulf by an occasional overflow of printers' ink in the form of a bombastic leaflet or at times setting up a 'pure' one hundred and fifty per cent revolutionary union. Insofar as the development of a revolutionary movement is concerned these efforts were worth no more than a rubber penny in an empty slot machine." Fortunately, the American Labor Alliance had brought to the new party "ability to display proletarian strategy in fighting the enemy and winning the masses" and a real "party of action" had been organized.[5]

But even as the call for the organization of the party was being considered by Communist organizations, defection came from an unexpected quarter. Max Eastman, editor of *The Liberator*, had

[4] *The Proletarian*, December, 1921.
[5] *The Toiler*, December 31, 1921.

been a spectator at the conventions of the Socialist Party and the two Left Wings in 1919 and had allied his publication with the general Communist movement. In October, 1921, he expressed marked dissatisfaction with the American movement. "Two years have passed since the triple convention at Chicago," he wrote, "when the revolutionists in the American Socialist Party split from the political and social reformers. Two years have passed, and except for the deepening and confirming of that split nothing of appreciable value to the cause of Communism has been done by the revolutionists. A good deal has been done to the detriment of the cause. In spite of an 'increasing misery' that surpasses the demands of any theory, the workers in America seem to be less friendly to Communism than they were two years ago." Eastman revolted against the policy of distributing "circulars advocating methods of terrorism," while Communists appear in court and plead that "the propaganda they are conducting is not in violation of the laws." The whole trend of the article was based upon the conviction that the policies of the American Communists ignored reality and could make no impression on American workmen.[6]

Eastman, however, represented only a small intellectual element which hovered around the Communist movement and who attempted to give the movement a certain literary tone. Two months after the Workers' Party had apparently united all Communist organizations except the Proletarian Party, another Communist organization appeared on the scene. On February 3, 1922, the Workers' Defense Conference of New England issued a call for a national convention to meet in New York City on February 28. This organization appeared to be one directed by Communists and it probably had its origin in the period of the Palmer raids when the hunted members of Communist organizations formed various groups and societies for educational or defense purposes. The call for the convention asserted that there was need for a "solid front"

6 *The Liberator*, October, 1921.

against the "forces of capitalism." The "burning questions" to be considered were the open shop, wage reductions, unemployment, defense of class-war prisoners and a national organization "to resist the onslaughts of the capitalist class." The following organizations responded to the call: the Workers' Defense Conference of New England; Alliance of Polish Workers of America; the Ukrainian Association; Lettish Publishing Association; Polish Publishing Association; Lithuanian Workers' Association; the Woman's Progressive Alliance, a member of the Shoe Workers' Protective Union, one of the Amalgamated Metal Workers of America, and a member of the Amalgamated Food Workers of America.

In welcoming the delegates the chairman stated that the Nonpartisan League, the Socialist Party, the Farmer-Labor Party, the Workers' Party and the Socialist Labor Party do not represent the working masses. The convention organized "the United Toilers of America" and declared that "the workers of America must present a solid front against the forces of capitalism." The purposes of the organization were stated to be: (1) to participate in the daily struggles of the workers; (2) unite them against the open shop, wage reductions and unemployment; (3) to hold mass meetings on "burning issues"; (4) to defend class-war prisoners; (5) to conduct educational and propaganda classes, arrange lecture courses, establish open forums; (6) to publish leaflets, pamphlets, books and papers. Nothing was said about proletarian dictatorship, Soviet organization, conquest of public power or fundamental aims. Branches of five or more members could be admitted and a number of such branches were permitted to form a city central committee. A National Executive Committee of seven members was elected and instructed to call another national convention "as soon as the preliminary work is completed." Late in March *The Workers' Challenge* appeared as the weekly organ of the United Toilers.

The character of the new organization soon became apparent. It was the creation of those underground groups of Communists who believed that the organization of the Workers' Party was a "betrayal" of the masses and of Communism itself. Its weekly organ did not and could not expound the views of the underground force groups, but week after week it devoted columns to attacking the Workers' Party and its prominent and active members. The leading editorial in the first issue announced its general policy of representing the masses on "all fronts," especially the "left elements," but succeeding issues were devoted to the Workers' Party. *The Workers' Challenge* fairly reeked with venom. In all the history of Labor journalism it has never been equalled in scurrility, hatred and a determination to literally destroy the detested organization. "That asinine assumption of humanity and pusillanimous purveyor of putrid punk that calls himself managing editor of the official organ of the Workers' Party," reads one editorial.[7] "We have charged the Workers' Party with harboring in its ranks most of the petty bourgeois reformists, 'revolutionary' adventurers, piecard artists, tricksters, fakers, charlatans, blatherskites, traitors and demagogues that the American Socialist movement has produced during its rather hectic career, and every report confirms our conviction that it is a dangerous enemy of the working class and should be avoided as one would avoid the plague," reads another.[8] The United Toilers represented the expiring phase of the old Communism which was reluctant to crawl from its underground retreat. The "open" party had compromised the revolutionary honor of Communism and the Workers' Party was more to be feared than the most reactionary of bourgeois organizations. One cannot read *The Workers' Challenge* during the short period of its existence without a sense of profound disgust that factional malice could bring human beings to the level of hurling the filth of the sewer. However, the future course of American Communism had been charted by the Workers' Party and the romance of

[7] *The Workers' Challenge* (New York), May 6, 1922.

[8] *The Workers' Challenge*, April 8, 1922. The proceedings of the convention that organized the United Toilers were reported in the issue of March 25, 1922.

underground adventure was being liquidated. Even the United Toilers were to join within another year with those whom they roundly cursed.

Two events within a few months after the organization of the Workers' Party contributed to shaping its course. At the beginning of 1922 there were three Internationals, the Second International organized at Geneva in July, 1920; the Communist International organized in Moscow in July and August, 1920, and the International Working Union of Socialist parties organized in Vienna in February, 1921. The latter organization was attempting to get all three organizations into one International and in January, 1922, it announced the possibility of an international conference in which all organizations would participate. The Communist International was already raising the cry for a "united front" of all political and economic organizations of the masses. This appeared to be an admission that the policy of "splitting" organizations was wrong, but whether the Communist International was willing to give up its independent existence and with the other organizations constitute one International was not certain. The executives of the three organizations met in Berlin the following April and we reserve consideration of this conference for another chapter.

The second event was the issuance of a call by the sixteen standard railroad unions for a progressive political conference to meet in Chicago on February 20-21, 1922. This call was the result of the initiative taken by the Socialists in the Detroit convention of the year before. The Socialists had released the initiative to the International Association of Machinists upon request of that organization on the ground that if trade unions assumed responsibility for calling a political conference there would be a larger number of organizations represented. For the first time since 1893 there was considerable discussion of independent poltical action in organizations affiliated with the American Federation of Labor and most of the railroad unions were active in politics although their activity was confined to support of candidates nominated by

the major parties. Wide distress among the farmers of the Northwest had also brought a radical political movement in that region.
The machinists and railroad organizations united in issuing the call
for the February conference and the political ferment of the period
was promising for a political movement independent of and in
opposition to the two leading parties.

A rough estimate would place the number of people represented
at the conference between 3,000,000 and 4,000,000. Besides the
organizations mentioned, others with delegates present were the
Farmer-Labor Party, the Socialist Party, the Nonpartisan League
and a number of independent state parties. It was evident to every
observer that if these organizations agreed to organize a Labor
Party through some form of autonomous political federation such
as that which has made the British Labor Party a power in British
politics, it would be a new situation which every radical organization would have to face. The Workers' Party and previous Communist parties had easily disposed of such a problem by condemning Labor parties and we have seen that one reason for organizing
the Workers' Party was that the Socialist Party had taken the
initiative in favor of just such a political conference as that which
was meeting in Chicago. A concrete situation now faced the
Workers' Party. What would it do?

The Central Executive Committee considered the matter and
sent a statement to the Chicago conference which revealed another
"retreat." The statement was not read or even considered by the
conference but it represents an important stage in the evolution
of American Communism. The document asserted that the Workers' Party is a revolutionary organization that believes that "social
and poltical maladjustments" cannot be remedied short of the
complete "abolition of the system of exploiting labor." But at the
same time there are "certain simple steps about which there can
be no sincere disagreement among partisans of the toiling masses."
All could agree to oppose the open shop, reduction in wages, industrial court laws and deportation of political offenders and all

could favor protection of the unemployed, a union standard of compensation, the right of Labor to strike, organize and picket, release of poltical and Labor-struggle prisoners, and extension of credit to working farmers. In other words, the Workers' Party favored a Labor Party if it accepted these "moderate" demands! These demands would "furnish a common ground upon which every Labor union and every political party of the workers can fight together." This document was drafted in February, less than two months after the organization of the party.

It then ventured into mysticism in its attempts to advise the conference what it should do. It claimed that "to grow dynamic power the Labor mass must organize within its boundaries" which was followed by the assertion that "to build upon any other outline is to build a shapeless mass without organic qualities." The authors go on to speak of "boldly clearing the outlines of a class made organic by common need." What this queer Communist sociology meant was never explained, but the language was probably intended to impress the conference with the learning its authors desired to place at its disposal. The document called for "a united front of Labor, politically and industrially," and assumed that the masses the delegates represented were eager to organize a Labor Party, but that the delegates intended to "betray" their constituents. As a matter of fact, while the masses were embittered and resentful the majority still hoped to use one or the other of the Republican or Democratic parties to obtain needed relief. A healthy minority favored organization of a Labor Party, but it could not press the issue to a decision without dividing the conference into opposing camps and probably breaking it up.[9]

The conference did little more than to recommend organization of political committees in each state and to arrange for another

[9] My source for this position of the Workers' Party is a copy of the document mentioned, drafted by the Central Executive Cmmittee, bearing date of February 18, 1922, and signed by James P. Cannon, Chairman, and Caleb Harrison, Secretary.

conference which met the following December in Cleveland. The Workers' Party took the further step of sending delegates to this conference. These delegates were excluded. Upon being asked why the Communist delegates were refused seats, Edward Keating of the credentials committee said that the Workers' Party was "un-American" and "did not stand for the Constitution and the flag." The Socialist delegates in a signed statement declined to be associated with this reason for the exclusion, stating, in part, that refusal of seats to the Communists, however, was justified because "actual experience has shown that the disruptive tactics" of Communists, their rejection of democracy and support of dictatorship made it impossible to cooperate with them. The excluded delegates immediately issued a statement asserting that the Socialist delegates had joined in voting against admission on the grounds stated by Keating!

How far the Workers' Party had moved within one year from the old Communist orthodoxy became evident in a "Proposed Statement of Principles of the Conference" which its delegates intended to submit. This program favored a bonus for ex-soldiers, restoration of all civil rights, a modified Plumb Plan, legislation to prohibit issuance of injunctions in strikes; abolition of industrial courts and wage-fixing boards; prohibition of the employment of children under sixteen years of age, etc., and, of course, organization of a Labor Party.[10]

In the meantime a faction of the underground Communists refused to acquiesce in the organization and support of the "open party." How many members assumed this attitude is not known, but the faction caused sufficient trouble to warrant the intervention of Moscow. One month before the Workers' Party was organized the Executive Committee of the Communist International

---

[10] *Report of the Proceedings of the Second Conference for Progressive Political Action, Cleveland,* December 11-12, 1922. *The American Labor Year Book, 1923-24,* p. 149. My references to the statement of the Communist delegates regarding their exclusion and their "Proposed Statement of Principles" are from copies of these documents in mimeograph form distributed at the conference.

had adopted a lengthy "thesis" entitled "Concerning the Next Tasks of the Communist Party of America," which contained instructions for the immediate organization of a legal party in the United States. This action was in accord with some resolutions adopted at the preceding congress of the Communist International, yet, despite this supreme authority, there were members of the underground organization who found it difficult to reconcile themselves to such a change. The "thesis" stated that care should be taken to assure underground "control over all the leading organs of the legal party" and to obtain "at least the majority on all important committees," while the "entire membership of the underground party, the real Communist Party, must join the open party and become its most active element." But in following this course Communists were warned against neglecting "illegal work," a tendency that would likely appear when members began to participate in the "open party." Upon finding themselves "in the easier life of legal activities, many will forget that no matter what maneuvers may be made upon the public stage, the final class struggle must be, until its end, a brutal fight of physical force."

In order to end the underground opposition to the Workers' Party, Moscow sent a representative to the United States and demanded compliance with the terms of the "thesis." The minority leaders refused and sent one of their number to Moscow, the minority contending that Moscow had been misinformed when it had adopted the "thesis." Moscow reaffirmed its decision and ordered the rebellious members to apply for reinstatement in the Communist Party, join the Workers' Party and submit to the discipline of the Communist Party. The minority had seceded from the Communist Party and its members were given until June 25 in which to comply with the orders of Moscow.[11]

The factional struggle, however, was soon to subside owing to a dramatic incident which occurred in the following August. The

[11] The important sections of the "thesis" were reprinted in the *New York Call*, July 23, 1922.

underground organization had taken elaborate precautions for holding a secret convention in the woods near Bridgman, Michigan. Among the delegates was Francis Morrow, an agent of the Department of Justice, known by the department as "K-97." Morrow had been turning over to the department all Communist documents that came into his possession and informed it of the proposed convention, which was to settle the party controversy. On the morning of August 22 the convention was raided. Upon his arrival at Grand Rapids, where he was told that the convention would be held in the woods near Bridgman, Morrow managed to get word to the Department of Justice. Seventeen delegates were arrested, including Morrow whose real name was Francis Ashworth. Sixteen other delegates who had escaped were later arrested. By this raid not only the leading members of the underground organization found themselves in custody, but practically all their secret documents came into the possession of the authorities. This disaster probably did more to sober the members obsessed with the romanticism of a secret organization than a week of discussion by the delegates at the Bridgman convention.[12] In April, 1923, the jury that tried William Z. Foster, one of the leading Communists, disagreed. He was released on bail and the following month Charles E. Ruthenberg was found guilty of "criminal syndicalism." His case was appealed.

In the same month that the jury brought in the Foster verdict the Communist Party held its convention in New York City. By a unanimous vote the delegates decided to dissolve the underground organization and by a similar vote recognized "the fact that the Workers' Party of America, of which the members of the Communist Party of America were a component part, has developed into a Communist Party."[13] One month before this convention

---

[12] *The American Labor Year Book, 1923-24*, p. 212. The spy's account of how he worked his way into the councils of the Communists appeared in the *New York Times*, April 8, 1923.

[13] Announcement appeared in New York papers April 17, 1923.

acted, the Central Executive Committee of the Communist Party had agreed on a statement to be sent to Moscow in answer to the latter's order to support the "open party." The committee complimented Moscow on its "ability to give concrete directions for the activities of the American party" and in a long document divided into ten sections and numerous sub-sections it presented what it believed to be a general analysis of economic and political conditions that warranted an "open party." Curiously enough, while commending Moscow for its "ability to give concrete directions" to American Communists, the committee observed that "we are also combatting a European psychology that persists to a degree in our foreign-born comrades, *which makes them look to Europe and their native countries for inspiration.*" [14]

In dissolving the Communist Party its leaders appeared to fear that some organization other than the Workers' Party might seize the opportunity to pose as the favored child of Moscow and in the same document which announced the dissolution of the party its authors warned all "the workers of the United States" that no other organization "has any relation with the Communist International except the Workers' Party" and that "any other organization using the name 'Communist' and pretending to represent the Communist International is an imposter." [15] No "impostor" appeared and Workers' Party fell heir to the membership, prestige and other assets of the underground organization. The United Toilers which had carried on a venomous campaign of opposition to the Workers' Party disappeared and its members were soon active in the "open party."

Not so the Proletarian Party. It attacked the Workers' Party and was attacked in turn. In the April number of its official organ the Proletarian Party charged that its rival was trying to destroy it. It ordered its members to give no further support to the Trade Union Educational League (we shall consider this organization

[14] The complete document appeared in *The Worker* (Chicago), March 3, 1923.
[15] Announcement in New York papers April 17, 1923.

below) and opposed the policy of forcing on the trade unions a Labor Party by "hothouse methods." It believed that Moscow had not been well informed when it approved the Workers' Party. It also contended that the Workers' Party was made up almost exclusively of alien workers and as such had no future in the United States.[16]

This charge regarding the alien composition of the Workers' Party was not only verified by the character of the organizations that founded it but was also admitted by the representative of Moscow in the United States, "John Pepper." Writing in the official organ of the party under this alias, Pepper presented a valuable analysis of the composition of the membership. He reported that the party had sixteen foreign-language federations and that it required great skill to "keep this modern Babel together in one party." It had 20,000 members, nine daily papers with a circulation of 90,000 and twenty-one weeklies with a circulation of 70,000, but the power of this press was "diminished" because it was "split into a score of languages" and a great part of the members were not citizens. "Be American!" was the caption to Pepper's article. Coming from the responsible agent of the Communist International in the United States his article was of unique importance. Because of the numerous nationalities of which the party was composed, certain reactions followed which Pepper described in the following paragraphs:

"And it is not only the languages which vary in our federations, but very often even the ideology. Our Russian comrades have a different historical tradition from the Italians, the Germans from the Poles. The workers belonging to various nationalities are still very deeply rooted in the social and political conditions of their old countries. The greatest event for the Italians is Fascism in Italy. For the German workers, the occupation of the Ruhr; for the

---

[16] *The Proletarian*, April, 1923. Some leading attacks on the Proletarians were made in *The Worker*, issues of May 5, May 26 and June 30, 1923. This organ was a daily established by the Workers' Party in Chicago.

Hungarian Communists, the White Terror of Horthy; for the Polish workers, the heroic election fight of our brothers in Poland; for the Russian comrades, the miracle of Soviet Russia, so dear to all of us.

"The agitation and propaganda of our comrades in the sixteen language federations centers mainly about these great events in their respective countries. And yet all the members of the language federations are living here in the United States. We likewise observe the most enthusiastic activities of our comrades in the federations to be in closest connection with their old countries. Our Italian comrades arrange a collection for the persecuted Communists of Italy, our German comrades send relief for the hungry children of German Communists; our Hungarian comrades put forth great efforts to collect money for political prisoners suffering in Horthy's prisons; our Polish comrades have made a collection for the support of the Communist election campaign in Poland; our Ukrainian comrades collect money for the support of the Ukrainian publishing activities in Europe; our Russian comrades are, of course, with heart and soul interested in relief of Soviet Russia; our Jewish comrades collect money for needy Jewish workers in the Ukraine.

"If we look through the press of the various federations of the Workers' Party, we find, with few exceptions, very little about the political and social struggle of this country. If we were to read the nine dailies and twenty-one weeklies of the Workers' Party carefully, one would get the complete picture of all European countries, but a very incomplete picture of political life in America." [17]

Pepper himself completed this portrait. He was the representative of the executive of the Communist International responsible for the direction of the Workers' Party, subject to orders received from time to time by this executive. The party members might

[17] Pepper's article appeared in *The Worker*, May 26, 1923.

hold conventions or discuss questions for weeks in the local organizations or in the press and reach a decision and have the decision reversed by Moscow. A majority in the party could be transformed into a minority by Moscow. If the numerous foreign-language sections reacted to what was transpiring in their homelands, the whole party was pledged to comply with orders of a small committee sitting in the capital of Russia, no matter what a majority of the party might decide on some matter related to the economic or political situation in the United States. So constituted, so divided and so ordered, the party could not be and has not been adapted to the economic, poltical and social conditions of the United States. It has been more of an order ruled by military discipline and officered by a small international staff playing at world strategy than a poltical party functioning in the politics of the United States.

Nevertheless, such an exotic growth could work havoc with other organizations more adapted to American life. With members fanatically sincere, fundamentally lacking in a knowledge of American history and psychology, honestly believing that the Russian Communists had founded a society and formulated policies that the working class of all nations must accept or be branded as "betrayers" and "counter-revolutionists," the Workers' Party, in response to the orders of the "staff of the world revolution," took up the policy of the "united front," which will now engage our attention.

CHAPTER VIII

THE "UNITED FRONT"

EARLY in the year 1922 the leading spirits of the Communist International decided on a course that apparently was a complete reversal of its central policy in international relations in the previous years. The first World War had disrupted the International, most of its affiliated sections having supported their respective governments in prosecuting the war. The Third International must be built upon more reliable material if it were to avoid a similar catastrophe, and to so build, the sheep must be separated from the goats. The problem was very simple. Those who had supported the imperialist war must be excluded as "betrayers of the working class" and "lackeys of the bourgeoisie," and war must be waged upon all Socialist and Labor parties that failed to accept the leadership of the Russian Communists in reorganizing the International. The same course must be followed in the case of the trade unions. This view required a policy of "splitting" these organizations and annexing the "purified" elements to the Communist International.

However, the Russians were not always consistent in enforcing this policy. The Italian Socialists had opposed the entrance of Italy into the war and remained in opposition to the end of the war. Marcel Cachin, the French Socialist, supported the French Government in the war, and was so trusted by the government that he served it in a special mission to Italy to induce the Italian Socialists to join in support of an Italian pro-war policy. The Italian Socialists declined to follow Cachin's advice. At the end of the war Cachin turned Communist and became one of the leading French spokesmen of the Third or Communist International, and was accepted as such in Moscow. On the other hand, the anti-war Italian Socialists were bitterly attacked by the Russians, while several pro-war

Italian Socialists turned Communist and were accepted by Moscow. The Italian party, in fact, was later "split" by the maneuvers of Moscow, and the factions became so weak that the march by the Fascists on Rome became possible.[1]

All over the world the parties had been divided into warring factions, when, early in 1922, the Executive Committee of the Third International called a special conference, to meet in Moscow on February 22. The call was headed, "For the United Front of the Proletariat" and addressed to "Workingmen and Women of all Countries." Communist parties were requested to send delegations "twice as large as usual." The call was a long and tedious document surveying the general world situation as it affected the working classes. Moscow believed that this situation justified "the union of all the forces of the international proletariat, the establishment of a united front of all the parties of the proletariat, regardless of the differences separating them." The call concluded with a challenge, not to the leaders, but to the organized masses. "You are not yet ready to renew the struggle," said Moscow; "you do not yet dare the armed conflict for power, for the dictatorship; you do not yet dare the great attack on the citadels of world reaction. Then at least join forces in a battle-front, unite as a proletarian class against the class of the exploiters and the pillagers of the world. Tear down the walls which have been built up between you; take your place in the ranks — whether Communist, Social Democrat, Anarchist or Syndicalist — for the battle against the misery of the hour."[2]

The result was negotiations between the Communist International, the International Working Union of Socialist parties, and the Second International, which led to a conference of the executives of these organizations in Berlin in the following April. The

---

[1] Henry Noel Brailsford in "The Socialist Battle for Existence in Europe," *Current History*, March, 1924, gives a vivid picture of the wreckage left in the trail of this policy.

[2] The call appeared in the first number of *The Worker* (weekly, New York), February 2, 1922.

initiative of the Communist International raised the question as to whether it was sincere or whether the proposal was not another maneuver to obtain contact with the rival organizations in order to effect more "splits." Suspicion was rife when the executives met in the Reichstag on April 2. Friedrich Adler of the Working Union opened the conference in a speech defining its purpose and limitations. There was to be no attempt at a fusion of the three organizations, as a common organization was not possible, but "common action" might be possible for "concrete ends."[3]

Clara Zetkin read a statement prepared by the delegation of the Third International. The Communists declared that because the working class was not ready to seize power "in revolutionary battle," organic unity "of the present international organizations of the proletariat, differing as to orientation in principle, is entirely Utopian and injurious." However, they also agreed that common action on some important questions was possible, and welcomed the proposal of the other two organizations "for the convocation of an International Labor Congress." But to make such a congress effective, they urged, the Amsterdam Trade Union International, the Red Trade Union International, independent syndicalist organizations and the American Federation of Labor should be invited. They also took occasion to open old sores, charging that their opponents had "helped world capital to repel the first attack of the proletariat" upon the bourgeois order.[4]

Vandervelde, for the Second International, declared that his organization would raise no objections in principle. The three organizations had two things to fear — "either that capitalists will be seized by the madness which leads them to the abyss, or that they will become reasonable, will try to come to an agreement and organize a vast consortium for the exploitation of the world, and primarily for the exploitation of Russia." Their aim appeared

[3] *The Second and Third Internationals and the Vienna Union*, Official Report of the Conference between the Executives, held at the Reichstag, Berlin, on the 2nd of April, 1922, and following days. London, 1922, pp. 5-12.
[4] *Ibid.*, pp. 12-18.

to be "the organization of a capitalist hegemony throughout the world, under the direction and aegis of that capitalism which is at once the most powerful, the most brutal, the most cynical — American capitalism." These dangers justified a union in action of the three organizations. But, he continued, the question of good faith is involved. Karl Radek had already sent from Moscow a confidential letter which justified apprehensions, and the Executive Committee of the Third International, in a document published the previous December, had "explained their real intentions."

Vandervelde had reached a crucial point in the negotiations by raising a question which every member of the conference knew would come up. "In this document," he continued, "there are passages which remind me irresistibly of that scene in the Nibelungen cycle where Mime tells Siegfried of her intention to poison him, at the same time overwhelming him with friendly and flattering speeches. An appeal is made for union, for the realization of the united front, but no secret is made of the intention to stifle us and poison us after embracing us. While we are all put in the same sack — pending the day when we shall all be put in the same basket — while we are being told, for example, that men like Jouhaux, Merrheim and Henderson, Vandervelde or Longuet, are serving the interests of the bourgeoisie, it is, to say the least of it, strange that these same men should be invited to take part in the defense of proletarian interests." Vandervelde put three questions to the Communist delegation: (1) would they attempt to strengthen common action or to create more divisions? (2) would they permit the peoples in the Ukraine, Armenia and Georgia to freely elect delegates to the general conference? (3) would they guarantee that "the trial of the Social-Revolutionaries shall be held under conditions which will satisfy international Socialism, and which, above all, will guarantee elementary rights of defense?"[5]

[5] *Ibid.*, pp. 19-28. The Social-Revolutionaries were accused of acts said to have been committed four years before at the period of the open civil war and they were to be tried despite several decrees of amnesty issued by the Soviet Government which included these acts.

It will be observed that Vandervelde was reluctant to quote from the document, which, he said, raised the question of good faith. J. Ramsay MacDonald believed that nothing should be concealed, and on the second day of the conference he quoted from the document sent out by the Executive Committee of the Third International the previous December. It contained the following paragraph: "Comrades of the Third International: There is a movement on foot in Europe for a united front. It does not matter whether we are in favor of it or not; *our tactics compel us to appear to be in favor of it;* but we ask the Communist sections all over Europe to take part in the creation of the united front, *not for the purpose of making it effective,* but for the purpose of strengthening the Communists through direct propaganda inside the organizations taking part in the movement."[6]

Karl Radek, speaking for the Communist delegation, ignored the document, and launched into an attack on Vandervelde and Socialists in general. If an agreement should be reached, he said, "this fight will decide whether it is a maneuver, as you say, in favor of the Communist International or a stream which will unite the working class."[7]

The conference agreed to set up an Organization Committee of Nine, to hold further conferences of the executives and to include representation of parties not affiliated with either of the three internationals. The committee was instructed to try to bring about conversations between the Amsterdam Trade Union International and the Red (Communist) Trade Union International, with the object of establishing a united front, while the Communist delegation agreed to allow the accused Social-Revolutionaries any defenders they desired, and a pledge was given that no death

---

[6] *Ibid.,* pp. 39-40. Zinoviev, President of the Communist International, was also quoted in the Moscow organ of the Communist Party as saying that the united front was a question only of "a tactical maneuver" to "expose the treachery of the leaders of the compromisers and centrists." Excerpts of translations of Zinoviev's speech appeared in the *New York Call,* February 25, 1922.

[7] *Ibid.,* pp. 65-77.

sentence would be inflicted. A public trial was guaranteed, and representatives of the three internationals would be permitted to attend the trial and take stenographc notes of the proceedings. It was agreed "to collect and examine the material to be submitted by the different sections on Georgia" and to call a general conference as soon as possible. Meantime united May Day demonstrations were urged to promote unity, in defense of the eight-hour day, against unemployment, for the starving Russians and resumption of political and economic relations with Russia. In a separate declaration, Grimm and Longuet of the Working Union noted that the Communist delegation had refused to accept a clause in the agreement that all parties should "work energetically for the immediate release of all political prisoners in their own countries, particularly those who were tried or condemned during a time of open civil war." Grimm and Longuet asserted that the Communists "considered of such importance the further detention of Socialist prisoners in Russia that they were prepared to abandon their struggle for the freedom of the proletarian political prisoners languishing in capitalist state prisons."[8]

The Organization Committee of Nine met in Berlin on May 23. Between the two meetings the Soviet Government had suppressed a Socialist rebellion in Georgia, and the Second International demanded immediate appointment of a committee on Georgia and that the document on Georgia promised by the Third International be immediately submitted. The Second International also reported that it had received from all its affiliated parties reports of "disruptive tactics" indulged in by Communists and declared that a general conference would be possible only when these difficulties were removed. The Third International promised to submit the documents to a committee of the three internationals only at a general conference, and demanded that a call for such

---

[8] *Ibid.*, pp. 83-85, where the full text of the agreement will be found. See also the *American Labor Year Book, 1923-24*, pp. 291-93, for a brief acount of the Berlin conference and its decisions.

a conference be immediately ordered. Negotiations were broken off and the Committee of Nine disbanded.[9] Mutual recriminations followed, the Third International issuing a long and bitter manifesto, concluding with the words, "Down with the united front of the Social Democrats and the bourgeoisie," and insisting that failure of the negotiations was due to its opponents.[10]

This attempt at unity of action and the trial of the Social-Revolutionists in Russia, which soon followed, determined the future relations of Communists and their opponents all over the world, and for this reason it is essential to understand them. The "trial" was of such a character as not only to arouse the resentment of the non-Communist Labor and Socialist movement in all countries, but to provoke a general protest on the part of liberal opinion, which was seeking to obtain diplomatic and trade relations between Russia and the other nations of the world. In accord with the Berlin agreement, Vandervelde, Waters, Rosenfeld and Theodore Liebknecht proceeded to Moscow to represent the Socialist workmen of Europe, and arrived on May 26. En route to the Soviet capital they faced numerous hostile demonstrations. In Moscow a huge hostile demonstration was planned and carried out. On May 28 thousands filled the Red Square to hear leading Communists denounce the accused Social-Revolutionists, and the first to speak was Piatakoff, *the president of the revolutionary tribunal that was to try the accused*. A mob was permitted to enter the courtroom, the judges listened to the orators, shook their hands, and thanked them for their loyalty to the Soviet Government.

In such an atmosphere the attorneys for the accused struggled hopelessly for a week, and finally withdrew from the case with the unanimous approval of the defendants. In a written statement, the attorneys declared that (1) the court had declined to admit

[9] *The American Labor Year Book, 1923-24*, pp. 292-94.
[10] The manifesto of the Third International appeared in *The Workers' Challenge*, July 1, 1922.

four new attorneys and, contrary to the Berlin agreement, had forbidden the defense to take a stenographic record; (2) the court had declared that under certain circumstances it would question the desirability of foreign counsel to continue participation in the trial; (3) Prosecutors Krylenko and Lunacharsky had declared that the Berlin agreement was not binding; (4) Bucharin, a representative of the Third International at the Berlin conference, had declared the Berlin agreement abrogated.

The four attorneys for the defense left Moscow, but not until after they had declared a twenty-four-hour hunger strike to compel the Bolsheviki to permit them to leave. They issued a long statement to the workers of Europe reviewing their experiences, adding that the home of one of the Russian counsels for the defense had been searched and that part of the material he had prepared was confiscated, and that two of the chief witnesses of the prosecution had admitted having planned the attempt to kill Lenin. Later it became known that three days after the foreign attorney withdrew from the trial, the Russian attorney for the defense, Muravioff, was indicated for contempt for protesting against the proceedings, and later was exiled to a distant part of Russia. The indictment against the accused charged that they had defended the Constituent Assembly with arms in their hands when the Bolsheviks attacked it, and upon the word of two informers, they were charged with attempting the life of Lenin.[11]

The character of the trial and the sentencing to death of twelve of the accused, also in violation of the Berlin agreement, made the breach between the Third International and its two rivals wider than ever. The former did not make matters any better by frequent declarations in which the Working Union and the Second International were ferociously attacked as "lackeys of

[11] The periodical Socialist and Communist literature here and abroad contains much material on the trial. The Communist press does not deny the essential facts mentioned above but justified the proceedings on the ground that "proletarian justice" differs vastly from "bourgeois justice." The most complete account of the proceedings is found in *The 12 Who Are to Die*, Berlin, 1922.

the bourgeoisie." On the other hand, the experience made it easier
for these two organizations to unite. In September the Independent
and Majority Socialists of Germany united, and in the same month
the executive of the Working Union declared that the Berlin
conference and the Moscow trial had made impossible any working agreement with the Communist International. A joint congress
of the two Socialist Internationals was held in Hamburg in May,
1923, and they united as the Labor and Socialist International.[12]

But the united front did not cease to be an issue with the Third
International and its affiliated sections in the various nations. They
explained the failure at Berlin on the ground that the masses
desired a united front in all countries, but that the "leaders" of
the Labor and Socialist International did not want it and were
standing in the way. The Hamburg congress was the subject
of a bristling manifesto from Moscow. "The capitalist offensive is
advancing," it declared. "The bourgeoisie is making the greatest
efforts to mobilize and concentrate all their main forces for the
decisive attack on the working class. Their accomplices, the
reformists, cannot remain separate from this business. They also
are gathering; the remainder of the Second and the Two-and-a-
half Internationals are about to unite and to form." The burden
of the document is that all outside of Communism is illusion,
"betrayal," "treachery," and that all Social Democratic parties
are "led by traitors."[13]

In accord with the view that leaders were constantly betraying
the masses, a new strategy was evolved. While these manifestoes
continued to come from Moscow, the approach to the organized
masses became indirect; that is, through special organizations
created for some particular purpose and with which Socialist
and Labor organizations were invited to affiliate. Organizations
for famine relief in Russia, Germany or China; for the release

---

[12] *The American Labor Year Book, 1923-24*, pp. 294-301.
[13] The complete manifesto appeared in *The Workers Weekly* (London), June
2, 1923.

and relief of political prisoners, Russia always excepted; for the protection of alien workers or to fight Fascism or to protect free discussion, freedom of the press and organization — again Russia excepted, and for a variety of other purposes, were formed upon the initiative of Communists with the view of establishing intimate contact with the organized masses outside the Communist organizations. All such organizations were formed in response to the cry for a "united front." Among such organizations formed in the United States were "The Friends of Soviet Russia," "The Federated Farmer-Labor Party," a number of State Farmer-Labor parties, "The Trade Union Educational League," "The Labor Defense Council," "The Irish Workers and Peasant Famine Relief Committee" and "The American Negro Labor Congress."

Early in the period of this new strategy Lenin outlined its policy for Communist work in the trade unions. In such work he advised his followers to "go to the whole length of any sacrifice, if need be, to resort to strategy and adroitness, illegal proceedings, reticence and subterfuge — to anything in order to penetrate the trade unions, remain in them, and carry on Communist work inside them, at any cost."[14] In the United States the Workers' Party issued a pamphlet of instructions for this work, of which Lenin was also the author, in which its members were advised "to practise trickery, to employ cunning, and to resort to illegal methods — to sometimes even overlook or conceal the truth" in order to penetrate the trade unions.[15] The results of this policy

[14] Lenin, *Left Wing Communism, An Infantile Disorder*, London (n.d.), p. 39.
[15] Lenin, *Should Communists Participate in Reactionary Trade Unions?* New York (n.d.). Published by the Workers' Party, p. 13.

In 1914 when Lenin was an exile in Switzerland he objected to this low code when applied to his comrades by the Czarist Government. On November 28 of that year he wrote to Shliapnikov, a Russian Bolshevik in Stockholm, stating that newspapers had confirmed the arrest of five Bolshevik Deputies in Russia and added the following comment: "A horrible thing. The government has decided, apparently, to have revenge upon the Russian Social Democratic Labor group in the Duma and will not stop at anything. The worst can be expecetd: *falsification of documents, fraud, planting material evidence, false testimony, a trial behind closed doors, etc. I think that without such methods the government could not have*

have proven demoralizing to organizations affected by it. It is no exaggeration to say that the non-Communist organizations that accepted some phase of the so-called "united front" were materially weakened by dissensions that followed, and some have been destroyed; yet the appeal for unity, for humanitarian or similar aims has always been put so adroitly that it has been occasionally accepted.

The most notable result of the policy of the "united front" was the election of a trade union delegation to Russia by the Hull Congress of the British Trade Unions in 1924. The result was a voluminous report[16] of 234 pages largely favorable to the Soviet Government, but in matters involving the rights of workers to organize, publish literature, hold meetings, participate in elections and speak freely, the committee was vague and obscurantist. The report provoked a storm of criticism by non-Communist organizations of workers in Europe. Its critics pointed out that the three members of the delegation who wrote the report had formerly been in the British diplomatic service, and that their obscurantist references to civil rights in Russia were characteristic of the British imperialists' explanations of arbitrary rule in India and Egypt. Yet the report admitted the dictatorship of an "inner ring"[17] in Russia, that "all opposition is as yet silenced,"[18] that the Communist Party was annually "purged" of those who may disagree with the "inner ring,"[19] and that a rigid control of all printed matter was maintained by the Soviet Government.[20]

obtained a conviction." The complete letter may be consulted in Gankin and Fisher, The Bolsheviks and the World War, p. 200. The Hoover Library on War, Revolution and Peace, Publication No. 15.
Lenin's protest also provides an interesting comment on the "trials" of dissenters in Russia during his dictatorship and that of Stalin.

[16] Russia, The Official Report of the British Trade Union Delegation to Russia in November and December, 1924, London, 1925.
[17] Ibid., p. 11.
[18] Ibid., p. 14.
[19] Ibid., p. 15.
[20] Ibid., p. 117.

Nevertheless, British workers faced a grave unemployment problem, and a number of the trade union leaders favored the "united front" which the Russians were urging, the British leaders believing that this unity would stimulate trade between Russia and Great Britain and offer substantial relief to the unemployed. An Anglo-Russian Alliance was formed between the trade unions of the two countries, but the terms of the agreement were rather limited, although they hoped that the alliance would lead to such a general conference as that which had failed to issue from the Berlin conference of the three internationals in 1922. The alliance remained practically an advisory body with consultative powers, and the European trade unions remained hostile to any "united front" that permitted the Red (Communist) Trade Union International to have any large measure of power.

In a critical analysis of the British report,[21] Friedrich Adler, Secretary of the Labor and Socialist International, declared that at the Hamburg congress, where the two internationals had united in May, 1925, Communists appeared with a plea for a "united front" against Fascism.[22] While this plea was being made at Hamburg in a carefully written document, another manifesto had been sent by the Communist International to all countries denouncing the Hamburg congress as a conference "led by traitors."[23] Adler enumerated the mixed organizations which they had formed in Europe in the name of the "united front" and asserted that in Communist circles these organizations were known as "Innocents' Clubs;" that is, non-Communist members and organizations affiliated with the "Workers' International Relief" and the "Hands

[21] Adler, *The Anglo-Russian Report.* London, 1925.

[22] This plea appeared in full in the *International Press Correspondence,* May 18, 1923. This was a weekly service maintained by Communists and which supplied publications all over the world with news of the Communist International and of the Soviet Government. It was later transferred to Vienna.

[23] See above, p. 145.

off Russia Committee" were innocent of the real intentions of Communists in forming these organizations.[24]

This background is essential to an understanding of a contemporary phase of the activities of the Communist Party in the United States. What is strange about the policy of the "united front" is that its advocates are themselves so innocent about the problem of human psychology which it involves. A union of human beings for common purposes can only be obtained on a basis of good faith, and yet while making fraternal advances to organizations in one document Communist organizations invariably publish other documents that clearly imply absence of good faith and the desire to intrigue and make trouble for those they would embrace. The same organizations that are asked to "fight the bourgeoisie" are also denounced as "agents of the bourgeoisie." The "betrayers of the working class" are urged to united for the welfare of the working class.

[24] Adler, *The Anglo-Russian Report*, p. 46. On page 47 Adler quotes a letter of the German Communist, Muenzenberg, who refers to these "Innocents' Clubs."

CHAPTER IX

THE FEDERATED FARMER-LABOR PARTY

WITHIN a few months after the Workers' Party was organized, in December, 1921, it was required to apply the policy of the "united front." As stated in Chapter VII, two months later the party sent a statement to the first Conference for Progressive Political Action, and in December, 1922, it sent delegates to the second conference, but they were not seated. Meantime economic discontent and political dissent were widespread in the agricultural sections of the West and Northwest and to a lesser extent in the industrial centers east of the Mississippi. In New York City an American Labor Party was organized in July, 1922, which consisted of some eighty trade unions, the Socialist Party, the Farmer-Labor Party, the World War Veterans, and several fraternal and cooperative organizations of wageworkers. A powerful farmer-labor political coalition had appeared in Minnesota as early as 1918, and a similar organization had appeared in Idaho which polled a large vote in November, 1922. In West Virginia a Farmer-Labor Party was organized in July, 1923, upon the initiative of the State Federation of Labor, and a tentative organization of the same type was formed in Missouri. In Los Angeles, San Francisco, Toledo and a number of other cities local political coalitions were organized. Near the end of the year 1923 influential members of the Non-Partisan League in North and South Dakota favored organization of an independent party of farmers and workers, and in Pennsylvania a Labor Party had been organized. The drift of this period was a pronounced tendency on the part of rural and urban workers in some states to disregard party ties and, as we have seen, to organize independently of the major parties.

The National Farmer-Labor Party, which grew out of the National Labor Party organized in 1919 at Chicago and which nominated Parley P. Christensen for President in 1920, held a national convention in Chicago in May, 1922. Seventeen states were represented by 72 delegates, and it appeared destined to fall heir to the state parties that were forming in the West. The party sent delegates to the second Conference for Progressive Political Action, which met the following December in Cleveland. The Farmer-Labor Party delegation introduced a resolution which, because of its subsequent effect on the course of the party and its relations with the Workers' Party, is important. The resolution reads: "Resolved, That the Conference for Progressive Political Action hereby declares for independent political action by the agricultural and industrial workers through a party of their own." A long debate followed, but the resolution was defeated by the narrow margin of 52 for and 64 against. The Socialists supported the resolution when it came to a vote, but they believed that it was a mistake to raise the question, because, they contended, a majority of the members of the powerful unions were not yet ready for independent party organization. As the conference closed, the Farmer-Labor Party delegation announced that the party would no longer affiliate with the conference.[1]

Early in the following year the Farmer-Labor Party issued a call for a national conference, to meet in Chicago in July. The call was sent to trade unions, state Farmer-Labor parties, the Non-Partisan League, the Socialist Party and the Workers' Party, the intention being to hold a national convention of the party and then confer with the other organizations with the view of uniting all of them in some workable political coalition. It believed that the conditions were favorable for this movement and that the Conference for Progressive Political Action was too timid and was moving too slowly to take advantage of a favorable situation. The Workers'

[1] *Report of the Proceedings of the Second Conference for Progressive Political Action, held at Cleveland, December 11, 12, 1922*, pp. 28-29.

Party immediately accepted the invitation, accepting it as the first fruit of its agitation for a "united front." A number of national and local unions also sent delegates, some, probably a majority, mainly in the capacity of observers.

The Socialist Party met in national convention in New York in May and considered this invitation and one from the Workers' Party for a "united front." In answer to the invitation of the Farmer-Labor Party to send delegates to discuss "such steps as may be necessary to bring about complete unity of the political forces of the entire working class" and establish a nation-wide Labor Party, the Socialist convention answered: "The Socialist Party fully agrees with the Farmer-Labor Party as to the desirability of uniting the workers on the political field. The only question is how soon and by what means this end can best be obtained. A necessary condition to the establishment of a really powerful political party of the working class is the active support of at least a majority of the great trade unions. Unless there is assurance that this support is now obtainable, any attempt at this time to effect the proposed unity of the political forces of the entire working class would result in disappointment." [2]

The proposal of the Workers' Party to the Socialist convention was to form a "united front" in order to promote (1) amalgamation of the trade unions; (2) to protect foreign-born workers; (3) to repudiate the Vienna Working Union, the Amsterdam International Federation of Trade Unions, and the Second International; (4) to support the recognition of Soviet Russia; (5) to remove certain governmental obstacles hindering the struggles of the workers; (6) to bring about a nation-wide Labor Party. The convention answered that if the Communists had urged a "united front" at the end of the World War, "this front would have been established five years ago. Instead of this policy, the Communist International pursued a deliberate policy of division. It ordered

---

[2] *The American Labor Year Book, 1923-24*, p. 132.

splits in every country. It sowed hatreds and dissensions among the working class. It destroyed all possibility of the solidarity of the workers of each nation. It brought civil war into the organizations of the workers." The answer proceeded to quote instructions of the Communist International on the "united front" which MacDonald read at the Berlin conference of the three internationals in April, 1922,[3] and continued: "There is no reason for our believing that the proposal of the Workers' Party is not of the same character. Nor can we believe that it is any more honest. It is couched in lauguage similar to the pleas which the Communist International made prior to the meeting of the Berlin conference."[4]

As matters stood, the Socialists declined to be represented at the Farmer-Labor conference and refused the offer of a "united front" by the Workers' Party. The Farmer-Labor conference was called to meet in Chicago, July 3, 1923. Officials of the party had been warned that the Workers' Party might not be acting in good faith, but they believed that these warnings were prompted more by factional differences than by any real danger. The Workers' Party in the meantime had transferred *The Worker* to Chicago and was giving publicity to the coming convention. It broadcast a "Manifesto" in favor of the "united front," a Labor Party and the Chicago convention, at the same time finding another example of "betrayal" in the Socialists' refusal to send delegates to the convention.[5]

Reports of the number of delegates and organizations represented at the conference are conflicting. Mr. Jay G. Brown, National Secretary of the Farmer-Labor Party, reported afterwards that four national labor organizations were represented, four state farm organizations, three national political bodies — the Farmer-Labor Party, the Workers' Party and the Proletarian Party — 123

---

[3] See above, p. 141.
[4] *The American Labor Year Book, 1923-24*, pp. 130-131.
[5] The "Manifesto" appeared in *The Worker*, June 2, 1923, and the same issue carried columns regarding the Socialists' "betrayal."

working-class fraternal societies, 246 local farm and trade union branches and 14 Farmer-Labor Party branches.[6] Robert Morss Lovett estimated the number of delegates at 440, which included representation from the Amalgamated Clothing Workers, the Maintenance of Way Men, the Mine Workers (45), the Machinists (28), the Workmen's Circle (32), and various farmers' organizations (81). He added, "When the sons of God assembled, Satan came among them," the invader being the Workers' Party.[7] The Communists, with probably less than 15,000 members, only 1,500 of whom were English-speaking, "captured" the convention and organized the "Federated Farmer-Labor Party."

How this happened is evident from the report of the convention sent out by the Workers' Party. The Communists were represented over and over again through various organizations and parts of organizations. Aside from the representation they obtained through their party and the Young Workers' League, their youth organization, they had delegates seated from the following organizations: "Lithuanian Workers' Literature Society," "Lithuanian Workers' Progressive Alliance," "Joint Conference of Lithuanian Societies," "African Blood Brotherhood," "Improvement Benefit Club," "United Federation of Rhode Island," "P. D. and P. H. of A.," "Arbeitergesang Bund Northwest," "Workmen's Gymnastic Association," "Roumanian Progressive Club," "Workers' Educational Association," "Sick and Death Benefit Societies," "United Workingmen Singers," miscellaneous unions, and so on. The roster of organizations represented is littered with such mysterious names. According to the report of the Workers' Party, the above organizations were credited with 54,000 members. The Workers' Party was credited with 20,000 members and its Young Workers' League with 2,500. A conservative estimate of all the organizations mentioned above gives them over 76,000 members, while the

6 *The American Labor Year Book, 1923-24*, p. 143.
7 Lovett, "The Farmer-Labor Fiasco at Chicago," *The New Republic*, July 18, 1923.

organized Communists of the whole country had less than 15,000 members.[8]

Charges were made after the convention that the Workers' Party had "packed" the conference, and this was vigorously denied, but the party has since provided the data itself to show that the charges were true. In its report to the fourth national convention of the Workers' Party, the Central Executive Committee presented detailed figures of the membership of the party month by month and from one year to another since the party was organized. The figures are accurate, as they are based upon the purchase of membership stamps each month by the affiliated organizations. This report shows that for the six months ending July 1, 1923, the total number of membership stamps purchased by the members was 89,199, which gives an average membership for each month of 14,866. The same figures show that the average membership of the English-speaking organizations was only 1,055, and these members are included in the total of 14,866. The figures show that when the Workers' Party claimed and obtained a representation for 20,000 members at the Chicago conference, it claimed representation for 5,000 more members than it really had.[9] It is practically certain that the claim of 2,500 members for the Young Workers' League was also an exaggerated claim. Small as the party's membership was, it obtained more representation through the mysterious organizations mentioned above, while the English-speaking section of a thousand members provided the leadership of the Communists in the conference.

As an organized, compact and disciplined group subject to the orders of a few shrewd leaders on the floor, the Communists outgeneraled the undisciplined groups of farmers and wageworkers.

[8] These figures are taken from a mimeograph report of the conference proceedings sent out from Chicago by Joseph Manley, Secretary of the Federated Farmer-Labor Party.

[9] The figures on the membership of the Workers' Party appear in *The Fourth National Convention*, Workers' (Communist) Party of America, held in Chicago, Aug. 21-30, 1925. The table for the membership in 1923 appears on p. 29.

As invited guests they "came into the house and carried off the ice cream," wrote Robert Morss Lovett. The intention of the Farmer-Labor Party was to hold a conference through which representatives of the invited organizations would confer and report back to their constituents any agreements that might be reached. The Communists came to the conference not to confer, but "with a program in conflict with the invitation and with the spirit of the meeting. Instead of a program for a plan to be carried back by the delegates to their several constituents, it was a plan for immediate organization, including the election of a new national executive committee, not in the future, but by that conference, then and there, which they had packed and which they controlled." Thus wrote Robert Buck, the editor of the Farmer-Labor Party's official organ.[10] This proposal was fought, but the Workers' Party won some support from delegates representing farmers' organizations who were impatient for immediate party organization. As one farmer delegate expressed it, "We farmers out West are not afraid of Bolsheviks. We have been called everything imaginable, and that does not bother us."[11] The farmers who favored party organization knew little and cared little about the intense feelings and convictions which had divided the workers of the cities.

Whether the Farmer-Labor Party considered the conference which it had called one of a tentative character, is not entirely clear. It was holding its own convention at the same time, and it may not have been entirely clear as to its intentions regarding the conference, but its delegates in the conference made it clear that they would not submit to any one group controlling it or forcing its program upon the conference, asserting that a Communist-led party could not win the confidence and support of the voting masses.

The Workers' Party had planned its work thoroughly. Large numbers of its supporters attended the conference each day to

[10] *The New Majority* (Chicago), July 21, 1923.
[11] *The Worker*, July 14, 1923.

provide the proper atmosphere by loud demonstrations in support of measures which the Communists favored. William Z. Foster and Charles E. Ruthenberg were the two generals in command of the Workers' Party delegates, and they enforced a rigid discipline. Charles Woll, a Chicago delegate and opposed to the Foster-Ruthenberg program, declared that the night before the conference opened "the Foster-Ruthenberg leaders called in the labor delegates and organized them in batches of ten, with a captain over each squad, and they were instructed to vote throughout the conference as the captain indicated, the captain getting his orders from Foster and Ruthenberg." [12] This organization and discipline was not something new. It had matured in the Left Wing when it waged its fight for the control of the Socialist Party in 1919. John J. Fitzpatrick of the Chicago Federation of Labor had been intimately associated with William Z. Foster in the organization of the steel strike in 1919 and had been active in the work of obtaining funds for the defense of Foster for his participation in the secret convention of the Communist Party in Michigan. Fitzpatrick, as a member of the National Executive Committee of the Farmer Labor Party, declared that "what they [the Communist delegates] have done is on the level of a man being invited to your house as a guest and then, once in the house, seizing you by the throat and kicking you out of the door. . . . It is silly to expect that the farmers of the United States will subscribe to the Third International or the Moscow program, whatever may be the individual's views as to these movements. They simply won't do it, and as practical men we know that." [13]

The Communist delegates obtained a majority for their program and organized the Federated Farmer-Labor Party. Of the 33 members of the National Executive Committee, at least 14 were known to be Communists and the remaining 19 were probably Communists too. Joseph Manley, a prominent member of the

[12] Quoted in an interview in the *Chicago Examiner*, July 7, 1923.
[13] *Ibid.*

Workers' Party, was elected National Secretary. Foster and Ruthenberg were also elected members of this committee. A "Statement of Principles" was adopted, which declared for "nationalization of all public utilities and all social means of communication and transportation," with increasing control and management extended to farmers and workers "through their own economic organizations." A program of social legislation was included which differed little from the Labor and Socialist platforms of the period. The final section was devoted to the farmers, which promised to eliminate landlordism and tenantry, which favored public ownership of "all means of transportation, communication, natural resources and public utilities, to be operated by and for the people," the issue and control "of all money and credit by the government, for service instead of profits, payment of all War debts by a tax on excess profits and a moratorium for five years for all indebted working farmers.[14]

Firmly seated in control of the new party, the Workers' Party broadcast the statement that the new party represented 600,000 affiliated farmers and urban workers. Mr. Manley addressed a letter to William H. Johnston of the Conference for Progressive Political Action, suggesting that a Committee of five of his organization meet a similar committee of the Federated Farmer-Labor Party "in order to discuss ways and means for a nation-wide organization campaign among the workers and farmers" with a view to united political action in 1924.[15] Nothing came of this suggestion.

The claim of 600,000[16] members for the new party was not warranted by any substantial evidence. The Farmer-Labor Party, immediately after the adjournment of the conference, declined to

[14] *The American Labor Year Book, 1923-24*, pp. 157-8.
[15] Leaflet of Federated Farmer-Labor Party, Chicago, August, 1923.
[16] *The Worker*, July 4, 1923. This claim of 600,000 members was also made to Moscow by John Pepper, the official representative of the Third International in the United States. He wrote a special article for the *International Press Correspondence*, Berlin, July 26, 1923, rejoicing over the achievement of the Workers' Party at the Chicago conference.

affiliate with the new party. However, its strong state organization in the State of Washington affiliated with the new organization, but its members drifted away, and by the end of 1924 the Washington organization became a handful and then disappeared. The Farmer-Labor Party itself inherited factional animosities as a result of its contact with the Workers' Party at Chicago, and it rapidly declined. In May, 1924, it announced that its national convention, which had been called to meet in Cleveland on July 4, had been abandoned "because the national office lacked the necessary funds." By the end of the year this promising party had ceased to exist. The Chicago Federation of Labor, which had taken the initiative in organizing the Farmer-Labor Party, reluctantly returned to the "non-partisan" political policy of the American Federation of Labor. Its political creation, the Cook County (Chicago) Farmer-Labor Party disbanded.[17] The Proletarian Party refused to affiliate with the Federated Farmer-Labor Party. The few large unions reported as being represented at the Chicago conference also declined to affiliate. The Chicago conference destroyed the Farmer-Labor Party, which had called it, and brought confusion and bitterness into other non-Communist organizations. The Workers' Party took out of the conference practically what it put into it, its own delegates and the delegates of the mysterious organizations that were admitted, together with another party name — the Federated Farmer-Labor Party. It had captured "nothing more substantial than its own padded enlargement." [18]

Much publicity was given to the new party, but it made no progress. The daily press had broadcast news of the proceedings of the Chicago conference and the character of the new party was known. In his report to the third convention of the Workers' Party in Chicago, December 30, 1923-January 2, 1924, C. E.

[17] *The New Majority*, May 24, 1924. Both announcements appeared in this issue.

[18] Benjamin Stolberg, "The Peter Pans of Communism," *Century Magazine*, July, 1925.

Ruthenberg, the Executive Secretary, explained the party's actions at the Chicago conference. He contended that his party had an agreement with the Farmer-Labor Party that if a half-million workers were represented at the conference, this number would serve for the basis of a new party. It was also agreed that "the structure of the Farmer-Labor Party should be used as the structure for the new Federation Farmer-Labor Party." Two days before the conference opened the executive of the Workers' Party constituted itself a "steering committee" for Communist delegates, and this committee informed the F.-L.P. "that only delegates from bona-fide affiliated organizations of the F.-L.P. should be seated in the preliminary convention." The F.-L.P. agreed with this view, according to Mr. Ruthenberg, but nothing is said in this report about the numerous disguised organizations whose delegates were then in the city and who were to be guided by the two Communist generals upon the floor of the conference. It would appear that if "bona-fide" organizations alone were to be represented, these mysterious organizations would certainly be excluded.

In any event, Mr. Ruthenberg reported that the F.-L.P. had broken faith with his "steering committee" by recommending that all the delegates present be seated. "The steering committee of the C.E.C. (Central Executive Committee) was ready to accept this decision," said Mr. Ruthenberg, "but during the process of debate on the question, amendments were made which would have seated all the local unions and central labor body delegates not affiliated with the F.-L.P., but would have excluded the Workers' Party and a number of international organizations. The steering committee could not permit such isolation of our delegates, and therefore insisted that either all delegates be seated or only the bona-fide Farmer-Labor Party delegates as per the agreement previously made. The motion of the steering committee for the seating of all delegates was carried in the convention." [19]

19 *The Second Year of the Workers' Party of America*, Report of the Central Executive Committee to the Third National Convention, Chicago. pp. 15-20.

What had happened was that the Farmer-Labor Party recognized too late that it faced a compact and disciplined group under the leadership of two men who were able to carry through any program they wanted. The host tried to either isolate or minimize this guest, but failed. Mr. Ruthenberg believed that the Chicago conference had "greatly strengthened the Workers' Party." He continued: "Through the maneuvers carried on by our party directly and by the Federated Farmer-Labor Party with our assistance, our party is now in a position which makes it impossible to challenge our leadership in the Labor Party movement. The Federated Farmer-Labor Party, although it has secured the affiliation of but 155,000 of the 600,000 organized workers represented in the July 3rd conference, enjoys a greater influence and prestige than the number of officially affiliated members would indicate. It has built for itself a position of powerful influence upon the whole Labor Party movement. On the basis of these facts and our cooperation in bringing about this situation, the C.E.C. believes that its view that the July 3rd conference and its results were a very great victory for our party cannot be successfully challenged." [20]

There was nothing in the general political situation of that period to justify this optimism. The Socialists and trade unionists who had sent warnings to the Farmer-Labor Party regarding the admission of the Workers' Party to the Chicago conference had their fears verified. Many embittered men left Chicago to give an unfavorable view of the Workers' Party and the Federated Farmer-Labor Party. The active members of the Farmer-Labor Party, who had spent nearly four years in organizing their movement, only to see it rent with dissensions and themselves attacked in Communist organs, were transformed into irreconcilable enemies. Even Mr. Ruthenberg's claims of membership for the new party had been reduced from 600,000 to 155,000, and the latter figure was an aspiration, not a fact. So blind were these men

[20] *Ibid.*, p. 21.

to the gaping wounds they had left in Chicago that they could believe with their Executive Secretary that they had won a "great victory," which made it impossible for anybody to "challenge our leadership in the Labor Party movement." Within a year after this rejoicing these men had themselves abandoned the Federated Farmer-Labor Party, and by June, 1925, they could report only 1,400 more members of the Workers' Party than the latter had when it "captured" the Chicago conference.[21] Apparently immune to the lessons of experience and lacking in comprehension of human psychology, they could broadcast a long greeting from the executive of the Communist International to their third convention that American Communists had demonstrated to American workingmen that they *are not only their best friends, but the only ones in the United States who understand the political needs of the working class.*" [22] Yet notwithstanding this claim of friendship and the ability to understand the needs of American workmen, the convention a few days later, when considering the matter of a Labor Party, by a unanimous vote referred "this problem to the Communist International before which all elements will be represented." [23]

How long the Workers' Party kept the Federated Farmer-Labor Party alive is not certain. No official announcement was ever made of its demise, but it was retained as a bargaining asset at least until June, 1924, when it was represented at a national political conference in St. Paul. Some time after this conference the name ceased to appear in the official publications of the Workers' Party. Had it retained even a portion of the 155,000 members claimed by Mr. Ruthenberg at the third convention of the Workers' Party, it is certain that it would have been continued in order to continue contact with its non-Communist members. That it was

[21] *The Fourth National Convention, Workers' (Communist) Party,* Chicago, 1925, table of membership, January-June 1925. p. 37.
[22] *The Worker,* January 5, 1924.
[23] *The Worker,* January 12, 1924.

abandoned some time after the St. Paul conference was equal to an admission that it practically only duplicated the membership of the Workers' Party, that instead of a "victory," it was a burden, and that as a means of acquiring leadership over the American masses it was a failure. Yet one cannot read the publications of the Workers' Party during this period without being impressed by the fanatical efforts of its members to induce American workers to accept the Federated Farmer-Labor Party as their instrument for political representation. The party's third convention formulated a comprehensive and detailed plan for the mobilization of all its members to effect this aim, but without any favorable results. Thus passed into history another organization created by American Communists, leaving the Workers' Party the sole survivor of Communist political organizations.

CHAPTER X

THE TRADE UNION EDUCATIONAL LEAGUE

WE HAVE now to consider an organization that had played an important role in American Communist history and which has been referred to·only incidentally,[1] the Trade Union Educational League. William Z. Foster, its founder, is one of the very few workers of native stock who has been attracted to the Communist movement. He joined one of the Socialist parties in 1900 and was expelled in 1909, and then became a member of the I. W. W. While abroad as a delegate to the Trade Unions Secretariat meeting in Budapest in 1910, he became convinced that the policy of organizing in opposition to the American Federation of Labor was futile. He helped to organize the Syndicalist League of North America in 1911, which became the International Trade Union Educational League in 1915. It expired the following year, but it was revived in 1920 as the Trade Union Educational League. Foster's participation in the steel strike of 1919 made him conspicuous because of his marked service to the unions in that struggle. In 1921 he went to Russia, where he attended the congresses of the Communist International and the Red International of Labor Unions, and upon his return to the United States he joined the Communist Party.[2] It will be remembered that Foster was arrested for having attended the secret convention of the party held in the Michigan woods in August, 1922.

Foster's pronounced Anarcho-Syndicalism had been outlined in his pamphlet, "Syndicalism," in 1912, and his transition to Communism was an easy matter. Before his visit to Russia the league was independent of political organizations here and abroad,

[1] See above, p. 59.
[2] *The American Labor Who's Who*, New York, 1925, p. 77.

but after his return Communists rapidly joined it, because the Communist International condemned dual unionism. Foster's admission to the Communist Party made the league an agency for Communist agitation in the trade unions and also an aid for waging "united front" campaigns for various purposes. This accounts for the fact that a Communist Left Wing did not appear in the trade unions until about two years after it appeared in the Socialist Party. Down to the period when Foster joined the Communist Party the Communists favored the I. W. W., and the latter was frequently approved in Communist programs. But when Moscow spoke, Foster says, "the militants, particularly those in the extreme Left Wing, came with a surprising change of front to see in it exactly the type of organization they needed. One after another, the Communist Party, the Workers' Party, the Proletarian Party and the United Toilers went on record in favor of its [the league's] general policy."[3]

Foster is practically the only man in American Communist organizations who appears to have any general knowledge of the history and evolution of American trade unions, and his original purpose appears to have been to make the modern league a genuine educational instrument in the trade unions by training members of the league for such service. The league especially emphasized the folly of progressive members of the unions withdrawing and setting up small radical unions of their own. Foster contended that the result was to continue to drain the unions of their best thinkers and most progressive men, leaving the field to the timid and unprogressive officials and leaders, while the dissenters became more sectarian, quarreled among themselves and always failed to do what they set out to do. This dual unionism, he insisted, had been the curse of the American trade union movements, and was the most important factor accounting for the very small percentage of the wageworkers organized in the United States. He reviewed the history of this policy of American trade union progressives

[3] Foster, *The Bankruptcy of the American Labor Movement*, p. 55.

and cited a mass of evidence to sustain his point of view.[4] Had the league followed an intelligent and sympathetic policy of education in the trade unions, it could have rendered invaluable service to the trade unions and inspired the members with a progressive outlook. Transformed into a Communist organization, the league has wrought more ruin in those trade unions where it has obtained a foothold than duel unionism has. It has had the same effect on the trade unions that the Left Wing had upon the Socialist Party in 1919.

The league obtained its inspiration and its guidance from the Communist International and the Red International of Labor Unions. Like the Federated Farmer-Labor Party, its sponsors credited it with great achievements. "In the brief years of its work," wrote one enthusiast, "the Trade Union Educational League has wrought a profound clarification in the entire labor movement. Starting out with a great campaign from coast to coast and in every labor union for amalgamation and a labor party — slogans expressing the two deepest and most fundamental needs of the American labor movement — the T. U. E. L. has reached the minds of hundreds of thousands of trade unionists and influenced the decisions of at least 2,000,000. From the broad slogans that stir the masses, it has intensively developed the issue of revolutionary unionism until today [1924] it represents the organized struggle wtihin the unions against every phase of capitalistic influence and bourgeois ideology. While it battles for the formation of an all-embracing farmer-labor party, it expresses the broad

___

[4] *Ibid.,* Chap. III. Foster, however, misstated the case regarding the Socialist Party when he says (p. 37) that this organization's dual unionism "has afflicted it ever since the party's foundation." This party was really organized as a protest against and a repudiation of the dual unionism of the Socialist Labor Party and its resolutions on the trade union question in every national convention rejected the idea of dual unionism. Some members of the organization on their own initiative did participate in dual movements but they never obtained the official approval of the organization. See above, Chapter I. Mr. Foster, first as a Syndicalist and then as a Communist, has never been careful in writing of Socialist organizations at home or abroad but he stated the case against dual unionism effectively.

political struggle of the toiling masses at the present moment of development. It is at the same time rallying the smaller groups of conscious revolutionary workers to the more bitter and intense struggle against the subtler forms of class collaboration. It is no accident that the T. U. E. L. is at once a leading factor throughout the labor movement in the struggle for a labor party in which millions are enlisted. . . ."[5]

These were very extensive claims, and, if true, indicated a profound influence at work stirring the working masses and effecting important changes in the policy and outlook of American trade unions. However, since the organization of the three Communist parties in 1919 each one of the numerous parties that were organized was acclaimed in extravagant terms, and to it was credited enduring achievements; and yet the organized movement had fewer members when the above was written than it had in 1919. The extravagant claims for the league were therefore far from convincing. Any organized group that could influence the "decisions of at least 2,000,000" members of the trade unions could easily change the general policies and program of the American Federation of Labor. Six months before the above claims were made for the league, William F. Dunne, an outspoken Communist, was unseated as a delegate to the convention of the American Federation of Labor because of his Communist activities within the unions. Only nine delegates voted against the motion to exclude Dunne.[6] If the league had influenced the actions of practically half of the members of American trade unions, the negative vote would certainly have been much larger.

With the passing of the league into the control of American Communists, the organization, like the Workers' Party, accepted the guidance and leadership of the Third International. It is there-

[5] Earl R. Browder, in the Introduction to Losovsky's *The World's Trade Union Movement*, published by the Trade Union Educational League, Chicago, 1924.
[6] *Proceedings of the Forty-third Annual Convention of the American Federation of Labor*, Washington, 1923, pp. 256-59.

fore important to understand the Russian trade unions, something of their history, experience and philosophy in order to understand what kind of leadership Moscow provided the league. The first form of labor organization that appears with the rise of capitalistic industry is the mutual benefit society, which took in masters and journeymen. Not until a later period, when the development of industry raises the master to the position of a capitalist owner and reduces the workman to a wageworker, does the trade union as an organization of combat and defense appear. The combative type appeared in the United States in the second decade of the nineteenth century, but not until about 1830 did it tend to become general.[7] This type also appeared about the same time in England.[8] Roughly speaking, the trade unions of the two countries have a hundred years of experience and history behind them. They have developed more rapidly and appeared earlier than in other countries, because modern industry has been freer to expand in England and the United States than in other nations. But even on the Continent the trade unions had appeared, roughly speaking, by the middle of the nineteenth century.

If we turn to Russia, we find a striking contrast. *The modern trade union did not appear in Russia till the first decade of the twentieth century.* The reason for this, of course, is obvious. The survival of a medieval and corrupt autocracy and the survival of feudalism well into the nineteenth century served as barriers to the development of capitalistic industry. Serfdom was abolished by the Manifesto of the "Czar-Emancipator" in March, 1861, but this did not lead to the rapid creation of a proletarian class. The corrupt bureaucracy continued as an obstacle to the growth of capitalism and the few great industries that appeared in Russia were generally owned chiefly by foreign capitalists. Russia continued to be a nation of small peasant producers.

---

[7] Hoxie, *Trade Unionism in the United States*, Chap. IV; Commons and Associates, *History of Labor in the United States*, Vol. I, Part II.

[8] Webb, *History of Trade Unionism* (rev. ed.), Chap. II.

It is said that the first trade union not confined to one locality in Russia was organized among the bristle workers of Poland in 1895, although there had been friendly or benefit societies in existence for years, a few dating back to 1821, but most of these societies properly belong to the last decade of the nineteenth century.[9] The very first sentence of the Communist historian of the Russian trade unions reads: "Trade unions as fighting organs of the working class against the capitalists arose in Russia only after 1905." He also adds the significant statement that "mutual aid socities among factory workers did not develop before the middle of the nineties."[10] One year later there were only 200,000 organized workers in Russia. The benefit societies were sufficiently numerous to constitute a problem when organizing a national conference of trade unions in 1905, and it was decided that only "the proletarian section of such organizations could have the right of representation."[11]

The contrast between the Russian trade unions and the trade unions of Western Europe also establishes a comparison between the development of industry in Russia and in Western Europe. The same contrast is found in South America. The more advanced nations like Argentina, Brazil and Chile had trade unions of the modern type. But Peru had little or no capitalistic industry, and labor organization took the same form there that it has in Russia. "One hears about labor organizations in certain industrial centers near Lima," says one writer, "and in the petroleum, sugar and mining districts. But when investigation is made, it is found that these are merely mutual societies, in which the workmen are associated for insurance and social purposes; they do not pretend to work for better contracts with their employers."[12]

Moreover, what there was of trade unions in Russia as well as

---

[9] Mavor, *An Economic History of Russia*, Vol. II, pp. 418-22.
[10] Losovsky, *Trade Unions in Soviet Russia*, London, 1920, p. 1.
[11] Losovsky, *op. cit.*, p. 9.
[12] Samuel G. Inman, "Organized Labor in South America," *Current History*, May, 1922.

their policies were shaped by the special conditions of Russian history. The modern trade union, which appeared about 1905, followed the appearance of the Zubatov organizations, or "Police Socialism," which were organized by police officials of the autocracy. Mixed motives influenced the government in organizing these unions through its agents, but they tended in some cases to become fighting organizations of the working class rather than pacific unions isolated from the growing revolutionary movement. At the same time, it became known that police agents were guiding the movement, and the more enlightened workers declined to have anything to do with them. Russian trade unionism, unlike Western European trade unionism, assumed a revolutionary political character, although it also had its aims of economic amelioration. It was not a matter of choice, but one of necessity. Every demand for better conditions and every strike brought it into conflict with the government. Moreover, it was forced to resort to physical force, armed insurrection. In the big strike of 1903 the manifestoes citing industrial demands were also accompanied by "manifestoes of a political character demanding the convocation of an All-Russian National Assembly, liberty of striking, of the formation of trade unions, and of public meetings, liberty of speech and of the press, liberty of conscience, and inviolability of the person." [13]

All these political concessions were essential for the normal development of the trade unions and for the exercise of economic pressure in wresting concessions from the employing class. When a strike drew in masses of workers of various trades, when it tended to become general, the movement tended to assume the form of a government. Out of the general strike in Moscow in 1905 issued the "Council of Working Men's Deputies." But a government without force to express its will is absurd, hence arose the idea of armed workmen, the arms sometimes being obtained by the pillage of armories. Even as this strike came to an

[13] Mavor, *op. cit.,* p. 446.

end, the council announced that "it was necessary for the working class to arm itself for the final struggle." [14] This conviction of the necessity for armed struggle grew out of the grim reality of Russian experience and history, and it became fixed in the minds of increasing numbers of workers. With the overthrow of the autocracy, the Communists gave this view a universal application, and the very words quoted above and which affirmed the necessity of armed insurrection in 1905 are found frequently in the publications of the Third International and the Red International of Labor Unions. A policy forced upon Russian trade unions by the autocracy has shaped their view of what trade unions should do in all countries.

It is essential to present this historical background in order to understand the leadership which the Trade Union Educational League accepts in the United States. It brought into the trade unions of the United States an alien factor in conflict with trade union policy and experience, a factor that had its ample justification in the old Russia, but which urged as a principle in the United States, would mean the ultimate disintegration of the trade unions. This is not to say that physical conflicts in the labor struggle are alien to the American trade unions. What is contended is that the insistence upon a policy of physical force as a recognized principle of action and ultimately aimed against the governing powers would lead to the destruction of the trade unions.

The Trade Union Educational League and its members worked with zeal to give Communism an ascendancy in the trade unions. It planted what it calls "nuclei" in such unions where a few of its adherents could be found, and these were pledged to follow the instructions of the league or the Workers' Party. The result has invariably been to bring these organized groups into conflict with the trade unions, and where the groups acquired considerable numerical strength, the factional warfare brought prostration to the unions. The struggle occasionally provoked physical con-

[14] Mavor, *op. cit.*, pp. 481-97.

flicts, with consequent demoralization of the unions. The chaos that ensued came not of dual unionism, but of *dual allegiance*. Presentation of the Communist point of view would not necessarily destroy the unity of the trade unions. The division occurs when the union, after long deliberation in conventions or by a referendum vote, decides on a certain policy and then a portion of its members are pledged to the policy of an organization independent of the union and which is seeking to obtain control of it. This dual allegiance results in misunderstanding, division into hostile factions and often in civil war. When the policy of dual allegiance is accompanied by ferocious attacks upon union officials or members who do not accept a program formulated by the league, personal animosities are added to the factional warfare. A policy of retaliation then appears and anger provokes the "regulars" to acts that in normal trade union development would not be resorted to. This widens the breach, effort to improve economic conditions is diverted into factional channels, members become discouraged, the union declines, and progress is impossible.

Early in 1925 Mr. Foster surveyed the work of the league in the trade unions with a view to showing its effectiveness in winning members to its general policies. He claimed considerable progress in the United Mine Workers, the Carpenters, the Iron, Steel and Tin Workers, the Machinists, the Fur Workers, the International Ladies' Garment Workers, the Amalgamated Clothing Workers, numerous local unions and a number of central labor bodies. The list of organizations was imposing, and it reveals considerable activity over a large section of the country, but its spirit may be judged from what the author writes of those who do not accept the league. The point of view is that league advocates are all honest men, its opponents dishonest — often worse. President Lewis of the Miners had degraded the organization "into a helpless victim of the rapacious mine operator." An official of the Carpenters is "like all other faker-autocrats." Officers of the Iron, Steel and Tin Workers were "ignorant, cowardly and corrupt" and "loyal aids of the United States Steel Corporation." The administration of the Machinists had a "long record of weakness, incompetency and corruption." In the Fur Workers, "there is a widespread revolt against the rotten administration, the yellow Socialist Kaufman machine." In the Ladies' Garment Workers, two presidents are "both tools of the yellow Socialist Vorwaerts."[15]

Four months later Mr. Foster again reported the results of the widespread activity of the league, and amitted that it had practically become isolated and outlawed by the trade unions. Curiously enough, he appeared to be completely oblivious to the relation between the type of propaganda which we quote above and its results, which we now consider. Although he believed that the league had made some gains, he regretted to admit that "within the past two years the influence of the league has, in certain respects, sensibly diminished in the unions." It had lost "leadership," and union members "are not responding to its slogans as they once did." In fact, the league had encountered a "ruthless campaign of expulsion and other forms of terrorism" in many unions, so that the league had become *an underground organizatoin in nearly every trade union in the country.*" Although its members had been accepted in good faith in the central labor bodies of Seattle and Minneapolis, they had been expelled from those bodies.[16]

Certainly the situaion could not be worse. In June, 1923, two organizers of the league were forcibly ejected from a district convention of the miners in Pennsylvania and physically assaulted by enraged miners, and a few months later William F. Dunne was expelled from the A. F. of L. convention at Portland. In September of the same year several shots were fired at Foster while he was addressing a meeting of Left Wing supporters in the Chicago section of the International Ladies' Garment Work-

[15] Foster, "The Left Wing in Trade Union Elections," *The Workers' Monthly,* February, 1925.
[16] Foster, "Party Industrial Methods and Structure," *The Workers' Monthly,* June, 1925.

ers' Union.[17] However good may have been the intentions of many members of the league, the admissions of Mr. Foster showed that, instead of bringing education into the trade unions, it had brought civil war. The needle trades unions in Chicago, and especially New York, have been centers of the struggle, and these unions have been the most progressive regarding workers' education, in favor of a labor party, and have been generous in their support of all other trade unions that have been involved in important struggles for better conditions.

The league, having realized this experience in the trade unions, turned its attention to the organization of shop and factory "nuclei" as the best means of obtaining influence in the unions, although not abandoning work in these unions. The Executive Committee of the Communist International gave attention to this plan in January, 1924, and worked out detailed instructions for Communist organizations to follow in all countries. It declared that "the nuclei must carry on an obstinate fight in the factories and workshops against the members and followers of other parties, also of the Socialist parties and labor parties," but the nuclei "should in no circumstances be confused with the Communist factions in the trade unions, cooperatives, etc., whose function cannot be replaced by the nuclei." The final clause in these instructions, which went into minute details and filled nearly four pages, reads: "At general meetings of non-party organizations, all faction members must act and vote as a unit on all questions. Disciplinary measures must be taken against any party members infringing this regulation."[18] These instructions enforced dual allegiance.

[17] The truth regarding this incident is not known. The Communists claimed that opponents of the League employed "gunmen" to kill Foster and this statement was answered by the assertion that the gunplay had been arranged by Foster and his friends to obtain sympathy and support for the League. *The Worker*, September 8, 1923, devoted columns to the attempted "assassination" but presented no evidence to support its contention.

[18] The complete instructions appeared in the *International Press Correspondence, Vienna*, February 27, 1924. This is a weekly medium of communication by the Third International with its affiliated organizations in all countries. See Appendix III.

The Workers' Party gave its attention to the establishment of shop nuclei, and Mr. Foster, speaking for the league, informed its members that they must give their attention to this work in order to "break through our isolation at all costs." Shop nuclei would help them to take the "leadership and initiative in all sorts of strike movements" and sweep large masses into the trade unions. Whereever an opposition to the administration in a union is found, the members must stimulate it and "lead it against our central enemies, the reactionary bureaucracy controlling the unions." [19] Isolated though the league members were in the trade unions, they must not give up their work. They must aid in setting up "united front opposition tickets to the administration candidates in all local unions, international unions, and central labor council elections, except in such cases, of course, where we are strong enough to make a substantial showing with our own revolutionary candidates." [20] The program of the league followed very closely the outline of the Communist International, and it continued to be the plan of Communist penetration of the trade unions.

In accord with the new plan of penetration, the league officially called a national Left Wing conference of its supporters in the needle trades section of the league, to meet in New York City on August 8, 1925. It outlined an agenda for the conference, which included many matters which properly belong to the respective unions in the trade and which alone can be acted upon by them because of their contractual relations with the employers in the trade. The character of such a conference not only implies

[19] The "reactionary bureaucracy" in the trade unions is a phrase that is repeatedly used by the League and the Communist Party regarding the officers of the trade unions. It is striking that those who willingly participate in a movement organized on the basis of a centralized bureaucracy, a movement that cannot adopt any important policy without obtaining the consent of a small executive committee in the capital of Russia, should refer to the administration of a trade union as "bureaucracy." The Communist parties are so many hierarchies attached to the central bureaucracy in Moscow.

[20] Foster, "Party Industrial Methods and Structure," *The Workers' Monthly*, June, 1925.

dual allegiance, but dual organization as well.[21] The Communist factions in the International Ladies' Garment Workers had already brought heated quarrels in the New York units of the organization. When the organization met in national convention in November, 1925, it was financially exhausted and considerably hampered in its effort to cope with certain economic changes in the industry that were undermining union standards which had been built up by two decades of sacrifice. In the convention itself, the league's members were organized as a compact bloc under the discipline of a few leaders who were more interested in factional advantage for the scattered nuclei in the industry than in restoring the union to its former power and helping it to solve some of the grave problems that impersonal economic forces had thrust upon it.

In some unions the members have genuine grievances against their officials for one reason or another. Some of these grievances are justified and others are due to lack of information or because of misunderstanding. The league was alert for such opportunities, and if it had members in the union so affected, they immediately capitalized the grievance and organized for a concerted effort to place its partisans in positions of advantage for the Communist movement. By the injection of an outside organized influence into such controversies, it becomes impossible to settle a grievance on its merits. Original issues fade into the background. Very often non-Communist members opposing the administration become the unwitting supporters of the nuclei leaders and are ranged in support of aims of which they know nothing. As a controversy passes from the plane of an issue of fact into one of bitter animosities a certain proportion of the non-Communist members are swept along and participate in the war of invectives. The administration leaders lose their heads, they reply in kind, and the union becomes a battleground, in which low cunning and unscrupulous strategy obtain the final decision. Whatever the decision may be,

---

[21] The call for the conference and the agenda appeared in *The Worker*, June 20, 1925.

the union is generally prostrated, and the members are the ultimate losers.[22] The league's founder, Mr. Foster, himself admitted that the league did not win the support of any considerable number of the organized workmen, and that it so conducted itself that it became an underground organization in the unions because of the resentment it provoked.

In the last month of the year 1925 Mr. Foster again surveyed the work of the Trade Union Educational League, and reluctantly admitted that its status in the trade unions had become desperate and that Communists were being expelled from many unions. He also observed a tendency for the unions to insist upon suspected members signing a pledge binding them to agree with the rules and decisions of the union and further agreeing that they would not affiliate with or give support, assistance or comfort to the league or any kindred organization. The feeling against his organization and its methods had become so menacing that he believed that "our fight against expulsion must be a flexible attitude." Its members "must be prepared to deny" their membership in the league and the Workers' Party "rather than be expelled from the unions." Such denial "means the occasional swallowing of nasty pills in the way of signing the various statements that are put up to us by the reactionary officials in the hope that our revolutionary gorge will rise against them to the extent that we will not sign them and thus make our expulsion more easy." He quoted one pledge drawn up for Communists to sign by the Carpenters' District Council of Cleveland. His counsel was for Communists to do everything to avoid signing such pledges. "Only where we are actually confronted with expulsion shall we adopt the expedient of denying membership," he continued, but in such cases members "must bear in mind the advice of Lenin and Zinoviev and sign a dozen such statements." [23]

[22] Miss Kopald, *Rebellion in Labor Unions*, New York, 1924, presents a good account of factional wars in the trade unions.
[23] Foster, "Drive Against Left Wing in Trade Unions," the *Daily Worker*, December 5, 1925.

Foster was completely oblivious to the conclusion to be drawn from the evidence which he submitted from this very survey. It is convincing to the most impartial observer that if the Communist signed the pledge because he was suspected, any Communist tendencies he later showed in the union would render him subject to expulsion for violation of his pledged word. If he had been an offensive Communist and refused to sign, he would be expelled. In the first case, the member would remain in the union, but be useless for Communism. In the second place, he is out of the union and just as useless. To stay in the union and serve the league was certainly impossible.

Mr. Foster and his associates charge that this union policy is a despotic method of dealing with them. But this policy is one which the Communist Party follows in enforcing discipline. It insists that its members must follow the orders of the party in the unions or be expelled. In January, 1925, the party mobilized its members in the Amalgamated Clothing Workers of Chicago to defeat certain union officers and to elect some of their own members. Eleven members were charged with not obeying the orders of the party in this union election. Five members were convicted and expelled, two were censured, one was suspended for three months and two for six months. This action was taken by the Central Executive Committee of the party, of which Mr. Foster was chairman.[24] His party adopted this method of enforcing rigid adherence to orders given its members in the unions, and after a number of years the trade unions began to adopt it. At its worst, the unions may be charged with meeting despotic methods with despotic methods. The Communist Party will permit no

---

[24] The expulsions and reasons therefor were reported in the *Daily Worker*, January 23, 1925. In December, 1925, an American Communist before the executive of the Communist International reported that his party had planted "a whole network of factions" in the needle trades of the United States. As for the League he said that "as soon as it is ascertained that a person belongs to the League he or she is immediately expelled from the trade union." *International Press Correspondence*, Vienna, December 21, 1925.

dual allegiance in its organization, and it rightly disciplines any person who attempts to carry into it orders received from any outside group. The trade unions are forced to follow the same policy. Dual allegiance will ultimately destroy any organization that permits it.

The league was fatally handicapped by its subjection to a few leaders in Moscow whose views of the trade union have been shaped by the special experience of Russia. This experience is the basis of a trade union philosophy attempting to function under a brutal Czarism, a philosophy that is certain to differ widely from the trade union philosophy of Western Europe and of the United States. Russian trade union policies under the old regime are no more adapted to the non-Russian nations than the trade union policies of the latter were adapted to the Russia of 1905. The attempt to impose one on the other can only bring conflict and civil war into the trade unions. This has happened, as Mr. Foster has reluctantly admitted in his writings.

CHAPTER XI

THE UPHEAVAL OF 1924

THE outstanding aspect of all political and economic organizations of labor at the close of the year 1923 was a decline in membership since the end of the first World War. This was in marked contrast with organizations in other countries where the trade unions and labor parties showed large increases. The American Federation of Labor had 4,000,000 members in 1920, which was reduced to 2,900,000 in 1923. It had realized some heavy increases during the war, but was unable to retain the new members. But what it lost, its rivals did not gain. In 1916 the I.W.W. claimed an increase in membership from 15,000 to 60,000, but the total number of membership cards it had issued to its members since its organization in 1905 was 500,000. Its convention in 1921, however, revealed that it was only a shadow of what it had been, and it continued to decline. The Workers' International Industrial Union, an offshoot of the I.W.W., a rival of it, and fostered by the Socialist Labor Party, could claim only 11,000 members in 1912. In spite of the loss of members by the A.F. of L., this organization continued to decline. In fact, in 1920 its membership had declined to 2,000, and the organization admitted that its finances were in a deplorable condition. The One Big Union, the American section of which was organized in Chicago in 1920 with 40,000 members, soon became involved in dissensions, and by the close of the year 1923 it had become moribund. The Socialist Labor Party had declined till its energies were devoted to maintaining one struggling English weekly in New York. We have seen that the national Farmer-Labor Party was "captured" by the Communists the same year and later disappeared. The Federated Farmer-Labor Party only survived on paper at the end of the year. The Socialist Party had a membership of 12,000, but obtained no new members. The Workers' Communist Party had a few thousand more, but only a fraction more than a thousand members were in the English-speaking branches. The Non-Partisan League of Farmers had become disturbed by dissensions, it was losing many members and was rapidly declining in influence.

Yet, as we have seen,[1] while there was a decline of membership in all these organizations, dissatisfaction with the two major parties increased. This was evident in the appearance of labor and farmer-labor parties in Idaho, Minnesota, West Virginia, Pennsylvania and a few other states, and similar organizations on a local scale in others. The organizations mentioned above were just emerging from the post-war reaction, the trade unions having waged a defensive struggle against the "open shop" campaign, while the political organizations had become all but exhausted by the years of government raids, arrests and suppression of newspapers, which was followed by what was known in radical circles as the "White Terror" of the American Legion and similar organizations. The Socialist and semi-Socialist movements as well as the trade unions were conscious of their losses, and resentment found expression in increasing political rebellion.

Another factor which tended to drive political dissent into in-dependent organization was contributed by the two leading parties in a number of states. The Non-Partisan League had been active in the Northwest since 1916, and at first confined its activities to farmers. At a later period it formed alliances with the workers of the cities. The league was organized to seize the machinery of the old parties. The primaries were often captured by troops of well-organized farmers and their allies in many districts and a few states. Naturally, the bourgeois politicians could not look on idly while insurgents took their party organizations. This led to legislation in the states affected by the insurgent movement to guard the

---

[1] See above, p. 135.

primaries against insurgent control. The major parties had no difficulty in agreeing on this legislation. This type of legislation became so apparent in the West that a Washington correspondent of a New York paper wrote that "there is no current political tendency more obvious than the disposition to get away from the primary and back to the party convention as a means of nominating candidates for office."[2] The tendency of such legislation was to exclude insurgents from voting in Democratic or Republican primaries. By such legislation the radicals were excluded from the primaries in Idaho and they organized their own party, which became the second party in the election of November, 1922. Similar legislation in Minnesota forced the farmer-laborities to organize their own party. In the meantime the British Labor Party in the elections of December, 1923, increased its membership in Parliament from 144 to 192, and on January 22, 1924, the first Labor Govrenment in the history of Great Britain took office, with J. Ramsay MacDonald as Prime Minister. This event also made an impression on the radical political movement in the United States.

Even the upper classes and conservatives in general were dissatisfied with the Administration at Washington, the conservative financial journals joining with many influential dailies and the liberal weeklies in expressing disgust. The *Journal of Commerce* of New York devoted a long editorial to the need of a new party, "a party of reasonable conservatism."[3] In an address before the American Bankers' Association, Frank A. Munsey declared that the old ideas of the dominant parties had been "converted into history," and he urged a union of the two major parties —" the Democratic-Republican Party, or whatever it might be" — as a "mighty wall of strength reared against the fast-rising tide of

2 *New York Evening Post*, May 20, 1922. For the league, see Russell, *The Story of the Nonpartisan League*, New York, 1920; and Gaston, *The Nonpartisan League*, New York, 1920.
3 May 20, 1922.

radicalism." [4] A few days later the proposal was approved by Nicholas Murray Butler of Columbia University.[5] The following week Charles Nagel, once a member of President Taft's Cabinet, said in St. Louis that party issues were obscured, that party lines had faded, and that "neither party faced the problems" of the period.[6] All evidence seemed to point to a political upheaval in the next general election and a possible realignment of political parties.

Only one factor appeared to serve as a restraining force, the leadership of the American Federation of Labor. It still favored the old policy of choosing candidates nominated by the two leading parties, although a considerable section of the members of the trade unions were affected by the general unrest, and in some states were acting with the independent movements.

When the third session of the Conference for Progressive Political Action met in St. Louis in February, 1924, the oil scandal was public property, and it eliminated William Gibbs McAdoo from any serious consideration by those delegates of the railroad unions who had favored him as a presidential candidate. The British Labor Government had taken office, and the conference cabled Premier MacDonald its fraternal greetings, while Samuel Gompers was writing long criticisms of the British Labor Party in the *American Federationist*. The cable to MacDonald showed that the unions in the St. Louis conference bore no prejudice against independent party organization and action in principle. The conference adopted a plan of permanent organization which provided for annual meetings, representation of affiliated organizations, a system of financial contributions, a national committee and state conferences. This was a near approach to the organization of a Labor Party on the federated basis which has made the British Labor Party conspicuous. Moreover, the conference granted to each state conference

[4] New York City, October 4, 1922. Reprinted by Mr. Munsey in pamphlet form.
[5] *New York Times*, October 18, 1922.
[6] *New York Herald*, October 23, 1922.

the power to decide whether it should try to capture the machinery of one of the old parties or nominate "by the method of independent political action." In the latter case the state organization was required to "adopt a distinctive political name." All these actions showed an expectant attitude towards the organization of an independent party. The conference also decided to call a national convention of delegates of trade unions, the Farmer-Labor Party, the Socialist Party, state labor parties and central labor unions, to meet in Cleveland on July 4 to take "action on nomination of candidates for the offices of President and Vice-President of the United States." [7]

In the meantime the successes of the Farmer-Labor Party in Minnesota had so encouraged the movement in that state that it called a conference of farmer-labor groups in other states, to meet in St. Paul, November 15-16, 1923, to plan for the election in 1924. Among the invited organizations was the Federated-Farmer Labor Party, the party created by the Communists in the ill-fated Chicago convention of the previous July. The St. Paul conference adopted a tentative platform, issued a call for a national convention, to meet in St. Paul, May 30, 1924, and elected a committee of five on arrangements. Considerable opposition to permitting the Federated Farmer-Labor Party to be associated with the May convention developed, and while some influential men in the Minnesota movement were considering this situation, the St. Louis conference met, and to it came some of the Northwest leaders. They became so encouraged with what appeared to be the progress made in St. Louis that they returned home, convinced that it would be wise to reconsider the call for the May convention and join with the organizations that were called to meet in Cleveland on July 4. The Northwest organizations, therefore, were summoned

[7] *Report of the Proceedings of the Third Conference for Progressive Political Action*, St. Louis, February 11-12, 1924, pp. 15-20. See also *The American Labor Year Book*, 1925, pp. 120-22.

to send delegates to a special convention to meet in St. Paul on March 10.

The prospect of the special St. Paul convention voting to urge its organizations to send delegates to the Cleveland convention on July 4 alarmed the Communists. The Workers' Party had been denied admission to other meetings of the Conference for Progressive Political Action, and it was certain that it would not be admitted to the July convention. The same was true of the Federated Farmer-Labor Party. The Communists, therefore, gave all their energy to controlling the decision in the special St. Paul convention. They succeeded by obtaining a majority in favor of a national convention, to meet in St. Paul on June 17. The resolution declared that the delegates to the latter convention would recommend "such a course of action in nominating candidates and adopting a platform as will leave the way open for cooperation for support of the same candidates and platform with the Conference for Progressive Political Action or any other group, provided, of course, that group endorses independent political action." [8] Enough farmer delegates were won to this point of view to give the Communists a majority. As matters stood in March, two nominating conventions were called, one by the Conference for Progressive Political Action in July and the other, with a powerful Communist bloc inside, in June. The Communist strategy appeared to be for St. Paul to make nominations first and thus give that movement prestige and bargaining power at Cleveland. [9]

In order to participate in the St. Paul convention, the Communists had to get the approval of the executive of the Third International. Consent was cabled to the Workers' Party, the cablegram reading: "Communist International considers June 17 convention momentous importance for Workers' Party. Urges Central Execu-

---

[8] Quoted in the *Daily Worker*, April 12, 1924.
[9] Murray E. King, in "Farmer-Labor Prospects," *The New Republic*, January 16, 1924, presents an excellent review of the Northwest background at this period.

tive Committee not to slacken activities preparation June 17. Utilize every available force to make St. Paul convention great representative gathering Labor and Left Wing." [10] This approval, however, was not surprising, as it was a fulfilment of the policy of the "united front." But it was also "a strategy and not an end in itself," as an influential Communist wrote. "The campaign will allow us to enter the third party wherever the opportunity presents itself, to form a left wing within it and split it away from the third party." [11] This was written for the information of party comrades in other countries. At home the executive of the Workers' Party adopted a "Thesis," declaring that "where the Farmer-Labor Party candidates have no chance to win and the third party can unquestionably win against the capitalist parties with our support, we will vote for the third party candidates." [12] The representative of the Third International in the United States declared that Communists "can and must vote for LaFollette if the mighty masses of workers and exploited farmers, who are not yet class conscious, put him up as a candidate." [13] C. E. Ruthenberg, Secretary of the Party, also supported this view. [14] These declarations are important because of the action of the Workers' Party a few months later.

The extensive preparations of the party for the St. Paul convention finally aroused the apprehensions of some of the leading Farmer-Labor men in Minnesota. They had discounted the fears expressed by others outside the state that St. Paul might repeat the experience of the Farmer-Labor convention in Chicago the previous July. The St. Paul organ of the Minnesota Farmer-Labor movement began to express these fears a few weeks before the convention met. It observed that the Communists had "become a seri-

10 *The Daily Worker*, May 16, 1924.
11 J. Amter, in *International Press Correspondence*, Vienna, February 28, 1924.
12 *The Worker*, December 1, 1923.
13 *Ibid.*, December 22, 1923.
14 *Ibid.*, April 10, 1924.

ous problem within the Farmer-Labor movement. The relationship between the two will have to be definitely settled at an early day, as the organized activity of the Communists has become a source of fear and irritation to a great many earnest supporters of this new movement." It objected to "a small group carrying on their intrigues and plots to control," which suggested "dictatorship of an insidious minority," which would make "their presence intolerable."[15] The day before this editorial appeared Senator LaFollette dissolved all doubts which the Workers' Party might have as to its relation to the campaign of 1924 by issuing a statement warning his supporters against the St. Paul convention. Among the documents quoted by Senator LaFollette was one showing that the Workers' Party had asked instructions of Moscow regarding the June convention and had received orders to participate in it.[16]

An unexpected result of the LaFollette letter was to strengthen the Communists in the St. Paul convention. Its organizers had estimated the number of delegates who would attend at 3,000, but the number was less than one third of this estimate, 542 from 29 states, according to the *Minnesota Union Advocate*, which also declared that La Follette's statement had kept many delegates away. But the Communist strength was more apparent than real. The Workers' Party repeated its work in the Chicago convention of July, 1923, by being represented over and over again through organizations created to give it representation. Having one state party in New York that had never been represented on the state ballot, it created another one, the Federated Farmer-Labor Party, and obtained representation for both. From the various states were reported the Woman's Shelley Club, the Negro Tenants' Protective Association, the Illinois Self-Advancement Club, the Red Eye Farmers' Club, the People's Voice Culture Club, the National Benefit Society, United Working Class Women, the Negro Broth-

[15] *Minnesota Union Advocate*, St. Paul, May 29, 1924.
[16] The LaFollette statement appeared in the daily papers of May 28, 1924.

erhood, Gymnastic Societies, Bohemian Central Body, Lithuanian, Slovak, Croatian and other societies and clubs.[17]

An astonishing aspect of the St. Paul convention was the method of apportioning the votes among the delegates. Each state was assigned as many votes as it casts in the Electoral College and one vote for each 5,000 "progressive" votes cast in the elections of 1922. This brought about the absurd situation whereby the Communists, who had practically no votes recorded in the elections that year, were permitted to vote on the basis of the votes cast by the Socialists in New York, Pennsylvania, California and some other states. How ridiculous this arrangement was is evident from the fact that the Socialist Party since 1919 had refused to have any relations with the Communists, and the latter regarded the former as enemies! The Minnesota organization, by this absurd apportionment of votes in the convention, placed itself at the mercy of a small disciplined group. This inept performance deprived it of the prestige it could have had at the Cleveland convention in the following July.

The convention nominated Duncan McDonald of Illinois for President and William Bouck of Washington for Vice-President. Within the committee on organization two views developed, one by the Communists and their sympathizers, who desired the immediate organization of a party, and the other by William Mahoney, who represented the Farmer-Labor forces of Minnesota and who believed immediate organization of a party would be premature. As a result of a struggle in the committee, a compromise was reached which provided for the appointment of a national committee to serve through the campaign, with power to replace or withdraw candidates and to negotiate combination with other groups. After the nomination of LaFollette in Cleveland, McDonald withdrew in favor of the former. The national committee set

[17] The reader will find an interesting comparison between these mysterious organizations and similar bodies for which the Communists obtained representation in the Farmer-Labor convention in Chicago in July, 1923. See above, pp. 138-139.

up by the St. Paul convention also formally withdrew the nominations. Dissensions followed in the Minnesota organization because of the St. Paul convention, and the *Minnesota Union Advocate* was soon involved in a long controversy with leaders of the Workers' Party. Robert Morss Lovett, who observed the convention, wrote: "If the party dies, it will die of that political malady the germs of which the Communists, in spite of their own robust immunity, seem like Typhoid Mary to carry among their associates." [18]

Thrown upon its own resources, the Workers' Party abandoned the Federated Farmer-Labor Party, which had been maintained in the hope that it might serve some purpose at St. Paul or Cleveland. Shortly after the St. Paul convention it called a conference in Chicago which nominated William Z. Foster of Illinois for President and Benjamin Gitlow of New York for Vice-President. In the following August the Central Executive Committee issued a platform which roundly denounced LaFollette as representing "the independent manufacturers, bankers and merchants, who are seeking greater power and profit for themselves." The candidates appeared on the ballot in 14 states. They received 33,076 votes. A farmer was elected to the North Dakota Legislature on the Republican ticket, and the Workers' Party claimed his election as a Communist victory. [19] The executives of the party met on November 14 to consider the party's prospects in relation to the election. Two factions, at bitter war with each other, had developed over political policies, and the Communist International had cabled to learn how many votes had been received for the presidential candidates in November. One faction moved to send the following cablegram: "Workers' Party vote very small. Will not exceed twenty thousand." This was voted down, and a motion was carried

---

[18] *The New Republic*, July 2, 1924. Also *The American Labor Year Book*, 1925, pp. 145-48; *Minnesota Union Advocate*, June 19, 1924; *The New Leader*, New York, June 21, 1924; the *Daily Worker*, issues during week of the convention.
[19] *The American Labor Year Book*, 1925, pp. 155-161.

"that we issue a statement claiming 100,000 votes and citing incidents in which votes were stolen from us." [20]

The heated discussion that followed in issues of the *Daily Worker* brought out a number of facts that came to the attention of the Farmer-Labor leaders in Minnesota. The substance of certain admissions, especially those made by C. A. Hathaway, an active member of the Workers' Party in Minneapolis, was that the Workers' Party had sent a special agent to the St. Paul convention to work in conjunction with a "steering committee of the party, and that at one stage of the proceedings the agent had given orders to "split the thing wide open." The advice was not followed, but the admissions of Hathaway convinced the Minnesota leaders that the Workers' Party had attempted to do at St. Paul what it did at Chicago. The Hathaway article was reprinted in the Minnesota organ of the Farmer-Labor Party,[21] and a few weeks later the affiliated organizations held a state conference in St. Paul. Relations with the Workers' Party were considered, and a resolution was adopted declaring that "members of the Workers' Party should be barred from all conventions and meetings of the Farmer-Labor Party." [22]

Meantime the Conference for Progressive Political Action met in Cleveland on July 4 and nominated Senator LaFollette for President. Nearly 600 delegates were present, representing international unions, state federations of labor, central labor bodies, cooperative societies, the Socialist Party, the Farmer-Labor Party, the Committee of Forty-Eight, state parties of labor, farmers or progressives, and some miscellaneous organizations. Socialists, Farmer-Labor men and those trade unionists who favored organization of a permanent party were disappointed to find that some of the most powerful organizations were not favorable, but they obtained some satisfaction in nominating a candidate for President

20 *The Daily Worker*, December 3, 1924.
21 *Minnesota Union Advocate*, January 1, 1925.
22 *Minnesota Union Advocate*, January 29, 1925.

opposed to the nominations of the old parties. Although federated in a political alliance for the support of LaFollette, each political and economic organization retained its own autonomy. The coalition was similar to the British Labor Party, and all that was required to make it such a party was a decision to make it a permanent union for all elections, city, state and national.

Certain actions of the convention suggested that this permanent union might be realized. It voted to increase the membership of its national committee to not less than fifty members, and gave this committee power to establish branch offices and to place organizers in the field. By a unanimous vote, the convention instructed its national committee to issue a call for a national convention, to meet the latter part of January, 1925. "The object of the convention," read the resolution, "shall be to consider and pass upon the question of forming a permanent independent political party for national and local elections upon the basis of the general principles laid down in the platform adopted by this convention, and for the transaction of such other business as may come before the convention." The unanimous acceptance of this resolution appeared to forecast the organization of a party in January controlled by political and economic organizations of farmers and workers.[23]

This expectation was enhanced when the American Federation of Labor decided to support Senator LaFollette. The nomination of a candidate for Vice-President was left to the national committee, and a few weeks later that body chose Senator Burton K. Wheeler of Montana.

The Socialist Party met in national convention after the adjournment of the Conference for Progressive Political Action, with 157 delegates and alternates in attendance. The party had looked forward to the Cleveland convention that nominated LaFollette in the hope that it would act in organizing a permanent labor party. The decision to defer action on this question to a special convention in January made it doubtful as to how the Socialists would act.

[23] *The American Labor Year Book*, 1925, pp. 122-26.

Two views were certain to find expression and these views appeared when the question was submitted to a special committee of fifteen. Out of this committee came two reports, a majority, signed by thirteen members, and a minority, signed by two. The majority report favored full cooperation in support of LaFollette, authorized the executive of the party "in its discretion to endorse the candidate for Vice-President," urged that increased representation on the enlarged National Committee of the Conference for Progressive Political Action be asked, that where independent candidates were nominated for local and state offices with the co-operation of the party they be supported, that the party should send a full representation to the January convention, and that its delegates be instructed "to vote and work for the formation of a party composed of economic organizations of labor, working farmers, the Socialist Party and other advanced groups; to be separate and distinct from and opposed to the Republican, Democratic and other capitalist parties; with a complete national, state and local form of organization and upon a platform containing as a minimum the planks of the platform adopted by the Cleveland convention."

The minority report declared that as the Cleveland convention had not organized an independent party and represented merely a "vague sentiment of unrest" which centered around one man, who had "never attacked the fundamental foundations of capitalist society," the party should nominate its own candidates and conduct a campaign "on a platform and with a program that states distinctly the fundamental problems that confront modern society." The minority further stated that it favored a Labor Party but was opposed to accepting an "indefinite promise that seven months from now a labor party may be formed, or sign a blank check for a vice-presidential candidate not yet named." It also could not approve a platform "so delightfully vague and indefinite as to the fundamental causes of social injustice."

The two reports brought on an extended debate, and during its progress Eugene V. Debs, five times the presidential candidate of the party, sent a telegram which read: "I think it wise for our party to make no nominations under the circumstances, but at the same time to hold the Socialist Party intact, adhere rigidly to its principles, and keep the red flag flying. I hope, above all, there will be no division, but that all will unite loyally in carrying out the program adopted by the convention." The majority report was finally adopted by a vote of 115 to 17.[24]

Organs of the Workers' Party were quick to see in this action of the Socialist Party another "betrayal" of the working class, and in August, William Z. Foster, the party's candidate for President, exchanged letters with Debs regarding this decision. Foster wrote him that his (Debs) approval of the Socialist convention's actions was an astounding document," and that it would "come as a shock to thousands of workers." Debs answered that if his endorsement of LaFollette seemed "shocking," it was strange, considering "that the St. Paul convention, dominated absolutely by the Communists, intended, according to some of its chief spokesmen, including Mahoney and Ruthenberg, to do that very thing . . . and it no doubt would have done so had not LaFollette, knowing the record of the Communists and understanding their game, publicly denounced them and positively refused their endorsement." [25] LaFollette received nearly 5,000,000 votes, and interest next centered on the January convention. The decision of this convention would determine the course of radical political history for some years at least, and all the groups represented at the Cleveland convention began to prepare for it.

The National Committee of the Conference met in Washington, December 12, 1924, to consider arrangements for the con-

[24] *The American Labor Year Book*, 1925, pp. 131-38; *The New Leader*, July 12, 1924, carried a complete report of the two conventions.

[25] *The New Leader*, August 2, 1924. It should be said that Mahoney was not a Communist but had accepted professions of good faith made by the Workers' Party leaders. He had already concluded that cooperation with them was impossible.

vention. Prior to this meeting prominent representatives of the railroad unions expressed disappointment over the vote polled by LaFollete, and this developed into a sentiment of indifference, and even opposition, to the convention, which had been ordered by the Cleveland convention. In this committee meeting the railroad representatives, excepting William H. Johnston of the Machinists, desired to abandon the convention. They were defeated by a vote of 30 to 13. They withdrew, and announced that they would consult the executives of their organizations. A few attended the convention at Chicago, the date of which was changed to February 21, and some sub-divisions of the railroad unions also sent delegates. The organizations represented were similar to those that were at the Cleveland convention which nominated LaFollette.[26]

When the convention assembled, it became known that the railroad representatives the night before had met and had decided that their organizations could not be induced to participate in organizing a permanent party. They contended that they had no mandate from their members to take this course, and in the convention asserted that the time was not opportune for independent party organization. For the present they believed that more could be accomplished by capturing nominations within the old party organizations and mobilizing their members and sympathizers as a bloc in elections for the candidates thus nominated. They introduced and supported a resolution in favor of continuing the Conference for Progressive Political Action on the basis of non-partisan political action.

Morris Hillquit presented a resolution representing the attitude of the Socialists and those trade unions that favored organization of a labor party. They proposed the organization of "the American Labor Party. The term 'Labor' to apply to all workers, agricultural as well as industrial, mental as well as manual, and all other citizens who accept the social and political ideals and aspirations of

[26] The American Labor Year Book, 1925, p. 131.

the producing classes." The resolution went on to outline a plan of national, state and local organizations, the election of a national organization committee by the convention and empowering this committee to undertake the work of organization and of calling another national convention in the following October "for the purpose of perfecting the organization of the party in all practical details." This plan also differed from the others that were presented in that it provided that the "national committee and all State and local committees shall also admit direct affiliation of organizations of workers and farmers and of progressive political and educational groups who fully accept its program and principles." This proposed admission of definite organizations became an issue in the convention.

J. A. H. Hopkins of the Committee of Forty-Eight offered a resolution providing that membership "shall be open to every citizen of the United States" subscribing to the party's principles "by individual enrollment in conformity with the requirement of our election laws," and in states "where a progressive party is already established" it shall be "recognized as the official organization" in the state. This implied organization after the pattern of other American poltical parties, and its adoption would mean that economic, political and cooperative organizations of workers and farmers would have no direct representation as organizations. A substitute which accepted this basis of organization was offered, but it also provided for the "cooperation of the organizations created during the last campaign," and proposed the appointment of a committee of five to call conventions in the states and election of delegates to a national convention.

The issue of group representation or individual enrollment became the subject of a long debate, which ended by Mr. Shepherd offering in behalf of the railroad organizations a resolution that the convention "adjourn and that those who desire to organize a new or third party, whatever they may term it, may assemble in this room at 8:30 tonight." This suggestion was unanimously accepted.

However, it also meant that the powerful railroad unions would not participate and that they were withdrawing to permit the question which other delegates were interested in to be decided by them. The adoption of the resolution proved to be the end of the Conference for Progressive Political Action. At night the delegates assembled as another body to establish a provisional organization of a third party. The convention had revealed three groups, and with the defection of the railroad organizations, only two groups were left in the new body, each favoring the organization of a new party, but differing as to its character and form.

When the delegates assembled in the evening they unanimously agreed "that this convention declare itself a convention of delegates to a new independent political party." The issue of group representation vs. individual enrolment, which also meant a Labor Party or a progressive party, was extensively discussed, and was finally referred to a committee of seven to report the following morning. Six members of the committee reported the progressive party plan and one the Labor Party plan. Following a lengthy consideration of the merits of the two proposals, the Labor Party proposal was tabled by a vote of 93 to 64. The Labor Party advocates remained to the end of the session, but took no more interest in its work. The progressives established a provisional organization and made tentative arrangements for a national convention later in the year, but their adjournment also proved the end of the new party. It never advanced beyond this provisional stage.[27]

This convention, however, presented a marked contrast with the Farmer-Labor convention of July, 1923, and the St. Paul convention of June, 1924, to which the Workers' Party was given representation. Both conventions developed bitter factions and were followed by personal and factional animosities. The Chicago

[27] The most complete account of this convention appeared in *The New Leader*, February 28, 1925. It is supplemented by a good digest of its proceedings in mimeograph form issued by Mr. H. L. Brunson, the secretary of the provisional conference, and a statement accompanying it by Mr. William H. Johnston for the executive of the provisional organization.

convention gave a death blow to the Farmer-Labor Party, which called it. The St. Paul convention brought bitterness into the powerful Farmer-Labor Party of Minnesota. The February convention, which we have just considered, divided into three groups, and yet they parted without leaving any trace of factional feeling or leaving any heritage of personal recriminations.

The Socialist Party delegates immediately met in their own national convention after the adjournment of the progressive convention and unanimously agreed to resume the independence of the party. The convention issued a statement declaring that the party had served the movement represented by the Conference for Progressive Political Action "from a high sense of duty, believing thoroughly in its value for the political education of the producing classes and hoping that in time it would develop into a powerful political instrument in the hands of the American workers, agricultural as well as industrial, mental as well as manual, in the protection of their interests and the promotion of their welfare in their struggle against exploitation and for their ultimate emancipation." As for the progressive party, the document declared that "it was clear that the party to be organized was far more likely to be a liberal party composed of the middle classes than a militant political organization of the toiling and producing masses of America." However, the convention agreed that in states and cities where the organized workers desired to establish or had organized a Labor Party the Socialists should cooperate with such movements after advising with the executive of the party.[28]

Thus ended the poltical upheaval of 1924, which began with expressions of fear by spokesmen of the bourgeois classes and their parties that the latter should form a united party against the rising tide of poltical radicalism. As the upheaval subsided, the apprehensions of the bourgeois spokesmen passed and the old two-party system found another lease of life.

[28] The complete proceedings appeared in *The New Leader*, February 28, 1925. A good digest appeared in the *Socialist World*, Chicago, March, 1925.

CHAPTER XII

NEUROSIS OF COMMUNISM

PSYCHOLOGISTS will find in the American Communist movement a profoundly interesting study. The movement has presented so many striking changes of opinion, numerous and conflicting policies and programs, recantations, affirmations and swift reversals of what but a few months before had been regarded as final, that the student is often left bewildered. Within six years it ran the whole gamut of ideas, from support of civil war to a demand for progressive reforms in politics. It rejected political action as a snare of the "bourgeois State" and ordered its followers to boycott elections, only to go into politics later as a political party. It sneered at labor parties as too "moderate" and then tried to organize them. It denounced all economic and political organizations of workingmen as "agents of capitalism," and followed this by appeals to these organizations for a "united front." It was eager to join the political coalition of 1924 to support Robert M. LaFollette, and then denounced all who gave that support. It vociferously proclaimed its faith in "dictatorship" and pleads for democracy when its members are in trouble. Believing once that an underground existence was the true test of loyalty to Communist principle, it eagerly came out of its hiding place to seek association with all those it stigmatized as "betrayers of the revolution." From 1919 to the end of the year 1921 twelve Communist organizations had been formed, an average of four each year. Each organization was heralded as the final type of Communist perfection, only to be abandoned for something else. The Workers' Party became the heir of all these experiences, and following the elections in November, 1924, factional struggles and personal antagonisms divided it into hostile groups. The documentary material related to these factional wars of two years is so bulky that it almost baffles any attempt to sift the important from the trivial. The issues had also been complicated by frequent appeals to Moscow, whose decisions were elaborated in long and wearisome documents which go into minute details of these internal wars. The numerous "Theses" and "Manifestoes" that have been issued by each faction and by the executive of the Communist International in relation to these quarrels are utterly incomprehensible to all but those who have studied them as a peculiar phase of labor history. One must go back to the obscurantist discussions of medieval scholastics to find anything similar to the debates that have accompanied the factional wars within the Communist movement.

The factional wars began over differing opinions regarding the maneuvering of the party for an important place in the political coalition of farmers and workers in the campaign of 1924. The official debate was opened in the *Daily Worker* of November 26, 1924, with a long "Thesis" by William Z. Foster and his faction, which filled fourteen newspaper columns, and was followed by a lengthy "Thesis" by Charles E. Ruthenberg and his faction in a later issue. Of the *Daily Worker*, a keen student of the history of American Communism wrote that it "is an incredibly inaccurate, misinterpretative and scurrilous sheet. Its references to American labor leaders, to the Socialists and to every one else who is not in complete accord with it are not merely malignant, but sometimes elaborately lascivious. The leading editor of the *Daily Worker*, Louis J. Engdahl, on the other hand, lives entirely in a world of fiction." [1]

The appearance of the leading "Thesis" was accompanied by an invitation to all party members to participate in the discussion in the *Daily Worker* and in the party branches. Four weeks were given for the debate, after which leading representatives of the two leading factions were assigned to debates before the membership in New York, Chicago, Boston, Detroit, Cleveland, Phila-

[1] Stolberg, "The Peter Pans of Communism," *Century Magazine*, July, 1925.

delphia, New Haven, Buffalo, Pittsburgh, Minneapolis and St. Paul. Rules were adopted by the Central Executive Committee for the branch discussions and for counting the vote in the referendum which was to follow. While there were a number of minor issues involved in the factional struggle, the leading one related to the question of the party's future attitude towards labor and farmer-labor parties. This issue was stated by the Foster faction in the following paragraph of its "Thesis": "No substitute for the Workers' Party. Nothing can replace the Workers' Party either as the leader of the proletarian revolution or as the practical leader in the everyday struggle. The idea that a 'farmer-labor party' is the natural and only possible leader of the workers and that it is the duty of the Workers' Party to create such a farmer-labor party is a petty bourgeois deviation; it is a revision of the fundamental theories of Leninism, and it leads directly to the liquidation of the Workers' Party." The conclusion from this reasoning was that the Workers' Party is the only party "of the working class," and that "no fake labor parties can be allowed to stand in the way." The true Marxian and Leninist policy required that the workers be taught that only by "accepting the leadership of the Communist International and its section, the Workers' Party, either by joining the Workers' Party or entering into a united front with it, can the working class fight for immediate betterment or final emancipation." This was the point of view of the Majority.

The Minority, led by Ruthenberg, in its "Thesis" contended that the World War "has developed the revolutionary crisis of the capitalist order," and that every attempt to save it "accelerates the climax of the crisis — the proletarian revolution," hence the "greatest task" of the party is "to win the leadership of ever greater masses of workers." This can be accomplished only by a "Bolshevized party," but building such a party "cannot be separated from the problem of setting in motion the proletarian and poor farming masses against the capitalists" under "Communist leadership." To do this it must still strive to build a farmer-labor party, amalgamate craft unions into industrial unions, organize the unorganized, demand relief for the unemployed, divorce "the working class from its treacherous trade union bureaucracy and petty bourgeois leadership." [2]

It is apparent that the Foster faction desired to abandon maneuvers to make the Workers' Party an intimate associate of a labor or farmer-labor party, while the Ruthenberg faction wished to continue these maneuvers. In the course of the long debate Fosterites ridiculed the claims made for the Federated Farmer-Labor Party organized by the Communists in July, 1923, as well as the maneuvers made by the party leaders at St. Paul in June, 1924. The factions became so bitter in this struggle for control of party policy that in the middle of December the Central Executive Committee issued a statement to the party members. The committee recalled that "under the statutes of the Communist International, permission must be secured from the Executive Committee of the Communist International before a convention of any of the sections can be held." The American party had requested permission to hold a convention in January, but this was answered by Moscow with the advice that the convention be not held until representatives of both factions had appeared before the executive of the Communist International. The Minority favored this proposal and the Majority opposed it. The latter cabled its fears of a "six months paralysis and crisis in the party" and renewed its request for permission to hold a convention in January. The Minority also cabled Moscow, admitting the "severe factional struggle within the organization," but also believing that a decision by the Communist International "will be the final guide for the party membership." [3]

Despite the bitterness of the discussion, the total vote polled in

[2] A good summary of each "Thesis" may be consulted in *The American Labor Year Book*, 1925, pp. 161-64. The discussion itself can only be followed by consulting the files of the *Daily Worker*, beginning November 26, 1924, and continuing for weeks thereafter.

[3] *Daily Worker*, December 19, 1924.

the referendum was rather small. The Foster, or Majority, faction received 1,516 votes and the Ruthenberg, or Minority, faction received 1,286.[4] The debate did not end with this vote. It continued in the form of a discussion of the methods employed by the factions to obtain an advantage. The charges and counter-charges revealed that "nuclei" and the intrigue planned by them for outside organizations had been resorted to by groups within the party to obtain control. Lenin's advice to "practise trickery, to employ cunning and to conceal the truth" had come back to plague the Communists themselves. Secret meetings were held by groups, underground documents were exchanged, and the Majority was charged with "vicious whispering campaigns" and "disfranchising hundreds of comrades." [5]

The Majority broadcast a long statement rejoicing in its victory, but it also charged that the Minority had organized a "nation-wide caucus" which had "literally flooded" the party branches "with anonymous documents, rumors, issues, etc." The result revealed a "complete defeat for the farmer-labor policy," but the Majority was "losing patience" with the obstruction methods of the Minority.[6]

Soon after the vote on the referendum was known, representatives of the Majority and Minority proceeded to Moscow, for even a decision of the party members decides nothing. The party leaders and the members may spend many weeks in discussing some issue and finally vote upon it, but the executive of the Communist International may modify it, set it aside or reverse it if it so chooses. Considering the time and energy wasted in these discussions, one is at a loss to understand why they are continued. Moscow's decision filled one entire page of the *Daily Worker*, going into details of the controversy, and while it had some criticism for both factions, it reversed the decision of the referendum

[4] Jay Lovestone, in the *Daily Worker*, January 9, 1925.
[5] Lovestone, *op. cit.*
[6] *Daily Worker*, January 17, 1925.

by deciding that the Workers' Party must continue to struggle for a Labor Party. During the factional struggle a third faction had appeared, the leader of which was Ludwig Lore, editor of the *New York Volkszeitung*, a German daily. This faction became known as "Loreism." It had attempted to combat the romanticism of the two leading factions and bring them to some knowledge of the reality of American life. The executive of the Communist International was aware of this third faction, and apparently decided to divert attention from the two-faction war by urging the extirpation of "Loreism." Both the Minority and Majority factions issued long and tedious statements, each congratulating itself that it had been sustained by Moscow, quoting from the latter's decision such statements as it could use for its purpose and indulging in caustic criticism of its rival. However, both agreed that "Loreism" must be liquidated, each contending that the other had been tainted with the deviation from "Leninism" with which Lore was charged.[7]

At the fourth convention of the party in August, 1925, the factions agreed by a unanimous vote that Loreism "is a right wing deviation from the revolutionary Leninist line of the Comintern and must therefore be relentlessly combatted." [8] Lore represented the German Language Group of the Workers' Party. The executive of the group met a few days after the decision of the Workers' Party convention became known and issued a statement declaring that the group had withdrawn from the Workers' Party because with "its present tactics and leadership [it] is getting daily farther away from its aim of becoming the awakener and leader of the American proletariat." [9] The elimination of "Loreism," however, did not abate the factional antagonism in the party.

[7] Moscow's decision and the Majority and Minority statements appeared in the *Daily Worker*, May 29, 1925.

[8] *The Fourth National Convention, Workers (Communist) Party*, pp. 93-95. "Comintern" is an abbreviation for Communist International.

[9] The complete statement of the group appeared in the *New York Volkszeitung*, September 2, 1925.

At this fourth convention the factional war became so grave that it was in session ten days, the factions being so evenly divided that fears of a secession and maneuvers to obtain a satisfactory truce prolonged the sessions beyond the period expected. Before considering this convention war, it is important to consider the illuminating report submitted to the convention by Secretary Ruthenberg. Detailed figures were presented of the membership of the party for each month and year since its organization, a summary of which the secretary presented in the following words:

> The above figures on new members taken into our party deserve the earnest consideration of our whole party organization. They show, first, that in the three and a half year period since the organization of the Workers' (Communist) Party, we have admitted into our party more members than we have in the party at the present time. At the time of organization of the party, some 10,000 members affiliated with it. Since that time, according to the table of new members initiated above, we have taken into the party over 20,000 new members. If we had held all of these members our party would now have more than 30,000 members. The dues payment figures for the past six months show an average of approximately 16,000, and we have therefore lost 14,000 members who entered our party in the last three and one-half year period. These figures show the necessity of more educational work within our party and also the need of assigning some activities to every party member in order to hold him in the party after he has joined.[10]

Beginning in September, 1924, the party made an industrial survey of its members, and of the 13,556 members reached, only 4,350 were members of trade unions. This was rather surprising considering that the party had continually urged its members to join the unions and become active in winning them for Communism. The party published twenty-seven periodicals in nineteen languages. Ten were dailies, one three times a week, two twice each week; eleven were weeklies, one three times a month, one twice each month, and one monthly. The combined circulation of all these publications was only 177,250. The reports of the

[10] *The Fourth National Convention, Workers' (Communist) Party*, pp. 27-41.

language sections of the party were interesting in that most of them show that these organizations were interested in the politics of their respective homelands. The Czechoslovak section had a "split" and its pamphlets were published in Czechoslovakia. The Greek section published a manifesto of the Communist Party of Greece; the Lettish section received large supplies of leaflets and pamphlets from abroad; the Lithuanian section raised funds for the Communist Party of Lithuania; the Polish section published a leaflet on the armed insurrection in Cracow, and so on.[11]

The call for the convention was issued late in July. In the meantime the Communist International, fearing that the factional struggles would wreck the party, issued a warning against their continuance. A Parity Commission of seven members, three from each faction and a representative of the Communist International, gave its attention to the struggle and sent a report to the party members about the same time that the call for the convention was issued. The commission observed that both factions had accepted the decision of Moscow regarding the issue which had arisen regarding work for a farmer-labor party and that the cause of the party war had been removed by this decision. But, the commission continued, "the factional war within the party not only has not ceased, but has assumed a much more bitter character" and was "intensified by personal attacks. . . . The party is going through an acute crisis; the party is in a dangerous situation." Not only was there a factional war raging in the party as a whole, but a "split" had occurred in Cleveland. In Philadelphia the division was so wide that the party "work is paralyzed." A dangerous schism had also appeared in the South Slavic section and "Loreism" was yet to be exterminated. The commission had agreed on a solution of the problems involved in all these cases, and it looked to the convention "to put an end to the factional struggle" and urged all party members to "consider seriously the critical situa-

11 *The Fourth National Convention, Workers'* (Communist) Party, pp. 43-51.

tion in the party."[12] The convention itself also showed trouble in the Finnish section and the Armenian section.

As the convention opened there were four factions in the party, the Majority, the Minority, "Loerism" and the Brahdy-Jampolski group, but it appears that only the first two factions were represented in the convention. The Brahdy-Jampolski group formulated a "Thesis" which in some respects was a remarkable digest of the contradictory actions of the party which we have presented in preceding chapters. It is a model of condensed history, and had it been presented at a period of intellectual calm, it would probably have made an impression, but the members and delegates were too possessed with the factional war to give it the attention it deserved. The "Thesis" concluded with the observation that a "great deal of the controversy in the party is of a purely factional nature and not upon any issues of principle. . . . Two groups in the party are brutally out for power, and [they] subvert everything else to attain their ends." [13]

It was several days before the convention could be organized because of the struggle between the two factions for control. Each had its secret caucus and formulated its strategy behind closed doors. There was even difficulty in agreeing upon the report of each day's session to appear in the *Daily Worker*. Although the convention opened on August 21 in Chicago, the city in which the *Daily Worker* was published, it was not until the issue of August 25 that the report of the first session appeared in this publication, and the report of each session thereafter was two or more days late. Except in the matter of "Loreism" and the removal of Askeli as editor of a Finnish organ, who was charged with "opportunist deviations," every important factional issue was decided by a strict factional vote, which showed that not a

[12] The complete report of the Parity Commission appeared in the *Daily Worker*, July 28, 1925. The call for the convention also appeared in this issue. The total number of delegates apportioned to the convention was 54.

[13] The Brahdy-Jampolski "Thesis" appeared in the *Daily Worker*, August 22, 1925.

single convert had been made by either side in the long discussions. The Majority vote was generally 40 and the Minority 20 or 21 on every such question.[14]

The Communist International had intervened twice to restore peace, and both factions had pledged support of its decisions, but the bitter feeling made peace impossible. Delegate Bittelman, of the Majority, reported for the Central Executive Committee. This was a long and tedious defense of Majority policies and a criticism of the views of the Minority, concluding with the observation that the Minority "cannot continue this fight without ruining this party" and urging peace. Ruthenberg replied for the Minority, beginning his address by saying: "As for Comrade Bittelman's closing remarks, I suggest that he should have thought of that yesterday in this caucus, when the caucus made its decision as to whether the Minority in this convention was to have what it won in the party or have a policy of extermination directed against it." He continued with a caustic criticism of Majority policies, concluding with the declaration that "we have no other resource than to say that you are in the right wing and that we must fight against you." [15]

Although the Foster faction constituted the Majority in the referendum and in the convention, a startling incident wiped out Foster's triumph. The Communist International intervened by cable, informing its representative in this country that "it has finally become clear that the Ruthenberg group is more loyal to decisions of the Communist International and stands closer to its views," and that the Foster group employed "excessively mechanical and ultra-factional methods." It ordered that the Ruthenberg faction should have not less than 40 per cent of the membership

[14] The discrepancy between this total vote and the 54 delegates originally assigned to the convention is probably due to an enlargement of the number of delegates. This increase was a compromise growing out of heated contests in the committee on credentials.

[15] Bittelman's long report and Ruthenberg's long answer appeared in the *Daily Worker*, August 29, 1925.

of the Central Executive Committee, that Ruthenberg should remain the party's secretary, and his group be given co-editorship on the *Daily Worker*. Although this order permitted Foster to have a majority in the party executive, he declined to take it in the face of the declaration that the Ruthenberg faction was more satisfactory to Moscow. Foster proposed equal representation of both factions, which was agreed to, but as the American representative of the Communist International serves as chairman and acts in accord with Moscow, the Ruthenberg faction became the Majority. The long discussions, maneuvers, caucuses and the bitter duel of the convention had decided nothing. Moscow decided.

One decision of the convention which also had its origin in Russia is unique, as it proposed a form of organization for the party which is unlike anything ever attempted by any political organization. This decision was formulated by the resolution on "Bolshevization of the Party." We have mentioned above[16] that as early as January, 1924, the executive of the Communist International had worked out a detailed plan of "nuclei" organization for Communists in all countries. The Workers' Party had experimented with this plan in a haphazard way for many months, and it was now decided to proceed to complete reorganization on this basis. The resolution asserts that the "territorial branch is a relic carried over from the Socialist Party," while the foreign-language branch tends to isolate its members and is "most fertile soil for factionalism and for the sharp division of the party members according to nationality." The resolution provided for the gradual dissolution of these forms of organization as their members were reorganized into "shop nuclei" and "street nuclei." Regardless of nationality, the members in a shop or factory or mine were to be organized into "nuclei" which were to become the units of organization of the party. The former branches were to become Workers' Clubs to which are to be admitted non-party members, but the Communist members of these clubs should in turn constitute them-

16 See above, pp. 156-157.

selves "nuclei" in these clubs "for the purpose of exerting the maximum influence over the non-party workers and drawing them close to the party." An extension of this "nuclei" organization into local, district and national conferences was also outlined in the resolution. Within a few weeks after the convention the party officials were issuing detailed instructions and explanations regarding the new form of organization, as it appeared that many members were unable to understand its intricacies and the relations between "nuclei" and Workers' Clubs. In fact, one has to read with very close attention to understand the complicated and cumbersome structure which was proposed as a substitute for the comparatively simple form of political clubs of which all political parties have consisted. How the party expected to function as a political organization participating in elections, it is difficult to understand. The frequency with which instructions and explanations appeared in the *Daily Worker* suggests that "Bolshevization" of the party would prove a big disappointment.[17]

A few weeks following the decision to reorganize the party on the basis of "nuclei," the Central Executive Committee sent to the membership an elaborate and detailed plan of reorganization. This communication explained the "street nucleus" as an international branch or "a group of party members, otherwise unattached, united on a street or neighborhood basis regardless of language grouping." The relations of the "street nucleus" with "shop nucleus" and their federation within given districts were described as follows: The subsection is the next highest unit above both types of "nucleus" and the subsection consists entirely of (a) "shop nuclei within a given industrial or working area; (b) of shop and street nuclei (international branches) within a given

---

[17] The documentary material for the convention is complete in *The Fourth National Convention, Workers' (Communist) Party*, Daily Worker Publishing Co., Chicago. However, this record of the convention gives no hint of the factional war in the convention. The reader will have to consult issues of the *Daily Worker* during the convention sessions to obtain an idea of the divisions and factional maneuvers for control.

industrial or working area; (c) entirely of street nuclei (international branches) within a given industrial or working area or a given territorial, residential area. Each of the units of the party, the shop nucleus, the street nucleus (international branch) or the subsection, is to have general and periodic meetings of all the members of the component units." Other details were presented, but it would only confuse understanding to attempt to summarize them.[18]

The previous experience of the party in attempting to experiment with this form of organization was not very successful. Shortly after the convention an American Communist reported that only about 60 "nuclei" had been established in all the states. In New York City, the most favorable city for the Workers' Party, there were only 32 members in seven "nuclei" in September, and in Detroit there were but fourteen members.[19] Late in January, 1926, four months after the party proceeded to reorganize, an active worker reported that "all of the large cities are now organized on the shop and street nuclei basis," but he was much concerned regarding the attendance of members at meetings, as reports showed a decline as low as 30 per cent. This he considered of "prime political importance," but later on observed that "attendance has risen to 50 and 75 per cent," and had even exceeded in some cases the attendance in the old form of territorial organization. This should be reassuring to the optimists were it not that the writer followed with a few pessimistic observations. He warned that the problem of attendance had not by any means been solved and that "the continuance of the present situation would involve at once a strong financial crisis in the party," which is "already manifested." The financial crisis implied a decrease in the revenue of the central party office because of a decline in membership,

[18] The detailed plan appeared in the *Daily Worker*, September 19, 1925. In the issue of September 17, both Ruthenberg and Foster also presented explanations of the plan.
[19] Bill Holden, "The Reorganization of the Workers' Party of America," *International Press Correspondence*, Vienna, January 13, 1926.

which in turn means that the new form of organization involved difficulties in retaining the members of the old organization. At best the writer seemed to be tossed between hope and fear regarding the results obtained four months after the party ventured on this new form of organization.[20]

The Proletarian Party was the only competitor which the Workers' Party had in the field on Communist organization. The Proletarian Party held its fourth convention in Detroit on November 26, 1925. The number of delegates attending and the organizations represented were not reported, but the party organ claims that it "was the largest convention the party had ever known." The convention adopted "Theses" on the agrarian question, the question of a Labor Party and on international relations. Although the party has never been accepted as an affiliated section by the Communist International — the latter recognizes but one party in each country — the convention declared "its support of the program and tactics of the Communist International." In its resolution on international relations the party presented a sarcastic review of the history of the Workers' Party, and declared that the latter would be extinct were it not that many of its members continue in the hope that the Communist International "will eventually clean up the mess." [21] Despite its adherence to the "program and tactics" of the Third International, the Proletarian Party paid no attention to the question of "nuclei" organization. The party restated its Manifesto and Program, but it contained few changes, and these were merely matters of phraseology. However, it continued to recognize the Communist International because its "militant leadership and its unceasing efforts are a source of hope and inspiration. . . ." [22]

One cannot follow the development of the Communist move-

[20] Martin Abern, "Attendance at Nuclei Meetings," *Daily Worker*, January 30, 1926.
[21] *The Proletarian*, January, 1926, p. 9.
[22] *Ibid.*, p. 10. The Proletarian Party did not nominate a presidential ticket in 1924. In fact, its members regarded the party mainly as an educational organization.

ment without being impressed by the fact that it is a special product of Russian history. It is as much so as tropical vegetation is peculiar to the equatorial zone. Given the institutional evolution of Russia, it was likely to shape some revolutionary group like that of the Bolsheviks. Russian economic and bureaucratic history weighs like a mountain upon the minds of Communists. They cannot shake it off. They think in terms of this history, they see the rest of the world through it, and everything else assumes the character, dimensions, coloring and importance of an experience that is Russian. Expounding the importance of the economic determination of history, they permit themselves to be its intellectual prisoners. The variation of climate, geography, language, customs, historical and psychic backgrounds that characterize each nation does not appear to impress the Communist.

This is especially evident in the matter of "nuclei" organization. The planting of cells in shops and factories and in the streets might well serve an oppressed class in the old Czarist bureaucracy, where political organization and voting were unknown. It might even serve in Soviet factories where workers are accustomed to hold meetings and even to vote for Soviet officials, but it appears cumbersome and unworkable for political purposes in the modern democratic countries. In any event, this phase of American Communist striving is the most bizarre that the movement ever attempted.

After several years of continuous factional war between the adherents of Josef Stalin and of Leon Trotsky in the Russian Communist Party, Trotsky was expelled in 1928 and then exiled. This brought another multiplication of sects, especially in the United States, each sect claiming to be the legitimate heir of Lenin, his views, policies and aims, and contending that Stalin and all the rival sects were imposters and betrayers of the "revolution." [23]

Lenin had become the philosopher and lawgiver of the move-

[23] For the first multiplication of sects, see Chap. VI above.

ment for all Communists, a man who had said the last word in economics, sociology and methods for the overthrow of capitalism. To question his views was to be guilty of an unpardonable sin. Of Lenin's activities and published works in the first quarter of this century, R. Palme Dutt, the leading Communist theoretician of Great Britain, wrote:

"Lenin's strength, which marks him out from all the other political thinkers and leaders of this period, was that *he alone*, from an early point, on the strong basis of Marxism, from well before the end of the nineteenth century, saw with complete clearness the whole character of the future period, prepared for it, drew the practical, concrete conclusions, and *was alone adequate to the demands of history* when the time came." [24]

Lenin also appeared to have this opinion of himself. Writing to Madame Kollontai in the United States on November 9, 1915, he informed her that within a few days his "group" in Switzerland would publish a pamphlet which would be the "first demonstration of the nucleus of the Left Social Democrats *of all countries who have a clear, exact and full answer to the question what to do and where to go.*" The letter may be found in Gankin and Fisher, *The Bolsheviks and the World War*, pp. 571-72. The Hoover Library on War, Revolution and Peace, Publication No. 15. As Lenin was the author of every important Bolshevik document published in Switzerland before he went back to Russia the "group" means himself.

This opinion is not exceptional among Communists. Hundreds of similar statements regarding Lenin may be found in Communist literature. Final knowledge had also been credited to Karl Marx to the period of his death in 1883 although Marx had again and again warned his followers against any tendency towards accepting his work and views as final. As Stalin through various party purges became absolute dictator, his name has been coupled with Lenin's as the last word in wisdom and the most humiliating spectacles in human abasement have been the "confessions" of "gross errors" by party hacks in Russia and other countries who

[24] *Lenin,* by R. Palme Dutt. London, 1933.

had strayed from the party line. These "confessions" did not always save the offenders. Many were "liquidated" by the dictatorship. Independent thinking had become a state offense and where all think alike no one thinks but the despot.

As thinking died in Russia it became a memory in the parties outside of Russia. Time was when the parties devoted five and six pages of their kept dailies discussing long and ponderous "theses" of equal length sent to the parties by Moscow. These consisted of periodical surveys of economic and political conditions all over the world, what prospects there were for revolution in many nations, the "errors" and "deviations" of the affiliated parties from the "party line" as laid down by the "revolutionary staff" in Moscow and warning each organization of penalties if it persisted in its "errors." These "theses" had been debated for many weeks in the local units of the parties but the outcome had always been hearty approval of the "revolutionary staff" and pledges to correct all "errors."

The savage purges of the Russian party brought colorless figures, like Earl Browder in the United States, to head each party outside of Russia, men who would obey orders. Each such leader was surrounded by sycophants who also paid homage to Stalin, exalted the latter as the unerring leader of the "world proletariat" and endowed him with attributes reminiscent of the virtues queer religious cults ascribe to their leaders. This change brought what the faithful called "monolithic parties," an admission that they are as lifeless as a pillar formed of a single block of stone. Hence the phenomenon of assent without question by these parties to every change in the "party line" ordered by Moscow. What was holy one month became sinful the next month and as the party turned heels-over-head in the air so its satellites, "innocents clubs" and fellow travelers did likewise.

All this gave the parties solidarity in dealing with those who deserted. On the other hand the deserters, having delivered themselves from this imprisonment, displayed delirious joy in working out their own programs. However, they had marched so long in the lock-step of Moscow that thinking was a new experience. The psychological shock of a sudden new life brought a multitude of odd, droll and fantastic programs, new factions and "splinters," which revealed that the Communist movement requires dictatorship if it is to function. Democracy cannot live within its pale.

The expulsion of Trotsky adherents from the Comintern in 1928 and from the American Communist Party was followed by a savage vendetta between the two organizations, the Stalin party resorting to attacks by organized bands to break up Trotskyite meetings. Jay Lovestone had become the leader of the party in this period of raids on the opposition but the following year the Lovestone followers failed to satisfy Moscow and they were expelled. They were also victims of assault by the "comrades" who succeeded the Lovestone leadership.

In December, 1928, while Lovestone was still leader, the Trotsky organization's office was burglarized, its official paper later listing the books, files and other equipment that had been stolen. It accused Lovestone and the Communist Party of the theft but took comfort in the fact that it had secreted copies of the most important of the stolen records.[25]

In February of the new year a Trotsky meeting in the Labor Temple, New York City, broke up in a riot in which brass knuckles and other weapons were used after the Lovestone partisans had howled down and sung down their opponents. A month later the Trotsky faction succeeded in holding a meeting after organizing a "workers guard" with the aid of brawny members of the I. W. W.[26]

This civil war brought many "splinter" Communist groups into the Communist arena, each trying to win converts from the others and from the parent organization which had spawned them.

[25] *The Militant*, organ of the Trotsky group, January 1, 1929.
[26] *Ibid.*, February 15, March 15, 1929.

The Communist League of Struggle organized under the direction of Albert Weisbord in March, 1931. In the following December, Weisbord also complained of a raid on his group, declaring that his headquarters had been pillaged, that his "whole Marxist library" had been stolen, and that he had obtained the confession of two Stalin partisans that they had participated in the burglary.[27]

In the following year, 1932, Lovestoneites and Trotskyites were both protesting against the violence of their former "comrades." The Lovestone faction, which had raided Trotsky faction meetings for a year, was expelled in 1929 and in July, 1932, the Lovestone group appealed to the Civil Liberties Union for protection, declaring that Stalinites had broken up meetings of the Trotskyites, Lovestoneites and Socialists. In one instance, it was charged, members of the International Labor Defense, armed with brass knuckles and knives, had dispersed a Lovestone meeting.[28]

The Trotsky faction followed up this protest the following September with a leaflet manifesto presenting details of the killing of two persons and the injury of a number of others on August 20 at 7th Street and Avenue A in New York City.[29]

In the same year the Labor and Socialist International reported similar raids on the Socialist parties of Europe by the Communist parties, indicating that they were not isolated events but due to a policy formulated in Moscow. These attacks were especially frequent in Poland where the "Bund," a Socialist organization, provided most of the victims. The Communist Party organized picked members for these raids and they were paid for their work. It was charged that the public authorities tolerated these attacks

[27] Circular letter by Weisbord, December 29, 1931.

[28] *Workers Age*, organ of the Lovestone group, July 23, 1932. See also the *New York Times*, July 17, 1932.

[29] Leaflet published by the National Committee of the Communist League of America (Opposition), September, 1932.

although the political agitation of both Communists and Socialists was persecuted by the police! [30]

Another splinter group, the League for a Revolutionary Workers Party, agitated for a Fourth International to replace the Comintern and it became involved in a civil war with other splinter groups and the Communist Party. It reported a fist fight at its headquarters in May, 1936, between a Field faction and a Demby-Stanley faction. The report was made by the Italian Left faction of Communism and the Revolutionary Workers' League which had conferred with the League for a Revolutionary Workers' Party regarding the possibility of a merger. The Left faction and the R. W. L., discussing the physical encounter, recalled their own experience "at the hands of the Stalinites and the use of gangster tactics by the Cannon-Schachtman (Trotsky) group in Philadelphia." They concluded that members who had not participated in the fist fight could redeem themselves "only by an immediate political declaration of the revolutionary road to the Fourth International." That was the "line" of the R. W. L. and the Left Faction.[31]

The most notorious example of "Red baiting" by Communists was the riot precipitated by the Communist Party in Madison Square Garden, New York City, in February, 1934. In that month the Austrian dictatorship of Chancellor Dollfuss directed its military might against the whole labor movement of Austria, the main center of the struggle being Vienna where the democratic Socialists, supported by the trade unions, ruled by an overwhelming majority of the voters. The shelling of Vienna's muni-

[30] *Bulletin of the Labor and Socialist International*, April 30, 1932.

[31] *The Fourth International*, July, 1936. Note two "splinters" with similar names, the Revolutionary Workers League and the League for a Revolutionary Workers Party. The "splinters" and split "splinters" become so numerous that it was difficult for some to choose a distinctive name and when names were abbreviated, as R.W.L. and L.R.W.P., the student gets a headache trying to distinguish between them. The Field faction mentioned above soon organized another "splinter" group.

cipal houses by artillery and the heroic fighting of the masses in the streets and provinces, was an epic in the long struggle of mankind against despotism which won the sympathy of democratic people in all countries.

In New York City powerful trade unions, democratic Socialists, and the Workmen's Circle called a mass meeting in Madison Square Garden for February 16. About 30,000 people attended but the meeting was broken up by Communist Party members. One day before the meeting the Communist Party held a meeting in the Bronx Coliseum where Clarence A. Hathaway, editor of the *Daily Worker*, and Earl Browder, secretary of the party, urged a "march" on the Madison Square Garden meeting while the *Daily Worker*, on the day of the Garden meeting, published a provocative editorial also calling on its readers to "march."

Communists came to the meeting as organized groups, each apparently under the direction of a leader. Trade union guards at the entrances relieved suspects of stink bombs, bottles, tailor's shears and other weapons concealed in newspapers, and confiscated stacks of provocative literature.

The chairman was greeted with boos and hisses and speakers were likewise treated. Claquers shouted, "We want Hathaway! We want Hathaway!" and the Communist editor rushed to the platform and tried to seize the microphone. The rowdyism continued for nearly an hour while Hathaway was severely beaten and taken to the hospital. Fist fights broke out in the immense auditorium, but due to the coolness of those in charge of the meeting many men, women and children were saved from injury. Not till March 4 were the meeting's sponsors able to hold their meeting, then in Carnegie Hall.

Sentiment rose to white heat against this shocking performance and for many months the Communists were isolated from the labor movement as diseased persons requiring quarantine. The outrage was also followed by an exodus of "innocents" from the Communist-controlled American League Against War and Fascism and the Socialist Lawyers' Association abandoned its co-operation with the International Labor Defense, declaring it to be a "legal mask for the Communist Party." [32]

In the early thirties these physical assaults on non-Communist meetings became general in the larger cities throughout the United States. Just as all criticism of the dictatorship was silenced in Russia so the Communist Party attempted to silence criticism here. It was not only an effort to extend the dictatorship to the United States but it was also considered training of party members as "combat units" in an armed rising against the government at some time in the future. Police officers who attempted to restore order were also attacked, yet no group was more vociferous in behalf of civil rights than the Communist Party when it failed to get a permit for a public meeting.

Meetings held by other organizations to obtain relief for the unemployed were turned into riots in several large cities. In San Francisco such a meeting to be addressed by Daniel W. Hoan, Mayor of Milwaukee, Morris Hillquit, National Chairman of the Socialist Party, and James H. Maurer, in March, 1930, was broken up. The Communists rushed the platform and some blood was spilled. Police who attempted to restore order was also attacked. Asked if they approved such actions, Communist leaders answered that they considered them "decidedly healthy in the interests of

[32] The New York dailies of the period carried extensive accounts of the riot and events leading up to it. The American Civil Liberties Union, of which the Rev. Harry F. Ward was chairman and who headed the American League against War and Fascism, submitted an obscurantist report to the press regarding the riot. It admitted that the Communist Party was responsible for it and had assumed the right "to determine" who the speakers should be but added that the attack on Hathaway "was disgraceful and wholly unnecessary." Ward had for years been a faithful follower of the Communist Party line. He said nothing about the provocations that led to the attack on Hathaway. Two members of the Civil Liberties Union, Robert W. Dunn, a Communist, and Mary Van Kleek, a "fellow traveler," practically justified the Communists in a casuist argument suggestive of medieval scholastics. The Civil Liberties Union report and press release was dated March 18, 1934.

the working class" and that the Communist Party "accepts moral responsibility for them." [33]

This period of Communist neurosis was also notable for the development of the theory of "social fascism," an accusation that was hurled at all democratic opponents of totalitarianism and dictatorship of the Communist type. "The united front is a method of struggle against the social fascists for the possession of the masses," wrote Earl Browder in the *Communist*, August, 1933. All high trade union officials and prominent men and women in the Socialist and Farmer-Labor parties were thus labeled.

Long and wearisome "theses" appeared in Communist periodicals regarding "social fascism" which were followed by interpretations offered by the very men who were practicing the fascist methods of Hitler and Mussolini before these two dictators came to power. These practices are precisely those adopted by the German and Italian dictators to silence or destroy men and organizations that formed barriers to totalitarian conquest.

These attacks continued even after the Communist Party became the Communist Political Association with the announcement that it had abandoned its Stalin ideology and methods. A notable example was the organized attempts to break up meetings addressed by Bertram D. Wolfe in Seattle and San Francisco in 1944 with Communist members of the C. I. O. National Maritime Union leading the assault. Wolfe had once been a member of the Communist Party but had abandoned it years before. Denounced as "a known Trotskyite" by the San Francisco unit of that union, its resolution also declared that Wolfe "was propounding a program of Hitler and Hitler's allies." In Seattle a band of Communists rushed the platform and attempted to break up the meeting. Commenting editorially, the *Christian Century* said: "Evidently the Communist Political Association has not, for all its change of name and announced purpose, learned the elementary a-b-c's of American democracy." [34]

Even the splinter sects have not abandoned raids on rivals. In 1945 the Shachman faction of the Trotskyites was reported as having "stolen the membership files of the Yipsels (Socialist youth group) and are using them to run meetings to recruit members from these lists." [35]

Floating with this official rowdyism and the neurotic sects have been professional men and women and declassed intellectuals, many without any serious preparation by a study of the social sciences and the labor movement, who joined either the parent organization or one of the sects. Each desired to be a member of something "left," but as "left" is a relative term he is always in doubt where to stop. If he does stop in this left ward trend humiliation may await him. To the left of him are those who brand him with the shameful epithet, "right." Or he may be said to be a "cowardly centrist" by trying to survive in some twilight zone between a "right" and a "left." This is distressing to him as he wants to experience the utmost in "revolutionary" faith and is afflicted with hesitation, doubt and fear as to his course.

Like phantoms, these deflated professionals and intellectuals pass from one group to another. Idle rich sons generally find an outlet for their revolutionary fervor by joining a fellow-traveler organization although a few secretly hold membership in the Communist Party. Both types, however, regard their venture as an interesting diversion, more satisfying than golf or tennis. To play with "proletarian dictatorship" is fun and a good thrill is obtained by following the current trends and discussing the latest change in the parent party line as it arrives from Moscow. They are playboys at revolution, those who enjoy the intoxication of vicarious fighting on the barricades with little risk to themselves.

[34] Wolfe presented a graphic acount of his experience in two articles in *The New Leader* of New York, October 7, 14, while the Seattle and San Francisco dailies carried news stories of these affairs.

[35] *Ibid.*, June 9, 1945.

If Stalin exterminates dissenters in the Russian party the war between the American party and its heretic sects and between the sects reveals that each seeks the extermination of the others. The civil war waged by them inspired a chapter in the late W. J. Ghent's book.[36] Titled "The Hanging List," the author declares that each group and party hate each other more than they do conservative and reactionary spokesmen of the old order. Each has a "hanging list" of prominent men and women in the other groups to be executed when "the day" arrives.

[36] W. J. Ghent. *The Reds Bring Reaction*. Princeton University Press.

CHAPTER XIII

FINANCING COMMUNISM

WITH the new year (1927) the decline of American Communism had become marked. This was apparent not only to the outsider but to those who read Communist publications. Pessimism gripped the membership and General Secretary Ruthenberg devoted a series of articles in the *Daily Worker* to this theme in the hope of dispelling the gloom. A long party resolution was also adopted to "combat pessimism." Ruthenberg went so far as to publish the names of active party workers who had failed to attach themselves to "nuclei." An uprising in the needle trades unions of New York City against Communism also induced the Communists to move the *Daily Worker* from Chicago to New York in January, where it has since been published with its one Yiddish daily, *The Freiheit*. The party forces concentrated in New York City to combat the rebellion in the needle trades which proposed to outlaw Communists so far as control of union offices is concerned.

Communism found a foothold only in the unions of the needle trades where many Jewish workers are employed. The problems of the garment industry are so complex because of the survival of small shops, seasonal work, rapid changes in fashions, uncertainty of work and numerous employers who are divided into outside and inside manufacturers, jobbers, sub-manufacturers and contractors, that discontent among the workers is rife. As many of the Jewish workers are also sympathetic to Russia, clever agitation on the part of the Communists enabled them to obtain control of the Joint Board of the Furriers and the Joint Board of the Cloakmakers. Practically all the ills of the industry were charged to the union officials, but Communist control was only obtained by making promises which, because of the nature of the industry, could not be fulfilled. In both instances the new leaders ordered the members out on long and disastrous strikes to fight for demands most of which were impossible of realization. The Communist leaders proved to be woefully lacking in the practical experience and generalship so necessary in the garment unions. They were unable to withdraw the men from the strike without serious losses. The settlements made for the Furriers and the Cloakmakers left the members stripped of some important gains which had been won by years of sacrifice. Moreover, the cost of the two strikes was enormous.

In the Furriers the Communists were more securely intrenched. Demands for an investigation of the strike resulted in an investigation by representatives of the American Federation of Labor and their report is interesting. According to the admission of some officials of the Furriers, the Communists had organized something like a Cheka to terrorize anti-Communist members. Close relations between Communists and police officials appear to have been established and large sums were paid to the police. Financial records were missing in many important transactions and important records were refused to the investigation committee. The bookkeeper of the Furriers admitted under cross-examination that the cashbook turned over to the committee was a substitute for the original. Large sums were paid of which there is no record as to who received the money.[1]

In the case of the Cloakmakers, the industry was left in a ruinous condition and the unions were nearly wrecked. The disaster that had come to the strikers after a struggle for July to December was so apparent that quite a number of influential members of the Workers' (Communist) Party and of the Trade Union Educational League resigned. Inconspicuous members of these organizations also deserted them. On December 9, 1926, representatives of a number of trade unions issued a call for a general trade union

[1] The important sections of the report appeared in *The New Leader*, January 22, 1927.

conference in New York, on December 21, to form a permanent alliance against Communism. Becoming alarmed at this revolt, the Communists arranged mass meetings in Chicago, Baltimore and Boston. To their surprise their opponents came to the meetings in these cities in such numbers that they were turned into anti-Communist demonstrations. After losing a number of meetings in New York, the Communist leaders of the Cloakmakers rented Madison Square Garden, calling all Cloakmakers to attend and protest against their opponents. Upon arrival at the Garden only Communists of the needle trades and other unions were admitted. At least 10,000 Cloakmakers demonstrated outside the Garden.

On December 21 the alliance of the trade unions against Communism was organized. Originally planned as a New York organization, it was expanded into a national alliance because of delegates who were present from Chicago, Boston and Philadelphia. Over 300,000 members of 17 trades were represented by 400 delegates. This body organized the Committee for the Preservation of the Trade Unions and adopted a program which declares that the Communist leaders seek to "make the trade unions conscripts of the oligarchy known as the Communist Party. For years we had supposed that members of this group could be reasoned with. We have presented reasons and facts, argument and persuasion, but to no purpose. All these methods by which civilized people adjust their differences of opinion have been spurned. We have been answered by malicious slander, atrocious falsehoods, unjustified attacks and secret plotting. . . . We submit that tolerance of these crimes would itself be a crime against the trade unions. We have endured this insolence long enough. We have resolved to end it." The activities of the organization were to be devoted to holding public meetings and publishing literature; to raising a fund to aid unions affected by Communist activities; to holding frequent delegate conferences; to surveying disguised organizations through which Communists gather funds that are used for their purposes; to maintaining a publicity service, and to "utterly root out of places of power and influence any members who take orders from the Communist Party or who have any friendly relations with the Trade Union Educational League, its officials and members."

Evidence of the intimate relations between the Communist Party and the officials of the Furriers and the Cloakmakers was confirmed by knowledge of the detailed instructions worked out for such relations by Communists in Moscow in February, 1926. The program outlined in detail the necessity of "nuclei" in the unions, the supremacy of the party leaders in directing the "nuclei" leaders and ordering strict obedience to the program. Representatives of Communist organizations of nine nations participated in the formulation of a program for "nuclei" organization in factories, streets, sport organizations and trade unions. A bulletin of 24 pages was devoted to the details of such "nuclei," their relations to each other and their control by Communist parties. A section devoted to "Model Directions for the Formation and Structure of the Communist Factions in the Trade Unions" throws considerable light on what happened in the needle trades unions of New York. The "model directions" declare that Communist members and officials of trade unions "must unite into a faction and carry on faction work" while the Communist Party officials must determine "the poltical and tactical line of the Communist factions." The party executive also "directs and instructs them and controls their activity." Rigid discipline of the "factions" and their strict obedience to the party officials are also commanded. The instructions continue:

"Important tasks of the factions shall be discussed in the trade union department in the presence of representatives of the factions. In case of serious differences of opinion between the faction and the trade union deparmtent, the party executive shall decide the matter in the presence of faction representatives. The decisions of the party executive must be carried out unconditionally by the faction. Non-fulfillment constitutes a breach of discipline.

"The faction executives are obliged to give regular reports to the party executive or to the proper department and higher faction executive.

"Candidates for all congresses, conferences and committees shall be nominated by the faction executive and approved by the proper party executive. If necessary, the party executive itself can nominate the candidates." [2]

From these instructions it is apparent that Communist members of the trade unions are required to maintain a secret organization in the unions and Communist officials must secretly confer with and accept orders of the Communist Party. Failure to carry out instructions "constitutes a breach of discipline" which generally brings expulsion from the party. Between sessions of Communist factions they are required to report to the party regarding union affairs and strikes while the party assumes the right to select candidates for office in the unions, and where the "factions" nominate union officials the nominations must receive the approval of the party. With this outside organization thrust into the heart of the trade union, directing its officials and making secret decisions unknown to the membership of the trade union, conflict is certain to be the result. Moreover, such control has for its first consideration the rule of Communists, not the improvement of the economic conditions of the members of the trade unions.[3] It is conduct in the strike of the Cloakmakers by the Communist leaders such as is outlined in the above "model directions," added to a disastrous settlement of the strike by these leaders, that resulted in the uprising of the trade unions in New York, Baltimore, Chicago, and Boston.

Previous to this uprising the Communist "factions" in the unions and the party "nuclei" have always concentrated their entire forces

[2] See Appendix III for instructions in organizing secret groups in other organizations.

[3] The "model instructions" framed in Moscow were printed in full in the *International Press Correspondence* (Vienna), May 5, 1926. The reader will remember that this is a bulletin published by the Communists and of which from one to five members are issued each week. A German and French Bulletin is also published. These bulletins are sent all over the world.

for any given purpose. For example, if they called a meeting of Furriers or Cloakmakers to demonstrate against their opponents the Communist "factions" of the particular union concerned would be insufficient. Communist painters, machinists, shopkeepers, tradesmen, clerks and members of street and factory "nuclei" were all ordered out. Concentrating all the Communist forces at a union demonstration gave it the appearance of great power in that union. At the Madison Square Garden meeting mentioned above the Cloakmakers were asked to come to a Cloakmakers' demonstration against the officials of the International Union. All known Communists in the city received notice to attend. Regardless of their occupation they were admitted, but with the cooperation of the police more than 10,000 Cloakmakers were excluded. President Sigman of the International Union, who was invited to attend the meeting and defend his official acts, was also singled out for exclusion.

The opponents of the Communists were at a disadvantage by this concentration of Communists in every dispute in the trade unions. By also acting in concert in a number of cities, the opponents of the Communists were able to easily take over meetings called by Communists themselves.

Faced with a rising of the members of the trade unions in New York, the Workers' (Communist) Party called a general meeting of all the "nuclei" members on January 5. To meet this uprising, the Communists decided to (1) increase their activities in the trade unions; (2) avoid dual unionism; (3) build "opposition blocs" in the trade unions and increase "the vitality of left wing organization"; (4) "further consolidation of party apparatus" and "increase the activity of leading comrades in sections and sub-sections." As all this is merely a restatement of Communist activities, presenting nothing new whatever, it appears that the Communists can think of nothing to meet the uprising but a continuance of the activities that provoked it.[4]

4 The meeting was reported in the *Daily Worker*, January 18, 1927.

Some financial help may be expected from the organization of what the European Communists call "innocents' clubs." These consist of special organizations ostensibly formed for some special purpose, such as protection of civil rights, release of poltical prisoners, etc. People unaware of the purpose of such organizations, and for that reason known as "innocents," are induced to join some such special organization. Having taken the initiative in organization, the Communists generally manage to place enough of their partisans on the executive committee of the organization to control it. They are especially careful to have a trusted member elected to the financial post. The "innocents" are thus associated with the Communists in a drive for funds to promote some worthy purpose. Literature is printed and meetings held. Communist speakers are sent out and find ample opportunity to engage in their own special propaganda.

A number of such "innocents' clubs" are maintained in this country. One organization has specialized in Philippine independence and for a time another club was maintained for the farmers. The largest of these clubs was the Federated Farmer-Labor Party to which we have devoted a special chapter. The "American Negro Congress" belongs to this type. Its organ is the *Negro Champion*, published in Chicago. Another is the "Labor Unity Publishing Association," a Chicago enterprise, with *Labor Unity* as its organ. It is intended to attract the support of progressive members of the trade unions. A third enterprise made its appearance in Chicago, the "Labor Sports Union," which maintains a mimeograph press service. The Communist International has frequently urged the importance of Communist "nuclei" in sport organizations. To this may be added the "All-American Anti-Imperialist League," also with headquarters in Chicago, which figured largely in Secretary of State Kellogg's absurd charge that Mexico was the base of a "Bolshevist" plot in Latin America.

For a year or two the Communists maintained another special organization, "The International Labor Defense," in Chicago. It devoted much of its time to collecting funds for the purpose of obtaining legal aid for Sacco and Vanzetti, two Italians convicted of murder in Massachusetts and by many who have investigated the case believed to be innocent. A Boston committee had this defense in charge for a number of years. In its *Monthly Bulletin* for December, 1926, the Sacco-Vanzetti Defense Committee, the Boston organization, declared that it had repeatedly asked the International Labor Defense "to send accounts of their activities and also accounts of the various Sacco-Vanzetti Conferences. To date, we received no satisfactory replies to our many letters regarding the purpose of the afore-mentioned organizations, or an accurate account of funds received and disbursed by them." A few weeks later Moscow reported that American Communists had reported having raised a half million dollars for "Sacco-Vanzetti relief work." [5] The reader may draw his own conclusion.

The International Labor Defense continued collecting funds for similar purposes in later years. A letter by Tom Mooney, the noted labor prisoner, on January 20, 1929, denounced the International Labor Defense for collecting funds in the name of Mooney and keeping the funds for itself. [6]

Despite protests and exposures the I.L.D. continued to obtain funds in this way. An especially shocking case was that of several miners convicted and sentenced to life imprisonment following a violent strike in Harlan County, Kentucky. The miners and their friends contended that the convictions were a "frame-up" and appeals were made for funds to take their cases to a higher court. One victim, W. B. Jones, wrote that the Communists through the I.L.D. "have collected thousands of dollars in our names but not

[5] The Moscow report was made by one who signs himself "A.G. Bosse (Moscow)" in the International Press Correspondence (Vienna), January 6, 1927.

[6] *The Monitor*, a New York weekly, published this long letter in its issue of February 2, 1929, and the *Weekly People*, organ of the Socialist Labor Party, New York, reprinted it September 14, 1929.

one cent have they expended in our defense." Friends were warned not to contribute to the I.L.D.[7]

One H. L. Doan swore to an affidavit in the same case. He had been called from Harlan County to Chicago to consult with Communists regarding aid for the convicted miners. Doan swore that the Communists "said that heaven is in Russia and that Hell is here in the United States, and that it wouldn't take but 24 hours to throw the White House into the river. They are soliciting $1,000 a day for the miners here and the miners are not getting any of it; they are soliciting clothing and they pick it over and just send the old rags down here."[8]

Denying that it was an agency of the Communist Party, the I.L.D. itself supplied the proof of its control by that organization. In 1929, Fred Beal, a member of the party, led a strike in Gastonia, N.C. During the struggle shots were fired and a police chief was killed. Beal was sentenced to twenty years in prison for murder. Awaiting results of an appeal, Beal fled to Russia but becoming disillusioned with the Communist dictatorship he returned to the United States and recanted his Communist views. The I. L. D., of which Vito Marcantonio, member of Congress from New York, was the head, had raised funds for Beal and defended him in his trial. Following Beal's recantation, the I.L.D. refused to defend Beal because of his anti-Communist views. Nothing could have better demonstrated the Communist domination of the I.L.D.[9]

A later case of chicanery by the I.L.D. brought a revolt of C.I.O. unions in California. The Los Angeles Trade Union Conference, composed of unions of the United Automobile Workers, the International Ladies Garment Workers, and the United Rubber

[7] *Workers Defense*, monthly, Chicago, November, 1932.

[8] *Machine Age in the Hills*, by Malcolm H. Ross (New York: The Macmillan Company) © 1933. Affidavit is in full on pages 184-185.

[9] Louis Waldman, labor attorney of New York, became the attorney for Beal after his desertion by the Communists. In his autobiography, *Labor Lawyer*, Waldman presents an excellent account of the Beal case in his chapter, Murder in in the Bible Belt.

Workers, in August, 1938, sent a letter to John L. Lewis, Chairman of the C.I.O., declaring that the unions mentioned had decided to withdraw from the Los Angeles Industrial Council and that they would not participate in the C.I.O. state convention called by Harry Bridges. The conference published many documents revealing activities of many Communist Party members to capture the C.I.O. unions with the support of Bridges.

One document, signed by Bill Busick, related experience the unions had with the Communists in collecting money for automobile strikers. Busick said:

"During and after the Douglas strike, known Communists circulated, and gave orders to circulate, subscription blanks on which appeared a statement to the effect that the International Labor Defense and the International Workers Order were sponsoring this collection of funds to help the Douglas strikers. These subscription forms were widely circulated in southern California and it was noticed that several forms had a large number of names on them with the amounts they had contributed set after each name.

"The records of the Douglas Strike Committee do not reveal that this money was turned over to it or used in the defense or in any way assisted the strike." [10]

How much money the Communists obtained by these methods through the I.L.D. is not and probably never will be known but it must have been hundreds of thousands of dollars. They also obtained funds through other "innocents' clubs" organized ostensibly for some worthy purpose but secretly controlled by the Communist Party. As a rule the financial post was given to a tried party member or to a reliable "fellow traveler" while agents and speakers in the field were of the same type. They were paid salaries and while in the field they quietly performed services for the party.

Considering the small membership and small vote polled by the Communist Party the layman is puzzled by the extensive activities

[10] Mimeograph document of the Los Angeles Trade Union Conference. August, 1938.

of this small group and wonders where it obtains the funds for its immensely costly work. Third party movements in the United States, the Populist Party, the Farmer-Labor parties, the Socialist Party, etc., were poverty-stricken organizations, although their membership and vote ranged anywhere from five to twenty times that of the Communist Party. They relied mainly upon dues, contributions and sales of cheap literature to meet expenses, and they were generally heavily in debt. On the other hand the Communist Party has always had unlimited funds and, no matter how small the movement has been in this and other countries it has enjoyed the same huge money vat.

We have pointed out one lucrative source of funds above. What are the others? Former members of the party who have recanted their Communism agree that the Communist parties receive subsidies from Moscow through the Communist International and the Red Trade Union International, the "Profintern" as it is called. When the Trotsky supporters were expelled from the party, James P. Cannon, their leader in this country, reporting the organization of the "Communist League of America (Opposition)," wrote of its intention to fight the "bureaucratic caricature of internationalism by the subsidized Stalin consulates." [11]

Thus as early as 1929 it appears that some of the subsidies came through Russian consulates. Whether through the consulates, the Comintern or the Profintern, many millions of dollars filched from the workers and peasants of Russia annually have been forwarded to Communist parties and their auxiliaries all over the world. It was also common gossip in the labor movement that the party in this country and Britain obtained a percentage of the profits realized by Amtorg, the Russian trade corporation, with large staffs in London and Washington. We have no definite evidence regarding this and it is obvious that it is not as easy to ascertain the facts as it is to probe the other sources.

[11] *The Militant,* organ of the Trotskyites, June 1, 1929.

Another substantial source of income for the party is a number of "rich uncles," wealthy men and women attracted to Communism, who have contributed lavishly to the Communist Party and its "innocents' clubs." [12]

The Communist Party is an enormously expensive apparatus for such a small organization. It publishes two English dailies and several in foreign languages. It publishes books and expensive pamphlets and maintains bookstores in many of our leading cities. These stores, periodicals and general literature are ventures that undoubtedly involve heavy deficits that must be made up from subsidies. The dailies carry little advertising and their circulation is small. Not one can survive six months unless its deficit is paid by sources outside its income.

On special occasions a Communist daily will publish an expensive edition that is purchased by few while the advertising is no more than in proportion to the regular small paper. The *Daily World* of San Francisco published a special edition in three sections with a total of 64 pages during the United Nations conference. The *Daily World* is a Communist Party paper the policy of which changes with each change decided upon in Moscow. No genuine small third party could possibly indulge in such luxuries without being subsidized. [13]

Another instance of shady financial transactions obtained publicity in the New York press late in October, 1945. The Scottsboro case involving a young Negro believed by many to have been

12 See article by Benjamin Stolberg in *The Saturday Evening Post*, February 15, 1941, "Muddled Millions: Capitalist Angels of Left-Wing Propaganda." This article is thorough and considers all the notable "angels" of the American Communist movement. *Time*, June 30, 1941, also carries an excellent account of a million dollars that were contributed primarily to radical causes in general by Charles Garland. He set up the American Fund for Public Service but as the Fund's directors consisted mainly of leading Communists and "fellow travelers," most of the fund and the income derived from it helped such Communist "fronts" as the Federated Press, the International Labor Defense, the Trade Union Educational League, the League for Peace and Democracy, and the New York Russian Communist Daily, *Novy Mir*.

13 *The Daily World*, San Francisco. United Nations Issue, April 28, 1945.

unjustly convicted of crime in a Southern state obtained much publicity for a number of years. The Communist Party and the I.L.D. seized upon this case to collect funds for the defense but no satisfactory accounting of the money had been made.

Benjamin F. Davis, Communist member of the New York City Council, was custodian of the funds and in the city campaign of 1945 a Liberal-Fusion candidate demanded that Davis gave a public accounting of an estimated $500,000 collected for the Scottsboro case. Morris Ernst, labor lawyer and prominent in the Civil Liberties Union, added his voice to this demand and publicly declared that it was time the Communists explain how much money went to the *Daily Worker*, how much to Communist committees, how much to secret underground organizers in the trade union movement.

That its income from dues is inadequate to finance its extensive activities is evident when we consider its monthly schedule of payments by members. The Communist Party held a national convention in New York City in July, 1945, and revised its constitution which provides that members earning less than $25 weekly shall pay 35 cents per month; $1 monthly for members earning from $25 to $60 weekly; $2 for members earning more than $60 weekly, and ten cents monthly for the unemployed.[14]

Louis F. Budenz, a member of the party for years, a national committeeman for six years and managing editor of the *Daily Worker*, resigned his membership in October, 1945, to become professor of economics at Notre Dame University, and in several statements to the press expressed his mature opinion of the Communist movement. Of the party's membership, he declared that there was a turnover of 40 to 50 per cent which indicates disillusionment of many once they obtain inside experience as party members. Such a heavy turnover does not promise substantial growth.

[14] *New York Times*, August 8, 1945.

Of the reasons for disillusionment, Budenz declared that the anti-religion of Communism destroys initiative, thinking and integrity of the individual, that the party "gets orders from somewhere," that it "substitutes abuse for thought, bureaucracy for democratic procedure" so that each member tends to become a "puppet." Each member, he concluded, "mutters phrases which he does not fully understand and he commits himself to actions of which he knows not the objective or consequence." [15]

This inside view based upon years of experience correlates with the opinions of outsiders who have studied Communism in theory and action. Despite the vast funds at the disposal of the American party, some obtained by questionable methods, it remains a sect whose primary purpose is to serve as the American agency of a totalitarian power.

[15] *United Press dispatch,* October 12, 1945.

CHAPTER XIV

TROTSKYISM IN AMERICA

ANOTHER branch of world Communism is the "Fourth International," whose founder and guiding genius was Leon Trotsky. A brief statement concerning Trotsky's part in the formation of Russian Communism, his break with Stalin, his underground activities, etc., is necessary in order to understand his influence in our own country. Lev Davidovich Bronstein, alias Leon Trotsky, left behind him a revolutionary record that is difficult to surpass. During the Czarist regime he spent several years in prison, was exiled to the prison camps of Siberia twice, and was forced to live in exile for twelve years. He was in New York when the Kerensky Revolution occurred in 1917 and returned to Russia in time to join Lenin in the sweeping Bolshevik revolution. Trotsky played a leading role in that epsiode. He became President of the Petrograd Soviet, the center of the revolt against the Kerensky Government, and when in October, 1917, the All-Russian Congress of Soviets constituted itself the supreme power in Russia, Lenin became the Chairman and Trotsky the Commissar of Foreign Affairs in the newly formed cabinet. The difficult task which confronted the newly appointed Commissar was peace negotiations with the Central Powers. Russia was crushed and the great majority of her people demanded peace — "peace at any price." Trotsky had to rely on his rhetorical ability as the only bargaining power since the Russian forces had surrendered unconditionally. His oratory attracted the attention of the world but had very little effect on Germany. The conditions imposed on Russia by the Brest Litovsk treaty were humiliating but the Bolshevik Government submitted rather than suffer further invasion of Russia. Trotsky, however, refused to sign the harsh treaty and Lenin appointed a new representative, Sokolnikov, to accept the German terms.[1]

Peace with Germany meant civil war, backed by the Allied Powers. The "White" offensive began early in 1919 and in June of that year, Trotsky was given command of the "Red" Army. He was an organizer of superior ability and before long he had a well-trained army, estimated at 400,000, which included about 30,000 officers from the old Imperial Army. With this select force, Trotsky carried on a successful war on sixteen fronts, and by October, 1920, the Red Army emerged triumphant on all fronts.[2]

Vladimir Ilyich Ulyanov, better known as Nikolai Lenin, passed away, January 21, 1924, and with his death began a new chapter in the career of Leon Trotsky. In his threefold capacity as Chairman of the Russian Communist Party, head of the Soviet State, and Executive Secretary of the Third International, Lenin wielded dictatorial power, not only in Russia, but also over the Communist parties in other countries. Whoever succeeded him would fall heir to a position of unlimited power.

Trotsky was, without question, the most outstanding man in world Communism at that time. He had displayed extraordinary abilities as writer, orator and organizer. He was opposed by Joseph Vissarionovich Dzkugashvili — "Old Man Joe" — of later Teheran, Yalta and Potsdam fame. Stalin had several advantages over his rival: he was the Secretary of the Russian Communist Party, attended Lenin's funeral, was an orthodox Bolshevik (Trotsky had been a Menshevik) and had succeeded in placing his own supporters in key positions in the party. Stalin, as the world has discovered, became the strong man of Bolshevism, as powerful a dictator as Lenin had ever been. Trotsky did not accept his defeat with good grace. He retreated, "for his health," to a village in Turkestan, Alma Ata, where he devoted his time to underground activities against Stalin and his "counter-revolutionaries."

1 Pares, Sir Bernard, A History of Russia, p. 480.
2 Jackson, J. H. The Post War World, p. 152.

The historical process, according to the "Marxian-Lenin" philosophy, through which Socialism may be realized, is revolution, and Trotsky devoted his time and energies to promote world revolution. Stalin, on the other hand, did not believe that a Bolshevik revolution would meet with success in any of the great capitalistic countries at that time; hence, he employed all his powers, dictatorial and otherwise, to establish Socialism in the Soviet Union and make it (the U.S.S.R.) the supreme power in Europe and Asia. The historical verdict seems to be that he has succeeded fairly well in these objectives.[3]

The Communist International had been created for the specific purpose of carrying on revolutionary propaganda in every country and to prepare the world for Bolshevism. Trotsky and Stalin also became rivals for the control of this agency and Trotskyism in America had its origin in this phase of the conflict. The Sixth World Congress of the Communist International met at Moscow in 1928 and all the factions of American Communism were represented at that congress. Among the delegates was James P. Cannon who was prominent enough to be placed on the Program Commission, and while serving on that commission, a document fell into his lap which decided his role as the "High Priest" of Trotskyism in the United States and "Patron Saint" of the Fourth International. This is what he has to say about that incident (or accident):

But that turned out to be a bad mistake — putting me on the Program Commission. It cost Stalin more than one headache, to say nothing of Foster, Lovestone and the others. Because Trotsky, exiled in Alma Ata, expelled from the Russian Party and the Communist International, was appealing to the Congress. You see, Trotsky didn't just get up and walk away from the party. He came right back after his expulsion, at the first opportunity with the convening of the Sixth Congress of the Comintern, not only with a document appealing his case, but with a tremendous theoretical contribution in the form of a criticism of the draft program of Bolshevism and Stalin.

[3] An excellent survey of this conflict is found in Langsam, *The World Since 1914*. Ch. XIX.

Trotsky's document was entitled "The Draft Program of the Communist International: A Criticism of Fundamentals." Through some slip-up in the apparatus at Moscow, which was supposed to be bureaucratically airtight, this document of Trotsky came into the translating room of the Comintern. It fell into the hopper, where they had a dozen or more translators and stenographers with nothing else to do. They picked up Trotsky's document, translated it and distributed it to the heads of the delegations and the members of the Program Commission. So, lo and behold, it was laid in my lap, translated into English! Maurice Spector, a delegate from the Canadian party, and in somewhat the same frame of mind as myself, was also on the Program Commission and he got a copy. We let the caucus meetings and the Congress sessions go to the devil while we read and studied this document. Then I knew what I had to do, and so did he — it was clear to us as daylight that Marxist truth was on the side of Trotsky. We made a compact there and then — Spector and I — that we would come back home and begin a struggle under the banner of Trotskyism.[4]

Cannon returned to America with his precious document fully determined to make the Trotsky program the basis for American Communism, but he and his followers soon experienced the same fate among their comrades in America that Trotsky and his followers had suffered in Russia: they were purged from the party, but since they could not be exiled, they were excommunicated to "outer darkness" of non-affiliation. However, Cannon and his supporters decided to remain in the party and organized themselves into a left-wing opposition, known as the Communist League of America. They lost no time in their anti-Stalinist activities. They were expelled from the party, October 27, 1928, and the following week the November issue of *Militant*, their official organ, came out with the Trotsky program, celebrating the anniversary of the Russian Revolution and "thus began the open fight for *American Trotskyism*." [5]

During the rise and defeat of Trotskyism in the Third Interna-

[4] Cannon, James P., *The History of American Trotskyism*, (New York: Pioneer Publishers) © 1944, p. 49.
[5] *Ibid.*, p. 55.

tional, the American party (the Stalinites) changed its name twice. Organized as the Workers' Party in 1921, by 1927 it was known as the Workers' (Communist) Party. In 1928 it adopted the name of the organization which had been outlawed in 1919 and again became the Communist Party and declared that it was the American section of the Communist International. Striking changes were also made in its national platforms in this period. In 1924 its platform urged a "proletarian revolution" to establish a Soviet system, and in 1928 the platform affirmed the necessity of a "dictatorship of the proletariat" as a substitute for the American form of government. In 1932 the platform dropped dictatorship and proletarian revolution but urged self-determination for the Black Belt, that is, organizing the Southern Negro people in a Negro autonomous republic. In 1936 the platform dropped the proposol for a Negro republic and declared that Communism is "Twentieth Century Americanism."

By the spring of 1929, the Trotskyites were convinced that the Communist Party would not follow true "Marxian" principles as outlined in the Trotsky program. On the advice of Comrade Trotsky, with whom they maintained underground connections, they decided to form an independent party. In the spring of 1929, they had a following of about a hundred members and they reckoned that this was sufficient for a successful convention. The leaders of Trotskyism called for such a meeting in Chicago, May, 1929, and 12 cities responded by sending 31 delegates and 17 alternates to the convention. This first conference against the "Stalinist hoodlums — met in a spirit of unanimity, enthusiasm and unbounded confidence in our [their] *great future*."[6] Their ultimate aim has been, and is, the "overthrow of capitalist rule in America and the creation of a Workers' State," and this could not be achieved by a small propaganda group. Fusion with other parties and control of other parties was the line of least resistance. With this in view the Communist League opened negotiations with the

[6] *Ibid.*, p. 79.

Workers' Party, headed by a former preacher, Mr. A. J. Muste. The negotiations resulted in a marriage between the league and the party in December, 1934, but it was not a happy union. The Trotskyites were looking for larger fields to conquer and the Socialist Party became their next field of conquest. The Musteites were in favor of building a strong party of their own, but the Trotskyites had discovered a superior strategy — the boring from within. This strategy had the approval of their commander-in-chief, Comrade Trotsky. After brief negotiations between the leaders of the two parties, it was agreed to admit the Trotskyites on the following terms: they could enter as individuals and not as a group or party, and they must discontinue their propaganda publications, the *Militant* and the *New International*.

That was rather humiliating to the members of the Fourth International but they were willing to swallow any humiliation for the good of the cause. The split which occurred in the Socialist Party at the Cleveland convention in 1936, offered the Trotskyites the opportunity they were looking for. They were advised not to dicker for terms but to get into the party as fast as they could, and once inside, see to it that the Trotsky *principles*, the *world-conquering ideas*, prevailed. The story of the Socialists' experience with the Communists is told in another chapter. It should be added here, however, that the strategy and tactics of the "ultra-revolutionary" Trotskyites became too radical even for the left wing, and the following year, 1937, they were officially ousted from the party. Fortunately for the Fourth International, these were the days of dark depression and the heyday of radicalism in the United States, especially among American youth, and the devotees of Trotsky salvaged enough radical material to launch a new party: the Socialist Workers' Party, founded in January, 1938.[7]

The leaders of this militant group boast of many important

[7] Gitlow, B., *I Confess*, p. 583; also Cannon, *History of American Trotskyism*, Ch. XI, XII.

achievements, especially in connection with strike activities of labor unions. Cannon has glorified these efforts in his lectures on American Trotskyism, devoting an entire lecture to "The Great Minneapolis Strikes." [8] Stolberg, in his history of the C.I.O., disagrees with Cannon. He calls them "a tiny, isolated sect." In their analysis of American labor, "they have been sectarian, unrealistic, and have amounted to nothing." [9]

Their greatest influence, without question, has been to publish and circulate the ideals of Leon Trotsky. They were, also, very active in bringing about the defence of their master, who was the central figure in the Moscow trials and purges of 1936-38. Trotsky was at that time in exile in Mexico, but his enemies, the Stalinites, feared that he was directing a world-wide conspiracy against the Soviet Union. The *History of the Communist Party of the Soviet Union* (Bolsheviks), authorized by the central committee of the Russian Bolshevik Party, sets forth in no uncertain terms that Trotsky and his

"contemptible lackeys of the fascists had set out to destroy the Party and the Soviet State; to undermine the defensive power of the country, to assist foreign military intervention, to prepare the way for the defeat of the Red Army, to bring about the dismemberment of the U.S.S.R., to hand over the Soviet Maritime Region to the Japanese, Soviet Byelorussia to the Poles, the Soviet Ukraine to the Germans, to destroy the gains of the workers and collective farmers and to restore Capitalist slavery in the U.S.S.R." [10]

Trotsky and his fellow conspirators were found guilty of treason against the Soviet Union as well as against the sacred cause of Bolshevism; the court sentenced the whole gang to be shot, and the Soviet people approved the annihilation of the gang, according to their authorized history.[11]

[8] These lectures were delivered in New York, 1942, and published in 1944 by the Pioneer Publishers.
[9] Stolberg, *C.I.O.* p. 30.
[10] *History of the Communist Party of The Soviet Union* (New York: International Publishers). p. 347.
[11] *Ibid.*, p. 348.

These purges created an intense interest in the United States. Many people who were neither Stalinites nor Trotskyites were eager to know the truth. A trial of Trotsky by an impartial jury might prove the most reliable method of getting a true verdict. A Commission was set up consisting of eleven outstanding Americans, including Dr. John Dewey who acted as chairman of the Commission. Dr. Dewey has been severely criticized for undertaking such a dirty task. Did he not know that he and his Commission would be smeared from head to foot by the most skillful smearing masters that our age has produced? Of course he did. But he had a strong conviction that "truth is the mainspring of all human progress," and if he and his jury could find the truth involved in the Moscow trials and executions that would have a great influence on the American people, especially on the labor unions which were at that time greatly stirred by various factions of militant Communism.

Dr. Dewey was laboring under the illusion that if American labor "knew the truth, the truth would make them free." The committee, on which no Trotskyites were allowed, devoted weeks and months to a careful investigation of all available evidence and, finally, reached the verdict that Trotsky and his son were "not guilty" of the charges brought against them. According to Dr. Dewey, "Trotsky never recommended, plotted or attempted the restoration of capitalism in the U.S.S.R. It was clearly established that the prosecutor of the trials fantastically falsified Trotsky's role before, during and after the October Revolution. In short, the report (of the committee) proves the Moscow trials to be a "frame-up." [12] The report of the committee furnished the Trotskyites with abundant material for their propaganda but had very little effect on their enemies, the Stalinites. The bloody purges were not limited to the U.S.S.R. but were extended far and wide, reaching Trotsky in Mexico, his son, Gedov, in Paris and

[12] Meyers, Agnes E., *Significance of the Trotsky* (Interview with John Dewey) *in International Conciliation*. (Feb., 1938.)

how many other Trotskyites will never be known. "These contemptible lackeys of the fascists forgot that the Soviet people had
only to move a finger, and not a trace of them would be left." [13]
That finger was Stalin's and the number obliterated by that finger
is a fertile field for historical research.

Trotsky is dead but many of his followers are not. In the United
States they are seemingly growing both in numbers and influence.
As an organized political party — the Socialist Workers' Party —
they have done very little in the national elections. They are, however, canvassing the field for possible merger for the next election.
In the labor movement they have gained a name for themselves as
the "Trotskyite Fifth Column," especially among their "friends,"
the Stalinites. George Morris, a Communist, exposed their activities
in the labor unions, as well as their anti-government activities
during the second World War, in a pamphlet published by the
New Century Publishers, 1945.[14]

They are obsessed with a revolutionary complex which mani-
fests itself in their literature as well as in their actions. Their activities in the labor movement have been primarily to promote strikes,
and the more violent the strike, the better they like it. Had it been
within their power to turn the war against the Axis nations into
a civil war, especially in Russia, they would gladly have done so.
Their anti-war and anti-Roosevelt activities caused the labor
unions, as well as the government, to take action against them.
Eighteen members of the Socialist Workers' Party (Trotskyites)
were convicted for seditious statements and activities against the
Government of the United States. Most of these seditionists were
members of labor unions and defended their actions as bona fide
union activities. That aroused the ire of the C.I.O., and at their
Minnesota State Convention, held at St. Cloud, September 1944,
they passed a unanimous resolution condemning their vicious
attacks against our Commander-in-Chief, President Roosevelt,

---

[13] *History of the Communist Party of The Soviet Union*, p. 347.
[14] Morris, George, *Trotskyites, 5th Column in the Labor Movement*.

their disruptive and seditious activities and branding them as *enemies of the labor movement.*[15]

One war is ended, but not their war. The Marx-Trotsky brand of Communism may take a new lease on life. Depressions, unsettled conditions and revolutionary activities which followed the first World War brought forth the Third International. Should similar conditions follow the second World War, the Fourth International may find the opportunity it has been looking for — "the overthrow of capitalism and the setting up of a workers' State." The future holds the secret.

[15] *Ibid.*, p. 30.

CHAPTER XV

COMMUNISM AND AMERICAN YOUTH

BOTH Fascism and Communism have given special care to the creation and expansion of their respective ideologies. They have scored their greatest success in this respect in the fields of training and "conditioning" the rising generation. In America, the "Communists have been far more successful than the Fascists in winning the youth to their program. Needless to say that they have followed the Russian pattern rather closely wherever it was possible to do so. There is this difference between the Russian and American training program. In Russia the entire educational system has been devoted to create a Bolshevik mentality which enabled the Communist organizations to devote all their energies to the selection and training of leaders for the proletariat masses. In America the Communists had to devote their major strength to win followers, and from these followers select and train leaders. During the revolutionary period of the 1920's, there were strong "radical" movements among the youth of America. The Independent Young People's Socialist League joined the Young Communist International in 1920. By 1922 the movement was known as the Young Workers' League and by 1924 the Young Communist League appeared, an organization that became very aggressive in the service of Communism. The pattern of this organization was a replica of the Communist Party and the technique was identical with that of the Comintern, of which it formed an important branch.

At first these young radicals devoted their attention almost exclusively to the farmer and laboring classes and neglected the student group. However, the "Hoover depression" opened new doors of opportunity. The millions of youth that graduated from the high schools, colleges and universities faced a future of unemployment and insecurity. Some graduating classes are reported as having adopted as their motto: "W.P.A., here we come!" It was an age of cynicism and frustration, and Communism thrives best in such an intellectual climate. This atmosphere was not confined to our educational institutions but that was where it produced a luxuriant growth of radical ideas. High schools and colleges were branded by Hearst and company as "hot-beds of radicalism," and even Wall Street began to show an interest in our educational institutions. The Communists took full advantage of the situation. They had a cure for all the ills of a moribund capitalist society. Through them a new day had come to old imperialist Russia and through them, especially the young Communists, a new era would be ushered in capitalist America where "people stood in the breadlines knee-deep in wheat."

The young American Communists took their mission seriously. In their handbook, compiled by Lewis Miller, their aims are clearly stated: "We Communists openly proclaim our aims. We tell the workers that under the leadership of the Communist Party and the Young Communist League, capitalism will be overthrown and a government controlled by workers and farmers put in its place." Furthermore, the youth organization was to serve as a training center "to prepare the working class for the final battles against capitalism"; also a center where defense squads could be formed and drilled; it was the school of Communism where leaders could be properly trained. Again we quote from this handbook: "A good way in which to illustrate Young Communist League work as a whole is to compare it to a machine operating on the belt system. The Young Communist League has numerous feeding belts connecting us to the masses of young workers and students — some of these belts connect us directly (as through our units), others, indirectly, through mass organizations. In turn, as a result of our mass work we recruit new members for the young Communist League." [1]

A large number of the "belt" operators were paid and others were volunteer workers, but whether paid or volunteer, they were certainly loyal to the cause and to the group. The last of their ten commandments warned against treason to the organization: "In case of arrest a Young Communist League member must not give any testimony to the police which could be used against other comrades, even if the police tell him that other comrades have already testified. A young Communist dares not allow either police tricks or force to make him a traitor to his class comrades and his organization." [2]

Through this "belt system" they were able to make connections with hundreds of organizations of youth controlled or influenced by the bourgeoisie, not for the purpose of destroying them, but to transform them from centers of bourgeois influence into centers of proletarian influence. The belt system proved very effective among the student groups, especially those who received "doles" from the NYA. The executive secretary of the Young Communist League, Gil Green, who was important enough to deliver a speech before the Seventh World Congress of the Third International, held as Moscow in 1935, stressed the importance of uniting with the "middle class youth, especially the student youth." By so doing it was possible to develop powerful student action. In the spring of 1935, they staged a student strike against war and Fascism. "On April 12th, 184,000 students walked out of their classrooms at one given moment, in the greatest demonstration of youth solidarity ever witnessed in our country." [3]

Their greatest opportunity for "peaceful penetration" into the bourgeois masses came with the founding of the American Youth Congress in August, 1934. The leading promoter of this movement

[1] American Legion, *Isms*, pp. 110-115.
[2] *Ibid.*, p. 117.
[3] Green, Gil, *Young Communists and Unity of the Youth*, p. 9.

was a young woman named Viola Ilma, who was motivated by a strong conviction that the interests of American youth could best be served by bringing all the youth groups into one great national organization. She had the misfortune of having traveled in Germany and was suspected of Fascist leaning for which reason she was deprived of leadership of the Youth Congress. The Communists and Socialists took credit for this action. The Communists evidently did more than oust Miss Ilma. At the famous Seventh World Congress of the Third International, Comrade Kuusinen informed the delegates that "the leaders of the Young Communist League of the United States, headed by Comrade Green, rolled up their sleeves and went to the congress at which an extremely variegated group of young people from most diverse strata was assembled. Our American comrades achieved great success at this youth congress. The agents of Fascism were completely isolated, and the congress was transformed into a great united front congress of radical youth." [4]

The Communist infiltration into the youth congress did not stop it from growing. "By the end of 1939 it represented a conglomeration of sixty-three national organizations, claimed 4,600,000 members, had an organizational structure as complicated as an Insul holding company — it was held together by a common concern with the future of 20,000,000 young people between the ages of 16 and 24 who have emerged into a world where jobs are scarce and problems are perplexing." [5]

The belt system of the Young Communist League seems to have been very effective in its efforts to transform the bourgeois youth organizations into a radical united front for peace and democracy. When it met at Washington, D.C., in February, 1940, it caused quite a stir because of its radical tendencies. Over 5,000 young people, representing 46 youth organizations, came from all over the

---

[4] Kuusinen, O., *Youth and Fascism*, p. 14.
[5] Gould, L.A., *American Youth Today* (New York: Random House) © 1940, p. 113.

land to bring pressure on the Congress and the Administration to help them solve their problems, especially the unemployment problem. In rain and slush they crowded the grounds of the White House in anticipation of messages from the President, the First Lady of the land and many other national dignitaries. If a message pleased them, they applauded; if it rubbed them the wrong way, they jeered and booed.

When President Roosevelt showed no better judgment than to class Russia as a dictatorship, he was jeered by the "united front" and in the halls of Congress members of the "front" did not hesitate to show their displeasure with certain actions of that body. These acts of "rank discourtesy" turned many people against them. Congress became very suspicious of un-American activities and the Dies Committee received moral and financial backing in its effort to uncover such activities. Opposition to the Communist steam-roller also raised its feeble voice but it was soon silenced. The attempt came when the congress was engaged in adopting a creed which would express the convictions of American youth. One of the paragraphs contained the expression: "I will oppose all un-democratic tendencies and all forms of dictatorship." One of the delegates felt that this was not specific enough and moved that the following phrase be substituted: "I oppose all undemocratic tendencies and I condemn Communism, Nazism and Fascism as forms of government equally oppressive of human rights and liberties." [6]

To condemn Communism as a form of government oppression of human rights and liberties would, naturally, draw fire from the Communists and fellow travelers. Gil Green, the leader of the Young Communist League, felt that the motion was directed at his organization. His compromise stand won the approval of the congress: "We do not expect in the congress to impose our ideas on others or have theirs imposed on us. . . . My organization takes a

[6] *Ibid.*, p. 100.

firm stand against dictatorship, against the advocacy or the use of force and violence." [7]

Browder's revisionism, Moscow's strategic retreat, won the day and the motion was defeated by an overwhelming majority, but 23 of the delegates left the convention in protest against the Communist domination. The creed to which the Communists did agree is a masterpiece. It begins with "I dedicate myself to the service of my country and mankind. I will uphold the American ideal, which is the democratic way of life," and it closes with "I pledge allegiance to the Flag of the United States of America and to the Republic for which it stands, one nation indivisible with liberty and justice for all." [8]

The press had very little to say about the creed, but the walkout of the 23 delegates, the booing of the President and the demonstrations in Congress gained the headlines. The war was raging in Europe. It was strictly a European war — let Europe stew in its own juice. The anti-British feeling was quite strong but the pro-Russian feeling was stronger than ever. The Berlin-Moscow Pact did not trouble them very much. It was a clever move on the part of Stalin and by the spring of 1941 he was fully justified in all that he had done, and by December, 1941, at the time of Pearl Harbor, the young Communists of America found justification for all their activities. The united front developed into the United Nations, and the Communists have been, and still are, strong supporters of the UNO, especially since Russia plays a leading role in that organization.

With Russia's entry into the global war, their objective changed from "peace and democracy" to that of "war for democracy"; and with America's entry, the "second front" became more important than the "united front." No one can accuse the young Communists of being slackers or pacifists; there were a few conscientious objectors among them, but very few. The attitude of

[7] *Ibid.*, p. 101.
[8] *Ibid.*, p. 299.

the Trotskyites was quite different. Stalin's Russia has been the main reason for the different attitude of these two groups.

The Young Communist League had another important function to perform. They helped to organize and to furnish leadership for the Young Pioneers and to train them for membership and to receive them as members at the age of 16 in the Young Communist League. The American Legion gives the following somewhat colored description of this organization: "The Young Pioneers is composed of boys and girls of grade-school age. Its programs are dedicated to hatred of American institutions and the American flag. Eighth-grade school children may form a nucleus of Young Pioneers and these nuclei or groups have been organized in our public schools in various cities throughout the country, including New York, Boston, Philadelphia, Chicago, Detroit, Los Angeles and other cities. They distribute Communist publications, such as *Young Spark*, praising the red flag." [9]

The Pioneers served a threefold purpose. They acted as fifth columns in the bourgeois youth organizations, especially in Scout groups; they served as feeders to the Young Communist League and, eventually, to the party; and they presented a golden opportunity for selecting and training leaders for American Communism. These young radicals acted very much like their elders. Whenever the Scouts held conventions, the Pioneers were sure to be there with their propaganda literature. When the Boy Scouts celebrated their twenty-fifth anniversary with a special Jamboree at Washington, D.C., in 1935, the Pioneers issued 100,000 copies of their propaganda sheet, *The New Pioneer*. "Distribution of this issue will have a great effect in counteracting and exposing, at least partially, the war mobilization character of the Jamboree." [10]

The Workers' International Relief established summer camps for the Young Pioneers in many parts of the country, especially in the State of New York. It has been estimated that these camps

[9] American Legion, *Isms*, p. 123.
[10] *Ibid.*, p. 129.

turned out over 15,000 young Communists every year. These young Americans had been thoroughly drilled in the tenets of Communism and many of them had sworn allegiance to the red flag. Radicalism among American youth passed through the same periods of development as it did among their elders. The destruction of the old order through violent revolution was the spirit of Bolshevism during the first period. Then Fascism menaced the Communist fatherland and the movement presented a united front against war and Fascism or for peace and democracy. Then came the great conflict and the Young Communists followed the American Communist Party and the Third International; they voted their organizations out of existence. The Communist youth of military age joined as willingly and fought as valiantly against the enemies of democracy as any of the bourgeois youth. Their loyalty has not been questioned. For once Uncle Sam was on the "right side" and as long as he remained on the right side, he could count on the loyal support of the young Communists.

How did Communist propaganda and indoctrination effect American youth? Their behavior has been severely criticized by some writers and praised by others. It depends very largely on the mentality of the writer. An impartial estimate is difficult. During the first period they seemed to take a special delight in shocking their elders. That applied to morals, religion, government — in fact everything that belonged to the bourgeois order. One of the plays presented by The Rebel Players bore the title *Mr. God Is Not In*. God was represented on the stage by a cigar-smoking individual, and his confidential secretary, St. Peter, by a man in golf knickers. God was not in to a poor widow, but he was pleased to do business with Reverend Ph.D's and opulent men of affairs, dressed in the garb of Knights Templars. Shocking blasphemy! Yes. The greater the shock to members of the old order, the better they liked it. This attitude changed with the coming of the united front and the Trojan horse tactics. During that period some of the comrades attended meetings and conventions which were opened with prayers. During the war there were plenty of Communists in fox-holes, but we have been informed that there were no atheists in those holes.

The war is over. The Communists who survived have returned or are returning. What will be the next move? Will the defunct Young Communist League and Young Pioneers be resurrected? The future of any movement depends on its success in winning and training youth. Communism is no exception to that rule.

CHAPTER XVI

DISSOLUTION OF THE COMINTERN

THE ANTI-COMINTERN PACT, signed by Germany and Japan, November 25, 1936, and by Italy, November 6, 1937, ushered in a period of great changes and activities in world Communism. The Tri-Partite Pact was a direct threat to the Third International and a most serious menace to the Socialist Fatherland, the Soviet Union. Aggressive Fascism must be met by an even more aggressive Communism. The defense strategy took the form of "anti" organizations and activities — anti-militarism, anti-imperialism, anti-imperialism, anti-New Deal and, above all, *anti-war and anti-Fascism.* The anti-Fascist front soon gave way to a more efficient propaganda, the "People's Front," which had met with great success in France, Chile and other countries. To unite all people with radical and liberal leanings, irrespective of class, creed or race, in a great drive for *peace and democracy*, became the main effort of the Communist leaders, beginning with the 1936 elections. The class struggle and proletariat dictatorship were kept in the background, the New Deal received their support and President Roosevelt became a great champion of world democracy. The civil war in Spain turned out to be a showdown between the forces of Fascism and the People's Front, sponsored by Moscow, and the outlook was rather dark for the latter. The United States and Great Britain seemed to be on the side of Fascism in the preliminaries to the second World War. Then followed the betrayal of Munich, which to Communist leaders meant that "Chamberlain was trying to trick the Soviet Union into a position of drifting into war, not on its own account or for its own interests, not even in support of any system of collective security, not even with the right to fight that war, but for the aims to be decided by Chamberlain, at a time decided by Chamberlain, and in a manner decided by Chamberlain."[1]

The Soviet Union was not to be "jockeyed" into war either on the side of Germany or Great Britain. Stalin played his own diplomatic game in such a manner that his country could watch the "Nazi Blitz" while it was getting ready for the inevitable. The Non-Aggression Pact between the Soviet Union and the Third Reich dazed the Stalinites at first but they soon discovered that "the Soviet-German agreement is the best current example of the way to peace — that the Soviet Union, which of course includes Stalin, wishes to do everything possible to limit and extinguish the wars that are going on, and to prevent the outbreak of any general war."[2]

The attack on Finland by the Soviet Union was heartily approved by Browder and his lieutenants. Finland was pushed by Great Britain "into an open provocation and threat of military action against Leningrad." The imperialist plan was "to transform Finland into a steel dagger at the throat of the Soviet Union." Even President Roosevelt was guilty of backing Great Britain against the Soviet Union. For a while the Communists withdrew all support of the New Deal and they accused President Roosevelt and his administration of trying to save the European bourgeoise at all cost, to advance American imperialism and to gain profits for American capitalists. This enthusiastic defense of the Soviet and strong opposition to American activities caused bitter resentment against the Communists. There was a strong suspicion among the American people that the whole affair was managed by Moscow. The American Legion, local, state and Federal authorities began a drive against the Communists, the Nazis and other subversive elements. The Soviet-German Pact united the Stalinites and the Hitlerites into a dangerous anti-American "Bund" which

---

[1] Browder, Earl, *The Second Imperialist War* (New York: International Publishers) © 1940; p. 107.
[2] *Ibid.*, p. 73.

frightened many patriotic Americans. If such a combination was directed by Joe Stalin with his efficient organization, secret agents and fanatical devotees, and if Stalin was aided by Joe Goebbels, America was in grave danger.

There was a strong movement in Congress to outlaw the Communist Party. Such a movement prevailed in many of the state legislatures, and in some states it was actually excluded from the ballot. The peacetime sedition act which forbade the advocacy of the overthrow of government by force or violence or propaganda creating disaffection in the armed forces, was aimed at the "Communist-Nazi" agents and the Trotskyites. Under such circumstances the Communist Party proved a liability to Stalin rather than an asset.

Whether advised from Moscow or not is of little importance, but the party severed its relations with the Comintern in November, 1939, shortly after the second World War had started. At last they were under one flag, the Stars and Stripes, free from all official foreign entanglements. As for a strictly American party, they felt that they were in a much stronger position to "defend the Soviet Union." This was more than a slogan — it was their main objective. Having no connection with Moscow, they could not be accused of "taking orders from Moscow." Stalin was still playing ball with Hitler, and the Stalinites contended that Britain and the United States were rooting for Hitler.

Anti-war mass meetings were held throughout the land at which they denounced President Roosevelt and his capitalist war party. "It is no accident," said Browder, "that a capitalistic world, raging in its dying agonies like a wild beast, and wanting to tear the Soviet Union limb from limb, when faced with the final decision to begin the job, turns from it and, instead, begins to tear one another limb from limb. . . . The second imperialist war, through the struggle of the masses to bring it to an end, will give birth to the Socialist system in one or more other countries." [3]

3 *Ibid.*, p. 298.

The Stalin-Hitler agreement placed the American Communists in a very awkward position. They were forced to collaborate with the Nazis against whom they had organized a united front. The first indication of a change for the better came in May, 1941, when Comrade Stalin for the first time assumed the premiership of the Soviet Government and stiffened his resistance to Hitler's demands. The following month, June 22, 1941, Hitler himself delivered the American party and other Communists and fellow travelers from their dilemma by attacking their beloved fatherland. The course that Stalin had followed became clear and he was praised for his clever strategy — he would still prove himself to be the savior of democracy.

This event ushered in a new period of activity for all Russian sympathizers as well as for their opponents. To the Communists and their fellow travelers Nazism, Hitlerism — any and all forces of Fascism — were the enemies of mankind and must be not only defeated but completely destroyed, and the Communists and all other forces of "democracy" must cooperate in their destruction. Hitler's grave blunder in invading Russia gave the pro-Russians a greater zeal and a clearer objective. "Democratic" Russia must be defended by all the democratic forces and especially by the United States — the world's greatest democracy. The anti-Russian forces also increased their activities. The isolationists still maintained that this was not America's war. Keep out of it and let Europe "stew in its own juice." Others maintained that now was the time to aid the "noble Aryans" in a holy crusade against atheistic and materialistic Bolshevism. In the midst of this rivalry and confusion another Fascist country saved the day for the pro-Russians: Japan's sneak attack on Pearl Harbor, December 7, 1941, put a stop to practically all pro-Fascist activities and the friends of Russia could now talk about the great allies: the U.S.A. and the U.S.S.R.

The Nazis, however, did not cease their propaganda. Their hope was to cause a split in the camp of the Allies. This war was a part of the Bolshevik Revolution. Stalin was the head of the Soviet State and the director of the Comintern and through these agencies, especially the Comintern, he hoped to Bolshevize the world. Comrade Stalin saved his fellow Communists from this propaganda by dissolving the Comintern. At a meeting of the executive committee, held at Moscow on May 15, 1943, that organization which had caused so much controversy voted itself out of existence. There are those who believe that it simply went underground and secretly continued to function. There is strong evidence that the world Communists maintained a secret central organization throughout the war. Be that as it may, officially it ceased to exist as a "democratic centralism" of the "national" Communist parties. Stalin gave four reasons for such a step: it would promote the organization of a common onslaught against Hitlerism; it exposed as a lie the oft-repeated Nazi charge that Russia tried to Bolshevize the world; it exposed as a lie, also, that the Communists within the labor movements in the United Nations were working against the war; it cleared the way to future organization of a companionship of nations based on their equality.[4]

The dissolution of the Comintern was, no doubt, a war measure. The Rome-Berlin-Tokyo Axis, joined by Spain, Hungary and Manchukuo, was an anti-Comintern pact. The Comintern was now dissolved. What about the pact? Was it more than a war measure? Are the gentlemen of the Round Table, referred to above, right in their assumption? "We are all agreed that the dissolution of the Comintern means the formal recognition of what has been the fact for quite a good many years — namely, that Russia is not interested in promoting either Communism or world revolution."[5]

Stalin's followers in America responded enthusiastically to any and all measures which would bring defeat to Hitler and the Nazi

[4] Chicago Round Table (No. 272), *The Death of the Comintern*, June 6, 1943.

[5] *Ibid.*, p. 22.

hordes. In their enthusiasm they almost forgot that America had a war in the Pacific. A united nation became their objective. "We American Communists," declared Browder, "make our first contribution to national unity by explicitly subordinating our most distinctive programmatic demand — the advocacy of Socialism for our country — to the common patriotic goal of victory. We declare that we will not bring forward our Socialist proposal in any way which could undermine or weaken our national unity. We were among the first and most energetic in urging upon the labor movement the most complete cooperation with the government and the employers for the common task of the war."[6] They soon discovered that their political organization was a hindrance to their war efforts. In May, 1944, they held two memorable conventions. The Communist Party of the United States followed the example of the Comintern and voted itself out of existence. Having done this, the Communist leaders called another convention and organized themselves as the Communist Political Association. In this new organization they could function more efficiently, especially in penetrating and controlling other political parties. They did not join any party as a group; individual Communists were at liberty to register under any party. Their duty was to "choose the best candidates from among those put forward by all parties."[7]

Thus was sacrificed on the altar of Mars the Third International, the Communist Party and other Communist organizations. Were these sacrifices made for the defense of Russia or America? For world democracy, they would answer. But actions speak louder than words.

[6] Browder, Earl, *Victory — and After* (New York: International Publishers) © 1942, p. 84.

[7] Browder, Earl, *Teheran* (New York: International Publishers) © 1944, p. 120.

CHAPTER XVII

UNDER TWO FLAGS

THE question of group loyalty has always played an important role in history. The nation-state represents the largest unit in modern society and nationalism the greatest force in contemporary history. Dual citizenship and hyphenated nationalism have been objects of grave suspicion on the part of the "hundred-percenters." Traitors are usually executed even in countries where capital punishment has been abolished. The Quislings, the Lavals, the Lord Haw-Haws and many others bear witness to the fact. Acts of sedition, especially in time of war, are also a serious offense against the nation, usually punished by imprisonment. Some members of the Fourth International (Trotskyites) can bear witness to that fact. "Subversive or un-American activities" are also investigated by the Federal authorities. American Communists have been under strong suspicion of being subversive in their attitude and behavior towards their country. The main reason for this has been their relation to the Third International with headquarters at Moscow. Earl Browder, for many years the Secretary of the American Communist Party, admits that this suspicion is current throughout the country. "Typical questions," he states, "that the Communist Party speakers meet everywhere are the following: Does the Communist Party take orders from Moscow? What is the Third International and how does it work? Is the Communist Party supported by Moscow gold?" [1]

These questions they find everywhere and their typical answer of No to the questions of "orders" and "gold" from Moscow has not been convincing and their explanation of how the Third International works has been evasive, often confusing. How did it

[1] Browder, Earl, *What is Communism?* (New York: The Vanguard Press) © 1936, p. 157.

work? What has been the relation of the American Communist Party to that organization? A brief survey of the party as well as the Comintern will aid us in understanding their relationship.

The Communists usually refer to their organization as "democratic centralism," and this is the nature of their centralism. At the bottom are thousands of nuclei or cells. These nuclei can be organized anywhere, in the factories, on the farms, in offices, schools, churches, even on the streets. They constitute the "atoms" that release the radical energy, and the Communists discovered long ago that they could "split the atoms" and thereby increase the energy. The greater the number of nuclei, the greater the energy when the Bolshevik explosions in the form of revolutions take place. Based on the nuclei are the section committees. These again are organized into districts. The districts elect the delegates to the national convention, which adopts policies, platforms, etc., and elects the central committees which choose their executive secretary. The central committee is the supreme authority of the party. The executive secretary of the central committee usually becomes the general secretary of the party and the presidential candidate for the party in national elections.

This democratic centralism is patterned after the Bolshevik Party of Russia, founded by Nicolai Lenin, the great "apostle of Marxism." The Comintern or Third International was also created by Lenin. "In March of this year, 1919," wrote Lenin, "there took place an International Congress of Communists in Moscow. This congress founded the Third, Communist International, the union of the workers of the whole world striving to establish Soviet power in all countries." [2] This Communist creation represented the essence of world democratic centralism. The nuclei or atoms for this body were the Communist parties of the various nations. These atoms could not be split, as only one party from each country could send delegates to the world congress, held from

[2] Lenin, *The Foundation of the Communist International*, quoted in *Isms*, p. 26.

time to time in Moscow. The delegates to this world congress elected their executive committee with its executive secretary which constituted the supreme authority in world Communism. Lenin became the first executive secretary of the central committee of the Bolshevik Party in Russia, also of the executive committee of the Third International, and Joseph Stalin, the successor of Lenin, fell heir to both.

For years Stalin was the center of democratic centralism. Since the Bolshevik Party controlled the government of Russia, he became the center of power in the Soviet Union without holding any official post in that government. Since he was the center of power in the Comintern he could control the executives of the parties affiliated with that body, and by 1936 there were 72 national parties in the Comintern, according to Mr. Browder.[3] These parties became known as "sections" of the Third International — Comintern for short.

Comrade Stalin has made excellent use of his extraordinary powers. Having gained control of the Comintern, his great ambition was to make the best use of it to promote the interests of Russia. Socialism in one country (the Soviet Union), and the defense of that Socialist country, became the ruling motives of the shrewd dictator. The 72 sections of the Comintern must serve this purpose. In order to achieve this, it was necessary to have a hand in selecting the executive secretaries of these sections. Earl Browder, according to Gitlow, was chosen by Stalin as Secretary of the American Communist Party in 1929, the main reason being that "Browder could be trusted to carry out orders implicitly." [4] Gitlow should know, as he was in Moscow when it happened.

The Communist Party of America, being a bona fide section of the Third International, was duty bound to abide by the constitution of that organization. (Printed as Appendix IV.) Paragraph 16 of that constitution states: "All decisions of the Congress of the

---

[3] Browder, Earl, *What Is Communism?* p. 158.
[4] Gitlow, B., *I Confess*, p. 329.

Communist International as well as the decisions of its executive committee are binding upon all the parties belonging to the Communist International." Paragraph 21 is very specific with regard to those who refuse to obey orders: "Those party members who, on principle, reject the conditions laid down by the Communist International are to be expelled by the party. The same thing applies especially to delegates to the special party conventions." Democratic centralism is a two-way affair. Questions and issues may be discussed in the nuclei, sections, district meetings, national conventions and world congresses, but once a decision is reached by the executive or central committee that ends the discussion. Whatever the supreme authority orders must be implicitly obeyed by those who are subject to that authority. Browder, at an investigation held June 30, 1938, by New York State, admitted that "the Communist Party of the United States is a part and parcel of the Communist International in Moscow — everything we had to pass upon we agreed with." [5]

This ingenuous democratic centralism became a mighty weapon in the hands of Stalin. Through the executive committee of the Russian Communist Party, of which he was the Secretary, he governed the Soviet Union, and being the Executive Secretary of the Third International, he governed the Communist Party of America through the executive committee of that party. In Browder he found a trusty and worthy lieutenant. The Red dictator had a very difficult task to perform. "Socialism in one country — Russia" was not easily achieved. The first Five-Year Plan was a full-speed-ahead signal for the collectivization of the land. Lenin had failed in this task. The peasants, especially the kulaks, the well-to-do farmers, had successfully resisted the government's efforts to deprive them of their property. Socialism in Russia would not be realized unless the land was socialized.

Besides, the kulaks represented a dangerous, counter-revolu-

[5] Sheen, Fulton J., *Liberty, Equality and Fraternity* (New York: The Macmillan Company) © 1938, p. 96.

tionary element which must be liquidated. By 1929 the second revolution, the elimination of the kulaks, was in full swing. "Thousands of Communists and Red Army soldiers were sent down to the villages; the local paupers pointed out the victims. The condemned man and his wife were deprived of everything they had — house, stock, implements and everything else — put into carts in what they stood in, and carried away to concentration camps, to work there as slaves of the government. There were heart-trending scenes. In many places there was the most stubborn joint resistance, culminating even in pitched battles interspersed with isolated assassinations. The government reckoned that there were as many as a million families on the list of the condemned, which in Russia, with an average of two parents and three children, amounted to five million persons. As kulaks they were liquidated; that is, they ceased to exist as such." [6]

Stalin and his Russian staff needed a smoke screen behind which they could carry out their ruthless policy of extermination, and their foreign satellites returned to their respective countries with specific orders to furnish such a screen. Browder and his lieutenants found the conditions in America favorable for their great offensive. The "Hoover depression," which had waited around the corner, was paraded up and down the streets in every city, town and hamlet. Thousands of "Hoovervilles" with their self-constituted Communist mayors and juntas dotted the countryside throughout the nation; hence, the leaders of American Communism found themselves in their native element and they lost no time in launching a great offensive against Hoover and his capitalist regime.

A critical analysis of Browder's keynote speech at the Presidential nominating convention of the Communist Party, held at Chicago, May, 1932, will help us to understand both the aims and the methods of Stalin's devotees in America at this particular period. "The Fight for Bread" was the topic and it was well chosen.

[6] Pares, Sir Bernard, *A History of Russia* (New York: Alfred A. Knopf) © 1944, pp. 142-43.

According to Browder's statistics, there were fifteen million workers without jobs, other millions with only part-time jobs; millions of farmers were being evicted from their farms because they were unable to pay taxes and interest on their mortgages. The country was in a serious crisis and there were only two ways out of it: the capitalist and the Communist ways. The one that the capitalist offered was one of "misery, suffering, starvation, war, death for workers and farmers. It is a way out only for the little parasite class of the capitalists and their servants." [7] The Communist Party, on the other hand, offered a different way out. It organized the workers and farmers "to create a revolutionary government which will confiscate the industries, banks, railroads, etc., from the parasitic capitalists who have proved they do not know how to run them, and to put the industrial machinery to work for the masses of workers and farmers." [8]

Herbert Hoover, the center of capitalism, was also, the head of American imperialism and in that capacity he was "one of the chief organizers of war against the Soviet Union, secretly and openly instigating Japanese imperialism to begin the attack in the East, hoping thus to destroy the Soviet Union, and at the same time weaken American imperialism's strongest rivals. Hoover and company are dragging the American working class into a world slaughter for redivision of the world. . . . We [the Communists] call upon the workers to fight and defeat the war plans of American imperialism, and build a living wall of defense of the workers' fatherland, the Soviet Union." [9]

Organized labor and the "oppressed Negroes" were the most promising fields for revolutionary propaganda. The officialdom of the A.F. of L. was hand in glove with Hoover and his capitalist imperialism. Organized labor was simply an agency of capitalism,

---

[7] Browder, Earl, *Communism in the United States* (New York: International Publishers). p. 96.

[8] *Ibid.*, pp. 94, 95.

[9] *Ibid.*, pp. 97-98.

promoting anti-injunction laws, yellow-dog contracts, imperialist wars, especially against the Soviet Union. The "oppression of the Negro masses in the United States takes on the most bestial forms — Negroes are burned alive in the public squares of our cities, and their bodies mutilated in the most horrible manner by crazed and drunken agents of the landlords and capitalists." [10]

Militant labor and oppressed Negroes gave the nominating convention a tip as to the most effective leadership in the Presidential election in 1932. William Z. Foster, the Presidential candidate, was well known in Moscow. He had many years' experience among organized labor as the head of the Trade Union Educational League, which had been transformed under his leadership to the Trade Union Unity League. He had been prominent enough in labor demonstrations to merit a few months in jail. Furthermore, there was no question as to his loyalty to the Red flag, the Hammer and Sickle. Monsignor Sheen, who has gained a reputation for converting Communists to Catholicism, records a testimony of Foster's before a special committee of the United States House of Representatives:

Q...."The workers of this country look upon the Soviet Union as their country, is that right?"
A..."The more advanced workers do."
Q..."Look upon the Soviet Union as their country?"
A..."Yes."
Q..."They look upon the Soviet flag as their flag?"
A..."The workers of this country have only one flag and that is the Red flag." [11]

Still, Comrade Foster was willing to run for the Presidency under another flag — the Stars and Stripes. What would have happened, had he been elected?

The policy regarding Negroes had already been decided upon

[10] *Ibid.*, p. 97.
[11] Sheen, Fulton J., *Liberty, Equality and Fraternity*, p. 96.

in Moscow at the Sixth World Congress of the Communist International in 1928. These instructions from Moscow included equal rights and national self-determination, "the ultimate objective of which was the establishment of an independent Negro state and government in the South." [12] These instructions from Moscow will explain, at least partially, the great concern for the Negroes. "The Negro question was injected into every situation, in every campaign. The Negroes were looked upon as the chosen people who were to be the vanguard of the Communist revolution." [13]

The social and economic conditions among the Negroes, especially in the South, were believed favorable for such a revolution. The candidate for Vice-President must be a Negro, and that honor fell to James W. Ford. He had several qualifications. He was a Negro, he was loyal to his superior, he had been a soldier in the first World War and he was an all-Southern football champion. Foster and Ford had the brightest prospects, not of winning the election, but of "painting America red" with the genuine Moscow colors. There were millions of young people graduating from secondary and higher institutions of learning with little prospect of finding employment; there were millions of small business men and farmers who had gone through the bankruptcy mills; millions were living on "doles" and the colored people of the "Black Belt" were in a revolutionary mood. It was a perfect setting for the long-delayed proletariat revolution.

Judging by the Communist literature of that period, America was riding on the crest of a world-wide revolutionary wave that threatened to wreck its social and economic order. Judging by what actually happened, this "revolutionary upsurge" had very little effect on workers and farmers. The Communists directed their efforts against other leftist groups and left the capitalists very largely undisturbed. "One of the principal revolutionary activities of the Communist Party was to break up Socialist meetings and

[12] Gitlow, Benjamin, *I Confess* (New York: E. P. Dutton & Co.) © 1940, p. 480.
[13] *Ibid.*, p. 482.

demonstrations. The blood that flowed in the major physical battles of the curious revolution was therefore the blood of comrades." [14] Some of these "physical battles" were rather sanguinary, especially the riot at Madison Square Garden in February, 1934, and the Red Press hailed these riots as a genuine proletariat revolution.

Comrade Stalin was highly pleased with this revolutionary upsurge in America, Asia and Europe. He could tell his fellow Bolsheviks that their ruthless drive against the kulaks and other counter-revolutionaries was a part of the world-wide proletariat revolution. Where Lenin had failed, Stalin was successful and Socialism in one country became a reality; "this was a second revolution, much more vital than the first." [15]

By 1935 the world situation called for a drastic change in the strategy and tactics of the Comintern. The terrific Red offensive brought about as terrific counter-offensives in many countries, especially in Germany. Adolf Hitler, first treated as a joke, soon became the most serious threat, not only to Bolshevism in Germany, but to the Comintern itself. When he became chancellor of the Reich in January, 1933, he made it perfectly clear that there would be no compromise with Communism: "There can be no middle of the course here," he declared. "Either the Red flag of Bolshevism will be hoisted soon or Germany will find herself again." [16] The general election of March, 1933, revealed the relative strength of the two opposing groups. The Communists cast 4,800,000 and the National Socialists, 17,000,000 votes. Backed by a plurality of voters, representing the upper and middle classes, Hitler was convinced that he could help Germany find herself, and this could best be done by liquidating the enemies within the

---

[14] Lyons, Eugene, *The Red Decade* (New York: The Bobbs-Merrill Company) © 1941, p. 79.
[15] Pares, Sir Bernard, *A History of Russia*, p. 505.
[16] Benns, F. L., *Europe Since 1914* (New York: F. S. Crofts & Co.) © 1941, p. 463.

gates, the Social Democrat Communists and the Jews. After the destruction of the Reichstag building in Berlin,[17] the Nazis and their sympathizers became hysterical in their anti-Communist feeling. After that event, Hitler found little opposition when he launched an uncompromising warfare against the Bolsheviks which finally led to an alliance of powers against the Comintern.

Comrade Stalin was not caught napping. The situation again called for a change in strategy and tactics and the strong man of Bolshevism was equal to the task. Russia's security demanded a united front with as many nations as possible, especially with the "have nations." Admissions to the League of Nations was of great importance. To gain the favor of the capitalist democracies was a necessity, but the great Western democracy, the United States of America, had stubbornly refused to recognize the Soviet Government. The first important step in the new strategy was to achieve that recognition. Fortunately for Russia, Franklin D. Roosevelt headed the government of the U.S.A., and his New Deal was a decidedly leftward swing. Japan had started on a rampage in Manchuria, the world situation was favorable for closer fellowship between the U.S.A. and the U.S.S.R. and Stalin took full advantage of that situation.

When Maxim Litvinov arrived in Washington in 1933, he found very little opposition to the establishment of diplomatic relations between the two great powers which were later to become allies in a global war. Among the several conditions for recognition accepted by the Soviet Union was one that caused suspicion and friction between the Communists and the United States Congress: "Not to permit the formation or residence on its territory of any organization or group — and to prevent the activity on its territory of any organization or group, or of representatives or officials of any organization or group which has an aim the overthrow or the preparation for the overthrow of, or the bringing about by force

[17] The Nazis deliberately put fire to the Reichstag as propaganda action against the Communists.

of a change in, poltical or social order of the whole or any part of the United States, its territories or possessions." [18]

Many of the American patriotic societies, chief among which was the American Legion, had a strong conviction that the Soviet Union disregarded this pledge of the American Government. The House of Representatives appointed a committee to investigate un-American activities and after a series of public hearings in December, 1934, at Washington, D.C., this committee reported that "the Communist International, acting upon Russian territory and controlled by the Soviet Union, has, since the giving of Litvinov pledges, directed the Communist Party of the United States and the Young Communist League of America to use every available means to prepare for the forceful overthrow of our government by propaganda and the organization of revolutionary trade unions, leagues, committees, and groups, and for the substitution in its place of a soviet form of government to be affiliated with the Union of Soviet Socialist Republics." [19]

Reports of that nature, given by government agencies, proved a serious threat to Stalin's anti-Fascist policy. The new strategy demanded new tactics in Communist propaganda, especially in the United States. Since the Third International had not held a congress since 1928, the executive committee deemed it expedient to call another congress of that organization where the necessary changes in strategy and tactics would have a world-wide application. Moscow, the capital of Communism, was the logical place and the summer of 1935 the most suitable time for such a convocation. It was a time well chosen as far as Russia was concerned. In February of that year the Soviet Union decided to adopt a new "democratic" constitution and had appointed a commission with Stalin as chairman to draft such a constitution. When the delegates from the Western democracies arrived they found evidences everywhere that Russia was changing. Stalin was fortunate also in

[18] American Legion, *Isms*, p. 5.
[19] *Ibid.*, pp. 61, 63.

having George Dimitrov as his spokesman at this congress. He was the General Secretary of the Comintern, and it was his pleasant duty to convey to his fellow Communists the new global strategy. A United Front Against Fascism was the core of this strategy, and no one in the "democratic centralism" disagreed with their leader.

We are mainly concerned with his instructions to the United States of America. That he was afraid of American Fascism which "tries to portray itself as the custodian of the Constitution and American democracy," goes without saying. What could be done to "prevent Fascism from winning over the wide mass of discontented working people"? The American conditions favored the creation of a mass party of working people, a Workers' and Farmers' Party. Such a party would constitute the People's Front in America. Such a party would be neither Socialist nor Communist, but it had to be anti-Fascist.[20] The Soviet Union is a farmers' and workers' republic, according to its new constitution, and a Farmer-Labor Party in America would run true to the Soviet pattern. Needless to say, the main issues of the Communist Party in the 1936 Presidential election in the United States were: a United Front and a Farmer-Labor Party. The American people were face to face with the greatest crisis since the Civil War. The reactionary forces threatened to bring it under the banner of Fascism and such a threat could best be met by uniting farmers and workers, Communists and Socialists and all other liberal forces in a united front against imperialist Fascism. A Farmer-Labor Party had the approval of Dimitrov, and the Communist nominating convention of 1936 adopted such a party as a strong plank in their platform. "The Communist Party unconditionally supports the building of a Farmer-Labor Party." [21] In the same platform it also pledged itself to work to bring the trade unions and all progressive forces into its ranks.

[20] Dimitrov, George, *The United Front* (New York: International Publishers) © 1938, p. 42.
[21] The Communist Election Platform, 1936.

The Communist strategy could be greatly strengthened, according to Dimitrov, if the leaders of the various parties would link up the present struggle with the people's revolutionary traditions of the past.[22] That suggestion certainly appealed to the American delegates. They discovered that they were the true followers of Jefferson, Lincoln and other great American revolutionary leaders. In a pamphlet containing material by Bowers, Browder and Franklin, *The Heritage of Jefferson*, they stressed the fact that Jefferson was a revolutionist, an iconoclast, a radical, that he had been accused of being a Communist, and had constantly stressed "the national friendship between the American and Russian peoples." With such a glorious revolutionary heritage, the American Communists were the defenders and promoters of Twentieth-century Americanism.

Strategy and tactics usually go hand in hand. In his long speech at the Sixth Congress of the International, Dimitrov suggested ancient and well-tried tactics: "Comrades," he said, "you remember the ancient tale of the capture of Troy. Troy was inacessible to the armies attacking her, thanks to her impregnable walls. And the attacking army, after suffering many sacrifices, was unable to achieve victory until *with the aid of the famous Trojan horse it managed to penetrate to the very heart of the enemy's camp*." [23]

This boring from within has caused much suspicion of and antagonism towards the Communists. American society was a very fertile field for this efficient technique. There were hundreds, if not thousands, of various kinds of organizations. In a democracy, most organizations are usually open to any and all who wish to become members. The Communists took full advantage of this golden opportunity. They wormed their way into unions, clubs, lodges, churches, schools and all kinds of organizations. Boring from within developed into a very efficient technique for spreading bolshevism in democratic America. The American Legion lists

[22] Dimitrov, *The United Front*, p. 78.
[23] *Ibid.*, p. 52.

fifteen of Moscow's Internationals with branches in America and sixteen Moscow agents in the United States.[24] These activities stirred both local and Federal authorities. Committees were appointed to investigate any and all un-American, subversive activities and the Communists received their share of free advertising through these investigations. The Texas Congressman, Martin Dies, and his committee spent millions of dollars to take an inventory of this strange animal, "The Trojan Horse in America," and they found a genuine Moscow stable in the very heart of America. These old "hippos" were found not only in the organization, listed by the Legion, but in practically all the government agencies, including the courts and the Congress. Such publicity helped to popularize Communism; if people in "high places" turned Communist, why should not people in other places do likewise? The leaders of the Communist Party never lost sight of the main objective: to enlist all forces and all people — especially the workers — for the defense of the Soviet Union. "The Seventh Congress of the Communist International put the question squarely before the toilers of the world. It pointed out that it was the revolutionary duty of every class-conscious worker to defend the Soviet Union — its defeat would be a defeat for the peoples of the whole world. It can be no effective fight for peace which does not involve as its task the defense of the Soviet Union." [25]

Loyalty to the Red flag and the Socialist Fatherland was their ruling passion.

[24] American Legion, *Isms*, p. 15.
[25] Browder, Earl, *What Is Communism?* p. 133.

NOTE: Here a note of caution regarding the work of the Dies Committee is necessary. That committee revealed much important and reliable documents and information but this was also accompanied by material that was biased and unreliable. Moreover, its Chairman, Martin Dies, indulged in propaganda of a dubious character without consulting other members of the committee and his methods aroused much protest. For these reasons the reports of the committee must be read with careful scrutiny if one is to sift the chaff from the wheat. The committee's work has been curiously like that of the Lusk Committee of the New York Legislature in the period of the first World War. See Reference 8, Chapter III, for the Lusk Committee.

CHAPTER XVIII

STRATEGIC RETREATS

PROLETARIAT revolution and dictatorship of the proletariat are fundamentals in the Communist dogma. Karl Marx considered revolutions as a method of speeding up the process of class struggle, especially in backward countries. In his famous *Manifesto* to the Communist League in 1848, he makes it clear that here

"The communists disdain to conceal their views and aims. They openly declare that their ends can be attained only by forcible overthrow of all existing social conditions. Let the ruling classes tremble at the communist revolution. The Proletariat have nothing to lose but their chains. They have a world to win. Workingmen of all countries, unite!"

Revolution would hasten the process of the inevitable downfall of the capitalist class, according to Marx. However, it contained the seed of its own destruction, revolution or no revolution. "What the bourgeoisie therefore produces, above all, are its grave-diggers. Its fall and the victory of the proletariat are equally inevitable!" [1] As to the dictatorship of the proletariat, Marx had very little to say. He looked upon it as temporary expediency during the period of transformation. "Between capitalist and communist society lies a period of revolutionary transformation from one to the other. There corresponds also to this a political transition period during which the state can be nothing else but the revolutionary dictatorship of the proletariat." [2] Such a revolutionary state would end, naturally, with the end of the revolution. The same idea was stressed by Marx in a letter to Weydemeyer, quoted in the same

[1] *Theory of the Proletarian Revolution* (New York: International Publishers) © 1936, p. 20.
[2] *The Dictatorship of the Proletariat* (New York: International Publishers © 1936, p. 34.

publication. In this letter he takes no credit for having discovered the existence of classes, nor the class struggle. That had been done by historians before him. What he did that was new was to prove: (1) "That existence of classes is only bound up with historical phases in the development of production; (2) That the class struggle necessarily leads to the dictatorship of the proletariat; (3) That this dictatorship itself only constitutes the transition to abolition of all classes and to a *classless society*." [3]

The Russian followers of Marx, Lenin, Stalin, Trotsky and others, have made great capital of these processes. Through the Bolshevik revolution they established a proletariat state under a rigid dictatorship and this dictatorship is still in power, consequently the revolution is still progressing.

American Communism is a replica of the Russian. Their differences consist in achievements rather than in objectives or technique in achieving the objectives. Since revolution and dictatorship are distasteful to most Americans, the Communist propagandists have used less offensive terms such as "class struggle," "labor government control by the working masses," etc. They call themselves the true followers of Jefferson and Lincoln and other revolu-

NOTE: As stated in Chapter I, Marx and his main followers abandoned the policy of force and dictatorship as trade unions and co-operatives developed and as democracy in general advanced. There were two Marxes: the early Marx who played with insurrection and the later Marx who abandoned it. Lenin and his followers adopted the early Marx, endowed him with the attributes of a seer, and gave his early statements regarding dictatorship the character of finality. It was this blind worship that induced Marx to say, "What is quite certain is that I am not a Marxist." There is also the fact that if Marx considered his early references to dictatorship of tremendous importance he would have expanded them in a book or pamphlet. He never wrote an article regarding it, while the Bolsheviks have devoted a vast literature expounding and expanding it as the core of "Marxist-Leninism." Finally, in a pamphlet, *The Civil War in France*, devoted to the defense of the Paris Commune, Marx pointed to the election results in the besieged city and remarked that here was a dictatorship of the proletariat. However, in this election *not one party but several published their own papers and obtained representation in the city legislative body*. The Paris example is the reverse of what the "Marxist Leninists" ascribe to Marx.

[3] *Ibid.*, p. 44.

tionary Americans. Some writers come out boldly and call a spade by its right name:

"Overthrow of the State power, and with it, of the capitalist system, grows out of the everyday struggles of the workers. One is historically inseparable from the other. . . . It is not necessary that this final blow, i.e., the revolution, should come in connection with an imperialistic war, although this is most likely. Capitalism will seek to prevent a revolution by plunging the country into war. . . . Here is how a general uprising should begin: workers stop work, many seize arms by attacking arsenals. Street fights become frequent. Under the leadership of the communist party the workers organize revolutionary committees to be in command of the uprising. There are battles in the principal cities. Army units begin to join the revolutionary fighters; there is fraternization between the workers and the soldiers, the workers and the marines. The movement among the soldiers and the marines spreads. The police as a rule continue fighting, but they are soon silenced and made to flee by the united revolutionary forces of workers and soldiers. The revolution is victorious." [4]

If the Communist revolution runs true to form, the next revolution in America will follow the pattern set forth in the above quotation.

Strategy and tactics have received careful attention by the Communist revolutionaries. Successful strategy in war often calls for *strategic retreats*. The retreat of the Russian forces during Napoleon's march on Moscow in 1812 led to his defeat. The famous retreat of the Red Army to Stalingrad in the second World War and its victorious counter-offensive is another example of the importance of strategic retreat. Both Lenin and Stalin have stressed the importance of strategic retreats in the struggle against the enemies of Bolshevism. The first strategic retreat was ordered by Lenin in 1921. "When, in the spring of 1921, it appeared that the vanguard of our revolution ran the risk of becoming divorced from the mass of people, from the mass of peasantry, which it was its duty to lead forward intelligently, we unanimously and

[4] Olgin, N.J., *Why Communism?* quoted by the American Legion in *Isms*, p. 50.

resolutely decided to retreat." [5] That retreat took the form of
the New Economic Policy which ushered in state capitalism to
the Soviet Union. A further retreat by Lenin established the state
regulation of trade and he justified all retreats on the ground that it
would enable them to make a "swift, extensive and triumphant
advance." [6] Under Stalin's leadership, Communism has more
strategic retreats than triumphant advances to its credit. The pact
with Nazi Germany, the agreements with the capitalist powers
at Moscow, Teheran, Yalta and Potsdam, the treaty with the
Nationalist Government of China, would all come under this
classification. Will they retreat still further before they launch a
victorious advance?

The American Communists have gone further than the Russians in their retreat. In their enthusiasm for the defense of the
Soviet Union, they not only severed their relation with the Third
International and dissolved their party but they almost made a
complete capitulation to their former enemies, the imperialist
bourgeoisie. Browder's revisionism was one of the most serious
blunders ever committed by the followers of Marx-Lenin-Stalin
and company. What was the nature of this serious error? The
dissolution of the party? Yes! Russia and other countries kept
their parties intact. However, that was not the most serious
offence. Comrade Jaques Duclos, one of the leaders of French
Communism, stated the essence of Browder's sin in an article
which appeared (in translation) in the July issue of *Political
Affairs*. Browder had become too optimistic about the "peaceful
co-existence and collaboration of capitalism and Socialism in the
frame-work of one and the same world. . . . The Teheran agreements mean to Earl Browder that the greatest part of Europe, west
of the Soviet Union, will probably be reconstituted on a bourgeois-
democratic basis and not on *a fascist-capitalist or Soviet basis*." [7]

---

[5] *Strategy and Tactics* (New York: International Publishers), p. 39.
[6] *Ibid.*, p. 61.
[7] *Political Affairs*, July, 1945, p. 655-656.

There were four basic errors in Browder's retreat: (1) It ended the independent political party of the working class in the United States. (2) It was a notorious revision of Marxism. (3) It transformed a diplomatic document (the Teheran accord) into a political platform. (4) It met with disapproval from the Communist parties in many of the Allied countries.[8] This radical departure from the straight and narrow path of Marxian doctrine met with opposition from a number of American Communists, chief among whom was William Z. Foster, former candidate for the Presidency of the United States on the Communist ticket. However, most of the comrades kept silent as long as the Socialist Fatherland was in danger, but once Germany was defeated, the opposition to Browder and his notorious revisionism resulted in speedy and drastic action. On May 7, 1945, Germany surrendered unconditionally, and the following month the National Committee of the Communist Political Association held a plenary meeting at which many of the leaders rehearsed the blunders and confessed their guilt in the revision of the "Marxist-Lenin" principles. The Communist Political Association held a special convention at New York, July 26-28, and voted itself out of existence and reconstituted the Communist Party of the United States of America. The first task of this reconstituted party was to stamp out revisionism. This it can best do by meeting four specific prerequisites of a "Marxist" party. (1) It must function as a vanguard of the working class. (2) It must gain the mastery of "Marxist-Leninist" theory. (3) It must understand the determining factor in all organizational and educational work and adopt the most effective strategy and tactics to help the workers to arrive at a correct understanding of the questions involved.

Special attention must be given to leadership. (4) It must have firm roots in the working class and guarantee that industrial workers comprise the majority of its members.[9] A new addition

---

[8] *Ibid.*, p. 670.
[9] *Political Affairs*, September, 1945, pp. 802-805.

has been made to the party machinery. The newly adopted constitution calls for a Review Commission whose chief duty is "to guard against violation of party principles and to maintain and strengthen discipline." This reconstituted party must steer its course strictly by the "Marxist-Leninist" compass. They are organized for advance rather than retreat, and the question is on what front will they launch their great offensive? Revolution and dictatorship of the proletariat must still be their objective if they are loyal to the oft-repeated "Marxist-Leninist" principle. The trouble is that there are legal restrictions on revolutionary propaganda and activities. They may have to limit their great offensive to the promotion of strikes by the labor unions and violent demands for racial equality among the Negroes. Collective bargaining is guaranteed by law, and the Communists will take full advantage of all opportunities within the law. "Strike while the iron is hot" is their motto, and they are opposed to the cooling off, fact finding and other delay measures proposed by the Truman Administration.

The Communists, however, have never been deterred in their revolutionary efforts by any legal restrictions. They are past masters in underground strategy and tactics. They mastered that technique in Russia during the Czarist regime and they have had golden opportunities to perfect it in the Nazi-occupied countries during the war. Nikolai Lenin was one of the greatest underground organizers and leaders of all time. In his "Proletarian Tactics," he urged his fellow revolutionaries to master all methods of warfare, especially the illegal. "Revolutionaries who are unable to combine illegal forms of struggle with *every* form of legal struggle are *very* poor revolutionaries." [10] Comrade Stalin owes his great success to the mastery of the illegal methods and he has had occasion to use it against the various enemies of Bolshevism. The American Communists would not be true to their great Russian leaders, if they neglect this form of struggle. We have

[10] *Strategy and Tactics*, p. 47.

no reason to believe that they are neglecting it. The Constitution of the Comintern anticipated conditions when entire parties would function illegally. "The Communist Parties must be prepared for transition to illegal conditions. The Executive Committee of the Communist International must render the parties concerned assistance in their preparations for transition to illegal conditions." [11] If it is possible for entire parties to pass from legal to illegal conditions, would not the same transition apply to the Comintern itself? Did it dissolve itself or simply go underground? There are strong evidences that very efficient underground transmission belts have been and are still in operation, and that these operations are directed from Moscow. The Russian Bolshevik Party and Soviet diplomacy are both past masters in the art of running underground transmission belts. Both of these agencies have retained legal status, consequently the Russian Communists have been in an excellent position to "combine illegal struggle with every form of legal struggle" even during the period of the war.

The American Communists are not very numerous but they are well organized for such a combined struggle. Their membership consists of two categories, the enrolled and the concealed, according to the findings of the *American Federation of Teachers*. The second group (secret members) is by far the largest and it will deny vigorously, even to the point of perjury, that it is affiliated with Communism.[12] Then there is still a third group, the fellow travelers, which has been described in another chapter.

The important fact about American Communists is that they are organized for advance rather than retreat. We shall watch their resumed offensive on various fronts. Are they still defending the Soviet fatherland? Stalin and his commissars seem to have reached a state of infallibility. They have never yet committed an error. All forms of imperialism, except the Russian, must be

[11] American Legion, *Isms*, p. 28.
[12] Childs and Counts, *America, Russia and the Communist Party*, par. 7.

stamped out. The American forces must be withdrawn from China, but the Russian forces evidently should remain in Iran. How about an American dictatorship of the proletariat? The American people are not clear as to the meaning of "the proletariat" and they are strongly opposed to all forms of dictatorship. In their recent writings, the Communists have avoided these terms, but they have stressed democratic centralism, the control by the masses, the labor-farmer government, etc. Expressions vary, but the objective remains invariable. Where do they stand today on the issue of revolution? They are still busy distributing revolutionary literature. Every large city has one or more book stores or propaganda centers where revolutionary pamphlets, journals and books are being sold at low prices.

At the Seventh Congress of the Comintern, held at Moscow, 1935, Comrade Dimitrov suggested that the Communists link their struggle with revolutionary traditions. It was very easy for the American Communists to persuade themselves that they represented twentieth-century Americanism and followed in the footsteps of America's great revolutionary heroes. The heritage of Washington, Jefferson and Lincoln, etc., has taken the place of proletariat revolution in recent publications. It even serves as a climax in the preamble of their new constitution: "In the struggle for democracy, peace and social progress, the Communist Party carries forward the democratic traditions of Jefferson, Paine, Lincoln, and Frederick Douglas and the great working class traditions of Sylvis, Debs and Ruthenberg. It fights side by side with all who join in this cause." [13] The order is forward march. The counter-offensive has begun and there will be no retreat or rest until capitalism has been overthrown and "Socialism" established in this fair land of ours. America's historic answer to such an offensive will be dealt with in the last chapter.

[13] *Political Affairs*, September, 1945, p. 834.

CHAPTER XIX

MORE FRONTS AND SPLITS

IN CHAPTER VIII we considered the "united front" maneuvers of Moscow and its party in the United States to the period of 1923-24. We now resume the narrative up to the period when Communist Russia established such a front with the nations at war with Nazi Germany.

The Workmen's Circle

By the end of 1924 Communist members of the Workmen's Circle, a fraternal society organized by Jewish imigrants in the early eighties, split that organization, taking probably a third of the members and organizing them in a rival organization — the International-Workers Order. Like all such factions the issue raised was "correct" orientation towards the Russian dictatorship.

The conflict had raged within the branches of the Circle since the Bolsheviks established their dictatorship in October, 1917. As in the Socialist Party in the period of the invasions of Russia, all who did not accept the numerous decrees of Moscow were placed in the same sack with the Czarist White Guards and as partisans of Kolchak, the leading White Guard general.

The Workmen's Circle had nearly 100,000 members. It provided sickness, accident and death benefits and maintained a sanatorium for aged and invalid members. There was no reason for normal human beings to bring such an issue into the society which imposed no party beliefs on its members. It was thoroughly democratic in administration and made complete periodical reports of its finances and activities to its members.

Since its appearance the I.W.O. has faithfully followed the changing "party line" of Moscow from isolationism, approval of the Hitler-Stalin pact, to support of the "united front" of Russia with Britain, the United States and other nations against Hitler and Mussolini. Included in its publications was a reprint of two speeches by Henry A. Wallace, Vice-President of the United States, in 1942, illustrated by Hugo Gellert, cartoonist for Communist and fellow-traveler organizations, and editions were also published in sixteen other languages.

The Fellow Traveler

The fellow traveler also plays an important role in united fronts. He follows the "party line" but always denies that he is a Communist. There are three types of fellow traveler: (1) one who is secretly a member of the party but always denies it; (2) one who is not a party member but accepts its aims; (3) one who is sentimental about the "great experiment" and willingly explains away the worst features of the Soviet dictatorship in the expectation that it will eventually yield its extraordinary powers to some future democratic pressures.

The fellow traveler of whatever type gives his name to various "innocents' clubs" and "transmission belts," that is, organizations with imposing "liberal" objectives that are founded by the Communist Party to influence public opinion, to penetrate and control non-Communist organizations, to undermine other groups by casting suspicion on their purposes and leaders, to restrict the circulation of books that are critical of Russia, denounce their authors in public meetings and by widespread publicity, thus extending, as nearly as possible, the Russian censorship of American literature relating to Russia and the Communist movement in general.

By these methods the fellow-traveler influence has restricted the circulation of important books. This influence has also penetrated some publishing houses where one fellow traveler may succeed in preventing the publication of a critical work on Russia or Communism. This Moscow-inspired policy is not confined to the United States. It is followed in other countries.

The fellow traveler is also often active in the major political parties and if accused of Communist ideology he points to the fact that he is a good Democrat or Republican. How can a Communist be a member of such a party? he asks. His accuser does not know that the loyal Communist is required by his "principles" to join such organizations and deny that he gets his directives from the Communist Party. Of course the third type, the sentimentalist, is generally unaware of what is going on behind the scenes. He drifts with the general course outlined by those who do know.[1]

Some individuals are induced to follow the fellow-traveler technique without being aware that they are being so used. This occurs when they are persuaded to add their names to the list of sponsors for some public meeting or to organize for some ostensibly laudable purpose. They are told that certain well-known liberals have signed and their signatures are given. Occasionally the real character of the meeting or organization is exposed in the press before it can get under way and the deceived liberals withdraw their names. However, it has often happened that some liberals, busy with other matters, have paid little attention to such exposures and they continue to serve as a flag for purposes outside the range of their real beliefs.

Sometimes these liberals resent the accusation that they are aiding some Communist venture. They want to be "fair," little knowing that fairness is considered a "bourgeois virtue" practiced by simpletons, according to the Communist creed. The result is that students of Communism are sometimes puzzled to classify the fellow traveler. We do not know which of the three types he represents or whether he is an innocent person who has been caught in an organized deception worked out in detail by Moscow in 1924.

[1] See Appendix IV for Moscow's instructions regarding this policy.

The Socialist Party

The Socialist Party, which had been free of Communist influence since the split in 1919, was finally destroyed by Communist infiltration in 1932-1936. This was accomplished by an inept new leadership which ignored what had happened to other organizations.

The first split had its origin primarily in members of immigrant origin; the second was due to American middle and professional class leaders who were intoxicated with the "Russian experiment" — the Five Year Plan and a desire to test "united fronts" with Communist organizations.

The outstanding leader in this policy was Norman Thomas, the party's Presidential candidate in three campaigns. Mr. Thomas also headed the League for Industrial Democracy and sponsored a youth organization, both providing booty for the Communists.

The policy that led to distaster began late in 1929 when new party members organized as "Militants" in New York City. In the next few years this group became a dual organization in the party. It expanded to other states while many members of the L. I. D. joined party branches as allies of the Militants.

The Socialist Party had declined in membership, votes and influence in the post-war period of prosperity. This decline was attributed by the Militants to ineffective leadership of the older generation, the "Old Guard," although the trade unions and various Farmer-Labor parties — except in Minnesota — had also declined. The objective conditions of the period did not favor the growth of economic, political and cultural organizations of the masses and all suffered reverses.

Early in 1932 the Militants published a pamphlet[2] to influence the actions of the party's national convention in May. The document was critical of the Old Guard and revealed the impact of Russia on its authors who declared that they had "every reason in

[2] *A Militant Program for the Socialist Party of America.* New York, 1932.

fact and theory to regard the Russian dictatorship as a necessary instrument for the industrialization of the Soviet Union."

In the same year the dual group decided to remove Morris Hillquit as national chairman. Mr. Hillquit was the outstanding thinker and logician of the American movement. In 1928 he had written that "the Soviet Government has been the greatest disaster and calamity that has ever occurred to the Socialist movement" [3] and this aroused the resentment of the Militants, Mr. Thomas recalling it in the national convention in May, 1932, in opposing Mr. Hillquit's re-election.

Mr. Hillquit was re-elected by a narrow margin but Communist influence continued to grow in the party and in 1934 the Militants issued another pamphlet [4] on the eve of the party's national convention in Detroit. This document was even more favorable to dictatorship. A number of pages were devoted to criticism of European Socialists for not including it in their programs, adding that "a number of comrades believe that it would be bad tactics to stress the idea of dictatorship of the proletariat at the present time. We will not quarrel about words." (p. 16)

But even this cautious approach to the Bolshevik aim was not satisfactory to an impatient section of the Militants. The Detroit convention of the party in May and June, 1934, adopted a new Declaration of Principles [5] by a roll-call vote of 10,822 in favor to 6,512 against, 99 delegates approving and 47 opposing it. However, the Militants did not satisfy a left wing within their group who wanted a clear statement approving dictatorship and armed insurrection. The new declaration favored "replacing the bogus democracy of capitalist parliamentarianism by a genuine workers' democracy." Its authors thought that this language would satisfy all elements except the Old Guard but these elements were rapidly turning to more definite Communist thinking.

[3] *The New Leader*, February 4, 1928.
[4] *Towards a Militant Program for the Socialist Party of America*. New York, May, 1934.
[5] *American Socialist Quarterly*, July, 1934.

Flushed with their victory over the democratic Socialists, the Militants, through their leader, Norman Thomas, issued an invitation to "homeless" radicals to join the party. The Trotsky Communists were admitted while others came in despite protests of the Old Guard. In November the left wing of the Militants published the first number of a quarterly [6] which accepted the complete Bolshevik program. Organized as the Revolutionary Policy Committee, this left wing repeated the history of the left wing in the Socialist Party in 1918. It declared "dictatorship of the proletariat" to be its aim and that "Workers' Councils organized in direct response to a growing revolutionary situation shall constitute the basic unit or organs by which the working class *can carry through an armed insurrection.*"

Meantime the party's youth organization, the Young People's Socialist League, was almost completely Militant and rapidly going Communist. Many young people in Europe and America charged the older generation with responsibility for a ruined world and were attracted to Communist or Fascist totalitarian ideology. They formed the shock troops of Hitler and Mussolini but here no promising Fascist movement appeared and young people turned to Communism. Our American Socialist youth, afflicted with a radical neurosis, short-cut plans for the overthrow of the government. They recommended extra-legal organizations and activities, establishment of workers' councils, preparation for "armed struggle to overthrow the bourgeois state," the establishment of "a proletarian dictatorship," and crushing the resistance of all who opposed the youthful terrorists.[7]

[6] *Revolutionary Socialist Review.* New York, November, 1934.

[7] The above is a brief summary of numerous documents collected in 1934. All are in mimeograph form and our summary gives no adequate idea of the morbid minds of their authors who discuss "tactics" and "maneuvers," methods of defeating armed forces of society, and present naive reasons for armed risings. Only mentally sick youngsters would give their time to such folly and yet the "Militant" party leaders opposed the exclusion of these young people from membership. As the youth organization's members joined the party when they came of age, the party was doomed to the destruction which followed a few years later.

Encouraged by the support the youth leaders received from the national party leaders, the youth organization was soon writing programs and making decisions independently of the party. It also condemned Labor and Socialist parties abroad as fatuous, cowardly and compromising. It presented a long and tedious "proclamation on War and the Ethiopian Crisis" to the party's National Executive Committee in 1935.[8] The international situation was reviewed for the elders who were told that if the democratic and Fascist nations became involved in war, *"the workers of the world would have nothing to gain from the triumph of either side."* No rebuke was administered for this amazing statement.

The National Executive Committee consisted of eleven members, seven of whom, including Norman Thomas, represented the Militants. Chairman Hillquit died in 1933 and Leo Krzycki was selected to succeed him. Following the recognition of Russia by the United States in November of that year, Mr. Krzycki issued a public statement that also revealed the Communist sickness. Approving recognition of Russia, the chairman added that because the Russian electorate "was uneducated and untrained in democratic methods," the dictatorship had to direct its repression not only against the old aristocracy "but against those members of the working class who had not enough vision to understand what they were doing." He added that the world's masses would eventually emulate the Russian example.[9]

Chairman Krzycki was repeating the arguments of conservatives in our state constitutional conventions a century before against the grant of suffrage to male adults. The Communist trend in the Socialist Party had become the political conservatism of

---

[8] Mimeograph document of the Young People's Socialist League, October 11, 1935.

[9] *Labor and Socialist Press Service*, November 24, 1933.

the rising banking, industrial and commercial interests of the early thirties of the last century! [10]

By 1934 the conflict of democratic and totalitarian ideas was sapping the energies and finances of the party, and the state elections in November of that year showed that in five states controlled by the Militants there was a catastrophic decline in the party's vote. In two years Illinois lost 54,000 votes; New Jersey, 33,300; Michigan lost half; California lost over 40,000; and the Militants had failed to get their candidates on the ballot in Ohio. The Old Guard, on the other hand, controlled in New York State and polled the largest vote the party had received since 1920, 126,580. Put to the test, the new Communist ideology was being rejected by the voters.

Norman Thomas admitted the distaster in a confidential letter to a few of his partisans in February, 1935. He declared that the party was becoming moribund, that it was losing to the Communists, and had fallen "a victim of paralysis." He continued: "We are rapidly losing in many parts of the country to (Huey) Long, to Dr. Townsend, to Upton Sinclair, and God knows who else. . . . I find it is a virtual impossibility to raise money from friendly sources because of the general belief that we are dead or dying." [11]

[10] In April, 1945, Mr. Krzycki was following the Communist Party line in speaking for the admission of the Lublin Polish regime at the United Nations Conference, a regime that was imposed on the Poles by the military might of the Soviet Union.

[11] Earl Browder quoted this letter in his report to the Central Committee of the Communist Party in May, 1935. It appears that he had his spies high in the Militant leadership, one of whom sent the letter to him. This may have been Powers Hapgood, a member of the Socialist Party's National Executive Committee, of whom Benjamin Gitlow, in his book, *I Confess*, wrote: "Powers Hapgood was one of the secret and most trusted members" of the Communist Party, and was "bound by its decisions and discipline." Moreover, the Communist press, including the *New Masses*, had for more than a year supported the Militants. Mr. Thomas's letter was an admission that Militant ideology could not withstand the inroads of Communism and the queer movements of the period and yet his faction continued its fatal policies into the next year when the party disintegrated. See the *Daily Worker*, June 8, 1935.

In January, 1936, the Militant National Executive Committee revoked the charter of the New York State organization and expelled the democratic Socialists who had fought to expel Communists who had slipped into the party in that state. The national convention meeting in Cleveland the following May confirmed the decision against New York and with some supporters from other states the democratic Socialists organized the Social Democratic Federation of the United States. However, the Federation was unable to expand its organization as many members were discouraged. The Socialist Party had experienced its second split over Communist ideology, some veterans retired from the struggle to rebuild a democratic Socialist organization, while radical youth was in general obsessed with Communist ideas.

The party of Mr. Thomas soon met the fate that had come to other organizations that collaborated with or admitted Communists to its fold. The Communists had been admitted as individual members, not as organized groups, but they acted as organized bands within the party and at the national convention of the Socialist Party in March, 1937, they were strong enough to control it. They enlarged the National Executive Committee to 15 and issued a manifesto declining to support any war, whether it be "democratic or fascist." It also pledged military support to the Soviet Union. The first was to satisfy the Trotskyists and the second the Stalinists.

Mr. Thomas is an ardent pacifist, opposing our entrance into the war against the Nazi dictatorship which was mastering Europe and this led him to a course that further weakened the Socialist Party. In March, 1941, he spoke at an "America First" mass meeting in New York City where followers of Hitler, Stalin and Father Coughlin demonstrated against our prospective entrance into the war on the side of Britain and cheered the speakers, including Mr. Thomas. Four of his friends on the National Executive Committee of his party resigned. Most of the Jewish branches collapsed or affiliated with the Social Democratic Federation while the German and the Yugoslav sections likewise deserted him.[12]

The decline of the Socialist Party as a result of its adoption of Communists and Communist ideology is evidenced by its continued loss of votes in national elections. It polled a vote in November, 1936, smaller than its vote in 1902 and its campaign fund was the smallest raised in the party's history. In 1944 the Socialist Party vote decreased to less than 75,000. The flirtation with Communism brought destruction to the organized Socialist movement in the United States.

The Militants had adopted two policies that doomed the Socialist Party. Mr. Thomas formulated the theory of an "all-inclusive" organization. That is, it should accept all applicants regardless of their views, including Communists, if they signed a pledge to accept party decisions. This brought all the theoretical conflicts outside the party into the various sub-divisions involving them in a civil war that was destructive to organization morale.

The official encouragement of new and inexperienced members, especially the youth, to oppose the Old Guard was also fatal, as a movement that had become weak needed the advice and support of veterans whose ability had been tested by many years of loyal service. Moreover, the youth were rapidly absorbing the totalitarian ideology of Communism and were becoming a liability rather than an asset.

One of the methods by which Stalin obtained his complete control of the Russian Communist Party was his encouragement of new and inexperienced members to eliminate the old Bolshevik veterans. Of this policy Alexander Barmine, one of the younger generation of Russian Communists who fled to the United States to avoid "liquidation," wrote: "Owing to our weariness of faction-

[12] See John Roy Carlson, *Under Cover*, New York, 1943, pp. 245-50, for an interesting account of the queer subversive elements that formed a united front in support of this and other meetings. Three months later the period of the Hitler-Stalin collaboration ended by the Nazi invasion of Russia and the Communists executed one of their complete reversals of policy. Overnight the "imperialist war" had, for them, become a holy war to be supported by any and all means.

alism and to Stalin's having flooded the party with raw masses of new members, *young and incapable of critical thinking*, they (the Opposition) could never muster more than ten or fifteen thousand among the million party members." [13]

The Farmer-Labor Party

The Farmer-Labor Party of Minnesota has had the usual experience with Communist infiltration of its ranks. It elected Floyd B. Olson as Governor in 1930 and a few years later Trotsky and Stalin Communists waged war to control the FLP. The Dunne brothers, Trotskyites, controlled a powerful A. F. of L. Teamsters Union in Minneapolis and a strike in 1934 gave them considerable prestige. However, Elmer A. Benson succeeded Olson as Governor in 1936 and the Stalinites became influential in FLP circles and also made great headway in C.I.O. unions.

Meantime many individuals, unions and local clubs were withdrawing from the movement and by 1938 the Communist penetration had become so obvious that it became an issue in the state elections of that year, bringing the defeat of Governor Benson, who was believed by many to have a working alliance with the Stalinites, and electing Harold Stassen, Republican, Governor. The Trotskyite leadership was broken during this period by Daniel Tobin, President of the International Teamsters, and in 1941 most of the Trotskyite leaders were convicted of sedition and sentenced to the penetentiary. This gave the Stalinites the opportunity to charge the Trotskyites with being a "fifth column" in the United States.[14] The Stalinites continue to direct the floating wreck of what was once the Farmer-Labor Party of Minnesota.

[13] Alexander Barmine, *One Who Survived* (New York: G. P. Putnam's Sons) © 1945, p. 165.
[14] See George Morris, *The Trotskyite Fifth Column in the Labor Movement*, a pamphlet circulated by the Communist Party. What is interesting about this publication is that it indicts the Trotskyites for maneuvers, practices and policies in trade unions and other organizations which the Communist Party itself followed during the Hitler-Stalin pact and which it again adopted in accord with the new "party line" in 1945!

The C.I.O.

The Congress of Industrial Organizations — C.I.O. — seven unions that seceded from the American Federation of Labor — A. F. of L. — in 1935, has been a source of Communist infiltration. The Trade Union Unity League of the Communist Party had about ten paper organizations affiliated with it after years of trying to seduce real unions to join it. During the period of 1928-1934 Moscow had ordered the organization of rival unions. This policy having failed, in 1935 Moscow permitted the new policy of penetration and the Trade Union League was abandoned in March of that year. The policy of "capture" from without was succeeded by the policy of "capture" from within, so that when the C.I.O. appeared the Communists gradually gave most of their attention to the new federation. The A. F. of L. had resisted all Communist approaches and intrigues and had little of this problem to face.

By 1938 the West Coast Longshoremen, the Cannery Workers, the National Maritime Union, the State, County and Municipal Workers, the American Newspaper Guild, the American Communications Association, the Office and Professional Workers and the Fur Workers were following the "party line" of Moscow. Some other unions were more or less shaken by Stalinist intrigues and disruption. Where Communist control became complete or fairly assured practically every trace of union democracy disappeared. Too often substantial sums were voted to "innocents' clubs" and "transmission belts" of the Communist Party. The members had little or no voice in union affairs. The dissenter was hissed and howled down and in some cases "framed" and expelled. Such unions were patterned after the Russian dictatorship.

John L. Lewis, the leading spirit in the C.I.O. and President of the Miners, is not a Communist but must certainly have known what was going on. His union's constitution barred Communists,

Fascists and Ku Kluxers from membership but the C.I.O. employed Communists as organizers and in other official capacities.[15]

American Federation of Teachers

Seeking power in schools and colleges, the Stalin Communists were successful in obtaining control of the American Federation of Teachers, an affiliate of the American Federation of Labor, in 1937. The Communists and fellow travelers elected a majority of the Executive Board, followed by the secession of non-Communist members in New York, the largest local in the union, who organized the Teachers' Guild. Jerome Davis was elected President of the Federation and during the years that he served in this office, according to George L. Googe, special representative of the A. F. of L., Davis "denied that he was a Communist, denied that the group he served were Communists, contended that he did not know a Communist when he saw one, but he served them in every instance, defended and protected individuals who were known Stalinites and admitted Stalinites, on every issue and roll-call vote."

Googe attended the annual conventions of the Federation and at one of them he had a resolution presented urging a pardon for Fred Beal by the Governor of North Carolina, as Beal, once a Communist, had repudiated Communism. Davis and other party liners, reports Googe, were "smoked out," opposing clemency for Beal. This was the beginning of the end of Communist domination of the union. Davis was defeated for president by George Counts, an able New York educator, and in 1940 the Communists were overwhelmingly defeated in elections for the Executive Board. The Teachers' Guild of New York returned to the union in 1941 after a national referendum adopted by an overwhelming vote a

15 See Benjamin Stolberg, *The Story of the CIO*, for a portrayal of the influence of the Communist Party in American trade unions.

proposal to revoke the charters of the Stalin-controlled unions in New York and Philadelphia.[16]

The Commonwealth Federation

The Commonwealth Federation of the State of Washington, the successor to the Commonwealth Builders organized in 1934 to influence progressive legislation, received what is called the "kiss of death" from the Stalin partisans and was officially disbanded in 1944 when it was apparent that it could not live. It was a federation of liberal, farmer and labor groups whose delegates organized the Federation in 1935. At first the Communist Party maintained a contemptuous attitude towards it but when the "party line" changed late that year party members and fellow travelers organized numerous clubs and societies and obtained representation for these paper organizations. Within about two years the Communist Party was the unseen director of the Federation. Readers will recall that this was the method by which Moscow's agents captured the Farmer Labor Party as related in Chapter IX.

A few men were elected to the Legislature, but when the Communist control became generally obvious the non-Communist members and organizations gradually deserted the Federation. However, the Federation was slow in dying as a few members who were inspired by democratic ideals hoped that in some way the organization would be liberated from control by its uninvited guests. The end came in 1944 when the Federation was officially buried, its last President being Hugh De Lacy, elected to Congress in 1944 as a Democrat and believed by informed former members to be a member of the Communist Party because of the policies he

[16] Our sources for the above are a letter by Mr. Googe to the authors, and American Federation of Labor *Convention Proceedings,* 1937-1941. In the fall of 1945, Mr. Davis, on a lecture tour, presented the thesis that Soviet Russia had been practically right in all of her foreign policies while Britain and the United States had been wrong.

followed. It is reported that the Communists in that state, aside from their activities in unions, are now working in Old Age Pension groups.[17]

International Labor

One of Moscow's biggest prizes in united-front maneuvers after more than two decades to obtain it was realized in Paris in October, 1945, when it succeeded in splitting the International Federation of Trade Unions and, with delegates from 45 countries, founded the World Federation of Trade Unions. Moscow had for years nursed and financed the Red Trade Union International, the Profintern, but it made little headway.

Three events in labor history barred united fronts with labor unions and parties. The fraudulent approach to the world Socialists at the Berlin conference in April, 1922, and the disclosure of secret Communist documents instructing the Communist representatives in a policy later described as "we will take them by the hand now in order that we may take them by the throat later," disillusioned many who thought that the outstretched hand of Moscow might be clean. This was followed by the period in Germany when, under Moscow's instructions, German Communists savagely attacked the Democratic Socialists and trade unions, not only refusing to cooperate with the latter against the rising menace of the Nazis but actually voting with the Nazis on some important measures in the Reichstag and several Diets, especially the Prussian, on the theory that if Hitler came to power he would last only a few months. Hitler was thus helped to achieve his ambition. He liquidated not only the Communist threat of dictatorship but all of the democratic forces of the Republic. When in 1939 Hitler and

[17] Documentary material on this movement is difficult to obtain and the above is based on recollections of William R. Snow of Everett, the Rev. Fred W. Shorter of Seattle, and those of James Oneal, one of the authors of this book.

Stalin signed the infamous pact that freed Hitler's hand to attack Britain and Europe, the Communists became pariahs in all nations except Russia. Attempting to hold street meetings in American cities they were driven from the platform by enraged masses of indignant citizens and in several nations their activities were prohibited by law. Not until after Hitler attacked collaborationist Russia were the Communists able to suggest a united front with the labor movement.

The organization founded in Paris claims to represent 75,000,000 members but this is an exaggeration. It probably represents a little over 50,000,000 of which about 27,000,000 are members of Russian "unions" that have no more power or independence than Hitler's Labor Front had in Germany. In both regimes wageworkers were and in Russia still are organs of a dictatorship and controlled by the ruling party. No strikes have occurred under either regime. The Russian delegates to the Paris congress represented the dictatorship, not free trade unions. They were faithful Communists and as such carried out the Moscow party line.

Moreover, quite a number of the organizations represented at Paris were of the usual paper variety and factions from several nations. There is practically no trade union movement in Egypt, Syria, Lebanon, Iraq, Iran, Arabia, Cyprus, and yet these countries were represented. That most of their delegates were agents of Moscow is certain and the same is true of the representatives of Communist-controlled Poland, Czechoslovakia, Rumania, Bulgaria and Yugoslavia. Through paper and Communist-dominated organizations Moscow has obtained an international which will largely be a representative of its Foreign Office.

One regret is that the democratic trade union movement of Great Britain was persuaded to aid in this enterprise but it is likely that it will be disappointed as the party line unfolds in the next year or two.

The American C.I.O. was also represented. It split the American labor movement and it has aided in splitting international labor.

Afflicted with Communist and fellow travelers, the course taken by the C.I.O. was to be expected.

The American Federation of Labor, having a consistent anti-Communist policy since the Communist counter-revolution in Russia in 1917, refused to send delegates. It not only objects to the servile Russian organizations, but it contends that acceptance of dual organizations and factions in any international is to invite strife and make unity impossible. The Communist International itself admitted only one organization from each country and has expelled dual groups and factions wherever they have appeared; but Moscow can use dual organizations in the Paris international, fostering conflicts among those not won to the party line and slowly eliminating those that fail to carry out directives intended to support Soviet foreign policies.

William Green, President of the American Federation of Labor, in opposing the Paris Congress, points out the inevitable consequences that face genuine unions that affiliate with it. He wrote:

"The first result of closer collaboration with the Soviet trade unions would be that the world body of organized labor would lose its freedom to criticise the Soviet Union and the Communist dictatorship. While opposition to and criticism of the so-called 'capitalistic' countries and governments would meet with the approval of the Soviet delegates, every word of disapproval or the slightest criticism of the policy or the methods of the Russian dictatorship would be vetoed by the delegates of the Soviet trade unions. Thus the world labor federation would practically be transformed, in the political field, into a 'yes-organization' of the Soviet government; and consequently of world Communism." [18]

That this is the price non-Communist organizations and members will pay for accepting this latest united front of Moscow is certain. Moreover, it begins with a split of labor into rival factions, the inevitable result that has followed all invitations of collaboration with Communists here and abroad.

[18] William Green, *The AFL and World Labor Unity*. *International Postwar Problems*. (Quarterly) July, 1945.

The American Labor Party

One of the most tragic and unnecessary disasters reaped by democratic elements in labor movement as a result of a united front with Communists came to the American Labor Party in New York State. Unnecessary because these elements had a decade of experience in deceit and devastating civil war with Communists which in several instances almost wrecked powerful unions and lowered the union standards of the members when Communists were successful in their drive for power.

The ALP was organized in 1936, primarily by unions in the men's and women's garment industry, other less influential unions, and the Social Democratic Federation, the democratic Socialist group which had been expelled from the Socialist Party because of its dissent from the policy of admitting Communists to that party. David Dubinsky, President of the International Ladies Garment Workers, and Sidney Hillman, President of the Amalgamated Clothing Workers, were the leading union chiefs sponsoring the ALP with the view of preserving the labor gains of the New Deal.

An agreement was reached with the SDF to exclude Communists who sought affiliation through trade unions, through other groups controlled by Communists, and individual Communists who applied for membership in local clubs under their own or other names. In the same year John L. Lewis, C.I.O. chief, appointed Hillman treasurer of Labor's Non-Partisan League which later became the C.I.O. Political Action Committee with Hillman as its chairman. The PAC also provided a home for the activities of many Communists.

ALP clubs were established throughout the state but the members were denied a voice in formulating policies, platforms and choosing candidates. All power was exercised by the state committee and the county committees, and within a few months the leaders quietly opened the door to Communists, admitting a few to the governing committees and nominating Michael Quill, head of the Transport Workers' Union and a follower of the Communist party line, as a candidate for City Councilman. He was elected.

Social Democrats who objected to this violation of the agreement by which they agreed to affiliate with the ALP were reprimanded by the top trade union leaders. Trade union members who objected to the secret united front with Communists were also reprimanded. Meantime the Communist Party through its agents slowly obtained increasing control of the new party while its members and fellow travelers enrolled in the primaries to capture it. Accused by Louis Waldman, Social Democrat and a founder of the party, of knowingly tolerating the Communists, the State Executive Committee publicly declared, in 1939, that "from the day of its inception the American Labor Party barred Communists from membership" and that it did not know of any ALP member "who is affiliated with the Communist Party."

However, in August of that year the Hitler-Stalin pact was signed and the Communist Party changed its policy in accord with Russia's interests, approving the Nazi-Communist alliance and declaring President Roosevelt an "imperialist warmonger." The top trade union leaders of the ALP suddenly discovered that there were Communist members in the party, following a public denunciation of the German-Russian united front.

Sidney Hillman and his union left the ALP in 1942, thus weakening the opposition to the Communists. But they returned to it in 1944 and formed a united front with the Communists although the latter had captured the legal party machinery in New York and Queens counties in 1937. In the year that the Hillman union returned to the ALP the Communists captured the legal state committee by an overwhelming majority.

The trade union leaders who had denied the Communist danger seceded, organized as the Liberal Party, and publicly announced that the ALP "is now the Communist-Labor Party." The Communist Party had accomplished its purpose — a split and capture of another organization. The defeat of the trade union leaders was further emphasized in the city election in 1945 when the Liberal Party lost about 130,000 votes compared with the ALP vote of the previous year.[19]

The Second World War Front

The most extensive united front realized by Communism was not due to seduction by Moscow and its fifth columns but to military necessity, the need of Great Britain and the United States to choose between two totalitarian regimes which had collaborated for nearly two years in war and then quarreled, one attacking the other. Britain and the United States chose to support Russia as the lesser of two evils. The net result is that without consulting her allies Russia became master of the bread basket of Europe and of millions of people in Esthonia, Latvia, Lithuania, Poland, Bulgaria, Yugoslavia and Rumania, completely absorbing the first three, transforming the remaining four into vassals under the dictatorship of Communist quislings, and adding 170,678 square miles of territory in Europe and Asia to the Bolshevik empire by December, 1945. In this booty must be included the pillage of industries, livestock, railroad equipment and other economic assets of the "liberated" nations, some of it being first seized by the Nazis in Belgium, Holland, France and Luxembourg and shipping the plunder to Russia. Hundreds of thousands of workmen and peasants were also deported to Russia as slave laborers while Moscow "negotiated" economic agreements with Finland and Hungary and with its quising dictators in other "liberated" countries which, if permanent, make these nations economic serfs of the Russian dictatorship. Raucous in pretense for liberation of colonial peoples, Moscow reduced much of Eastern Europe to a status of helpless subjugation that makes the condition of today's colonial peoples appear to be a honeymoon of happiness by comparison. Facing the measureless

[19] See Louis Waldman, *Labor Lawyer*, especially the chapter titled "The American Labor Party," with its excerpts from important documents, the whole revealing the folly of men who insisted on following a course which a decade before had reaped the same result in their unions.

daring and exactions of Stalin and his associates, Britain and the United States yielded again and again in the hope of appeasing the Red imperialism only to find themselves dangerously near being accomplices in a gigantic Munich that makes the Hitler-Chamberlain Munich look like a venture in philanthropy. How account for all this?

One does not have to turn to critics of the pseudo-philosophy of Communism for an answer. All that is necessary is to consider what Lenin, Trotsky, Stalin and other leaders have said of themselves and their aims. They have been as frank as Hitler was in his *Mein Kampf* and their course in bad faith, intrigue, unilateral action, repudiated treaties and broken pledges, is the logical result of their published views of history, of labor, of democracy, of dictatorship, of revolution, of terror, and their contempt for non-Communist nations and individuals who trust them. In methodology the Communist movement does not differ at all from the methodology of the Nazis and had puzzled statesmen, editors and radio news commentators consulted the basic literature of Communism as they have Hitler's *Mein Kampf* they would not have been perplexed by the course the Russian dictatorship has taken in the war and the post-war period.[20]

The eminent journalist, Dorothy Thompson, in her column of November 21, 1945, presented a caustic rebuke to those who have failed to go back to reliable Communist sources to understand Russia's course. "We say Russia is an 'enigma wrapped in a mystery' because the men who direct our affairs of state are politically illiterate," she wrote, and added: "They are constantly being surprised by events that any person really familiar with revolutionary movements could clearly foresee. They do not listen to the men in the State Department who have historical sense; they listen, instead, to self-appointed ignoramuses, who are sometimes innocent dupes of others not innocent."

[20] See the next chapter, Summation, for a brief consideration of Communist views of the world and Communist methodology.

A harsh judgment, to be sure, but much has happened to provoke such bitter criticism.

Two outstanding facts regarding the global war are that *Stalin and Molotov freed Hitler's hands to attack Europe and also freed Tojo's hands to attack the Dutch Indies, the Philippines and Pearl Harbor.* Moreover, the evidence indicates that they knew what they were doing.

While British and French representatives of their respective military staffs were consulting with the Russians in Moscow, to stop Hitler's measureless aims in Europe, the Russians were also secretly negotiating with the Nazis for a plan of mutual collaboration. Consternation swept through the democratic nations when the Nazi-Soviet Pact was signed on August 23, 1939. Stalin and Molotov had deliberately chosen the Nazi dictatorship as a non-aggression partner! Articles II and IV especially bound the two powers in an iron-clad defensive alliance, each pledging the other that it would not "associate itself with any other grouping of powers which directly or indirectly is aimed at the other party." Had Hitler kept the bargain Stalin would have been his aid in attacking not only Europe and Britain, but North, Central and South America.

The Berlin correspondent of the *New York Times*, considering this pact, wrote that "a German and a Russian who had played important roles in the negotiations sank into each other's arms with the Russian exclaiming, 'At last we have found each other.' " [21]

The sinister agreement was signed August 23, 1939, and on September 1 the Nazi armies attacked Poland.

Nearly two years later Soviet Russia repeated this sordid performance when the Soviet-Japanese Neutrality Pact was signed in Moscow on April 13, 1941. *Pravda*, official organ of the Communist Party declared that Britain and the United States feared a Japan free to act in the Pacific and that the pact was a bewildering blow at these two nations. *Pravda* cynically added that Washington

[21] *New York Times*, August 27, 1939.

had sought friendly relations with Russia only with the hope *"that strained Soviet-Japanese relations would deter Japan from attacking Britain's South Pacific naval base at Singapore and the Netherlands Indies."* [22]

The Soviet-Japanese Pact did free Japan to attack not only Singapore and the Dutch Indies but also the Philippines and Pearl Harbor the following December! Thus "freedom-loving" Stalin freed one dictatorship in Europe and one in Asia to begin the most frightful war of all times. At the end of the war Russia was most vehement in demanding stern punishment of all collaborationists who served Hitler's and Tojo's aims!

Fifteen days after the Nazis attacked Poland, Russia declared all Soviet-Polish treaties cancelled, that the Polish state no longer existed, sent troops into Poland, the Polish cabinet fled to Rumania, and Russia notified Britain and the United States that she was still neutral in the German-Polish war! On September 24, Hitler's troops delivered Brest Litovsk to Russia, followed by a joint parade of rejoicing Nazi and Russian armies. Four days later "disintegration of the Polish State" was the text of a statement by Molotov and Ribbentrop as they divided prostrate Poland between Germany and Russia. The statement also warned that if British-French negotiations with Hitler failed, Russia and Germany "will consult with each other on the necessary measures." On October 2, Secretary of State Hull announced continued recognition of Poland which was the victim of force. On October 31, Molotov charged Britain and France with "fomenting war with Germany" which established "the imperialist character of this war," adding that *Poland would never be restored.*

Dripping with the booty of the Polish war, on November 28, Molotov informed Finland that the Non-Aggression Pact of 1932 was cancelled, severed relations with Finland the next day and on November 30 invaded that nation. On December 1, Soviet troops

---

[22] A.P. Moscow news story in the *New York Times*, April 20, 1941.

set the fashion which Hitler followed by establishing a "People's Government" with a Finnish quisling, Otto Kuusinen, as Chairman and Minister of Foreign Affairs. Kuusinen, a Communist and active in the Comintern, had resided in Moscow for years. A mutual assistance pact was signed by Molotov and this puppet. Finland appealed to the League of Nations to brand Russia an aggressor and Molotov wired that the Soviet "maintains peaceful relations with the democratic Republic of Finland," that is, the Kuusinen regime. On December 14, Russia was expelled from the League.

Here was the pattern followed by Hitler in conquered nations and continued by Stalin in the countries "liberated" by Soviet armies later when Russia was driven (she had no choice) to fight with the coalition against the Nazi power.

These events shocked the peoples of the democracies and the American press, except the Communist and Nazi publications — the German-American Bund, like the Communist Party, was then following the Moscow-Berlin party line — vigorously condemned the Soviet dictator, one cartoonist portraying Stalin as the red vulture swooping down on the prostrate body of a young woman. Addressing an American Youth Congress on the White House lawn, President Roosevelt declared that "the whole world is shocked, horrified and amazed at this attack on Finland," and added: "The Soviet Union, *a dictatorship as absolute as any other dictatorship in the world*, has invaded a neighbor so infinitesimally small that it could do no conceivable possible harm to the Soviet Union. . . ."[23]

After heroic resistance Finland finally capitulated on March 12, 1940, and Stalin imposed a harsh peace. In June, 1941, the two dictators, Hitler and Stalin, ended their collaboration and the Nazis

[23] *New York Times*, February 12, 1940. Some boos and hisses greeted this statement of the President. It is interesting to note the evolution of Stalin in the American press and through radio news commentators who transformed him from the Russian dictator and Red Vulture to Premier Stalin and eventually Uncle Joe!

made war on Russia but in this same month Russia again attacked Finland and the latter defended herself which prompted Moscow to charge that Finland was allied with Germany. *At no time was a defensive or any other kind of alliance contracted by Finland with Hitler!* Our State Department issued a statement to the press on December 18, 1941, stating that on June 22, 1941, "Germany invades the Soviet Union; *the latter raids Finland.*" [24]

Following Stalin's acceptance of collaboration with Britain and France, later with the United States, after Hitler attacked Russia, clever propaganda by Moscow and its "transmission belts" here, gave the impression that Finland was an ally of Nazi Germany. A crushing armistice was imposed on the beaten nation in September, 1944, with the view of making it a helpless economic vassal. Russia had "protected" herself against the "menace" of this tiny nation!

The fate of the Baltic republics — Latvia, Esthonia and Lithuania — was also sealed by the Russian dictatorship in June, 1940, while Hitler and Stalin were collaborators. They were swallowed up, followed by deportations to the Russian interior and the subjection of their populations to the dreaded NKVD, the ruthless Russian secret police. When Hitler broke with Stalin in June, 1941, the Nazis wrested these republics from Russia and Russia later reconquered them. Two united fronts, one with Nazis and one with the Allies by Russia, made no difference in the fate of the Baltic peoples.

The limitations of this work do not permit a thorough presentation of the fruits of Russia's united front with the Allies but a few of its sordid aspects may be mentioned. The martyrdom of Poland, the most notable of Russia's victims and an ally of the anti-Nazi coalition, is familiar to all. Her fate is all the more shocking because Poland was the first nation to fight to the bitter end against the German hordes. Moscow's propaganda against Poland took the

---

24 *New York Times*, June 23, 1941. See two pamphlets, *Are the Lights Going Out in Finland?* and *Is Finland Worth Saving?* Save Finland Committee, Duluth, Minn.

course of denouncing its government as one of landlords and reactionaries. This was largely true of the government that fled to
Rumania but the Government in Exile, at first in France and then
later in London, was an entirely different government. It represented all the democratic organizations of the old Poland and yet
Moscow continued to accuse the new government of being controlled by landlords and reactionaries. Many people in the democratic nations were deceived by this falsehood. Moscow set up its
puppet Lublin regime, and Britain and the United States eventually acquiesced in this unilateral act of usurpation. Polish democracy was crushed, the Government in Exile faded out, and Poland
became a satrapy of Russian imperialism. [25]

Bulgaria, Rumania and Yugoslavia were also required to march
in the lockstep of Bolshevik imperialism. In Eastern Europe an iron
curtain descended barring it to the scrutiny of press correspondents
of Britain and the United States and in two instances American
military officers were expelled from Bulgaria. Moreover, the
Premier of this Soviet-dominated country, Kimon Gheorgieff, and
the Minister of War, Damien Veltcheff, were leaders of the Pan-
Slavist, Fascist *Zveno* Party! Following the "liberation" of Bulgaria by the Red Army, the Fascist-Communist Government
headed by these two men arrested the veteran democrat, Nikola
Mushanoff and other pro-Allied men and women as "war
criminals."

The "liberation" of Rumania by the Red Army was followed by

[25] One of the most clever of the Communist transmission belts in the United
States is the National Council of American-Soviet Friendship which published a
pamphlet titled *The Case of the 16 Poles*, i.e., sixteen Polish patriots who were
arrested by Soviet authorities after being promised immunity. They were tried
with the usual "confessions" featuring the case as in others in Russia. And yet this
pamphlet is really a vindication of Polish democracy for it shows that all that
these Poles and tens of thousands of others did was to oppose totalitarian Russia
as vigorously as they did totalitarian Germany, that their only "crime" was to
fight on their own soil for the liberation of their country from their latest
despoilers! The authors of the pamphlet were apparently too dull to understand
that the evidence they cite places them and Russia in the dock as the accused,
not as the accusers.

a similar experience, except that the Moscow Foreign Office directly staged a *coup d'état* by sending Andrei Vishinsky, Soviet Assistant Commissar, identified with Moscow blood purges, to Bucharest by plane where he ordered King Michael to dismiss the pro-Allied government headed by General Nicola Radescu. With a million Russian solders in Rumania the King complied. A nonentity, Petru Groza, was installed as Premier, and George Tatarescu, head of King Carol's former pro-Nazi dictatorship, became a member of this government! The Ministries of Justice, Transportation and Propaganda were placed in the hands of Communists. The Ministry of Propaganda is reminiscent of the same office set up in Nazi Germany and administered by the late Joseph Goebbels.

Yugoslavia differs little from Moscow's other satrapies. During the period of the Stalin-Hitler collaboration, Tito refused to fight the Nazis while General Draja Mihailovich, Chetnik leader, who fought the Nazis with arms was denounced by Moscow as a traitor and Axis collaborator! In fact, *every Communist who holds public power of any type in Russia's puppet regimes in Europe collaborated with the Nazis and defended the Hitler-Stalin pact.* Many of them are not even citizens of the nations they help to hold in servitude. They are citizens of Russia.

Tito has also rewarded Fascists. His ambassador to London is the notorious Dr. Luba Leontitch, a Croat lawyer and founder of the Yugoslav Fascist organization known as "Orjuna." Of this worthy and his Fascist group, London *Time and Tide*, June 23, 1945, declared: "Leontitch assumed the title of 'Veliki Chalnik! (Grand Fuehrer). The organization, founded after Mussolini's march on Rome, was a copy of the Italian Fascist original — it even adopted the black shirt as its uniform. It was used to break up meetings and strikes, and had a special body of storm troopers, who perpetrated deeds of violence."

Iran is another case of broken faith with the Allies, and the Soviet policy towards that nation is remarkably like Hitler's towards Czechoslovakia. Hitler's threats and support of Nazi fol-

lowers in the province of Sudeten was followed almost in detail by
Soviet Russia in aiding a separatist rising in the province of
Azerbaijan and prohibiting the Iran Government from suppressing
this conspiracy against its sovereignty.[26]

Azerbaijan became a provincial vassal to the Soviet dictatorship
and the Moscow radio, on the eve of the meeting of the foreign
ministers of Britain, the United States and Russia in the Russian
capital, declared "unsatisfactory" a note from Turkey answering
a Russian protest against anti-Russian demonstrations in Istanbul.

As this is written (December, 1945) the situation in China is still
too confused to warrant more than a casual consideration but one
thing may be said of those who contend that the Chinese Communists are independent of Russia. Mao Tse-tung, leader of this movement, was a member of the Presidium of the Communist International for years and no man can enter that holy of holies of Bolshevism unless his organization is a faithful affiliate of it.[27]

Other high personages in the dictatorship over five provinces are
Communists trained in the Moscow school while the Moscow press
and radio, at a period when Chunking was fighting the Japanese,
openly accused Chiang Kai-shek and his aides of conduct little
short of treachery. Typical of this arrant breach of faith with an
ally of Britain and the United States was the attack by *Izvestia*,
the official Soviet Government organ, on December 2, 1944.

Here was an armed secession against the Central Government
similar to the secession in 1861 that brought on a civil war in the
United States. And while these secessionists shouted loudly for
"unity" their very existence made unity impossible, especially
when they had the support of the Russian dictatorship which has

[26] Readers may well compare the news accounts of the Soviets in Iran in
November and December, 1945, with the vivid story of Hitler's collaboration
with Sudeten Nazis, which brought the whole of Czechoslovakia under the Nazi
yoke, as told by G.E.R. Gedye in his remarkable book, *Betrayal in Central Europe*.

[27] See special supplement to *The New Leader*, May 26, 1945, which presents
an informing survey of the plight of China because of the armed secession of the
Communists, Moscow's role in that unhappy country over many years and the
war with Japan.

made armed insurrection against governments a matter of Communist policy.[28]

In Burma, Indo-China and Korea, Moscow's fifth columns, following the collapse of Japan, were also active in various phases of the united front. Occupation of northern Korea, for many decades a victim of Japanese brutality, was the signal for the descent of the iron curtain of secrecy and censorship by Russia, the barring of Allied correspondents from the area, and the systematic dismantling of factory and mining equipment and shipping it to Russia. Had Korea been an ally of Japan she could not have been more unfairly treated than she was by her "liberators." [29]

The story of the united front throughout its history through trade unions, cooperatives, sports organizations, Labor and Socialist parties and their internationals, to the war alliance with Russia by the democracies, is a tale of broken promises, intrigues, bad

[28] In November and December, 1945, the Communist front in the United States rose in defense of Russia's policy in China. All sectors of the front revealed their loyalty to the "fatherland." While members of the party picketed the White House demanding return of our soldiers from China the party held meetings in New York and protested American "armed intervention in China's internal affairs." Upon his return from Moscow, James Curran, head of the National Maritime Union, called for a 24-hour strike against alleged slowness in returning American soldiers from overseas while Harry Bridges, head of the Longshoremen's Union, joined Curran in calling a similar strike. Both have been faithful followers of the "party line." Even more interesting, Congressman Hugh De Lacy of Washington and five other pro-Russian members of the House made a vicious attack on Chiang's government in terms that recall *Izvestia's* tirade against Chiang and his administration. Curran's return from Moscow and the mobilization of all fronts against the Chinese Government are reminiscent of the visit of Jacques Duclos, French Communist, to Moscow. He wrote an article critical of the American Communist Party which was followed by the removal of Earl Browder from leadership and a return to the old policy of the party. These incidents convincingly show that all these fronts owe allegiance to the Russian dictatorship, not to the American people, their government and democratic institutions.

[29] See dispatches by Richard J. H. Johnston from Seoul, Korea, in the *New York Times*, particularly the issues of October 25 and November 30, 1945. A. T. Steele, correspondent of the *New York Herald Tribune*, also gave attention to revolts fostered by fifth columns in Southeastern Asia — French Indo-China, New Guinea, Malaya and Burma. In Burma the Communist organization's flag "is patterned after that of Marshal Josip Broz's (Tito's) party in Yugoslavia." See especially Steele's story from New Delhi, India, of December 3, 1945.

faith, secrecy and unilateral action, despite agreements and understandings. Following the end of the war the rift between Russia and the democracies developed steadily from the time that Foreign Commissar Molotov appeared at the United Nations Conference in San Francisco. By the end of the year 1945 it had become a war of nerves. The press, radio news commentators, members of Congress and diplomats were puzzled to account for Russia's conduct. Explanations were offered that did not explain.

Meantime, the Communist Party organizations, their "transmission belts" and fellow travelers in all of the democratic nations faithfully approved each tortuous turn of the "party line," echoed each defense of Russian aggression and broken pledges in Europe and Asia, no matter how absurd, how false, and how much they were in conflict with the glaring facts.

Had perplexed outsiders considered the history of Bolshevism they would not have been puzzled over this phenomenon. We may now turn to a consideration of this history.

NOTE: The sources consulted for this final section of the united front, in addition to those previously cited, are many. The reader will find the sections on Foreign Affairs and War Chronology in the *World Almanac* for each year invaluable for a brief digest of the most important events. The *New York Times Index* is also helpful in directing the reader to daily sources. Two excellent publications are *Russian Affairs* (monthly) New York, which merged with *The New Leader* late in 1945, and *International Postwar Problems* (quarterly) New York. The *New Leader*, of the same city, has also carried much valuable information, its special monthly supplements being invaluable, its issue on *The Balkans, Battleground of Two Worlds*, being an admirable tabloid history of that region "liberated" by Russia. *The Saturday Evening Post* has carried several notable articles including the following: "The Soviet's Iron Fist in Rumania," by Leigh White, June 23, 1945; "Our Communists Are So Sorry They Were Good Boys," by Stanley High, December 1, 1945; "Russia Still Suspects Us," a surprising contribution by Edgar Snow, generally pro-Russian, November 17, 1945, as he presents the Russian masses almost as inmates of a prison and screened from the rest of the world by censorship. *Red Book*, August, 1945, presented the frankest fellow-traveler article by Vincent Sheean, whose ostensible theme is how we should deal with Germany. He is very candid in saying that "we must undertake to study and understand what Russia wants with regard to Germany, and we must adjust our conceptions, accommodate and integrate them, with the Russian conceptions." Evidently, Britain and the United States were in the war solely to assure Russia everything she desires in Germany! Finally, the periodical publications of the Communist Party reveal no departure from loyalty to Russia before, during and after the war.

CHAPTER XX

SUMMATION

CONSIDERING the incredible history of the Communist movement here and abroad and the fact that democratic organizations have never been able to act in concert with that movement without being fatally divided or destroyed, the reader will naturally ask, is such cooperation possible within the United Nations Organization? Naturally, we cannot answer as the answer will unfold in the coming months or years. However, it is obvious that the peoples of the democratic nations are apprehensive of the future, as unilateral action, "strategic maneuvers" and direction of fifth columns abroad by any power are as dangerous to world peace and stability as the use of the atomic bomb by one power or a few powers.

Several theories have been offered to explain Russian conduct in international affairs. It has been said that Moscow has been arrogant because of Bolshevik immaturity in foreign affairs, or that Russia is partly Oriental and not appreciative of Occidental ways, or that her actions are due to poor translations of agreements with the Allies. We doubt whether any one or all of these theories throw much light on the problem, especially when the theorists ignore certain aspects of Bolshevism which are evident from its history, its theory and practices.

In the first place, Bolshevism contends that it has found the final answer to the social and economic problems of our time, that Marx, then Lenin and, finally, Stalin are the sole custodians of this solution. Any person that holds to any other view, the Communists contend, is either a simpleton, a "betrayer" of the masses, or a scoundrel who deserves to be liquidated. Therefore, the united front with such persons or organizations they represent is not for the purpose of cooperation but to destroy leaders and their organizations and to absorb the remnants that can be assimilated.

All this is outlined in thousands of Communist periodicals, resolutions, books, pamphlets and leaflets. It is the core of Communist pseudo-science. The Communist Party in each nation is not a political party. It is an agency of the Russian dictatorship pledged to carry out the aims and policies of Moscow in the expectation that eventually a Communist dictatorship will be established in each nation and the "world revolution" become a reality. The Communist in France, in China, in the United States and in all other countries does not regard the nation in which he lives as his. Russia is his "fatherland" and Communist literature in all countries refers to Russia as the "fatherland," or the "worker's fatherland," or the "socialist fatherland." It is not a matter of Russia first and his own nation second; it is Russia *only*. There is no second choice unless the servitude he plans is extended to the nation where he lives and even then Russia is the mother country with the responsibility of guiding or punishing its new offspring. Need it surprise one, therefore, that the children dutifully respond to the commands of the parent no matter how ridiculous such a response may be?

The most striking example of the policy of the parent inducing recantations and reversing policies considered sacred occurred in 1941 when the Nazis invaded Russia. Four years before, General Tukhachevsky and seven other generals were shot in a bloody general purge of the army by Stalin on the ground that they were seeking collaboration with Hitler. Now Stalin made an open pact of collaboration with the German dictator. Communists in the United States and other countries were horrified that "fascist mad dogs" had been found in high army circles in Russia in 1937, but when Stalin and Molotov did what the executed generals were accused of trying to do the party liners supported Nazi-Communist collaboration! The "fatherland" must be supported no matter what degree of human abasement such support requires.

Russell B. Porter surveyed the turnabout of the American Communists in the *New York Times* as revealed by contradictory decisions of the Communist Party and its "transmission belts" before and after the Hitler-Stalin pact was signed. In addition to the party, the Young Communist League, the American Peace Mobilization, the American Youth Congress, the League of American Writers, the American League for Peace and Democracy, the Progressive League to Rebuild the American Labor Party, and the Greater New York Industrial Council (C.I.O.) — all party-line organizations — hastened to repudiate their approval of the Hitler-Stalin pact. *Daily Worker* editorial policy regarding the war changed overnight. The young Communist League, the American Peace Mobilization, the American Youth Congress, the League of American Writers, headed by Dashiell Hammett of Hollywood, and the greater New York Industrial Council (C.I.O.) had just a few weeks before publicly denounced President Roosevelt as a "warmonger" but each recanted and blessed him.[1]

Never had the party and its "transmission belts" and members so demonstrated their loyalty to the "fatherland." It was a bitter pill for them to swallow but as the ape-like faculty of imitation is required of the faithful they responded with pretended patriotic fervor. This was repeating the contemporary history of Russia, for there, too, meetings were held throughout the country and resolutions adopted bitterly denouncing the alleged "fascist mad dogs" of 1937 while similar meetings later approved the Hitler-Stalin pact. In Russia, however, the masses had no choice. To openly express dissent was to invite imprisonment or death.

Another factor must be taken into account in speculation regarding the kind of cooperation Russia may give to other nations. Russia is totalitarian, in fact the parent totalitarian dicta-

[1] See amusing article by Mr. Porter in the *New York Times*, July 27, 1941, in which the author quotes statements by these organizations shortly before the Hitler-Stalin pact and contrasts them with other statements following the signing of the pact.

torship, and the barriers to cooperation between democratic and totalitarian nations are numerous. Their ways of life are fundamentally different and they anticipate the future of social evolution in terms that are in basic conflict. Democracy trusts the people; totalitarianism does not. In fact, it fears any independent thinking and action by the masses. The White House can be picketed in Washington by dissenters; the Kremlin has never been and will never be picketed so long as the dictatorship survives.

The Communist movement since its inception in 1903 has never trusted the masses. It has based its appeal on the interests of the so-called proletariat but in Lenin's party the proletariat was assigned the serf role of blind obedience. He denied that workmen could be conscious agents in effecting social changes through self-controlled democratic organization. He urged an organization with iron discipline imposed on its members by professional revolutionists. A serf-like loyalty and strict obedience to orders from the top were required and departure from this code was punished by expulsion by the party dictatorship. His contempt for democratic procedure is evident throughout. "Bureaucratism against democracy — that must be the organization principle of the revolutionary Social Democracy," wrote Lenin, and added that it is the mission of such an organization "to guide all other organizations of the working class." [2]

Among Lenin's followers in other matters was Rosa Luxemburg who was aghast at his proposal. She ascribed the origin of this advocacy of despotism to the despair that had possessed some fighters for freedom, its net result being acceptance of a Czarist concept which they opposed in the Russian Government. "The ego which has been beaten down by Russian absolutism," she

[2] *Lenin, One Step Forward, Two Steps Backward,* and his *What is to be Done?* See also *History of the Communist Party of the Soviet Union* (Bolsheviks), authorized by the Central Committee of the C.P.S.U., pp. 33-4, 48, 49 and 51, for revealing quotations from Lenin's writings in the formative period of his party in 1903-1906.

wrote, "takes revenge by setting itself on the throne in its revolutionary thought-world and declaring itself omnipotent — as a conspiratory committee in the name of a non-existent 'popular will.' " [3]

Coupled with this distrust of the masses was Lenin's attitude towards every person who disagreed with him. His views were declared with pontifical certitude accompanied by vitriolic denunciation of his opponents. Dissent was not only impious: one who differed with him was a "renegade," a "bourgeois simpleton," or just a plain scoundrel and this characteristic runs through the literature of the Communists in all countries.[4]

Never having trusted workingmen and peasants, to say nothing of professional men, in the party, it was logical to extend the inner party dictatorship over party members to the nation over the workmen, peasants, professional men and women and the whole of Russian life "in the name of a non-existent popular will," to quote Rosa Luxemburg again.

Moreover, Communist and fellow-traveler literature has obscured one important fact regarding the Russian Revolution. *Not one of the leading Russian Communists participated in the democratic revolution that destroyed the Czarist regime!* [5]

The democratic revolution in Mrach, 1917, was an example of a whole nation rising against a hated regime. The Communist

---

[3] This is quoted from a pamphlet which has gone astray. But see Karl Kautsky, *Communism and Socialism*, p. 15, for a similar view by Rosa Luxemburg.

[4] See *History of the Communist Party of the Soviet Union*, pp. 324-28, for scurrilous language employed against all who differ with Stalin. They are "lickspittles," "wreckers," "fascist hirelings," "gang of assassins," "Judas Trotsky," "despicable tools," etc. Also pp. 346-48 — "dregs of humanity," "villains," "Whiteguard pigmies," "Whiteguard insects," "contemptible lackeys," "fiends," etc.

[5] This includes Lenin, Pavlov (P. V. Bergin), Trotsky, Rakovsky, Kollontai, Krasin, Litvinov, Lozovsky, Piatakov, Radek, Riazanov, Solkolnikov, Stalin and Zinoviev. All except Stalin were not in Russia when the Czarist system was overthrown and the democratic revolution released Stalin from Siberian exile. See Gankin and Fisher, *The Bolsheviks and the World War*, Biographical Notes, for an extensive list of revolutionaries.

leaders hastened to return to Russia. Having no trust in the great masses who had removed the barrier to democratic development, the returned exiles gave their time and energy to the overthrow of the republic and substituting their dictatorship for that of the Romanov clique. They were a tiny minority but, like Hitler later in Germany, they utilized the chaos, confusion and destitution of the masses as well as the mistakes of the democratic leaders as propaganda for Communism. Many informed workmen and peasants were won to the Communist banner and in October the Communists, much stronger but still a minority, organized a successful military rising against the republic. The democratic honeymoon was over and the hopes of millions soon vanished under the new dictatorship.

Lenin and his partisans organized a military "putsch" against the Constituent Assembly and dispersed the delegates to that body the elections to which they had themselves made an important issue. Why disperse it? The elections followed a few weeks after Lenin's armed bands had overthrown the Kerensky Government but the election returns showed that of 36,000,000 votes cast for delegates the Bolsheviks cast only 9,000,000. They were overwhelmingly defeated in this popular election which revealed 27,000,000 voters opposed to them.[6]

This violent overthrow of the Republic gave the Czarist generals their excuse for starting the civil war of which the Bolsheviks complain. The intervention of the Allies followed as the Lenin victors called for armed risings in the Allied nations to which American Communists responded on each May Day and Labor Day from 1919 to 1922 by distributing manifestoes urging the masses to armed insurrection against the American Government. The counter-revolution against Russian democracy took refuge in nation-wide espionage and terror against the people its partisans had declared they would emancipate. Henceforth in elections

[6] See Karl Kautsky, *Communism and Socialism*, for a discussion of this and the only genuine democratic election the Russian people ever had.

the people either voted Bolshevik or "non-partisan" because they were not permitted to organize and vote for anything else.

Having no confidence in the free choice of their own people in elections, need one be surprised that Russian Communism declined to risk its future in neighboring nations after the war and resorted to intrigue, coercion, and military might in rigged elections to obtain control of the people?

American apologists for Russia assert that she must have "friendly neighbors" and is entitled to them. Does she fear the exhausted peoples of these little nations and is it possible to make friends by suppressing their aspirations for control over their own institutions?

The United States has friendly neighbors in Latin-American countries because we have abandoned the old policy of coercion, intervention and dollar diplomacy. Had we continued these practices it is likely that Argentina would today be the recognized leader of the Latin-American nations. Moreover, the so-called Pan-Slavism of the Russian dictatorship dooms the promise of a genuine Pan-Slavism which the democratic elements of the Balkan nations have desired and worked for through a voluntary Balkan federation. Moscow makes the Slav nations conscripts while a democratic federation would make them free nations. Moscow's policy in Eastern Europe has planted dynamite in a region that has been a fruitful source of conflict for generations.

At best, a government committed to such policies is an uncertain partner in the attempt to organize the nations of the world for peace and security. Its internal policy of "liquidating" all critics in the party, the Army, the Air Force, the Navy, the "trade unions," etc.; its maintenance of espionage throughout the nation by means of the dreaded secret police; the periodical "purging" of the party of hundreds of thousands of members suspected of the slightest "deviation" from the party line; the control of the press, radio, meetings, elections, theatres, publishing plants, scientific research, art and educational institutions; sealing up the nation against travel abroad, unless one is on a mission for the government or is a diplomatic agent,[7] are phases of what the Communists of all countries now call the "higher democracy!"

Encouragement of children to spy on their elders, even their parents, and "confessions" extorted from accused persons in "trials" are also revolting phases of a system approved by American Communists. The espionage system that recruits children as well as adults is similar to the Hoko, or hostage system, in pre-war Japan which made every Japanese a spy upon other Japanese in ferreting out "dangerous thoughts." Of this system an American newspaper correspondent in Tokyo wrote:

"Originally the key men were hostages to the authorities for the thoughts and actions of the rest, and today each keyman is a trusted ally of the police. There has evolved a system of ethics in which tattling is a duty instead of a disgrace and what a man thinks is more important than what he does because thinking leads to doing." [8]

That paragraph is as apt in reference to Russia as it was to the vanished regime of old Japan. Just as repellent are the frequent "confessions" of crimes against the Russian dictatorship, so frequent that it suggests that there is something in a Bolshevik system which breeds apostates on a vast scale, or that those who confess are victims of intense coercion, or that the dictatorship is so intolerable that men are willing to risk their lives to destroy it. Considering that all of the instruments of intellectual coercion are monopolized by the dictatorship, as they were in the old Japan,

[7] See Alexander Barmine, *One Who Survived*, index under Stalin, for a vivid account of the liquidation of high officers of the Air Force, Army, Foreign Office, Navy, diplomatic corps, etc. Even a majority of the commission that drafted the Soviet Constitution were "liquidated"!

[8] Frank L. Kluckhorn, "The Menacing Shadow: Japan's Old Order," the *New York Times Magazine*, September 16, 1945.

and that the hostage system is also employed in Russia, of the numerous "confessions" made by the accused at "trials" it is certain that many are forced.

American colonial history reveals one parallel with these Russian "trials," the witchcraft trials at Salem, Massachusetts, in the seventeenth century where the informer and incredible confessions were also conspicuous in obtaining convictions. There, too, was a dictatorship, its leaders being the bigoted Increase Mather and his son, Cotton, who ventured upon a "purge" of those accused of being in league with witches. The criminal nonsense of some Boston children regarding a washerwoman resulted in denunciation of her as a witch. Beginning in the spring of 1792, by October, wrote Brooks Adams, a distinguished New Englander and descendant of two Presidents of the United States, "it seemed as though the bonds of society were dissolving; nineteen persons had been hanged, one had been pressed to death, and eight lay condemned; a number had fled, but their property had been seized and they were beggars; the prisons were choked, while more than 200 were accused and in momentary fear of arrest; even two dogs had been killed." [9]

Moreover, the claims that the dictatorship does not persecute Jews and that the constitution adopted in 1936 and its subsequent amendments assure democracy for Soviet citizens will not survive analysis. It is true that the Jew is not imprisoned or executed because he is a Jew. Neither is the Russian, but thousand of Jews and Russians have been imprisoned and executed because of their opinions. In short, there is equality of status before the hangman for Jews and all nationalities in Russia. In Nazi Germany the Jew and German were imprisoned and executed, the first because of his "race" *and* opinions and the German *solely* because of his opinions. It is no consolation to the Jew to know that under one

[9] See Brooks Adams, *The Emancipation of Massachusetts* (Boston: Houghton Mifflin Company) © 1919, especially his burning chapter, The Witchcraft. See also James Truslow Adams, *The Founding of New England*, pp. 451-56.

dictatorship he is executed because of "race" and under another because of his opinions.

As for the Soviet Constitution, Articles 125 and 126 presume to guarantee all the civil rights Americans enjoy but there is a "joker" in Article 126 which declares that the Communist Party *"is the leading core of all organizations of the working people, both public and state."*

In practice this has meant and still means that no organization can be formed or can function unless its chief officers are tested members of the Communist Party and faithfully carry out the policies of the dictatorship. Article 126 declares that the dictatorship extends to all organizations, *"both public and state,"* so that the civil rights mentioned in Article 125 are simply a mockery. Under such a ruthless system it is not surprising that in Communist Russia as in Nazi Germany national elections have given as high as 98 per cent of the vote to the candidates of the dictatorship.[10]

Has Moscow abandoned world revolution, armed insurrection, terror and dictatorship? The evidence indicates that it has not, for despite every change in *policy* these aims do not change. Every new "party line" has been followed by the publication of new books and pamphlets expounding it and the suppression of the old "party-line" literature, but no matter what the "party line" has been in each change of policy since 1919 one type of literature has not been called in, one type that has been and still is available in all Communist bookstores. *This is the literature of world revolution, armed insurrection, terror and dictatorship.*

If the Communist movement has at any time abandoned these doctrines, why has it continued to market such literature and bring out new editions as they are exhausted? This fact reveals a continuous changing of policy to realize an unchanging aim —

[10] *Constitution of the U.S.S.R.* American-Russian Institute. This edition contains all the amendments except one reported in a Miscow press dispatch of October 12, 1945, which provides for direct, secret, universal suffrage but does not alter the monopoly of the Communist Party.

a dictatorship for the United States as ruthless as that which rules helpless millions in Russia.[11]

Indeed, it appears that even the Soviet Embassy at Washington has become bold enough to openly market similar ideas. Its official *Bulletin* of November 17, 1945, quotes from a speech by A. Y. Vyshinsky at a celebration of the Bolshevik Revolution when he stressed "revolutionary struggle" and added:

> "Lenin developed the teachings of Marx and Engels on the State, especially on the important question of 'smashing the bourgeois state apparatus' and of utilizing the State for the purposes of the proletariat." [12]

When one adds to such views the use of falsehood as a weapon against political opponents, a course which Lenin recommended in the early days of the movement and followed throughout his life, we have some comprehension of the anti-social character of Communism. Lenin in his *Left Wing Communism* (see Note 14, Chapter VIII) advised his followers to follow this course, but as early as 1906 he also had urged it. In that year the Russian Social Democratic Labor Party split over Lenin's conception of organization, Lenin obtaining a majority, his followers being called Bolsheviki, or Majoritaires, while his opponents became

---

[11] This literature is available in Communist bookshops in the large cities throughout the United States. The following list does not exhaust such items. Lenin: *The Tasks of the Proletarian Revolution; State and Revolution; Left Wing Communism; A Letter to American Workers; The War and the Second International.* Stalin: *The Road to Power.* The following are compilations from the writings of various authors presenting the counter-revolutionary dogmas of Bolshevism in systematic form: *The Dictatorship of the Proletariat; Theory of the Proletarian Revolution; Strategy and Tactics.* All of these pamphlets and books bear the imprint of International Publishers, 381 Fourth Avenue, New York, a publishing agency of the Communist Party. The same agency publishes the *History of the Communist Party of the Soviet Union* which expounds these Bolshevik dogmas over the entire period of the Russian movement.

[12] *The New Leader,* December 8, 1945, quotes two leading paragraphs of this speech as it appeared in the Soviet Embassy *Bulletin.* This use of an Embassy publication shows how bold even diplomatic representatives of the dictatorship can be.

known as Menshiviki or Minoritaires. Lenin then wrote a pamphlet (in Russian) whose title would read in English: "The Hypocrisy of the Thirty-one Mensheviks," in which he accused the minority delegates of having "sold out" to the enemies of Socialism.

The pamphlet caused a scandal, some of Lenin's colleagues sharply condemning the false statement. Defending himself, Lenin freely admitted that his accusation was not true and that it was not permissible to make false statements regarding a party member, but it was legitimate to use falsification in attacking party opponents. The 31 were no longer party members, therefore it was permissible to slander them.[13]

Thus at this early period of the Communist movement Lenin justified this code of low cunning and it has been observed by his followers in all countries in their relations with other men and organizations. That such conduct destroys confidence, decency and fairness, giving "united fronts" no more cohesion than a rope of sand, is obvious to all. Employed in relations with other nations it leaves the Russian dictatorship a suspect and yet there are those in the United States who plead in extenuation of Russian conduct in international affairs that Russia is "suspicious" of other nations' intentions!

The doctrines of violence, terror, falsehood and dictatorship have brought servitude to millions in Russia while this counter-revolution against civilization has also devoured all but a handful of the old Bolsheviks who participated in the overthrow of the republic. They have died in prisons or have been executed for the slightest deviation from the thought rations passed out by the dictatorship. They praised the regime and were crushed by it. Our Communists and fellow travelers would have us adopt it.

[13] No English translation of this pamphlet has been made and we are indebted to Algernon Lee, President of the Rand School of Social Science, New York, and Boris Nicolaievsky, Russian scholar, Social Democrat and refugee from Russia, for this information.

Their approval recalls an incident that J. S. Buckingham, the British traveler, mentions having observed in a Southern city in the days of slavery. In his *Slave States of America* he wrote:

"Every evening, the bell of the Christian church is tolled at nine o'clock, to warn all slaves and colored people to repair to their homes, as it is not permitted them, without a pass, to be in the streets after a fixed hour of the night. When the church bell has ceased its office of warning, the drums of the military guard house take up the strain, and continue the admonition for a quarter of an hour longer. The last time I passed the guard house, and saw the Negroes hurrying to their masters' houses, from the different quarters of the town, the drums and fifes were playing the air of —

> *'Who would be a traitor knave?*
> *Who would fill a coward's grave?*
> *Who so base as be a slave?'*

"The musicians were themselves slaves!"

CHAPTER XXI

POST WAR TRENDS

THE preceding chapters were completed in February, 1946. Since then events at home and abroad have not required any alternation of our interpretations.

The outstanding feature of this period has been increasing "toughness" by Moscow, Russian objection to British and American firmness, and loyal devotion of American Communists and fellow travelers to Moscow. Scarcely a week passed that the Moscow radio or press did not hurl invectives at the democratic nations, the continuous barrage recalling the Hitler technique before following up words with armed force. This hot war of words reached a climax in Moscow's denunciation of the Atkinson articles in the *New York Times* in July and the acquittal of a Soviet official in Seattle who had been charged with espionage. Canada had already been a target for having investigated a Russian spy ring.

Having practically annexed Poland, Rumania, Yugoslavia and Bulgaria, through quisling dictators, Moscow in March declared that Russia "is not thinking of seizing foreign territory," that the dictatorship is a "stranger to any expansionist desires," that it was "only consolidating peace and security," while "Churchill and his friends have put on the shoes of warmongers." On June 1, three such attacks came from Moscow, one in the *New Times*, the second in *Izvestia*, and the third over the radio.

In July the attacks soared to a high pitch when Nicolai Redin was acquitted of espionage in Seattle and the *New York Times* published a series of articles on Russia by a correspondent recently returned from Moscow. Redin's acquital would have brought rejoicing from a normal government, but a Moscow journalist, writing in *Pravda*, denounced the "American secret police . . . for participation in a filthy conspiracy" against "international collaboration of the states united in the struggle against fascism."

The *New York Times'* articles were written by Brooks Atkinson and the same Moscow journalist declared the author a "bandit" unfit to be whipped, an unprincipled "informer" and "untalented calumniator" who had been hired to "fan enmity in the world."

This war of words also became an undeclared war against the United States. By late August the *New York Times*, in a striking editorial, declared that the "battle of words is being punctuated by the more dangerous bursts of machine-gun fire" which was "full of explosive possibilities." The *Times* listed 15 attacks on American forces in Asia and Europe by Russian forces from August 29, 1945, to August 19, 1946.[1]

This shift from the insolence of words to the audacity of physical attack brought Yugoslavia into the spotlight when the United States rapped dictator Tito over the knuckles. Several notes were exchanged over Yugoslav violence, which included the shooting down of American planes. At first arrogant, Tito became conciliatory, yielded to a 48-hour ultimatum, and consented to the payment of an indemnity for the lives of American fliers shot down in Yugoslav territory. Tito's insolence apparently was a Stalin-Tito test of how far Bolshevik "toughness" could go without provoking war.[2]

Limitations of space will not permit consideration of other actions of Russia and her vassals in relation to Greece, the Dardanelles, the Danube, unification of Germany, Austria and Korea, the frustration of General Marshall's attempts to stabilize China, international control of the atom bomb, the economic strangulation of certain European areas, and frequent use of the veto to continue the chaos, confusion, destitution and despair that Bolshevism regards as favorable to its aims.

Considering the absence of any ethical code which Communist history, theory and practice disclose, one wonders whether inter-

[1] Editorial in issue of August 20, 1946.
[2] The text of the several notes exchanged by the State Department with the Tito dictatorship may be consulted in *World Report*, August 29, September 5, 1946.

national problems can be settled with Russia and her conscript states.

Elsewhere in this work we have shown the debasement of Communists who are required to abandon all ethics, to practice subterfuge, conceal the truth and to lie. This revolting code is also described by an ex-Communist as "the two truths," one intended for the inner party circle and the other for the rest of the world. Victor Kravchenko, a former Soviet official, wrote:

"Foreigners who try to understand Stalin's policies or the 'Soviet mind' by studying the Soviet press and the Kremlin's public action usually come up with a truckload of gibberish. Not one in a thousand among them has grasped the Bolshevik idea of 'two truths' — one for the masses, for the world at large, and another for the party faithful; the initiated, the insiders. At a time when a certain line of propaganda or action is being conducted publicly, party people might be instructed to disregard it or even instructed to believe the exact opposite." [3]

The author was impatient with "experts" who hailed the proclaimed disolution of the Third International, the alleged break with the idea of world revolution, and the tale that the dictatorship was slowly giving way to democracy. He continued:

"Had any one of these experts sat in at our closed weekly party sessions for the higher personnel, he would have been shocked. For us the 'retreat from Leninism' was simply a temporary tactical maneuver. . . . Bourgeois moralists who prate about double-dealing and perfidy are, to the Bolshevik 'realist' just ludicrous left-overs from a dead past and hypocrites to boot." [4]

[3] *I Chose Freedom*, by Victor Kravchenko (New York: Charles Scribner's Sons) © 1946.

[4] See the amazing Chapter XXIV, The Two Truths, in Victor Kravchenko's book, *I Chose Freedom*, the story of a disillusioned Soviet official. Considering this shocking code one may ask, What reliance can be placed upon *any* statement, oral or written, that comes from any Moscow official? Those who explain Russian behavior in terms of a virtuous suspicion of the Western democracies will better understand the dictatorship and its foreign agencies by studying this code. William C. Bullitt, our first Ambassador to Communist Russia and for years sympathetic to the Russian "experiment," reveals one result of this code — 28 violations of Soviet treaties, agreements and assurances, which he compares with 26 similar violations by Nazi Germany. Bullitt, *The Great Globe Itself*, Appendix I.

This behavior is no puzzle to those acquainted with the history of Bolshevism. Communists believe it permissible to compromise their allies in a united front, to circulate falsehoods, and to undermine them in every way.

The Paris Peace Conference last year repeated in detail the history of united fronts of private organizations with Communist organizations. Before the conference met, the Moscow press and radio carried on a malicious campaign of innuendo and direct attack against the nations assembled to draft peace treaties. Dripping with the fruit of its pillage of Eastern Europe, terrorizing several helpless nations with armed forces, Moscow accused the Western Allies of "imperialist" designs! This was occasionally repeated even at the conference.

The accusation of imperialism has no foundation whatever. The old imperialism is passing out while Russia is expanding an imperialist dictatorship in Europe. She is also seeking imperialist control of China and the whole of Asia.

While Moscow's radio and press in 1946 were hurling this charge the Philippines celebrated their independence while the British Labor Government tossed independence into the hands of the people of India! Moreover, there is little doubt that Hawaii will soon be admitted as a State to the Union while Puerto Rico is also far advanced towards self-government and is represented by a Resident Commissioner in Washington. One may imagine what would be the fate of all these peoples if they came under the Russian dictatorship.

Our Communists and fellow travelers repeat Moscow's attacks against Britain and yet the whole history of British imperialism shows that it is, like ours, passing into history. Beginning as a regime rulling dependent peoples, wholly self-governing communities like Canada, Australia, New Zealand and the Union of South Africa have emerged in the past half century. A second class of communities are on the road to a self-governing status, the home government appointing only part of the legislative body and the governor. These include the Channel Islands, Malta, Cyprus, Ceylon, British Guiana, Jamaica, Rhodesia, etc.; some of them, like Rhodesia, are now approaching full Dominion status.

The history of the British Empire shows that it is evolving into an international commonwealth, the change being "gradual, halting, uneven, and incomplete: an evolution rather than a revolution." Following the end of the first World War the Dominions practically became independent nations and the "full equal sovereignty of the self-governing portions of the Commonwealth received formal recognition by the Imperial Conference of 1926 and by the Statute of Westminster of 1931." [5]

Dutch and French foreign policy is certain to follow the British and American trend. Indeed, in October, 1946, the Indonesian Republic signed a truce with Dutch representatives while negotiations were resumed for recognition of the independence of the Netherlands East Indies. The old imperialism is passing out, and a ruthless Russian imperialism now threatens all the peoples of the world.

This new imperialism not only threatens the "backward" peoples; its clammy hand has been grasping the peoples of Eastern and Central Europe. In this area no Communists have been chosen in a free election as the ruling party. The contention of Communists and fellow travelers that peasant nations like Rumania, Bulgaria, Poland and Hungary have popular Communist governments runs counter to what we know of peasant ideology in all countries, including Russia. The peasant's mode of life, his semi-isolation from urban influences, and his tillage of small acres, make him a fierce individualist. Even the Communists discovered this when they "collectivized" Russian agriculture. Millions of peasants resisted when their farms and other possessions were seized. The number of

[5] See Chapter XXXIX, From British Empire to British Commonwealth, in *History of the English-Speaking Peoples*, by R. B. Mowat and Preston Slosson (New York: Oxford University Press) © 1943. This work is an excellent account of the history of the American and British peoples in their migrations, settlement and expansion overseas.

horses, cows, goats, and hogs declined by millions, the peasants consuming them, while millions of dissenters were either shot or transported in cattle cars to slave labor in Siberia. Other millions perished of famine. The victims ultimately submitted for the same reason that convicts submit to penitentiary discipline. They could do nothing else.

Moreover, the partition of large estates by the Communist regimes in Russia's vassal states of Poland, Rumania, etc., is not a permanent program. The peasants will eventually be treated to "collectivization" as the Russian peasants were.

Peasant aversion to Communism is also evident from the fact that the Communist parties in Rumania, Bulgaria, Poland and Hungary never polled any large vote before the first World War, despite financial aid given them by the Comintern. To all this must be added the fact that peasant individualist ideology is supplemented by the Catholic faith of many millions in Rumania, Poland and Hungary, and Catholicism has been a potent enemy of Communism in all countries. The social, economic, ideological, and religious factors show that Communist dictatorships are imposed upon, not chosen by, the peoples of those unhappy countries.

Having sketched this brief background of Communist actions abroad, we now turn to the American movement. The status of Earl Browder, fuehrer of the party for many years, has been a puzzle since February, 1946, when he was expelled by the national committee by a unanimous vote of 54, on the grounds that he had deserted his duties and began publishing *Distributors' Guide* to "advise Big Business along a political line that coincides with the interests of employers and of American imperialism." This action coincided with a marked change from the party line of collaboration in winning the war. It resurrected the old "revolutionary" policy that was abandoned when Hitler attacked the Communist "fatherland." The shift was effected when, in the spring of 1945, Jacques Duclos, French Communist leader, visited Moscow. Returning home, he attacked Browder for collaborating with American capitalism. This was Moscow's way of declaring that as the Kremlin was getting "tough" in its imperialist policies, collaboration here and in international affairs no longer served the "fatherland." [6]

Browder declared he was the victim of a frame-up, slander and espionage, and that leaders at the national convention denied him the right to defend himself. Outside critics asserted that it appeared that Browder had encountered the "justice" of a Moscow trial. A. A. Heller, a wealthy New York Communist and President of International Publishers, resigned his membership in protest against Browder's expulsion, while the party's national secretariat, headed by the new fuehrer, William Z. Foster, issued a solemn proclamation, pillorying Browder as an "expelled renegade" who had "abandoned Marxism." [7]

The proclamation was issued because of persistent press stories that Browder had obtained a visa to visit the "fatherland." He did go to Moscow, occupied a suite at the Hotel Moskva, was cordially treated by high Bolsheviks, and obtained a contract as sole representative of Soviet publishing houses in the United States. Heller also visited Moscow at the same time. [8]

This episode is extraordinary in Communist history. In all other cases of expulsion of top Communists in all countries they have faced a hot fire of denunciation, some of them being pursued and destroyed. As we have seen, the secretariat publicly denounced Browder as a "renegade," the favored epithet for all "traitors," but this "renegade" not only was welcomed in Moscow but was gra-

[6] The *Daily Worker*, February 24, 1946, presented long excerpts from the report of the national committee explaining the excommunication of Browder. Those who care to read the complete story of this tempest in the Communist teapot should consult the nine documents, including the Duclos article, reprinted in *Marxism-Leninism vs. Revisionism*, New Century Publishers, New York, another publishing agency of the Communist Party.

[7] *New York World-Telegram*, March 11, 1946. The *Daily Worker*, April 30, 1946, carried the full text of the statement by the secretariat.

[8] See Moscow dispatch to the *New York Times*, June 19, 1946. Other dailies of that date carried similar information.

ciously received by Foreign Commissar Molotov! Was the expulsion of Browder genuine, or was it a mask for concealing some sinister work assigned to the ex-fuehrer, work that he can do better in his present role?

The new fuehrer of the Communist Party, William Z. Foster, as we have seen in Chapter I, was formerly an Anarcho-Syndicalist who expounded the necessity of force and abandoning all ethics to achieve Syndicalist aims. The Communist creed, therefore, was acceptable to him. He has openly urged a dictatorship for the United States on the Russian model. He wrote in 1932 that under the rule of his party *"all the capitalist parties — Republican, Democratic, Progressive, Socialist — would be liquidated, the Communist Party functioning alone as the party of the toiling masses."* [9]

Moreover, Moscow's fifth column does not rely on political action to accomplish its purpose as it knows that it can never win a popular majority. Therefore, the basic units of the party have been organized as shop, factory, mine, store and street nuclei, as described in Chapter XII and Appendix IV. *This type of organization is adapted for intrigue, conspiracy and insurrection, not for poltical action.* The Communist parties in all countries have been organized on this basis as it enables the members to go underground at a signal from the top leaders to engage in various forms of violence.

It is never possible to report the number of "innocents' clubs" or "booby traps," as they are sometimes called. These groups are founded by the party for some alleged worthy purpose to which liberal men and women are lured to give them a "respectable" front. A recent survey reports more than seventy nation-wide organizations of this type. Of these more than half did not exist in 1940 "while three fourths of the Communist-controlled committees and associations active in 1940 have been liquidated since." Some are wholly, some partly, controlled by the Communists and of the

---

[9] William Z. Foster, *Toward Soviet America* (New York: Coward-McCann) © 1932, p. 275.

more than seventy listed last October the following are outstanding "fronts": American Youth for Democracy; Protestant Associates; International Labor Defense; National Committee to Win the Peace; Independent Committee of the Arts, Sciences and Professions; National Lawyers Guild; Screen Writers Guild, etc.

By the time this is read some of the seventy "booby traps" will have disappeared, but new fronts appear nearly every month. Some are abandoned because the Communist control had become notorious, some are merged with others, or a front's name is changed for some reason.[10]

The main trap for Negroes for ten years has been the National Negro Congress which, in June, 1946, asked the United Nations to halt "oppression" of 13,000,000 American Negroes. Herbert Aptheker, an "interpreter" of American history for Negroes, whose pamphlets are published by a Communist Party agency, resented the indictment, while the noted Negro baritone, Paul Robeson, a Soviet propagandist who sent his son to Moscow to be "educated," at a mass meeting denounced President Truman and praised the Russian dictatorship in terms similar to those heard over the Moscow radio.

The indictment carries the usual exaggerations typical of Communist agitation. It ignores the fact that since the Civil War the Negro people have made remarkable advances in every phase of American life, that even in the South they are not only voting in primaries and elections in several states, but that their social status is slowly improving with the cooperation of intelligent whites. Moreover, there has been an enormous decline in lynchings in the part forty years, and the revived Ku Klux Klan for the first time

[10] See survey of American Communist underhand activities, by Norbert Muhlen in the liberal *New Leader*, supplement, October 12, 1946. The author also presents a partial list of various "literary" and "news" services inspired or secretly directed by the Communist Party in this country to which is added an interesting short biography of Willi Muenzenberg who met Lenin in Switzerland during the first World War. Muenzenberg became the key man in organizing "booby traps" for the unwary in all nations.

faces vigorous opposition in the South. The resolution of the bogus Negro Congress could aid only the illiterate opposition to further advances in the welfare of our Negro citizens.[11]

The resolution is typical of the hackneyed approach to social problems. In fact, an outstanding phase of the Communist movement in all countries is its poverty of thought, the dull level of mediocrity of its leaders, theoreticians, editors, organizers, publicists and pamphleteers. One who reads the output of the German, Russian, French, Chinese, American and other Communists is impressed by its intolerable dullness, its sameness, its uniform ideas, words, "slogans" and methods of presentation. Trained in the slave ethic of dictatorship, the mind cannot function. Platforms, resolutions, manifestoes, books, pamphlets, periodicals, etc., have an insufferable sameness that indicates a common source — the Russian dictatorship. Of the thousands of books and pamphlets the Communists have published in this country, not one stands out as an original interpretation of American history and American problems. There is little doubt that the same is true in other countries.

In 1927, David Starr Jordan published a book on the "Higher Foolishness," in which he outlined what he called "sciosophy," which in turn he defined as "systematized ignorance." Bolshevik pseudo-science may well be included as a branch of "sciosophy."

Communist mediocrity is also evident in the changing party line. William C. Bullitt presents its history for the period of July 1, 1939 — September 2, 1945. This includes policy on the Munich appeasement of Hitler, the Roosevelt policy of arming for the eventual struggle with Nazism, the Nazi-Bolshevik pact which released Hitler's hands for the attack on Europe, the declaration of

11 AP dispatch from Detroit, June 1, 1946, reporting the resolution. As for Aptheker, see review of his "Essays in the History of the American Negro" in the *American Historical Review*, April, 1946. Aptheker justifies "insurrections, arson and murder to change the system"; infers that the "poor white was an ally of the slaves and wanted them freed"; some of his opinions contradict historical facts, some "of them are silly," and some "are gross exaggerations based on omissions and distortion." In short, Aptheker is a Communist "historian."

war against Germany by France and Britain, the attack on Poland by Germany and Russia, the latter's attack on Finland, followed by Russia's expulsion from the League of Nations, the invasion of Norway and Denmark by Germany, the occupation of the Baltic nations by Russia, the attack on Russia by Germany, Japan's attack on Pearl Harbor, the several conferences of Roosevelt, Churchill and Stalin, the "abolition" of the Communist Party and its restoration, etc. Direct quotations from the *Daily Worker* reveal the tortuous changes in the party line by the American Communist Party as it changed in Moscow, convincing evidence that the party members are willing conscripts of the Kremlin.[12]

The twisting party line exacts servile submission of party members in all nations. An American ex-Communist reveals thorough preparations made by the party to break up public meetings arranged by rival groups who had been expelled, incidentally relating a joke that was current in the Communist Party regarding its servility to Moscow:

"Why is the Communist Party of the United States like the Brooklyn Bridge?" a member would ask.
"Because it is suspended on cables," was the answer. Moscow generally cabled its orders to its affiliates.[13]

Despite increasing knowledge of what international Communism is there still remain a few who favor appeasing Moscow. A sensational effort of this kind was a mass meeting in New York last September addressed by Secretary of Commerce Henry A. Wallace, Senator Claude E. Pepper of Florida, Paul Robeson, and Florence E. March, movie star. Arranged by the Independent Citizens Committee of the Sciences, Arts and Professions, a party front, and the Political Action Committee which, in New York, is nursed by

[12] See Bullitt, *The Great Globe Itself*, Appendix II, for quotations from the *Daily Worker*.
[13] Benjamin Gitlow, *I Confess*, pp. 220-22.

the C.I.O. Industrial Council which, in turn, follows the party line, the speakers did not wander far from this line in international affairs.

Mr. Wallace declared that he was "neither anti-British nor pro-British, neither anti-Russian nor pro-Russian," yet he pleaded for most of what the Russian dictatorship was demanding. A few criticisms of Russia brought hisses and boos from the Communist faithful, the *Daily Worker* following with sharp criticism of this section of the address, but when the Moscow radio and press approved Wallace, the Communist organ dutifully came to his support.

Five days after the meeting the White House press secretary released a letter Wallace had sent the President on July 23 in which the author stated his views on what should be American policy towards Russia. Mr. Wallace was so pro-Russian that he urged yielding to Russia on every issue that had then emerged, even admitting that this could be construed as appeasement!

This episode caused consternation in the democratic nations; only Russia and her vassals expressed satisfaction. President Truman later requested Wallace's resignation, which was given, and announced that American foreign policy had not changed. The incident revealed how Moscow's fifth column and some innocent offshoots can cause confusion and division. Three years before, Mr. Wallace spoke in terms of appeasement in Delaware, Ohio, and declared that unless there was "understanding" with Russia "there is grave probability of Russia and Germany sooner or later making common cause." It did not occur to him to ask, How is it possible to reach a satisfactory understanding with an ally that was likely to perpetrate such treachery? [14]

Appeasement and fellow-traveling, however, was fading out in

---

[14] This earlier address was delivered March 8, 1943. See dailies of the next day. We have not cited references to the later Wallace episode as the press carried many stories and editorials regarding it in the period of September 13-31, 1946.

1946 and the national elections in November swept a number of men out of Congress who had followed a course sympathetic to the Soviet Union in foreign policy. An exception was Vito Marcantonio of the 18th Congressional District in New York City. He was returned with a smaller vote. First elected in 1934, he was accused of attending Communist and Italian Fascist meetings, a photograph portraying him seated with the Italian Consul and other Fascist officials. In the campaign last year a liberal New York weekly published a photograph of the Congressman seated with a group of underworld characters. The weekly also presented the police careers of several characters. Marcantonio was supported by the American Labor Party which had been captured by Communists while the *Daily Worker* generally treated him kindly.[15]

Probably the most audacious venture in 1946 was the organization of the American Authors Authority which, if successful, would extend Communist and fellow-traveler domination over screen, radio and magazine writers and intimidate publishers of books not satisfactory to this totalitarian control. Through various front organizations Moscow has for years attempted to ban American books critical of Russia, and the Authors Authority proposed to expand this dictation to other fields. The proposal brought quick resentment from more than 75 journalists and authors who organized the American Writers Association to combat it. Dorothy Thompson declared in her syndicated column that the AAA "is much closer to the Goebbels methods of thought control than to the Communist."[16]

Revolt against Communism was also apparent in veterans organizations, the American Legion refusing a permanent charter to the Duncan-Paris Post in New York because of the Stalinology of

[15] *The New Leader*, August 24, and October 19, 1946. According to this record there was a short lapse in the Congressman's fellow-traveling in the period of August, 1939, to the following January. Then "Vito was back in the Communist camp, the most belligerent isolationist in the House."

[16] See articles in *The New Leader*, September 21, by Raymond Howard, and September 28, 1946, by Eugene Lyons.

some of its members. J. Edgar Hoover stirred the delegates to the national convention in San Francisco in October by stating that Communism had made its deepest inroad into our national life in the previous five years. It is probable that the Canadian investigation of Soviet spies had revealed the network extending into private organizations and institutions as well as the government itself. Hoover expressed confidence in the Legion's ability to expose Communism which is "built and supported by dishonor, deceit and tyranny and a deliberate policy of falsehood."

In the previous June, delegates of the American Veterans Committee met in their first national convention at Des Moines, Iowa, and erected a barrier to the admission of Communists who for months had been planning to either control the convention or to obtain a large measure of power. However, the history of all new organizations warrants the assertion that the Communist Party will continue its intrigues to obtain control.[17]

The year 1946 also witnessed the most determined upheaval against Communism in American trade unions. The American Federation of Labor has not been much affected by this disruptive influence, but the Congress of Industrial organizations has been plagued by it and the revolt was mainly in C.I.O. organizations. One reason for the democratic revolt against the totalitarians is the frequent support of Russia's foreign policy by C. I. O. unions under Communist control. This tends to give outsiders the impression that the whole C.I.O. approves this policy, which is not the case. Only eight national C.I.O. unions are controlled by Communists: the Fur Workers, the Office Workers, the Public Workers, the Transport Workers, the Longshoremen, the Farm Equip-

17 One of the most revealing contributions to an understanding of how Communists act in concert in other organizations and under the orders of a party committee will be found in an article by Raymond Postgate in *The American Mercury*, July, 1934. The author had been a Communist but deserted the movement as he observed the methods of Stalin's agents in attempting to control the London Trades Council. A sample of the orders they received shows that such documents are almost impossible for others to understand.

ment Workers, the Food and Tobacco Workers, and the American Communications Association.[18]

These unions are not large and powerful, but the Longshoremen and the American Communications Association hold strategic positions in our economy.

Probably the most extensive revolt against the Communists occurred in June when Morris Muster, President of the United Furniture Workers (C.I.O.), resigned and issued a blistering statement against the Communists charging that less than a thousand of them controlled the 42,000 members. By the following October the Upholsters International Union (A.F. of L.) reported that thousands of the C.I.O. members had joined the U.I.U.

It is this strengthening of the A.F. of L. by rebel C.I.O. members that gave high C.I.O. chiefs much concern. Asked how a tiny minority of "fatherlanders" could obtain control over so many members, Muster declared that they planted switchboard operators and secretaries in the office, likewise an educational director and secretary-treasurer. None, of course, admitted party membership. Thus an inter-office espionage system was established and control was obtained of finances, education, the union paper, the membership lists and correspondence. Other techniques were interesting. The Communists assigned a woman in two cities to cultivate local officials. An unknown Communist would be planted in a town to be organized, then made an official. In other instances the Communists spent lavish funds entertaining union members with reliable girls as a feature attraction. Communists came early to meetings and remained late, this being an old method of tiring out those who fought them.[19]

In May the United Steel Workers, a C.I.O. giant, warned Communists, Socialists and other outsiders not to meddle in the union's

[18] See the short but informative article by William Hard and J. O. Blachly, "Communists Invited Out," in *The Reader's Digest*, November, 1946.

[19] Victor Riesel in the *New York Post*, July 2, 1946, in an interview with Muster.

affairs, and the previous month Walter Reuther, new President of the United Automobile Workers (C.I.O.) included a similar warning in a long statement on policy. Reuther had been elected over R. J. Thomas, who had held the office for several years. Reuther won after a bitter fight with Communists. In the following September, however, the left wingers obtained a vote of five to one at the Electrical Workers convention to admit persons of all parties to membership. A resolution directly attacking every form of totalitarianism never came to a vote.

So the struggle within the C.I.O. against totalitarians produced a stalemate in some instances, in others a victory. A notable triumph was registered for the anti-Communists in April when the convention of the Utility Workers Union (C.I.O.) changed its constitution to bar members of Communist, Fascist and Nazi organizations from membership by a vote of 371 to 6.[20]

The National Maritime Union (C.I.O.), of which Joseph Curran has been president for years, was also shaken by the revolt of Curran against Communist control. Like Muster of the Furniture Workers, he appears to have been a hostage of Stalin's agents. This is also a strategic union in our economy and in a crisis with Russia it would be capable of great harm to the United States. Curran declared that the organization department employed organizers who spent much time campaigning for Communist candidates at union elections in various states, this course having cost a payroll of $1,600,000 a year, the union running a deficit of about $12,000 a week.[21]

The anti-Communist delegates to the C.I.O. convention, held at Atlantic City, September 1, 1946, were determined to bring the "Red issue" to a showdown. However, President Philip Murray adopted an "appeasement policy." A well-balanced committee, consisting of three "leftists" and three "rightists," was appointed to prepare and present to the convention a resolution which would

---

20 *New York World-Telegram*, Aprin 10, 1946.
21 Victor Riesel, in the *New York Post*, July 9, 1946.

express the sentiment of the majority, if not all, of the delegates. The resolution, which was unanimously adopted, pledged the C.I.O. to "only one National allegiance, and that allegiance is to our own country, the United States of America, to resent and reject efforts of the Communist Party or other political parties and their adherents to interfere in the affairs of the C.I.O." Even the Communists and fellow travelers voted in favor of the resolution. Unity of action was of great importance to President Murray as well as to the delegates.[22] This resolution seems rather weak to the anti-Communists. However, it may prove to be a powerful weapon in dealing with subversive activities in local and state councils.

President Murray announced to the convention that the executive board of the C.I.O. had made drastic changes in the rules which govern state, county and municipal industrial union councils. These councils are prohibited from sending delegates and make contributions to organizations not recognized by the C.I.O., and they are to be guided in their activities and statements by the general policy of the national organization. The president has the right to expel Communists from the leadership of local and state councils, to seize the funds of offending councils, and hold such funds in trust till the national convention disposes of them. The reason for this drastic change is not difficult to find. "More than a few of these councils have fallen into Commies hands, and their declarations of policy and political activities more nearly reflect the international aims of the Kremlin than the aspirations of the American Workers." [23]

There is a growing feeling among American scholars who have studied critically the teachings of Karl Marx that his "gospel" needs to be freed from the deadly dogmatism of Lenin, Stalin, and other Russian misinterpreters. The Russian brand of Communism with its brute force and terrorism came closer to the teachings of

[23] *The Progressive*, December 2, 1946. . . . .

[22] See the *New York Times* for September 25, 1946.

Michael Bakunin than to the teachings of Karl Marx. Bakunin was expelled from the first Labor International in 1872 by the followers of Marx. Lenin, however, incorporated many of Bakunin's ideas into his "Scientific Materialism." The "intellectuals" of today will find a truer and more efficient exponent of Marxism in Karl Kautsky, a German author, very little known in America.[24] However, a new exposition of Marxism would have very little influence on the Lenin-Stalin brand of Communists. It would, no doubt, present Marx in a truer and saner light than that given him by his Russian expositors.

The transition period which followed the global war has been one of Communistic inflation. That period is drawing to a close and, judging by strong present-day trends, Communism in America is heading for a serious deflation. The labor unions, as we have noticed, are hot on the trail of the "strangers" in their midst. The government will spare no efforts in exposing subversive activities and purge all "disloyal" persons from the Federal payroll. Recent revelation of "underground" activities has made labor, capital and government suspicious of "foreign intervention," not only in our country, but in many other countries where the Communist Party is strong.

In April, 1946, the Research Institute of America released a report based upon an extensive investigation, which declared that "Soviet foreign policy is the barometer of the activities of a Communist Party-dominated Unions," that "American C.P.'ers live

---

[24] Karl Kautsky was a voluminous writer and much that he wrote remains in the original German. Thoroughly imbued with the Marxian philosophy, he contended that it is basically democratic in ideology, aims and methods, and subjected Lenin and his colleagues to continuous criticism. The latest compilation of Kautsky's anti-Communist writings, although only a small part of this phase of his work, was published by the Rand School Press, New York, in 1946. With an Introduction by Sidney Hook, it bears the title, *Social Democracy versus Communism*.

Also note discussion of Bakunin in Chapter I above and compare his views with those of the modern Communists.

by one principle — Russia First." [25] Little wonder that the Education Board of the C.I.O. made drastic changes in the rules governing local and state labor councils.

Of the Communist International it may be said that there is no reason to believe that the Moscow announcements of May 15 and June 10, 1943, that it had been dissolved, are true. The uniform following of the party line by Communist organizations in all countries since the "dissolution," indicating the continuance of the international lock-step, is supplemented by additional evidence. In August, 1946, translation of a document issued by the Central Political Bureau of the Chinese Communist Party revealed that it had the approval of the Far Eastern Bureau of the Communist International. [26]

Just as convincing is the evidence contained in the report of the Royal Commission of Canada on the activities of the Russian spy ring in Canada. Here documentary evidence is presented showing that the Communist International was still directing the activities of Canadian leaders in 1945. [27]

The above citations are typical samples of recent disclosures of subserviency to Moscow. Nationalism is a little too strong in America to tolerate loyalty to any foreign power. The months ahead will be a period of intense investigation. The Congress, the Federal Bureau of Investigation, the American Legion, and other national

[25] *New York World-Telegram*, April 27, 1946.

[26] Parker La Moore in the *New York World-Telegram*, August 26, 1946. Other dailies carried this item about the same time.

[27] *The Report of the Royal Commission*, Ottawa, Canada, 1946, pp. 37-41. This volume of 733 pages is an amazing exposure of the extensive ramifications of Russian espionage. Enforced by reprints and photographs of important secret material, it reveals that even the Russian secret police functions in Canada and that every Communist Party is a potential spy for the Russian dictatorship. Prospective secret agents are secretly investigated and all data regarding them is checked in Moscow before an appointment is made. The Canadian investigation is the first to reveal the systematic organization of treachery by Moscow in other countries and there is little doubt that what has been disclosed in Canada exists in Britain, the United States, Mexico, China, and all other nations on the condemned list of the Kremlin.

and semi-national agencies will vie with one another in exposing this foreign issue which is "built and supported by dishonor, deceit and tyranny and a deliberate policy of falsehood." [28]

Will American Communism survive such exposures? It is closely tied with Russian Communism and many people believe that some day — probably with the passing of Joseph Stalin — it too will pass into oblivion.

Just before *its* departure into oblivion, Mrs. Shelley's Frankenstein monster declared it had hoped to meet other beings who, "pardoning my outward form, would love me for the excellent qualities I was capable of bringing forth." Anticipating impending death, it lamented, "When I die, I am well satisfied that abhorrence and opprobium should load my memory."

The regret and lamentation might well be that of Russian Communism. Seeking the affection denied it by humanity, it found this affection in another monstrosity — the Nazi dictatorship in Germany, and collaborated with it. The normal processes of social evolution had condemned it at birth to be what it is. It was incapable of developing those excellent qualities which sentimental travelers to the Bolshevik Mecca sought, for, as Enrico Ferri, the criminologist once wrote, whether misshapen things are the product of social or organic life, "nature inexorably blasts them with degeneracy and sterility."

28 J. Edgar Hoover in his address before the American Legion Convention, held in San Francisco, October, 1946.

CHAPTER XXII

ALTERNATIVES

> Desperate men are liable to destroy the structure of their society to find in the wreckage some substitute for hope.
> — PRESIDENT TRUMAN

> Mankind can be uncivilized and well fed, but he cannot be civilized, moral or even decent if famishing. Famished people will not be law-abiding or peace-loving, but beasts of the jungle; and social jungles, like natural ones, always encroach upon civilized gardens.
> — DOROTHY THOMPSON

IT IS NOW evident that the three decades that ended with the atomic bomb in August, 1945, and the surrender of Japan, have brought a new era in world history. Two world wars, a worldwide depression, and the rise of totalitarian dictatorships — each a counter-revolution against all the nobler achievements of civilization — have taught the discerning that the convulsions following widespread economic depressions and modern war bring the charlatan, the unscrupulous demagogue and adventurer into prominence as leaders of distressed and desperate human beings. The result is the servitude to totalitarian dictatorship for all outside the small group of ruling despots. Whether this totalitarianism bears the label of Communism, Fascism, or Nazism; whether it be Russian, Italian, German, Spanish, or Japanese; whether it is our own recent native varieties of the late Huey Long, Father Coughlin, or Gerald L. K. Smith; whether it is atheistic as in Russia, pagan as it was in Germany, Emperor-worship as in Japan, Catholic as in Spain, or Protestant as in the cases of Huey Long and Gerald L. K. Smith — the aims and the results are the same.

Three years after the first World War, James Harvey Robinson observed the "sickness of an acquisitive society" as it emerged from that great conflict. "When we contemplate the shocking derangement of human affairs which now prevails in most civilized countries, including our own, even the best minds are puzzled and uncertain in their attempts to grasp the situation," he wrote. It was his conviction that "we must undertake the arduous task of reconsidering a great part of the opinions about man and his relations to his fellow-men which have been handed down to us by previous generations who lived in far other conditions and possessed far less information about the world and themselves. We have, however, first to create an *unprecedented attitude of mind to cope with unprecedented conditions, and to utilize unprecedented knowledge.*" [1]

Ten years after this was written the world was in the throes of a general depression and late in April, 1933, Secretary of State Cordell Hull, in a lecture before the American Society of International Law, declared that "the awful plight of all countries offers proof conclusive of the bankruptcy of statesmanship in every part of the world."

The following passages from that address are indicative of the free reign of private enterprise, isolationism and international anarchy:

"The present utterly chaotic and dislocated conditions, political, economic and moral, in every part of the world, present a terrifying crisis.

"International treaty obligations are flouted, the sanctity of contracts is complacently ignored, while force and violence are either indulged in or threatened in different parts of the world; the international exchange and money situation loudly call for

---

[1] James Harvey Robinson, *The Mind in the Making* (New York: Harper & Brothers) © 1939, pp. 4, 5. Italics in the original.

stabilization; the commodity prices in world markets are in a state of collapse; international finance and trade are almost dried up.

"The internal affairs of each nation are in a still worse plight, with vast unemployment, damned up surpluses, price dislocations, depreciated currencies, and extreme agricultural distress.

"Hundreds of millions of suffering and desperate people in the various countries *are not in a state of mind to function normally* or to manifest serious concern about other problems and conditions, no matter how important, until and unless they first secure release from their economic ills. They are hopelessly engrossed with the frightful and unbearable conditions.

"Another phase of this psychology, significant as it is dangerous, is the possibility of social disturbances and uprising, easily leading to widespread disorders.

"It is also true that most modern military conflicts and other serious international controversies are rooted in economic conditions, and that economic rivalries are in most modern instances the prelude to the actual wars that have occurred."

The above address was delivered as the nation was in the throes of the most terrible industrial crisis in its history and when the third totalitarian dictatorship, Hitler's, was consolidating its power. One month before, March, 1933, President Roosevelt delivered his remarkable Inaugural Address in which he declared that "plenty is at our doorstep, but a generous use of it languishes in the very sight of the supply.

"Primarily," he continued, "this is because the rulers of the exchange of mankind's goods have failed through their own stubbornness and their own incompetence, have admitted their failure and abdicated. . . .

"Stripped of the lure of profit by which to induce our people to follow their false leadership, they have resorted to exhortations, pleading tearfully for restored confidence. . . . The money changers have fled from their high seats in the temple of our civilization."

We have quoted two Presidents of the United States, a noted woman journalist, a renowned historian and philosopher, and a gifted American Secretary of State, and the reader will note that their thoughts regarding the economic sickness of modern civilization are similar. These quotations could be multiplied by including opinions of eminent statesmen and scholars in other countries. Confidence in the old order out of which came two world wars and at least five brutal dictatorships is giving way to widespread skepticism. It is also becoming the conviction of many thoughtful people that the old order cannot and should not be revived. This conviction has already found expression in international affairs through the United Nations Charter which substitutes the collective principle for the rampant isolationist nationalism of the old order.

Collective internationalism, however, is only in its initial stage. It is a planned experiment that resuires patience and good will, cooperation and understanding of the nations and peoples of the world. Although planned, the United Nations is also the end result of more than a century of wars and rivalries between nations. It is a gratifying phase of evolution from a hit-and-miss nationalism to conscious international control of many important factors that lead to war. It promises the realization of one of the Four Freedoms — freedom from fear.

However, the United Nations Charter, excepting certain social and economic reforms some of its agencies will promote, does not and cannot consider the maladjusted economy of each nation. That is a problem for the people of each nation to solve. That economic distress is still widespread throughout the world is obvious. The United States Department of Labor recently declared:

"Two-thirds of the people on earth have never enough to eat — though two-thirds work at producing food. About 75 percent of the people of Asia and 30 percent in advanced industrial countries live on a diet below a minimum standard of health. In some countries 200 out of every 1,000 babies born die during the first year. Approximately 50 percent of the adults of the world are unable to read or write. The majority of the factory workers of the world, including women and children, endure sweatshop conditions at substandard wages." [2]

Despite the vast productive powers of the United States we also have depressed areas where masses of men, women and children live in unsanitary conditions even in periods of prosperity. In short, while freedom from fear appears to be in the process of realization, freedom from want is a yearning which still haunts many millions of human beings throughout the world and it is generally recognized that economic impoverishment is one of the reasons that lead masses of human beings to seek content and plenty through one of the several forms of totalitarian dictatorship only to learn that they have escaped the uncertainties of the old order by accepting the certainty of brutal servitude.

The thought therefore arises, Is there no alternative between the chance-world of so-called "free enterprise" — with its uncertainties, recurring industrial depressions and widespread unemployment, its human wreckage in disease and malnutrition, its blighted hopes and despair for millions — and the dictatorship of a few despots? Has democracy no answer to this problem?

We believe that democracy not only has an answer but that it has the *only* answer that is satisfactory to freedom-loving human beings and that it may be found in the evolution of industrial society itself.

First as to "free enterprise." Our economic history shows that it has not always been free and that it has not always been enterprise. Throughout American history reliable records show that the more powerful forms of business enterprise have often relied upon colonial and, later, municipal, state and congressional legislative aid by direct subsidies, grants, gifts, taxation or tariffs. Reliance

[2] *Monthly Labor Review*, Journal of the United States Department of Labor, June, 1945.

upon its own resources and initiative has been typical of small business enterprise, not of the big and strong. The latter, because of its size, has been able to exercise pressure on legislative bodies and often to get its agents in legislative bodies to serve it directly. Too often, it must be said, its enterprise has been somewhat shady and certainly rarely free in the sense of relying on its own unaided efforts.[3]

The old concept of American individualism is a nationalistic phase of isolationism in international affairs and yet this individualism, as we have seen, has often been fiction, not fact. Our ranking American historian, Charles A. Beard, has shown in his monumental writings that in our political thinking fiction has often been its basis. Fifteen years ago when the great depression had already washed out this idea, Beard returned to this theme in a satirical article. Considering only the modern period, he cited fifteen of the major Federal measures that interfered with the individualist philosophy of business and noted that in every instance some phase of private enterprise itself had inspired and welcomed this interference. Of this he wrote:

"The point is that the Federal Government does not operate in a vacuum, but under impulsion from without; and all of the measures which put the Government into business have been supported by rugged individualists — business men or farmers or both. The current tendency to describe the Government as a meddling busybody, prying around and regulating for the mere pleasure of taking the joy out of somebody's life, betrays an ignorance of the facts in the case. The Government of the United States operates continually in the midst of the most powerful assembly of lobbyists the world has ever seen — the representatives of every business interest that

[3] The economic histories of Ernest L. Bogart, Catherine Coman, Walter W. Jennings, Edward C. Kirkland, and the massive three-volume *History of Manufactures in the United States*, by Victor S. Clark, to mention only a few, contain a wealth of material on this aspect of American life from the colonial period to recent years. See also the article by James Oneal, *The Umpire of Fairness*, in *The American Mercury*, June, 1929, for a short sketch of such legislative history in the colonial and constitutional periods.

has risen above the level of a corner grocery; and there is not a single form of government interference with business that does not have the approval of one or more of these interests — except perhaps the taxation of incomes for the purpose, among other things, of paying the expenses of subsidizing and regulating business." [4]

Double thinking and double talk regarding free enterprise and American individualism are barriers to an intelligent comprehension of our economic and social problems and it is time that we face facts rather than philosophical phantoms in our approach to the great tasks that confront us.

On the other hand, no one will question the fact that capitalist enterprise, a little over a century old in the United States, has on the whole been progressive and that the greatest powers of production the world has ever known have developed under its dominion. It is also true that the working masses in general have realized the highest standard of living of any nation, while literacy is more and more widespread each year. Conceding all this, it is also true that there are urban and rural slum areas that are a disgrace; that in various occupations the income of wageworkers and farmers is insufficient to maintain a decent human existence; that hundreds of thousands of proprietors of small businesses eke out a precarious existence, many disappearing in the abyss of bankruptcy; that when an economic crisis occurs, not only millions of farmers and wageworkers, but hundreds of thousands of professional men and heads of small business firms are swallowed up in the disaster, while many of the major industries are closed to millions of workmen whose very lives and the lives of their families depend upon access to these industries.

Moreover, the people of the United States, through the Federal and state governments, have again and again had to interfere with private enterprise to check and repair its ravages in polluted

[4] Charles A. Beard, "The Myth of Rugged American Individualism." *Harper's Magazine*, December, 1931.

waters, destruction of the soil (of which the Dust Bowl is a tragic result), restore our disappearing forests, engage in flood control of waters released by extensive private exploitation of soil and timber lands, protect our health by legislation against dangerous drugs and impure foods, guard against accidents and disease in mills, mines and factories, build public roads and bridges, establish traffic codes for our highways, bring order and democratic equity in radio broadcasting, and, finally, there is the whole system of social legislation to provide relief for the aged, the unemployed, widows, dependents, and other human by-products of private enterprise. All this is collective action for equitable social ends and no intelligent person will question its necessity.

Indeed, collective action, either voluntary or legislative, is as old as private enterprise itself. Many of us forget that the pioneers on each wave of our moving frontier across the continent, individualist as they were, also turned to collective action in many important matters that affected their well-being. This included co-operation in erecting communal stockades and storehouses, planting and reaping crops, corn and quilting bees, manufacturing and direct exchange of various articles without any profit motive, and organizing their caravans on the same principle to protect them against Indian raids.

Moreover, the pioneers and their sons in the eighties and nineties, while still retaining many individualist characteristics, also turned to legislative action in the Granger and Populist movements to modify the harsh conditions they faced. Of this period the leading authority on the American frontier wrote that the Western settler

"as he began to adjust his life to the modern forces of capital and to complex productive processes; as he began to see that, go where he would, the question of credit and currency, of transportation and distribution in general conditioned his success, he sought relief by legislation. He began to lose his primitive attitude of individualism, government began to look less like a necessary evil and more like an instrument for the perpetuation of his democratic ideals. In brief, the defenses of the pioneer democrat began to shift from free land to legislation, *from the ideal of individualism to the ideal of social control through regulation by law.*" [5]

American pioneers were also associated with a type of industry as old as private enterprise, a type that was non-profit in character and based upon consumption as its primary incentive. "The household, making goods for its own consumption, is the primordial unit of production," declares Edward C. Kirkland in his excellent *History of American Economic Life.* Throughout the colonial period a mass of useful articles was made in the homes of the people and this form of production survived into the middle of the nineteenth century. It was a family collectivism, a cell of industrial democracy, that never knew industrial depressions. This production was the "egg" from which many of our modern industries were hatched.

With the rude hand tools of the period, men women and children transformed raw materials into articles adapted for their use. The spinning wheel and handloom were always busy. Men made shoes or supplied the materials to the itinerant shoemaker. Hats, harness and nails were made in the home. Wheat was ground into flour and baked by the women. Animals were butchered and meat was cured and packed for use. The family clothing, candles, soap, dyes and preserves were manufactured. Livestock provided fats and hides, the former for making candles and the latter for making harness and shoes. Furniture — tables, stools, cradles, benches and beds — was manufactured of the material of the forests, while the same source also provided rakes and other farm tools, platters, spoons, bowls and other kitchen utensils.

Each home was a family collectivism of producers. Each member produced and each shared in the consumption of the output in accord with his or her needs. There was no employer and no wageworker, no hiring and no firing, no production for a market; supply and demand was a matter of family production and wants.

[5] Frederick Jackson Turner, *The Frontier in American History* (New York: Henry Holt and Company) © 1920, pp. 267-77.

Consequently, there was no "overproduction," no unemployment. Consumption balanced production and no "industrial depression" afflicted these family collectives. Moreover, the family owned the workplace, the tools and raw materials, and the members could work or play as they chose. They were not required to supply an uncertain market; they constituted their own market. Within this cell of democratic, cooperative and collectivist production, such words as "capital," "interest," "wages," "market," "supply," "demand," "profits," "price" and "value" had no meaning whatever. It housed infant industries that were to escape the producers' control and develop to vast proportions in later decades.

Space does not permit consideration of all the factors that led to the destruction of this household production — increasing population, specialization in the production of one or more articles, transfer of the workplace from the home to a shop, employment of one or more apprentices and payment of wages, extension of roads and canals and consequent growth of a market outside the home, the invention of machines to replace hand tools, the evolution of the shop into a modest factory, the multiplication of shops requiring itinerant wageworkers to serve them, the appearance of the merchant capitalist and industrial capitalist and complete emergence of the wage system, followed by the phenomenon of periodical industrial depressions.[6]

The reader will understand the profound revolution in our economic life wrought by this shift from family cooperation to private enterprise by noting the following eighteen contrasts between the two:

---

[6] The reader will find an informative account of the transition from the old system to the new in the following works: Rolla M. Tryon, *Household Manufactures in the United States, 1640-1860;* Blanche Evans Hazard, *The Organization of the Boot and Shoe Industry in Massachusetts Before 1875;* Richardson Wright, *Hawkers and Walkers in Early America;* Commons and Associates, *History of Labour in the United States,* Vol. 1, Chapters 2 and 3; Edward C. Kirkland, *A History of American Economic Life,* pp. 83-87.

COMPARISON OF THE TWO FORMS OF PRODUCTION

Household Production	Private Enterprise
Ownership of plant. Family.	Ownership of plant. Capitalist.
Ownership of tools. Family.	Ownership of machines. Capitalist.
Ownership of raw materials. Family.	Ownership of raw materials. Capitalist.
Ownership of product. Family.	Ownership of product. Capitalist.
Type. Collectivist.	Type. Private or corporate.
Control. Democratic.	Control. Often arbitrary.
Production. For use and enjoyment.	Production. For sale and profit.
Production-Consumption. Balanced.	Production-Consumption. Unbalanced.
Product. Use values.	Product Exchange values — Commodities.
Market. The family.	Market. Unknown.
Income. Product to family.	Income. Profits to owners: wages to workers.
Supply-Demand. Reciprocal.	Supply-Demand. No reciprocal relation.
Hiring and firing. None.	Hiring and firing. General.
Classes. None.	Classes. Owners and wageworkers.
Class conflicts. None.	Class conflicts. Frequent.
Labor power. Self-directed.	Labor power. Bought by owners, sold by workers.
Labor security. Assured.	Labor security. Precarious, uncertain.
Industrial Crisis. None.	Industrial crisis. Periodical.

It may be added that while family production was the primary source of modern private enterprise, there were also two minor sources. The first was a small type of industry generally outside the home, sometimes a family venture, occasionally the enterprise of one or several individuals. This type included gristmills, flour-mills, sawmills, ironworks, bloomeries, slitting mills, etc. These industries merely awaited the application of steam-driven machines to join the procession of factory enterprises emerging from old shop production, and the machine revolution brought what is known as "capitalist industry."

A large amount of private capital had also been invested in commerce and fisheries in New England, while a number of wealthy merchant princes engaged in the slave trade. The Napoleonic Wars and the War of 1812 prostrated New England commerce; and in the first two decades of the nineteenth century large sums of commercial and merchant capital were transferred to the development of industrial enterprise.

The stabilized industrial democracy of the home gradually vanished. Private enterprise multiplied, producing its own progeny, which in turn produced for markets the capacity of which no one knew. A mad scramble for business followed, chaotic and planless, like wild urchins escaped from parental control. Each ventured upon a career of individualism that became an American philosophy, heedless of the conflict and chaos produced by rivalries for conquest and power. Each carried within it the depression disease which has baffled mankind, the first prostration occurring in 1819-1822.

It is beyond the range of this work to consider this industrial evolution in its succeeding stages, through partnerships, corporations, trusts, cartels, etc. However, no matter what form the organization of modern industry and finance has taken each economic prostration has been more severe than the one that preceded it, while its range has gradually extended beyond our shores to include other nations with the same economy until nearly all nations were swallowed up in the convulsion that followed the first World War. Its outstanding characteristic is *a vast accumulation of usable but unsaleable commodities, idle machines, idle men, idle capital. Millions of people can use what they cannot buy but they cannot buy what they want to use!* There is a conflict between human wants and inequitable distribution of the products of private enterprise.[7]

Three congressional committees investigated the depressions of 1873 and 1886. Representatives of various groups and professions testified and Commissioner of Labor Wright listed their explanations under 68 main heads, including the following: undue influence of agitators, want of confidence, municipal corruption, an impractical common school system, devotion to new dress fashions, harmful indulgences, intemperance, disfranchisement of women, free passes on railroads, faulty collection of government revenue, tariff agitation, adulteration of food, inadequate training of girls for future duties, excessive use of tobacco and — "want of employment"!

It would be interesting to review the statements relating to depressions by our ruling parties in their platforms but we shall be content with two. The Democratic platform for 1920 declared:

"For fifty years before the advent of this Administration periodical convulsions had impeded the industrial progress of the American people and caused inestimable loss and distress. By enactment of the Federal Reserve Act, *the old system, which bred panics, was replaced by a new system which insured confidence.*"

---

[7] All of the economic historians agree that peace-time periodical depressions had their beginnings in the rise of private enterprise, the appearance of machine and factory production served by wage labor. In addition to the economic histories cited in Note 3 above, the reader will find invaluable material and discussion of American industrial depressions in the following: Samuel Rezneck, *The Depression of 1819-1822, A Social History, American Historical Review*, October, 1933; same author, *The Social History of an American Depression, 1837-1843, American Historical Review*, July, 1935; Reginald C. McCrane, *The Panic of 1837;* Carrol D. Wright, *First Annual Report of the Commissioner of Labor, Industrial Depressions;* Henry M. Hyndman, *Commercial Crises of the Nineteenth Century;* O. C. Lightner, *The History of Business Depressions.* The volumes of John Bach McMaster's *A History of the People of the United States,* that fall in the periods of the first three depressions, 1819-1857, also carry much interesting material, especially the reaction of the masses to each disaster and absurd "explanations" by eminent men regarding its causes.

By the end of the year 1920 a depression set in and continued to 1922.

The Republicans made a similar boast in their platform for 1928, saying:

"By unwavering adherence to sound principles, through the wisdom of Republican policies, the *foundations have been laid and the greatness and prosperity of the country firmly established*."

The platform added that "the mighty contribution to general well-being" made by the party and its leaders should not blind one "to the consequences" that would follow if they were not continued in office. Surely, a cynical fate was sharpening a sword for those who adopted this platform on the eve of the greatest industrial convulsion in the history of the world!

If many party leaders and statesmen were unable to understand the economics of the prevailing order the same proved true of others. From the presses had come many books by economists and publicists stressing the theme that the United States through mass production had assured permanent prosperity to the people. These gathered dust in old bookshops after October, 1929, with no buyers except collectors of curios.

Following the crash in Wall Street eminent financiers, traders, industrial executives, editors, publicists, educators, the President and members of his Cabinet in public statements rationed optimism, each insisting that the nation was sound, that the people were facing only a temporary setback, that prosperity was just around the corner, etc.

Early in 1931 a New York publishing house brought out a delightful little book of 60 pages[8] quoting these men on the soundness of our economic system through the year 1928, followed by their comments and soothing assurances beginning with the collapse on October 24, 1929. The latter section provides rare

8 Edward Angly, compiler, *Oh Yeah?*

comedy in that each assurance of health and recovery is followed by evidence of further sinking of industry to a new low level while unemployment was mounting into the millions. It was evident that all were guessing and were indulging in wishful thinking.

President Hoover obtained a pledge from a conference of big industrialists that they would not discharge any more workmen but the discharges continued and the idle army continued to increase. In the face of the overwhelming disaster, the employers were not heartless — they were helpless. They would have been foolish to produce useful but unsaleable goods. The need for those goods is almost unlimited but human needs do not mean *effective demand*. The only effective demand is money in the hands of the masses and they lacked this demand because of the general paralysis.

The farmer is little better off than the city workman. In an address to his neighbors in West Branch, Iowa, in August, 1928, President Hoover recalled the revolution that had come to the farms he had known. "Many farms," he declared, "were still places where we tilled the soil *for the immediate needs of our families.* We ground out wheat and corn on toll at the mill; we slaughtered our hogs for meat; we wove at least a part of our clothing; we repaired our own machinery; we got our own fuel from the woods; we erected our own buildings; we made our own soap; we preserved our own fruit and grew our own vegetables. Only a small part of our living came by purchases from the outside. . . . In a half century the whole basis of agriculture has shifted."

In short, industrial change has robbed the rural home and often left it with the rags and bones of industry. Credit and transportation are controlled by others. The farmer had reached a local market with his team but the market expanded to include the nation and the world. His team has been replaced by the great railroads' and ocean freighters owned by powerful corporations. At one time when he needed credit he obtained it from the neighbor he knew; today credit and finance constitute a vast web with its center in the great financial houses. Even if he knows the local banker the latter is often little more than a clerk in a financial chain. Gamblers in the grain and cotton markets, commission men, brokers and middlemen line the routes along which the products of the farmer flow. At his forge and anvil he once made his simple instruments or obtained the aid of the village blacksmith. These instruments have been transformed into costly machinery concentrated in industrial corporations. His productive yield per acre has enormously increased in the past hundred years, because of better soil analysis, improved fertilizers, control of insect parasites, deeper plowing, better adaptation of crops to the soil, and the use of machinery, but millions of farmers have not reaped the reward of increased production. *The farmer has largely become a helpless dependent of great industries which, as infants, left the homes of his ancestors and, during depressions, he is like Tantalus of Greek mythology who was plunged up to his chin in water with ripe fruit above his head, both of which receded when he attempted to drink or eat.*

Such contradictions between widespread want and widespread plenty not only affect urban and rural workers but millions of small storekeepers, retail merchants and professional men. It is out of such general economic and human decay that the demagogic totalitarian emerges to sell his false wares to millions in distress. What's to be done about it?

The authors do not pretend to have any final answer, but the historian can at least point out the general course of industrial evolution and indicate the character of the measures that promise intelligent control of our social order for the general good. The course taken must correlate with our democratic philosophy and aim away from the old isolationism and individualism towards the ideal of cooperation for human needs.

During the period of the Great Depression there were some shortsighted people who asserted that we face a choice between Fascism and Communism. This was saying we must accept totali-

tarian dictatorship, the only choice being the label. Such thinking unwittingly surrenders the whole democratic philosophy
which has been evolving out of social development and human
struggle and experience for several centuries. We may dismiss this
view as unworthy of consideration.

Considering the historical trend of American democracy, a
trend that is also apparent in the other English-speaking nations,
the Scandinavian countries, and among other peoples, it appears
that there are three courses before us. We may attempt to return
to the old order of unrestricted private enterprise which brought
the nation to its greatest crisis; we may decide to move forward to
a democratic and cooperative collectivism; or we may venture on
the path of a mixed economy, moving cautiously within the range
of democratic policy and administration.

Few of us want to return to the old era of isolationist-individual-
ism in domestic and foreign affairs. Moreover, to get back to the
age of "rugged individualism" we would have to rip out the Federal and state statutes that embody collective responsibility for
the welfare of farmers and city workmen and this would invite
widespread disorders and, probably, social upheavals. These
statutes cushion the hardships that come to millions of human
beings, hardships which are intimately related to unrestrained
private enterprise. This legislation is also especially essential to
those facing unmerited misfortune when private enterprise sinks
into a periodical depression.

Whatever may be said of democratic collectivism, it is certain
that the American individualist complex is too recent to forecast
any large-scale installment of it in the United States for many
years. However, the economic collectivist trend in American life
has received reluctant recognition even in conservative thought.
An illustration of this tendency was the brochure published in
1943 by the editors of *Time, Life and Fortune* magazines after two
years of research and study of American economic history. Commended by eminent men of finance and industry, instructors in

colleges and universities, members of Congress, state governors, publicists, economists and sociologists, this study revealed how outmoded the individualist maxims and general ideas of the economists of private enterprise had become because of vast economic changes since the days of Adam Smith, Charles Darwin, Herbert Spencer and William Graham Sumner.

Titled *America and the Future*, this study noted the drift from the old order towards mass production with its "collectivized Americans." The authors believed that by overhauling the tax structure, loosening up capital markets, prosecuting monopolies, re-examining corporate charters, reforming the patent system, and advance planning of public works, something like a mixed economy can be realized with security and freedom for all. Whether this is possible only the future can tell, but the authors certainly blasted with atomic force many of the ideas associated with the old concepts of private enterprise.

Just as significant of this thought trend in the upper ranges of society was a remarkable article by U. S. Senator Joseph C. O'Mahoney of Wyoming, in 1946. He had been Chairman of the Temporary National Economic Committee which in 1938 made a study of the concentration of economic power and is a member of the Special Post-War Economic Policy and Planning Committee. His services on these committees enabled him to explore the vast reaches of corporate development and power and to draw conclusions that challenge old concepts of private enterprise. "It is absurd, for example," the Senator wrote, "to think of General Motors or United States Steel as examples of private enterprise. They are collectivist economic states which exercise an influence upon the welfare of the people and which are as far beyond the powers of cities and counties and states to regulate in the public interest as is the airplane that hops from New York to San Francisco through the stratosphere."

The author noted a contradiction in the thinking of business executives who object to a state-managed economy and yet set the pattern for it "by insisting that private management shall have a free hand in running the hugh collectivist economic units of modern times." Such a free hand means a corporate-collective sovereignty over hundreds of thousands of human beings and society is compelled to intervene through state regulatory measures with a view to preventing gross inequities. If we are to successfully cope with the problems posed by these giant off-shoots of the old competitive era, we must think of them not in terms of private enterprise but as new types of economic organization that are stamped with the collective character.[9] And yet the collectivist trend in the United States since 1929 has been marked. It has not been a response to radical agitation but to grim necessity. The abyss that yawned for American economy was so grave that citizens of all classes and all political opinions acquiesced in various Federal measures — the New Deal, for example. Each violated the economic maxims and major party slogans of generations but so appalling was the national crisis that no one recalled them as it was evident they had failed.

These measures included the Civil Works Administration, the Agricultural Adjustment Act, the Tennessee Valley Authority, the Emergency Housing Division, the Public Works Administration, the Home Owners Loan Corporation, and the Farm Relief Act, to mention only a few of the major ones. Each measure empowered public agencies to assume some of the functions which in the old era had been considered as belonging solely to private enterprise. Of this dramatic phase of American history the Beards wrote:

"From decade to decade it had been revealed in the census returns of industry, agriculture, and labor, that the self-sufficing homestead and community were dying and that all the interests, occupations, properties, and callings of the nation were being drawn into a tighter and tighter web of

[9] This able and thought-provoking article appeared in *Dun's Review*, April, 1946.

economic interdependence. The commodities and articles produced in each center or region were scattered broadcast throughout the Union in exchange for goods of use and consumption. The complete independence of the farming family that satisfied all its own wants had almost vanished. For isolated individualism, always overemphasised in American thought and teaching, *was substituted an interlaced system of exchange and mutuality, correctly described as collectivism.*" [10]

In short, through no conscious design but because of general economic decay the nation had been shifted to a mixed economy, partly of private and partly of collective initiative. Old theories yielded to new facts which in turn are fostering social thinking adapted to a mixed economy.

The same period witnessed a similar revolution in the thinking of American trade unions. Like all other citizens union members were under the spell of American individualism. At its national convention in 1923 the American Federation of Labor adopted a long statement of its philosophy in which it opposed "state regulatory powers under the guise of reform and deliverance from evil." It was a renunciation of government as an agency for human welfare. Not until the Great Depression was there the beginning of a change; and it was late in 1932, when the American economy was sinking to its lowest level, that the A. F. of L. approved unemployment insurance which two years before it had condemned as a degrading "dole" and a policy that would "seriously interfere with freedom" by requiring "registration not only of the aliens among workers but of all workers." In the years following 1932 American trade unions completely abandoned their policy of opposing collective responsibility through legislative action for social welfare and have approved the whole body of Federal social legislation. The evolution from individualist to

10 Charles A. and Mary R. Beard, *America in Midpassage* (New York: The Macmillan Company) © 1945, Vol. I, p. 253. Readers may well consult Chapters IV, V and VI of this illuminating history of the period, including the last years of what are now vanished illusions and the emergence of public intervention and control to avert complete social and economic disaster.

collectivist thought in the A. F. of L. in the period of the depression is striking. The C. I. O. also accepts this social policy.[11]

Correlating with this marked change in the thinking and policy of urban worker has been the remarkable development of voluntary collectivism among American farmers — cooperatives in production and consumption. American agricultural cooperatives now constitute one of the biggest enterprises in the nation, doing an annual business of $2,400,000,000. They are organized in every state, their greatest foothold being in the North Central States of Minnesota, Wisconsin and Iowa, a section pronounced in its individualist philosophy and devotion to private enterprise fifty years ago.

About 2,000,000 producers own and control their cooperatives. The profits that normally go to private enterprise are retained in the capital structure of the co-ops or are distributed to members as patronage dividends. Each member has a voice in determining the policies of his co-op.

Nearly every product of the farm, including livestock, goes through co-ops to market. There are also 2,600 co-op farmers' elevators, over 500 cotton gins, and a number of seed-cleaning and processing plants. Co-ops provide members with farm machinery, paints and building materials; hardware and farm implements; binder twine and dynamite to remove stumps. Some 2,500 co-op water companies water dry Western soils, and a nation-wide co-op credit system provides loans at reasonable rates. Moreover, co-op insurance provides fire insurance of $11,000,000,000, and windstorm insurance in excess of $5,000,000,000.[12]

The development of this form of voluntary democratic collec-

---

[11] A.F. of L. *Convention Proceedings*, 1923, and for the years 1929-1936, inclusive. The discussions and decisions of these years vividly reveal the impact of changing economic conditions on the minds of the delegates. The year 1923 was one of prosperity, the other years a period of adversity with consequent abandonment of ideas and policies no longer adapted to serve the working masses.

[12] See *Producer Co-ops in Action*. Farm Credit Administration, Washington, D.C.

tivism is an amazing example of the change in the habits and thinking of an economic group whose members have been the most typical individualists in American history.

This form of cooperation is also obtaining increasing support of city dwellers. In various parts of the country, in 1943, about 4,500 cooperatives, declares a Federal Government publication, "are supplying themselves with one or more of nearly all kinds of goods and services," including housing associations which "provide apartments and individual dwellings." [13]

Late in 1945 the Labor Department reported that "continued expansion in both membership and business was exhibited by the consumers cooperative movement in 1944. The distributive and service business of the local associations reached an all-time high of $568,000,000, and the regional and district wholesale associations supplying them had an aggregate business of over $155,000,000. Service federations reported a total business of over $700,500,000. Nearly $8,000,000 was declared in patronage refunds to the membership associations."

Cooperative production has also been increasing "very rapidly in the past few years. In 1944 the value of goods produced in cooperative plants reporting amounted to $65,000,000 — more than twice the value produced in the preceding year." [14]

Voluntary collectivism is a notable phenomenon of many nations, Great Britain leading the world and on such a scale that the most recent comprehensive survey declares that the British co-ops have created the "world's Biggest Business." [15]

[13] *Monthly Labor Review*, January, 1944.
[14] *Ibid.*, September, 1945.
[15] See Sydney R. Elliott, *The English Cooperatives*. Yale University Press, 1937. An excellent world-wide view of the development of this movement may be consulted in the *Encyclopedia of the Social Sciences*, Vol. IV (1930), some forty pages being devoted to it. The various types of collectives in Finland, Sweden, Norway and Denmark indicate that private enterprise has yielded a third or more of the field to the collective principle, while in Denmark it yielded so much before Hitler's invasion that this little nation has been frequently referred to as a cooperative commonwealth.

Moreover, the four biggest enterprises in the United States are of the collective type, the Panama Canal Zone, the Post Office, the manufacture of the atomic bomb, and the Tennessee Valley Authority. The first three are completely collectivized in that they are national property, while in Panama private enterprise is completely eliminated! The government owns the two railroads on the Isthmus and two lines of steamers. It owns restaurants, hotels and homes, foundries and repair shops and inherited a large cooperative in groceries when it took over. It owns its bakery, ice plant, laundry, printing plant, department store and other enterprises. Labor unions are recognized and encouraged and the administration is democratic in spirit although, as in the District of Columbia, there is no suffrage.[16]

Readers are too familiar with the Post Office and the manufacture of the atomic bomb to warrant more than the above reference to them, but TVA is a unique variation in the application of the collective principle. As a regional collective venture TVA is what President Truman called a "two-way" partnership with state, local and private agencies under the direction of three members who have the power to issue securities; build dams, reservoirs, powerhouses and transmission lines; to produce fertilizers and produce and sell electric power to corporations, states, counties, cities, rural cooperatives and individuals. It has provided unified development of an important valley and its low retail rates have especially encouraged cities, towns and cooperatives. Speaking at the dedication of TVA's Kentucky dam on October 10, 1945, President Truman declared that TVA policy should be followed in other river valleys of the nation. As a half-way departure from private enterprise this type of regional collective has possibilities of expansion into other fields.

Significant of the economic-collective trend has also been the

---

[16] See Ralph Edwards (A. Bullard), *Panama: The Canal, the Country and The People*, especially the chapter, Experiments in Collective Activity.

emergence of the great corporation, undemocratic in structure and management compared with the voluntary cooperatives. Its history, legal and economic; its structure, purposes, control and trends are portrayed in a remarkable work [17] prepared under the auspices of the Columbia University Council for Research in the Social Sciences. Convinced that "American industrial property, through the corporate device, was being thrown into a collective hopper wherein the individual owner was steadily being lost in the creation of a series of huge industrial oligarchies," the authors contend that perhaps "two-thirds of the industrial wealth of the country" has been transformed "from individual ownership to ownership by the large, publicly financed corporations" which "vitally changes the lives of property owners, the lives of workers, and the methods of property tenure. The divorce of ownership from control consequent on that process almost necessarily involves a new form of economic organization of society."

The authors also show with a convincing wealth of argument that the old concepts of Adam Smith and other classical economists regarding private property, wealth, private enterprise, individual initiative, the profit motive and competition have little or no application to the great corporation. *There is little private property left within its range.* They add that our problem is how to democratize this undemocratic collective so that it will serve "not alone the owners or the control but all society." Unfortunately, this nonviolent revolution in our economic life is far advanced without any general recognition of its significance.

Finally, the Full Employment Bill, passed by the Senate and now (October, 1945) before the House, is another phase of the evolution towards a national policy of collective responsibility for human welfare. It would not have the government take over any

[17] Adolf A. Berle, Jr., and Gardiner C. Means, *The Modern Corporation and Private Property.* New York, 1932. See also Charles A. and Mary R. Beard, *America in Midpassage*, Vol. II, pp. 873-80, for an informed discussion of the facts and trends presented in this and other studies.

industries but it would vest the President with authority to submit an annual budget on production and employment to Congress, to estimate the total labor force seeking jobs, the number of non-federal and private jobs available, and recommend measures to cancel any disparity between the two. As a last resort, if a deficit of jobs is still evident, the Federal Government shall engage in public works and improvements.

Here again, necessity rather than agitation is responsible for this idea of a partnership with business in assurance of jobs to the jobless. Fearful of another depression and its consequent dangers, knowing that a policy of drift in the American economy is hazardous, this policy, which would not have received even casual consideration at the beginning of the Great Depression, is now approved by many conservative men.

In testimony supporting this bill, Reconversion Director John W. Snyder declared that the depression of the thirties cost the nation 300 billion dollars in goods and services that "we could have produced but did not due to economic stagnation." That some over-all planning by a national agency is necessary is evident from our history. The executives of each great enterprise know their own business. They have a fairly good idea of market prospects but the inter-relationships of the whole national economy in terms of finance, production, distribution, transportation, communications, labor force — private and public — agriculture, wholesale and retail business, are beyond the ken of executives of any particular business. This was evident in the absurd statements made by many for several years after the collapse in Wall Street in October, 1929.[18] The mass of information necessary to an over-all understanding of our complex economy is available in the various departments and bureaus of the Federal Government and, supplemented by the studies and reports of reliable private research organizations, the American people have a vast reservoir of data

[18] See Reference 7 above.

which will enable the President and his advisers to aid in bringing some order and coordination in to our economic life. Moreover, to prevent economic disaster or to render it less acute should another depression occur is more humane and less costly than to let the malady slowly accumulate and then overwhelm us by its elemental force.

It is obvious that social and economic evolution is modifying the old social order in the democratic nations and the tendency is towards a mixed economy of private and collective initiative with a large installment of democratic collectivism in some countries. Our survey of American history shows that we are not a nation apart from this general trend. Moreover, far from impairing the democratic ideal this shift from an irresponsible individualism to collective responsibility for human welfare is fulfilling this ideal.

A mixed economy also allows for cautious experiment, for a policy of trial and error, advance and retreat, in feeling our way out of the complex dangers which thirty years of wars and depression have brought to humanity. Democratic controls now available and others which we may set up to inspect and recommend, to reject and approve, will guard against bureaucracy and give an alert democracy a consciousness of its responsibility.

We have traced the evolution of the collective principle in American history and we have seen that it has advanced from thinking to action from the colonial period to the present; that it has accompanied private initiative, voluntary and legislative, and that it has emerged from crises, emergencies and human experience rather than its being the result of long agitation by "dreamers." Changed conditions have modified old ideas and policies and these in turn have modified the old order through voluntary and legislative action, the general trend being away from a hit-and-miss irresponsibility towards national collective responsibility.

This trend is enhanced by the sudden precipitation of humanity into the Atomic Age with all of its fears, uncertainties and problems. We had not yet completely adjusted ourselves to the steam and electric-power age when this new and terrifying energy was released by science. General comment includes its profound effects upon industry and our whole social order, the forecasts all correlating with the collective principle discussed above. Typical of this reasoning is the assertion that "man now has it within his grasp to emancipate himself economically. If he wills it, he is in a position to refine his competitive impulse; he can take the step from competitive man to cooperative man. He has at last unlocked enough of the earth's secrets to provide for his needs on a world scale." [19]

The satanic possibilities of this new power, if employed in war, are also so staggering that its control to avert the destruction of civilization is thought of only in terms of the collective principle, national and international. George Bryan Logan, Jr., anticipated this in a remarkable book published nearly twenty years ago. The disparity between our material and moral cultures, declared Logan, is aptly dramatized in the uses to which modern science has been put in war. "This way lies madness," he wrote. "Sooner or later the end of everything we know as civilization will go down in destruction, should this Frankenstein, science, uninformed with moral sense, break from our control and in sheer horror of its own fiendish aspect strike blindly to left and right." [20]

There is little doubt that the people of the world have entered a period of profound changes that recall the destruction of the remnants of feudal society as a result of the Napoleonic Wars.

[19] Editorial in *The Saturday Review of Literature*, August 18, 1945.

[20] George Bryan Logan, Jr., *Liberty in the Modern World*. University of North Carolina Press, © 1928. The disparity between our material and moral cultures is also responsible for the failure of this notable book to win a high place in the literature of American democracy. Published in the last year before the Great Depression, Logan's work, because of the general engrossment in material success, fell on deaf ears. In nine essays the author explored the implications of democracy and liberty in terms of law, thought and expression, government, work, history, science, humanism and religion, with a literary power and charm recalling some of the best passages of Emerson. This work still has a contemporary ring, is an antidote for stodgy thinking, and deserves a better reception.

For a time the Holy Alliance attempted to dam Niagara and return to the old era but its nostalgic dream vanished in the flood of new social, economic and political trends. Today many would still follow the course of these powdered-wig, impractical visionaries. On the threshold of a new epoch, they recall Matthew Arnold's graphic reference to those

> *Wandering between two worlds — one dead,*
> *The other powerless to be born.*

We cannot change the new tides, and to drift would be to yield to a policy of fatalism. We can control and guide the forces that are shaping a new civilization. We are part of those forces, the conscious element that can decide whether the democratic pattern shall continue; or we can yield to the wild, the ill-informed and the destructive misfits of humanity whose triumph can only result in the Cattle State of totalitarian dictatorship.

PROGRAM OF LEFT WING SOCIALISTS, 1919

IT is the task of a revolutionary Socialist Party to direct the struggles of the proletariat and provide a program for the culminating crisis. Its propaganda must be so directed that when this crisis comes, the workers will be prepared to accept a program of the following character:

(a) The organization of Workmen's Councils; recognition of, and propaganda for, these mass organizations of the working class as instruments in the immediate struggle, as the form of expression of the class struggle, and as the instruments for the seizure of the power of the State and the basis of the new proletarian State of the organized producers and the dictatorship of the proletariat.

(b) Workmen's control of industry, to be exercised by the industrial organizations (industrial unions or Soviets) of the workers and industrial vote, as against government ownership or State control of industry.

(c) Repudiation of all national debts — with provisions to safeguard small investors.

(d) Expropriation of the banks — a preliminary measure for the complete expropriation of all capital.

(e) Expropriation of the railways, and the large (trust) organizations of capital — no compensation to be paid, as "buying-out" the capitalists would insure a continuance of the exploitation of the workers; provision, however, to be made during the transition period for the protection of small owners of stock.

(f) The socialization of foreign trade.

These are not the "immediate demands" comprised in the social reform planks now in the platform of our party; they are not a compromise with the capitalist State, but imply a revolutionary struggle against that State and against capitalism, the conquest of power by the proletariat through revolutionary mass action. They imply the new Soviet State of the organized producers, the dictatorship of the proletariat; they are preliminary revolutionary measures for the expropriation of capital and the introduction of Communist Socialism.

1. We stand for a uniform declaration of principles in all party platforms both local and national and the abolition of all social reform planks now contained in them.

2. The party must teach, propagate and agitate exclusively for the overthrow of capitalism, and establishment of Socialism through a proletarian dictatorship.

3. The Socialist candidates elected to office shall adhere strictly to the above provisions.

4. Realizing that a political party cannot reorganize and reconstruct the industrial organizations of the working class, and that that is the task of the economic organizations themselves, we demand that the party assist this process of reorganization by a propaganda for revolutionary industrial unionism as part of its general activities. We believe it is the mission of the Socialist movement to encourage and assist the proletariat to adopt newer and more effective forms of organization and to stir it into newer and more revolutionary modes of action.

5. We demand that the official party press be party-owned and controlled.

6. We demand that officially recognized educational institutions be party-owned and controlled.

7. We demand that the party discard its obsolete literature and publish new literature in keeping with the policies and tactics above mentioned.

8. We demand that the National Executive Committee call an immediate emergency national convention for the purpose of formulating party policies and tactics to meet the present crisis.

9. We demand that the Socialist Party repudiate the Berne Congress or any other conference engineered by "moderate Socialists" and social patriots.

10. We demand that the Socialist Party shall elect delegates to the International Congress proposed by the Communist Party of Russia (Bolsheviki); that our party shall participate only in a new International with which are affiliated the Communist Party of Russia (Bolsheviki); the Communist Labor Party of Germany (Spartacans), and all other Left Wing parties and groups.

THE 21 POINTS OF THE THIRD INTERNATIONAL
Adopted in Moscow, July-August, 1920

THE second congress of the Communist International adopts the following conditions for membership in the Communist International:

1. The entire propaganda and agitation must bear a genuinely Communistic character and agree with the program and the decisions of the Third International. All the press organs of the party must be managed by responsible Communists who have proved their devotion to the cause of the proletariat.

The dictatorship of the proletariat must not be talked about as if it were an ordinary formula learned by heart, but it must be propagated for in such a way as to make its necessity apparent to every plain worker, soldier and peasant through the facts of daily life, which must be systematically watched by our press and fully utilized from day to day.

The periodical and non-periodical press and all party publishing concerns must be under the complete control of the party management, regardless of the fact that the party as a whole being at that moment legal or illegal. It is inadmissable for the publishing concerns to abuse their autonomy and to follow a policy which does not entirely correspond to the party's policy.

In the columns of the press, at public meetings, in trade unions, in cooperatives, and all other places where the supporters of the Third International are admitted, it is necessary systematically and unmercifully to brand, not only the bourgeoisie, but also its accomplices, the reformers of all types.

2. Every organization that wishes to affiliate with the Communist International must regularly and systematically remove the reformists and centrist elements from all the more or less important posts in the

labor movement (in party organizations, editorial offices, trade unions, parliamentary groups, cooperatives and municipal administrations) and replace them with well-tried Communists, without taking offense at the fact that, especially in the beginning, the places of "experienced" opportunists will be filled by plain workers from the masses.

3. In nearly every country of Europe and America the class struggle is entering upon the phase of civil war. Under such circumstances the Communists can have no confidence in bourgeois legality.

It is their duty to create everywhere a parallel illegal organization machine which at the decisive moment will be helpful to the party in fulfilling its duty to the revolution.

In all countries where the Communists, because of a state of siege and because of exceptional laws directed against them, are unable to carry on their whole work legally, it is absolutely necessary to combine legal with illegal activities.

4. The duty of spreading Communist ideas includes the special obligation to carry on a vigorous and systematic propaganda in the army. Where this agitation is forbidden by laws of exception it is to be carried on illegally. Renunciation of such activities would be the same as treason to revolutionary duty and would be incompatible with membership in the Third International.

5. It is necessary to carry on a systematic and well-planned agitation in the country districts. The working class cannot triumph unless its policy will have insured it the support of the country proletariat and at least a part of the poorer farmers, and the neutrality of part of the rest of the village population. The Communistic work in the country is gaining greatly in importance at the present time.

It must principally be carried on with the help of the revolutionary workers in the city and the country who have connections in the country. Renunciation of this work or its transfer to unreliable, semi-reformist hands is equal to renunciation of the proletarian revolution.

6. Every party that wishes to belong to the Third International is obligated to unmask not only open social patriotism, but also the dishonesty and hypocrisy of social pacifism, and systematically bring to

the attention of the workers the fact that, without the revolutionary over-throw of capitalism, no kind of an international court of arbitration, no kind of an agreement regarding the limitation of armaments, no kind of a "democratic" renovation of the League of Nations will be able to prevent fresh imperialistic wars.

7. The parties wishing to belong to the Communist International are obligated to proclaim a clean break with the reformism and with the policy of the "center" and to propagate this break throughout the ranks of the entire party membership. Without this a logical Communist policy is impossible.

The Communist International demands unconditionally and in the form of an ultimatum the execution of this break within a very brief period. The Communist International cannot reconcile itself to a condition that would allow notorious opportunists, such as are now represented by Turati, Kautsky, Hilferding, Hillquit, Longuet, MacDonald, Modigliani, et al., to have the right to be counted as members of the Third International. That could only lead to the Third International resembling to a high degree the dead Second International.

8. In the matter of colonies and oppressed nations a particularly clear-cut stand by the parties is necessary in those countries whose bourgeoisie is in possession of colonies and oppresses other nations. Every party wishing to belong to the Communist International is obligated to unmask the tricks of "its" own imperialists in the colonies, to support every movement for freedom in the colonies, not only with words but with deeds, to demand the expulsion of its native imperialists from those colonies, to create in the hearts of the workers of its own country a genuine fraternal feeling for the working population of the colonies and for the oppressed nations and to carry on a systematic agitation among the troops of its own country against all oppression of the colonial peoples.

9. Every party wishing to belong to the Third International must systematically and persistently develop a Communist agitation within the trade unions, the workers' and shop councils, the cooperatives of consumption and other mass organizations of the workers. Within these organizations it is necessary to organize Communist

nuclei which, through continuous and persistent work, are to win over the trade unions, etc., for the cause of Communism. These nuclei are obligated in their daily work everywhere to expose the treason of social patriots and the instability of the "center." The Communist nuclei must be completely under the control of the party as a whole.

10. Every party belonging to the Communist International is obligated to carry on a stubborn struggle against the Amsterdam "International" of the yellow trade unions. It must carry on a most emphatic propaganda among the workers organized in trade unions for a break with the yellow Amsterdam International. With all its means it must support the rising international association of the Red trade unions which affiliate with the Communist International.

11. Parties wishing to belong to the Third International are obligated to subject the personnel of the parliamentary groups to a revision, to cleanse these groups of all unreliable elements, and to make these groups subject to the party executives, not only in form but in fact, by demanding that each Communist member of Parliament subordinate his entire activities to the interests of genuinely revolutionary propaganda and agitation.

12. The parties belonging to the Communist International must be built upon the principle of democratic centralization. In the present epoch of acute civil war the Communist Party will only be in a position to do its duty if it is organized along extremely centralized lines, if it is controlled by iron discipline, and if its party central body, supported by the confidence of the party membership, is fully equipped with power, authority and the most far-reaching faculties.

13. The Communist parties of those countries where the Communists carry on their work legally must from time to time institute cleansings (now registrations) of the personnel of their party organization in order to systematically rid the party of the petit bourgeois elements creeping into it.

14. Every party wishing to belong to the Communist International is obligated to offer unqualified support to every Soviet republic in its struggle against the counter-revolutionary forces. The Communist

parties must carry on a clean-cut propaganda for the hindering of the transportation of munitions of war to the enemies of the Soviet Republic; and, furthermore, they must use all means, legal or illegal, to carry propaganda, etc., among the troops sent to throttle the workers' republic.

15. Parties that have thus far still retained their old Social Democratic programs are now obligated to alter these programs within the shortest time possible and, in accordance with the particular conditions of their countries, work out a new Communist program in the sense of the decisions of the Communist International, or as a rule the program of every party belonging to the Communist International must be sanctioned by the regular Congress of the Communist International, by its executive committee.

In case the program of any party is not sanctioned by the executive committee of the Communist International, the party concerned has the right to appeal to the Congress of the Communist International.

16. All decisions of the Congress as of the Communist International, as well as the decisions of its executive committee, are binding upon all the parties belonging to the Communist International. The Communist International, which is working under conditions of the most acute civil war, must be constructed along much more centralized lines than was the case with the Second International.

In this connection, of course, the Communist International and its executive committee must, in their entire activities, take into consideration the varied conditions under which the individual parties have to fight and labor, and only adopt decisions of general application regarding such questions as can be covered by such decisions.

17. In connection with this, all parties wishing to belong to the Communist International must change their names. Every party wishing to belong to the Communist International must bear the name: Communist Party of such and such a country (section of the Third Communist International). The question of name is not only a formal matter, but is also to a high degree a political question of great importance.

The Communist International has declared war upon the whole bourgeois world and all yellow Social Democratic parties. It is necessary to make clear to every plain working man the difference between the Communist parties and the old official "Social Democratic" and "Socialist" parties that have betrayed the banner of the working class.

18. All the leading press organs of the parties of all countries are obligated to print all important documents of the executive committee of the Communist International.

19. All parties that belong to the Communist International, or that have applied for admission to it, are obligated to call, as soon as possible, but at the latest not more than four months after the second congress of the Communist International, a special convention for the purpose of examining all these conditions.

20. Those parties that thus far wish to enter into the Third International, but have not radically changed their former tactics, must see to it that two-thirds of the members of their central committees and of all their important central bodies are Comrades who unambiguously and publicly declared in favor of their party's entry into the Third International before the second congress of the Communist International.

Exceptions may be allowed with the approval of the executive committee of the Third International. The executive committee of the Communist International also has the right to make exceptions in the cases of the representatives of the center tendencies named in paragraph 7.

21. Those party members who, on principle, reject the conditions and those laid down by the Communist International are to be expelled from the party. The same thing applies especially to delegates to the special party convention.

APPENDIX III

INSTRUCTIONS FOR COMMUNIST FACTIONS

THE instructions of the Executive Committee of the Communist International to all affiliated organizations, adopted in Moscow on February 27, 1924, make a document of over 10,500 words. It is divided into three sections. The first is titled "Resolution of the Executive Committee of the Communist International on the organization of Factory Nuclei"; the second, "Introduction to Instruction for Communist Factions in Non-Party Institutions and Organizations;" the third, "Instructions for Communist Factions in Non-Party Institutions and Organizations." The entire document is too long to be included in this Appendix but the third section is printed below.

The aim of Communists in all "united fronts," as the three documents reveal, is to compromise opponents, sow suspicion in their ranks, divide democratic forces, exhaust them by dilatory methods at meetings, and split the organization if it cannot be captured.

The three documents were carried in *International Press Correspondence*, Vienna, issue of February 27, 1924, an official publication of the Communist International. The third section follows.

1. Wherever there are not less than three communists in workers' and peasants' organizations and in various institutions — trade unions, cooperatives, educational, athletic and other societies, factory and unemployed committees, as well as at congresses, conferences and in municipal councils, parliaments, etc. — it is essential to establish a communist faction with the object of increasing Party influence and introducing the policy of the Party into non-party masses.

2. All communist factions, regardless of their size and importance, must be subordinate to corresponding party organs — the nucleus (the executive committee of the nucleus), group, local, district (in America, nucleus, branch, section, local, district) or central committee, according to the positions occupied by the given communist faction

(local or national). Such Party organs must issue the necessary instructions to the communist factions (thus, for instance, the executive committee of a factory nucleus must control and direct the work of the communist faction in the factory committee, in accordance with the directives received from the higher Party organs. District committees must control and direct the work of the communist factions in all the non-party organs and organizations in its district, etc.). In all questions on which decisions were made by corresponding Party organizations, the factions must strictly abide by these decisions.

3. When discussing in the Party committees questions concerning a faction, the committee must carefully prepare these questions and organize preliminary conferences with the representatives of the faction wherever existing police conditions allow.

4. Communist factions, with the consent of the corresponding Party committee, elect their executive committee, which is responsible to the corresponding Party organ for the work of the factions.

5. During the interval between congresses (conferences), the communist factions within the executive committees of local trade unions and cooperatives are the guiding and unifying organs of all communists in these organizations. The communist faction in the executive boards of trades councils (in America, central labor councils, state federations of labor) and of district cooperatives, are the guiding and unifying organs for all communists in these organizations.

These factions are all subordinate to the control of the local or district Party committee, but must also report to the factions in local conferences or district conventions of trade unions and cooperatives. Candidates to the executive boards of the above-mentioned organizations are nominated by the factions of the corresponding conferences and conventions in agreement with the local or district Party committee. The above regulations apply also to the national trade union and cooperative congresses or conventions.

6. The corresponding Party committee has the right to install or recall any member from the faction, notifying the faction of the reason for such action.

7. Communist factions must come to an agreement with the corresponding Party organs with respect to candidatures to the executive boards of all the organs mentioned above. The same procedure is to be adopted with respect to recalls or transfers from one faction to another.

8. Factions have complete autonomy in questions of their inner life and current work. Party committees must not interfere with their everyday work. They must, on the contrary, allow factions as much freedom of action and initiative as possible. In the event of serious differences of opinion between the Party committee and the faction on any question within the competence of the latter, the corresponding Party committee must once more investigate this question together with the representative of the faction, and arrive at a final decision by which the faction must abide.

9. All questions having a political significance and subject to discussion by the faction, must be discussed in the presence of representatives of the committee. The committees must delegate their representatives immediately on receipt of a notification from the faction.

10. Every question subject to the decision of non-Party institutions and organizations in which the faction works, must be previously discussed at a general meeting or in the executive committee of the faction.

11. Party organizations [nuclei, group (branch) local and other bodies. Party conferences and conventions or committees elected by them] should receive reports on the work of factions, decide on the tactics and political lines of their further work, etc.

12. At general meetings of non-Party organizations, all faction members must act and vote as a unit on all questions. Disciplinary measures must be taken against any Party members infringing this regulation.

APPENDIX IV

CONSTITUTION OF THE THIRD INTERNATIONAL

THIS document is not easy to obtain as it is intended only for members of the Communist Party. It is reprinted from a pamphlet, *Program of the Communist International*, published by the Workers Library Publishers, New York, 1936, an agency of the Communist Party. Its first paragraph shows that Moscow plans a world dictatorship, just as Tojo and Hitler did. Considering the general uniformity of action by the affiliated parties in all countries since the announcement of the "dissolution" of the Comintern, there is reason for believing that it is still functioning or that a substitute for it is directing these parties.

Section 36 shows that each party is required to hold itself in readiness to go underground.

To the Constitution we also append sections of the Program which show that Communism plans for the "violent overthrow of bourgeois power," not by the acquisition of political power through popular elections.

PROGRAM OF THE COMMUNIST INTERNATIONAL

N.Y. WORKERS LIBRARY PUBLISHERS, 1936

CONSTITUTION OF THE COMMUNIST INTERNATIONAL

I. NAME AND OBJECT

1. The Communist International — the International Workers' Association — is a union of Communist Parties in various countries; it is the world Communist Party. As the leader and organizer of the world revolutionary movement of the proletariat and the protagonist

of the priniciples and aims of Communism, the Communist International strives to win over the working class and the broad strata of the property-less peasantry, fights for the establishment of the world dictatorship of the proletariat, for the establishment of a World Union of Socialist Soviet Republics, for the complete abolition of classes and for the achievement of Socialism — the first stage of Communist society.

2. Each of the various Parties affiliated to the Communist International is called the Communist party of ....
name and country (Section of the Communist International). In any given country there can be only one Communist Party affiliated to the *Communist International* and *constituting* its *Section* in that *country*.

3. Membership in the Communist Party and in the Communist International is open to all those who *accept* the *program* and *rules* of the respective Communist Party and of the *Communist International*, who join one of the basic units of the Party, actively work in it, abide by all the decisions of the Party *and* of the *Communist International*, and pay Party dues.

4. The basic unit of the Communist Party organization is the place of employment (factory, workshop, mine, office, store, farm, etc.,) which unites all the Party members employed in the given enterprise.

5. The Communist International and *its Sections* are built up on the basis of democratic centralism, the fundamental principles of which are:

(a) election of all the leading committees of the Party, from the lowest to the highest (by general meetings of the Party members, cpnferences, congresses and International congresses);

(b) periodical reports by leading Party committees to their *constituents:*

(c) decisions of the *higher* Party organs to be *obligatory* for the *lower* organs, strict party discipline and *prompt execution* of the *decisions* of the *Communists International*, of its leading committees and of the leading Party centers.

Party questions may be discussed by the members of the party and by party organizations until such time as a decision is taken upon them by the competent party organs. After a decision has been taken by the congress of the Communist International, by the congress of the respective Section, or by *leading committee* of the *Comitern*, and of its various Section, the decision must be unreservedly carried out even if a part of the party membership or of the local Party organizations are in disagreement with it. In cases where a Party exist illegally, the higher Party committee may appoint the lower committees and co-opt members for their own committee, subject to subsequent endorsement by the competent higher Party committees.

6.   In all non-party workers' and peasants' mass organizations and in their leading committees (trade unions, co-operative societies, sport organizations, ex-servicemen organizations, and of their congresses and conferences) and also on municipal elective bodies and in parliament, even if there are only *two Party members* in such organizations and bodies, *Communist factions* must be *formed* for the purpose of *strengthening* the *Party's influence* and for *carrying* out its *policy* in these organizations and *bodies.*

7.   The Communist factions are subordinated to the competent Party bodies.

NOTE: *A.* Communist factions in international organizations (Red International of Labor Unions,* International Labor Defense, Workers International Relief,** etc.,) are *subordinate* to the *executive* Committee of the *Communist International.*

B. The organizational structure of the Communist factions and the manner in which their work is guided are determined by special instructions from the executive committee of the Communist International and from the Central Committee of the respective Sections of the Comintern,

---

* In United States known as the T.U.U.L. Trade union unity league.

** In United States known as the I.W.O. International Worker's Order.

8.   The supreme body of the Communist International is the World Congress of representatives of all parties (Section) and organizations affiliated to the Communist International.

The World Congress discusses and decides the programmatic, tactical and organizational questions connected with the activities of the Communist International and of its various Sections. *Power* to *alter* the program and Constitution of the Communist International *lies exclusively* with the *World Congress* of the Communist International.

The World Congress shall be convened once every two years. The date of the Congress and the number of representatives from various Sections to the Congress to be determined by the Executive Committee of the Communist International.

The number of decisive votes to be allocated to each Section at the World Congress shall be determined by the special decision of the Congress itself, in accordance with the membership of the respective country. Delegates to the Congress must have a free mandate; no imperative mandate can be recognized.

9.   Special Congresses of the Communist International shall be convened on the demand of Parties which at the preceding World Congress had an aggregate of not less than one-half of decisive votes.

10.   The World Congress elects the Executive Committee of the Communist International (E.C.C.I.) and the International Control Commission (I.C.C.)

11.   The location of the headquarters of the Executive Committee is decided on by the World Congress.

III. The Executive of the Communist International and its Subsidiary Bodies

12.   The *leading body* of the Communist International in the period between Congresses is the *Executive Committee*, which gives *instructions* to all the Sections of the Communist International and *controls* their *activity*.

Appendix

The E.C.C.I. publishes the central organ of the Communist International, in not less than four languages.

13. The decision of the E.C.C.I. are *obligatory* for all the *Sections* of the Communist International and *must* be promptly carried out.

14. The Central Committees of the various Sections of the Communist International are responsible to their respective Party Congresses and to the E.C.C.I. The latter has the right to *annul* or *amend decisions* of Party Congresses and of Central Committees of Parties.

15. The E.C.C.I. has the *right* to *expel* from the Communist International, *entire Sections*, *groups* and individual members who violate the program and constitution of the Communist International or the decision of the World Congress or of the E.C.C.I.

16. The programs of the various Sections of the Communist International must be endorsed by the E.C.C.I.

17. The E.C.C.I. has the right to accept affiliation to the Communist International of organizations and Parties sympathetic to Communism, such organizations to have a consulative voice.

18. The E.C.C.I. elects a Presidium responsible to the E.C.C.I. which acts as the permanent body carrying out all the business of the E.C.C.I. in the interval between the meeting of the latter.

19. The E.C.C.I. and its presidium have the right to establish permanent bureaus (Western European, South American, Eastern and other Bureaus of the E.C.C.I.), (*) for the purpose of establishing closer contact with the various Sections of the Communist International and in order to be better able to guide their work.

NOTE: The scope of the activities of the permanent bureaus of the E.C.C.I. shall be determined by the E.C.C.I. or by its presidium. The Sections of the Communist International which come within the scope of activities of the permanent bureaus of the E.C.C.I. must be informed of the powers conferred on those bureaus.

20. The Sections must carry out the instructions of the permanent bureaus of the E.C.C.I.

21. The E.C.C.I. and its presidium have the right to send their representatives to the various sections of the Communist International. Such representatives receive their instructions from the E.C.C.I. or from its presidium, and are responsible to them for their activities. Representatives of the E.C.C.I. have the right to participate in meetings of the Central Party bodies as well as of the local organizations of the Sections to which they are sent. Representatives of the E.C.C.I. must carry out their commission in close contact with the Central Committee of the Section to which they are sent. They may, however, speak in *opposition* to the *Central Committee* of the given *Section*, if the line of the Central Committee in question diverges from the instructions of the E.C.C.I. Representatives of the E.C.C.I. are especially *obliged* to *supervise* the carrying out the decisions of the World Congresses and of the E.C.C.I.

The E.C.C.I. and its Presidium also have the right to send instructors to the various Sections of the Communist International. The powers and duties of instructors are determined by the E.C.C.I. to whom the instructors are responsible in their work. (*) On the France Communist Party Convention last fall Earl Browder was elected as honorary Chairman, which means that next to Stalin he is of the presidium in the rest of the Countries.

22. Meetings of the E.C.C.I. must take place not less than once every six months.

23. Meetings of the Presidium of the E.C.C.I. must take place not less than once a fortnight.

24. The Presidium elects the Political Secretariat, which is *impowered* to make *decisions*, and which also draws up proposals for the meetings of the E.C.C.I. and of its presidium, and acts as their executive body.

25. The Presidium appoints the editorial committees of the periodical and other publications of the Communist International.

26. The Presidium of the E.C.C.I. sets up a department for Work among Women Toilers, permanent committee for guiding the work of *definite groups* of Sections of the Communist International and other *departments* of work.

IV. THE INTERNATIONAL CONTROL COMMISSION

27. The International Control Commission investigates matters affecting the unity of the Sections affiliated to the Communist International and also matters connected with Communist conduct of individual members of the various Sections.

For this purpose the I.C.C.

A. Examines complaints against the actions of Central Committees of Communist Parties lodged by Party members who have been *subjected* to *disciplinary* measures for *political differences.*

B. Examines such analogous matters concerning members of central bodies of Communist Parties and of individual Party members as it deems necessary, or which are submitted to it by the deciding bodies of the E.C.C.I.

C. Audits the accounts of the Communist International.

The headquarters of the I.C.C. are fixed by the I.C.C. in agreement with the E.C.C.I.

V. THE RELATIONSHIP BETWEEN THE SECTIONS OF THE COMMUNIST INTERNATIONAL AND THE E.C.C.I.

28. The Central Committees of Sections affiliated to the Communist International and the Central Committees affiliated sympathizing organizations *must send* to the E.C.C.I. the minutes of their meetings and *reports* of their *work.*

29. Resignations from office by individual members or groups of members of Central Committees of the various Sections is regarded as disruptive of the Communist movement. Leading *post* in the Party do not *belong* to the *occupant* of that post, but to the *Communist International*, as a whole. Elected members of the Central leading bodies of the various Sections may resign before their time of office expires only

with the consent of the E.C.C.I. Resignations accepted by Central Committees of Sections without the consent of the E.C.C.I. are invalid.

30. The Sections affiliated to the Communist International must maintain close organizational and informational contact with each other, arrange for mutual representation at each other's conferences and congresses, and with consent of the E.C.C.I. exchange leading comrades. This applies particularly to the Sections in *imperialist countries* and their *colonies*, and to the Sections in *countries* adjacent to each other.

31. Two or more Sections of the Communist International which (like the Sections in the Scandinavian countries and in the Balkans) are politically connected with each other by common conditions of struggle, may, with the consent of the E.C.C.I. form federations for the purpose of co-ordinating their activities, such federations to work under the guidance and control of the E.C.C.I.

32. The *Sections* of the Comintern must *regularly pay affiliation dues* to the *E.C.C.I.;* the amount of such dues to be determined by the E.C.C.I.

33. *Congresses* of the various *Sections*, ordinary and special, can be convened only with the *consent* of the *E.C.C.I.*

In the event of a Section failing to convene a Party Congress prior to the convening of a World Congress, that Section, before electing delegates to the World Congress, must convene a Party conference, or plenum of its Central Committee, for the purpose of considering the questions that are to come before the World Congress.

34. The International League of Communist Youth (Communist Youth International) is a *Section* of the *Communist International* with full rights and is subordinate to the E.C.C.I.

35. The Communist Parties must be *prepared* for *transition* to *illegal* conditions. The E.C.C.I. must *render* the Parties concerned *assistance* in their preparations for transition to illegal conditions.

36. Individual members of Sections of the Communist International may pass from one country to another only with the consent of the Central Committee of the Section of which they are members.

Communists changing their domicile must join the Section in the country of their new domicile. Communists leaving their country without the consent of the Central Committee of their Section must not be accepted into other Sections of the Communist International.

PARTS OF THE

PROGRAM OF THE COMMUNIST INTERNATIONAL

(adopted at the forty-sixth session of the sixth World Congress of the Communist International September 1, 1928) Reprinted in the U.S. Feb. 1936.

CHAPTER THREE

THE ULTIMATE AIM OF THE COMMUNIST INTERNATIONAL WORLD COMMUNISM

THE ultimate aim of the Communist International is to replace world capitalist economy by a world Communist society.

CHAPTER FOUR

"PROLETARIAN revolution, signifies the *forcible invasion* of the proletariat into the domain of property relationships of bourgeois society."

"The conquest of power by the proletariat does not mean peacefully "capturing" the ready-made bourgeois state machinery by means of a parliamentary majority. The conquest of power by the proletariat is the *violent overthrow* of bourgeois power, the destruction of the capitalist state apparatus (bourgeois armies, police, bureaucratic hierarchy, the judiciary, parliaments, etc.) and substituting in its place new organs of proletarian power."

"The Soviet form of state, being the highest form of Democracy, namely, proletarian democracy."

The confiscation of all large private capitalist undertakings (factories, plants, mines,) and the transference of all state and municipal enterprises to the Soviets."

"The confiscation of railway, waterway, automobile and air transport services commercial and passenger air fleet, telegraphs, telephones and wireless, and the transference of state and municipal transport and communication services to the Soviets."

"The confiscation of all landed estates in town and country (private, church, monastery and other lands)."

"Monopoly of foreign trade. The repudiation of state debts to foreign and home capitalist."

"The dictatorship of the proletariat is a continuation of the class struggle under new conditions. The dictatorship of the proletariat is a stubborn fight — bloody and bloodless, violent and peaceful, military and economic, pedagogical and administrative — against the forces and traditions of the old society."

"In destroying the capitalist monopoly of the means of production, the working class must also destroy the capitalist monopoly of education, that is, it must take possession of all the schools, from the elementary schools to the universities."

"One of the most important tasks of the cultural revolution affecting the wide masses is the task of *systematically* and *unswervingly* combating *religion* — the *opium* of the people.

APPENDIX V

NAZI-COMMUNIST PARALLELS

COMMUNISTS and fellow travelers deny that there is any similarity between Nazi totalitarianism and Communist totalitarianism and yet their frequent cooperation before and during the second World War, and even their literature, shows a marked identity between them in about thirty aspects of their history, methods and aims. This is to be expected of totalitarian dictatorships. Comparison also reveals that in these respects both are the spiritual heirs of the force-Anarchism of Michael Bakunin whose career we presented in Chapter I. The following record verifies this view.

Both Nazis and Communists came to power in a counter-revolution against a Democratic Republic.

Both established a ruthless dictatorship and destroyed all dissent by persecution and endless terror.

Both crushed all other political parties and imprisoned or executed all leaders of these parties who refused to join the ruling party.

Both established a secret police system with arbitrary powers of arrest, imprisonment and execution.

Both sealed up their respective nations against foreign travel by their citizens unless the citizen was sent abroad on a mission for the government and even then he was constantly shadowed by secret police until he returned.

Both dictatorships controlled the radio, press, meetings, schools, universities, etc., no point of view being permitted that deviated from the thought rations of the dictatorship.

Both dictatorships confiscated the trade unions, cooperatives, cultural organizations and civic groups and attached them as servile organs to the dictatorship.

Both declared their aim to be a world revolution, organizing all nations under a totalitarian dictatorship.

So thoroughly have both dictatorships controlled their respective peoples through a one-party system that general "elections" have been carried by the ruling clique by a vote as high as 98 per cent.

In the "Parliament" of Nazi Germany and Communist Russia there has been no independent view, no debate, no differing opinions of the members, as dissent marked a man for the attention of the secret police. The members, as robots, voted the dictator's views and adjourned.

Both dictatorships have pursued members who renounced their views and fled to other countries and in many instances these refugees have been murdered.

Under both dictatorships the membership of the ruling party has been frequently "purged" by expulsion, by imprisonment and even by execution.

The Nazi and Communist dictatorships taught children to spy on their parents, to report any conversations that could be construed as "disloyalty" to the ruling class.

A primary article of faith in the Nazi and Communist creeds is the duty of the faithful to regard promises and agreements as outmoded "bourgeois virtues," to conceal the truth, to compromise opponents and to lie if it would advance the "cause."

Both dictatorships maintained international organizations composed of servile units in all countries, each dictatorship imposing an iron discipline over its units and members.

Both dictatorships functioned behind an iron curtain, all news and views of the home front and of other nations being filtered through the radio, press, schools, meetings, universities and publishing houses controlled by agents of the dictatorships.

Each dictatorship maintained concentration camps for persons suspected of being or known to be heretics to the state-kept party and the party-kept state.

In the war period both Nazis and Communists imposed dictatorships on weak nations with quisling agents controlling them.

Both through the press and radio waged a war of nerves to obtain concessions from other nations or before taking by force what they wanted.

Both pillaged conquered countries of foodstuffs, machinery and industries, impoverishing the victims and making the latter dependent upon their despoilers.

Both protested against "encirclement" while expanding their rule by military might.

Both accused the democratic nations with starting wars although both collaborated in the attack on Europe.

Both insisted on "friendly" neighbors while making their neighbors vassals of their respective dictatorships.

Both dictatorships were, in several respects, also the spiritual heirs of Michael Bakunin, the Russian founder of force-Anarchism. Bakunin, Hitler and Lenin each founded an international world staff to undermine all governments through intrigue, propagating falsehoods and violence. All three practiced the "propaganda of the deed," that is the assassination. The force-Anarchists attacked rulers of governments while the dictatorships of Hitler and Lenin-Stalin pursued deserters into other countries where they were often destroyed as "traitors to the fatherland."

INDEX